Unle

Voice

Unlocking Confidence and Power
in Every Woman's Story

HANNA OLIVAS
Along With 82 Inspiring Authors

Published by She Rises Studios Publishing **www.SheRisesStudios.com**.

ISBN: 978-1-969463-57-0

TABLE OF CONTENTS

INTRODUCTION

Welcome to **UnleashHER Voice: Unlocking Confidence and Power in Every Woman's Story**—a bold, unapologetic collection of stories that speak to the heart, soul, and strength of womanhood.

This anthology was born from a simple yet powerful truth: *every woman has a voice, and every voice deserves to be heard.* Within these pages, you'll find the unfiltered journeys of women who have dared to rise—who have turned silence into strength, fear into fuel, and struggle into stories of triumph.

These are not stories polished by perfection. They are real. Raw. Honest. They speak of self-doubt, heartbreak, resilience, and breakthrough. They invite you into deeply personal moments—where voices were once hidden in the shadows, now stepping into the light with power and purpose.

Each chapter is a celebration of authenticity and a testimony to what happens when a woman chooses to speak up, step out, and own her narrative. Whether she's navigating loss, healing from trauma, reclaiming identity, or rediscovering her worth, her voice carries wisdom that resonates far beyond her own journey.

You'll find voices that reflect diverse experiences, cultures, and perspectives—but each united by one mission: to inspire other women to rise, too.

As you read, we hope you see yourself in these pages. May you feel seen, heard, and empowered to embrace your own story with courage. Let this book be a mirror, a guide, and a rallying cry to unleash the voice within you—because your voice is not just powerful; it's necessary.

This is more than a book.
This is a movement. This is UnleashHER Voice.

Hanna Olivas

Founder and CEO of SHE RISES STUDIOS

https://www.linkedin.com/company/she-rises-studios/
https://www.facebook.com/sherisesstudios
https://www.instagram.com/sherisesstudios_llc/
www.SheRisesStudios.com

Author, Speaker, and Founder. Hanna was born and raised in Las Vegas, Nevada, and has paved her way to becoming one of the most influential women of 2022. Hanna is the co-founder of She Rises Studios and the founder of the Brave & Beautiful Blood Cancer Foundation. Her journey started in 2017 when she was first diagnosed with Multiple Myeloma, an incurable blood cancer. Now more than ever, her focus is to empower other women to become leaders because The Future is Female. She is currently traveling and speaking publicly to women to educate them on entrepreneurship, leadership, and owning the female power within.

UnleashHer Voice

By Hanna Olivas

There was a season in my life when silence felt safer than truth. I didn't choose that season. It was shaped by the world around me long before I ever understood how heavy silence could be. I learned, like so many women do, that the easiest way to survive was to swallow my words and shrink my presence. I mastered the art of being strong without making noise, responsible without asking for help, and present without ever being fully seen.

People praised me for it.

"She handles everything."

"She never complains."

"She's so strong."

But the truth was this: my silence wasn't strength. It was suffocation dressed as survival.

Silence becomes a prison when your voice was designed to change rooms.

For years I lived inside that prison. I let the expectations of others wrap around my throat like vines. I quieted myself in boardrooms so I wouldn't intimidate anyone. I hid my pain in hospital rooms so my family wouldn't worry. I stiffened my spine in moments I should have fallen apart. And every time I muted my voice, a piece of my identity slipped through my fingers.

What I didn't understand then, what I had to learn through heartbreak, illness, motherhood, marriage, and the relentless grit of building an empire while fighting for my life, is that the voice God gave me was not meant to lie dormant. It was meant to lead. To heal. To disrupt. To ignite.

A woman's voice is not fragile.

It is fire.

And the moment she unleashes it, the world around her starts to shift.

My own shifting came slowly at first, like a whisper. A tightening in my spirit. A quiet knowing that my silence was costing me more than my truth ever could. But like all women who have spent a lifetime being told to be quiet, I tried to push it down. I told myself not to make noise. I told myself to play it safe. I told myself that staying silent kept everyone comfortable.

But comfort is rarely where purpose lives.

One night, after a long day of treatments and an even longer history of pretending I was okay, I realized I couldn't keep quiet anymore. I realized that silence wasn't protecting me it was erasing me. And I refused to spend the rest of my life living as a dimmed-down version of the woman God created me to be.

So I made a decision, not out of confidence but out of exhaustion: I stopped shrinking.

I unleashed my voice.

Not the neat version. Not the "acceptable" version. Not the version that makes people clap politely. I unleashed the version that trembles, the version that carries scars, the version that has fought through hell and still rises. I unleashed the voice that was forged in grief, sharpened in adversity, and strengthened through faith.

When a woman speaks from that place, from the depth of who she truly is, she becomes unmistakable.

She becomes undeniable.

She becomes unshakeable.

And she becomes dangerously free.

Of course, the world reacts when a once-silent woman begins to speak. They called me intense. Emotional. Dramatic. Too much. The same words they use for every woman who refuses to fold herself into the small boxes she outgrew. The same words designed to scare us back into silence.

But I wasn't going back.

Because I realized something that changed everything:

The moment a woman unleashes her voice, she becomes uncontrollable.

Not in a wild way, but in a purposeful, God-led, destiny-driven way. When she stops apologizing, stop diluting, and stops asking for permission, she unlocks the part of her that was always meant to change lives.

The truth is, your voice isn't just sound.

It's identity.

It's power.

It's your spiritual fingerprint.

Your voice is the thread that stitches your past to your purpose. It carries the stories of the women who came before you and the hope of the daughters who will follow. Your voice is the reason your heart still beats with resilience. Your voice is the masterpiece of everything you've survived.

People ask me often, "Where does your courage come from?"

And the most honest answer is: I stopped waiting for courage.

I spoke anyway.

Courage isn't the absence of fear.

Courage is the decision to speak even when your voice shakes.

And yes, unleashing your voice will make some people uncomfortable. Let it. A woman rising is always a disruption to someone who benefits from her staying small. But you were not created for their comfort. You were created for your calling.

Some people will fall away when you start speaking your truth.

Let them.

Your destiny is not built on fragile connections.

Some people will misunderstand you.

Let them.

Your voice is not meant to be translated for anyone who refuses to listen.

Some people will judge you.

Let them.

Judgment is often the echo of someone else's fear.

What matters is you, the woman you are becoming, the woman you are remembering, the woman you are reclaiming.

Unleashing your voice is not about volume.

It is about ownership.

It is not about shouting.

It is about standing rooted in who you are, even when the world tries to shake you.

Sometimes unleashing your voice is saying "No."

Sometimes it's saying "This is who I am now."

Sometimes it's saying "God called me to more, and I refuse to shrink for anyone."

And sometimes, it's simply saying, "I'm done being silent."

Your voice is the key that unlocks everything you've been praying for.

Your voice is the bridge between your pain and your purpose.

Your voice is the spark that lights the fire of every woman who crosses your path.

So this chapter isn't just a story.

It's an invitation.

A signal to the woman reading these words, the woman who feels that stirring, that pull, that familiar whisper saying it's time.

It's time to speak.

Time to rise.

Time to be heard.

Time to be seen.

Time to unleash her.

Unleash her courage.

Unleash her truth.

Unleash her power.

Unleash her faith.

Unleash her voice.

Because when a woman unleashes her voice, she doesn't just free herself, she frees generations.

And you?

You were born for this kind of freedom.

You were born for this kind of fire.

Your voice is your legacy, and it's time the world hears it.

Hunyah Irfan

CEO of HunyahTravels

https://ca.linkedin.com/in/hunyah-irfan-blogger351
https://www.instagram.com/officalhunyahtravels/?hl=en

Hunyah is a content creator ,and model .Hunyah has perfromed spoken word virtually and in person many times .Hunyah does food reviews and different types of reviews .Hunyah is a editoral has recently walked runway at Brampton Fashion Expo 25,Mother Day Craaf 25, Carabram 25 and Label Blue Khushi Boutique .

Finding My Voice After Trauma

By Hunyah Irfan

Hi, I'm Hunyah and I'm from Brampton, Ontario. My story is about how I recovered from my accident and the trauma I dealt with from a guy back then.

Now, I'm going to share with you how I found my voice after the trauma.

My Story

I was in my early 20s when I spent time and dated this guy, who is also my cousin. By 2025, I found out in the end that it was only a one-sided relationship.

A month before my accident, I was done with college and I spent time hanging out with a guy.

Since I started recovering from my accident, I have been trying to convince everyone that I'm going to marry this guy. But no one seemed to agree. The minute I said I wanted to marry this guy, I have been getting picked on for this since then.

For more than 10 years, I haven't been able to see the guy, even now, because of the no-cousin policy. This cousin policy is like if you are breaking a rule when really my story was unplanned the whole way through.

For the past six years, this guy, who has not been coming, suddenly appeared only to make a legal statement against me. That is when my trauma started. This happened once on my 26th birthday and one time before that. And it caused me to stay at home for three months and from going to the malls.

At that time I didn't know that the guy was abusing me, something that I didn't control.

My intention was to get married and get the word out somehow, but not in a rude sense. I got misguided on that a few times. The year after, when the guy got married to someone else in 2019, I cried a lot. After being abused by this guy and then being told he is married, it hurt me a lot.

I was informed that he went on a honeymoon with his wife the day after the wedding. Simply thinking about that made me very upset because everything that he does and gives to his wife now should have been mine.

Despite that, I continued working on my blog, which I started when I was still with the guy but he discouraged me from doing it because he thought that I did not have the potential to excel in this field.

I know that it's not right for me to remain crying over this heartache. Then someone advised me that the only way to get over my feelings for this guy is to stay in touch with him—which I later did.

In 2025, I was trying to help the same guy with the problem we were dealing with in the community. I was being nice to my ex-boyfriend and did not show any feelings for him but his wife didn't seem to like it.

My aunt and my whole family were in a rage and expressed their dislike on WhatsApp for what has happened between me and my ex's wife.

I regretted my decision to have listened to the advice given to me that time. In April 2025, I declared I was done with that guy. I stayed away from them and I became active on social media instead.

That is the story behind my trauma, which I never expected would lead me to where I am now.

My Career

Starting a blog wasn't easy to begin with.

I'm self-taught in content creation, but I also took time taking masterclasses, certifications, and training in content creation while starting my career. I had been brought down many times for small accomplishments in my career.

Having accomplished a lot in a short time has surprised a lot of people around me.

It was through faith that I got successful.

The guy who abused me indirectly still says it's not long-term material.

I worked hard and collaborated with a lot of people. I believe that being a content creator is the right path for me and no one can bring me down—not even my past relationship and the trauma it brought to me.

No matter how I try to avoid it, I still receive negative comments from the guy and his family. But I told myself that their words and comments are not for me to deal with anymore.

Opportunities

I am now a "creative" entrepreneur. To be creative means you have to create opportunities instead of waiting for them to come to you.

Opportunities can either be voluntary or paid. Sometimes, voluntary opportunities lead you to paid opportunities.

The choice is yours.

This is my story of how I found my voice after trauma. I hope you find yours, too!

Martha Payan

Empowered by Faith Coaching & Consulting
Kingdom Wealth & Empowerment Coach

https://www.linkedin.com/in/marthapayan/
https://www.facebook.com/martha.payan/
https://www.instagram.com/empoweredbyfaith_coaching/
www.marthapayan.com
https://payhip.com/UpliftedCoaching

Martha Payan is a Kingdom Empowerment Coach, educator, and visionary leader passionate about helping others unlock their God-given potential. With a Master's in Education and years of experience teaching English and Spanish internationally, she blends creativity, faith, and practical strategy to inspire transformation. Martha is the founder of Shooting Star Art & Theater Productions and host of the Faith Empowered Life podcast, where she empowers audiences to step boldly into their calling with confidence and clarity. Her mission stems from her deep faith: to build what endures, cultivate wealth with purpose, and empower others to live lives of abundance, wisdom, and impact. She creates courses, workshops, and faith-based resources that equip people to rise to leadership, strengthen their voice, and live in alignment with their Kingdom purpose. At her core, Martha is a faith-filled visionary, devoted wife, and mother, whose journey is guided by God's favor and grace.

Stand in Power on Your Stage: From Fearful Voice to Confident Presence

By Martha Payan

The stage lights were blinding, but I could still make out the silhouettes of the audience waiting for me. I could feel their anticipation; there is a special connection between an audience and the person about to perform. My heart pounded as the first notes of the song filled the theater. What I was feeling was not just from nerves but from the sheer challenge ahead. *Let It Go* isn't an easy song to sing; it stretches your voice, demands strength, and leaves no room to hide behind hesitation. And yet, I knew I had to sing it. This wasn't just another performance—it was my declaration.

For years, I had carried the question: *What if nobody cares about what I have to say? What if my voice doesn't matter?* But preparing for that moment, and now standing on stage, about to sing words that had become symbolic for my life, I felt powerful. Confident. Free. That night, with every lyric, something inside me changed. For the first time in a long time, I wasn't just singing. I was reclaiming my voice.

To understand why this moment meant so much, let me share a bit about myself.

I grew up as the "nice girl." I obeyed my parents, was polite at the table, never interrupted adults, and always tried to do what was expected. On the surface, it seemed like maturity and discipline. But behind it was something else: a deep need for approval.

I became the fixer in my family—the one people turned to when problems needed solving. Relatives and friends, not just my immediate family, leaned on me for answers, solutions, and support. Helping others wasn't the problem. I genuinely loved it. But somewhere along the way, I lost sight of balance. I put other people's opinions, expectations, and needs ahead of my own, time and time again.

The pattern ran deep: I didn't say no, even when I wanted to. I held back my voice, convinced it was better to keep the peace than to speak my truth. I measured my worth by how well I met others' standards and how I seldom disappointed anyone.

And while I seemed confident academically or professionally, emotionally, I was not. My thoughts whispered: *Who do you think you are to try something as big as this? Haven't you learned anything from previous experiences? You have to give even more, overcompensate to keep your friends. Don't risk rejection.*

Four years ago, something inside me changed. I looked at my daughters—bright, full of life, growing into young women of their own—and asked myself: *What kind of role model do I want to be for them?*

If I kept silencing my needs, pushing my voice to the background, what was I teaching them? That their worth was tied to pleasing others? That their voices weren't worth being heard? That they should limit their dreams, goals, and aspirations in life?

I knew I couldn't keep living that way. God was stirring something in me, reminding me that He hadn't created me to live small. He had given me a voice for a reason, and it was time to use it.

So when my theater company had the chance to do a show featuring Broadway hits, and I saw *Let It Go* on the list, something inside me leapt. I knew—*that's my song.*

This wasn't just about singing. It was about declaring who I was becoming.

In rehearsals, the lyrics hit me differently than they ever had before. *I don't care what they're going to say.* That line pierced me. For most of my life, I had cared far too much about what others thought. I wanted to be liked, accepted, admired. I wanted to belong. And even though I've worked on releasing that, the truth is—it's still a part of me I wrestle with.

Then came another line: *And the fears that once controlled me can't get to me at all.*

Fear had been my shadow for years. Fear of rejection. Fear of not fitting in. Fear of failure. Fear of speaking up and being misunderstood.

But that night on stage, something shifted in a way I hadn't expected. As I sang, I became aware of the gown I was wearing, a flowing, luminous blue that caught the lights at every turn. I felt like a Queen. Not just because of the dress, but because in that moment, for the first time, I embodied the truth I had come to internalize: We are daughters of the King. Every ounce of courage, every bit of authority, every spark of power I needed was already inside me. The gown was a symbol, a physical reminder of that truth. I didn't have to become someone else or wait for approval; I only had to stand tall, lift my crown, and claim the authority that was already mine. God had already approved me.

The adrenaline of the stage, the technical challenge of the song, the presence of the audience—all of it merged with a powerful awareness: Confidence wasn't something I had to earn from others. It was something I already had, waiting for me to claim it, right there, stepping fully into my strength and voice, fully aligned with who God created me to be. With every note, every lyric, I wasn't just performing. I was reclaiming my voice, embracing my identity, and standing in the power that had always been mine.

That performance became a turning point. The adrenaline of being on stage wasn't new—I've always loved speaking, teaching, and performing—but this time it was different. It wasn't just about the song. It was about stepping into full ownership of my voice.

It was about saying no when I needed to, setting boundaries without guilt, and choosing values that truly mattered to me—living by them instead of bending under the weight of other people's opinions.

Life isn't black and white. For too long, I tried to live by rules that others set, believing that was the "right" way. But God reminded me that He created me uniquely, with my own shades of color, my own tones, my own design. When I stopped comparing myself, stopped silencing myself, and began trusting Him, I felt a freedom unlike any I had ever known—the freedom that comes from living authentically, fully aligned with who I was meant to be.

That night, as I sang those powerful lyrics, I wasn't just performing. I was destroying lies. I was embodying truth. I was showing my daughters that their voices mattered. I was stepping into the woman God designed me to be.

Maybe you're reading this, and you see a bit of yourself in my story. Perhaps you've been the nice girl, the fixer, the one who keeps quiet to avoid conflict. Maybe you've held back your voice, thinking it wasn't worth hearing.

Let me tell you: Your voice matters. And here are a few things I've learned along the way:

Step in before you feel ready. Confidence grows when you take a step, even if it's not a big one, not when you stand still.

Anchor your identity in God. People's opinions will vary. God's truth about you never does.

Reframe the "what ifs." Stop asking, *"What if no one cares?"* and start asking, *"What if my words change someone's life?"*

Set boundaries with grace. Saying no doesn't make you unkind; it makes you authentic.

Find your song. For me, it was literally *Let It Go.* For you, it might be a conversation, a prayer, a creative project, or a step in faith. Whatever it is, let it be your declaration of freedom.

That night on stage, I felt powerful—not power over others, but power within myself. The kind of power that comes when you finally realize you don't need permission to live fully.

And that's what I want for you.

I want you to imagine standing on your own stage, singing the lyrics to *your* song. I want you to feel the rush of knowing that fear no longer controls you, that you don't need approval to be worthy, and that God designed you for impact.

Because your story, your experiences, and your voice matter more than you know. Every moment you've lived, every lesson you've learned, has the power to encourage someone else, to spark hope, to set them free. When you speak, you allow others to do the same.

So step forward. Speak. Sing. Share. Don't wait until you feel ready. Do it now because God has already approved you, equipped you, and placed the words on your heart for such a time as this. Stand tall, lift your crown, and let your light shine boldly. The world needs the fullness of who you are, and your voice is exactly what someone else has been waiting to hear.

Marlene Gravenberch

Founder of Leadership Refocused

https://www.linkedin.com/in/marlene-gravenberch-5655a61a
https://www.facebook.com/MMIGravenberch
https://www.instagram.com/marlenegravenberch
https://leadership-refocused.com
https://www.facebook.com/LeadershipRefocused

I am Marlène Gravenberch, a personal and professional development coach, empowerment advocate, and writer, born and raised in Suriname's rich, diverse culture. With over thirty years of experience across education, HR, and leadership, I founded Leadership Refocused to help individuals — especially women — lead with authenticity, courage, and alignment. My own journey of resilience, starting to rebuilding my life at the age of 50 and founding my coaching business at the age of 58. I believe true leadership begins with knowing yourself, setting healthy boundaries, and honoring your core values. I am also the author of Re-Embrace You: A Journey of Self Re-Discovery to Build Conscious Connections and co-author of research publications on customer centricity and mentorship. Today, I combine storytelling, coaching, and lived wisdom to empower others to heal, grow, and create lasting impact in their personal and professional lives.

Voice, Values, and the Courage to Lead

By Marlene Gravenberch

How Knowing Yourself Transforms the Way You Lead, Love, and Live

Leadership often gets defined by titles, strategies, or results. But the truth is, leadership begins long before the boardroom. It begins in the quiet moments when you are alone with yourself, asking, "Who am I really?"

For years, I thought leadership was about delivering results, meeting deadlines, and showing up strong for everyone else—even if I was not feeling okay. I believed excellence meant keeping the machine running, no matter the cost. But I've learned, often the hard way, that true leadership isn't about wearing the mask of success; *it's about taking that mask off.*

The most powerful leaders I now know are not the ones with the loudest voices or the biggest teams. They are the ones who have taken the time to know themselves: their values, their boundaries, their strengths, and even their scars. They lead with integrity because they've learned how to be honest with themselves first.

Taking the time to learn about yourself is like meeting someone, and you are curious who this person is, what they do or don't like, what they stand for, their values, what triggers them, and much more.

That's the same with you being curious about yourself: your values, what you like or don't like, how to set healthy boundaries, and how to communicate your values and boundaries can transform not only your leadership but also your relationships, your business, and your legacy.

This chapter is not just about leadership in business. It's about the leadership of your own life. It's about what happens when you stop performing, stop pretending, and start leading from alignment.

If you've ever felt the tension between the life you show the world and the one you feel inside, this chapter is for you.

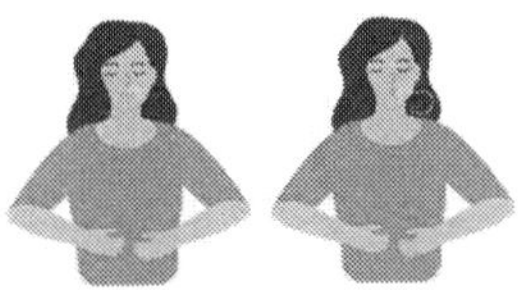

So take a deep breath with me—in through your nose, out through your mouth—and set aside the pressure to have it all figured out. I invite you to walk next to me in my story of what it really means to be a woman who knows herself and leads from that place of truth.

Leading on Empty

There was a time in my life when everyone thought I was doing great. I was the dependable one, the one people could call and the one who also had the answers most of the time. I felt that it was my duty and responsibility to carry and solve everyone's burdens like they were my own. Being the eldest and my role as an HR manager contributed a lot to that feeling too.

My days were packed with responsibilities. In meetings, I smiled and always had words of empowerment for everyone. On the outside, it looked like I had it together. I was the strong one at work, the fixer at home, and the woman who held it all together for everyone else. But when I got home at the end of the day, I felt like I was missing something, that I was not myself. I felt life was living me and not me living life.

I remember one afternoon, after one of these long days, I sat in my car and whispered to myself, "*Who am I doing all of this for?*"

My kids were grown and doing well. I didn't need to provide for them. They have their own family and are doing well for themselves. So why was I still carrying the weight of the world?

What I later learned is: This is what happens when you lead disconnected from yourself. *You give and give, but you lose sight of your own voice. You're performing, not leading. You're surviving, not thriving.*

I realized I had been leading everyone—except myself. This wasn't new. For almost 30 years I stayed in a relationship that looked fine to others but was breaking me inside. Telling myself, "*This infidelity is only a flaw. Other women have it worse.*" I minimized my pain, wore the smile, and played the part just as I did in leadership.

For years, I mistook endurance for strength and silence for dignity. But the truth was, inside I was breaking into a thousand pieces.

That moment in the car was my wake-up call. Leading on empty is not leadership; it's performance. And performance has an expiration date.

When leaders don't stop to check in with their own hearts, they drift into burnout. Worse, they build businesses and relationships that look stable but crack under pressure.

Reflection:
Am I leading from a place of overflow, or am I running on empty?

Discovering My Core Values

That day in my car, I asked myself, *WHAT REALLY MATTERS TO ME*? Not what my parents taught me, not what society expected or rewarded, but what I could not live without.

During my forgiveness journey, which I wrote about in another anthology, I learned something life-changing: Fidelity was my non-negotiable. When my then-husband said he loved me but could not promise to be faithful, I realized I had to honor my own values. For years, I had betrayed myself by staying in a relationship that tore me apart. In 2013, just before I turned 50, I looked at myself in the mirror and asked, "*Marlène, are you going to end like your mother? Slowly dying of heartbreak?*"

These questions forced me to name my core values. **Integrity. Compassion. Growth.**

Core values are not just words on paper. They're anchors? Mine reminds me who I am when everything around me feels shaky. Naming them was both liberating and terrifying, but once I named them, I couldn't go back. I couldn't keep saying yes to things that didn't line up. Once I had clarity, I could no longer hide behind excuses. I had to align my choices with what I said I stood for.

That's when I also discovered the power of *boundaries*, and here's the truth: Values and boundaries go hand in hand. You cannot live your values if you don't protect them with boundaries.

For me, boundaries were not walls to keep people out. They are bridges, showing others how to connect with me in healthy ways. They also mean walking away from opportunities that looked good but didn't feel right and protecting my energy for what truly mattered.

If you know your values but never set boundaries, you'll keep betraying yourself. And if you set boundaries without values, you'll seem harsh instead of grounded.

Reflection:
Write down your top three core values. Then ask yourself: Where in my life or leadership am I betraying these values? What boundary would protect them?

Personal and Professional Development as a Leadership Advantage

We often think personal development is separate from leadership and that journaling, reflection, therapy, or coaching are "private matters." But the truth is, personal growth fuels professional excellence.

Personal development saved me. Without the inner work of forgiveness, self-reflection, and healing, I would still be stuck in a cycle of pleasing, performing, and pretending. But personal growth didn't just heal my heart; it opened doors.

Once I anchored in my values, I also realized that I could no longer neglect my own growth; opportunities began to flow. I was blessed with better jobs, I bought my own home in 2017, and I eventually founded *Leadership Refocused.* My story became my strength.

You see, professional development was the other half of the equation. I invested in learning how to empower others through coaching to lead themselves. Learning new skills multiplied my impact. My personal healing gave me resilience; my professional training gave me tools. Together, they built a foundation strong enough to carry my business and my clients.

This is what I've learned:

- Personal growth fuels character. It makes you resilient, humble, and self-aware.
- Professional development fuels competence, sharpens your skills, and makes you effective.
- Leaders who develop self-awareness make wiser decisions.
- Leaders who practice emotional regulation lead calmer, stronger teams.

- Personal and professional development for sustainable business excellence. A leader who is aligned, resilient, and innovative is the leader every business needs.

Today, my big vision is scaling regionally and globally, leaving a legacy for my children and grandchildren that isn't built on quick wins. But built on the daily choice to keep growing personally and professionally.

Mini Exercise:

1. Identify one area of personal growth you've been avoiding (maybe it's dealing with your inner critic or challenges setting healthy boundaries).
2. Now identify one area of professional growth you've neglected (perhaps delegation, systems, or strategy). Write down one small action to move each forward this month.

Leading with Alignment

When I began aligning my actions with my values, everything changed. Decisions became clearer. My relationships became healthier. In business, it meant walking away from collaborations that compromised my integrity. In leadership, it meant being consistent: the same Marlène in public as in private.

Alignment meant I no longer said "yes" to things out of fear. Alignment gave me peace. Decisions became simpler because I frequently ask myself, *"Does this align with my values or not?"*

Boundaries also became a form of love. By saying, *"This is how I work best, this is what I need, and this is what I cannot compromise on,"* I wasn't rejecting anyone. To me it was clarity, and clarity builds trust.

Alignment is not about perfection; it's about consistency. When your values, words, and actions are aligned, people notice.

Reflection:
Think about one area where your words and actions don't yet match. What's one small step you can take this week to bring them into alignment?

Courage, Confidence, and the Ripple Effect

When a woman knows herself, she can't be knocked down so easily anymore. Confidence stops being about titles or applause; it's more about living truthfully. And when that happens, it flows into everything she does. After reading my book *Re-Embrace You*, women came to me and said, *"You too? I thought I was the only one."*

My personal healing gave me the courage to share my story, which gave others courage to share theirs. This is how cycles break—one honest story at a time. *When you show up as you,* it gives others permission to do the same.

This is what courage in leadership looks like:

- Name your values out loud.
- Communicating values openly and respectfully creates cultures where trust thrives.
- Communicate clearly and respectfully, so people know where you stand.
- Teams flourish under leaders who are both clear and compassionate.
- Authentic boundaries in leadership model respect and balance for others.

This kind of leadership builds long-lasting, meaningful relationships. Teams feel safe. Families heal, and communities grow.

Exercise:
Write your own "Values & Boundaries Statement."

- What do you stand for?
- What boundaries protect those values?
- How will you communicate with them with love?

An Invitation to You

Leadership is not about being perfect or having all the answers. It's about showing up as you, without the mask, aligned, and committed to growth.

Business excellence does not start with systems, strategy documents, or KPIs—it starts with the leader. When you grow, your business grows. When you align, your team aligns. When you communicate with clarity and courage, your relationships deepen.

I invite you to:

- Invest in your personal development. Heal, reflect, and grow.
- Invest in your professional development. Keep learning. Stay curious.
- Name your core values. Protect them with healthy boundaries. Communicate them with love and courage.

The world doesn't need more leaders who are burned out and disconnected. The world needs you—whole, authentic, and aligned.

And when you lead from that place, you don't just achieve business excellence. You build legacies. You create lasting, meaningful relationships that will carry your influence far beyond the boardroom.

And that, my friend, is the leadership of a woman who knows herself!

Isaura Martinez

Writer & Coach | Making AI Marketing Human

https://www.facebook.com/profile.php?id=100048230917535
www.isamartinezcoach.com
www.isamartinez.es

Writer & Coach blending AI innovation with human creativity. Inspiring growth with clarity, storytelling, and strategic insight.

May Your Voice Get Louder

By Isaura Martinez

Are you truly listening to yourself?

In a world that so often leaves us unseen and unheard, it's no wonder we crave recognition. Yet how can we expect others to listen when we refuse to hear our own voice first? That's the invisible grip of the *Good Girl Syndrome*—quietly silencing us, suffocating our dreams, and stealing our truth before anyone, including ourselves, notices.

Growing up, I wasn't just a "good girl." I was a perfectionist. Being good never seemed enough; only excellence counted. I longed to be *someone*: to earn the grades, the degree, and the respectable job with the respectable pay. I chased every box society told me to tick.

But ambition was not welcomed where I grew up, in a Catholic Latin American school run by nuns. Good girls were expected to become perfect wives, perfect mothers, with perfect homes. Yes, we could study, but our true "duty" was already decided. And if we strayed, the system was quick to punish us, especially while we were still too young to defend our dreams or speak our truth with confidence.

How can confidence grow when authority is the first to tell you to be quiet? How can you trust your voice if it's silenced before it even has a chance to speak?

If you're still reading, maybe you recognize yourself here. I'm talking about me, but I'm also talking about you and about the countless women who have never felt truly seen, heard, or validated in what their hearts were trying to say.

The Grip of Fear Holds Us Back

I often wonder why I never told my parents about what happened at school. Sometimes the bullies aren't classmates at all; they're authority figures. I was shamed in public for no reason, scolded for celebrating good grades, and reminded that "God doesn't like proud girls."

My parents would have defended me—and eventually, they did—but for years I kept silent. At home, there were already enough problems. As a "good girl," I couldn't add more weight to their shoulders. So I carried it alone, convincing myself I could manage the pain in silence.

Even then, I knew I was being treated unfairly. But I couldn't make sense of it. That's the trap: When you try to "understand" behavior that comes from a place of harm, it doesn't set you free. It disarms you. Empathy can heal conflicts when both sides care, but with those who abuse power, it only gives them more room to wound you.

You cannot truly understand a mindset built on values you don't share. And trying to "understand" doesn't make you better, or kinder, or holier. It just silences you further.

And keeps you *living in fear*.

Fear thrives in that silence. The stronger its grip, the quieter your voice becomes, until it disappears completely. And when that happens, the system wins—not just the teacher, or the job, or the family, but the collective mindset that feeds on keeping women quiet and "compliant."

They take everything, while we're left with crushed dreams and lives shaped by other people's expectations.

But here's the truth: Silence is not a virtue, and fear is not destiny.

How long will you keep paying the price of someone else's comfort with your own voice?

I realized the price was far too high. I am done paying it. From here on, I choose to create my life on my own terms.

What Do You Need?

When a former supervisor once asked me, *"What do you need?"* I froze. I had no answer. Not because I was afraid of speaking in that moment, but because I had no real awareness of my own needs or desires. I could have asked for more time, training, resources, or support. But I didn't know what could make things better other than me trying to make everything better alone.

Years later, the "good girl" still appeared whenever I felt threatened. She was still afraid of wanting too much, still hesitant to speak up, and still convinced her needs were less important than everyone else's. That's what happens when silence becomes a survival tactic: You lose touch with your desires, your dreams, and your very self, buried under layers of people-pleasing.

The more disconnected you are from your own truth, the easier it becomes to put others first—every single time—until something breaks inside you, forcing change.

Good Girl Syndrome whispers that the quieter we become, the more dependable we'll seem, and the more people will like us. And if they like us, they'll reward us with open doors, meet our needs, and protect us in this unpredictable world.

But it doesn't work that way. And when the illusion shatters, we're left with nothing but the heavy price of silence—our dreams buried, our voices muted.

Because silence can be a gift, yes—but it can also be a trap. We give it away hoping for safety, approval, and love. And often, we get none of it.

So I ask you: What do you believe you need from others?
And what if the very thing you long for is something you can give yourself?
What if the power to meet your deepest needs has always been in your own hands?

If this resonates, please remember:
You are not powerless.
You never were.
Your voice matters.
Your message matters.
And you were never meant to shrink in order to fit someone else's comfort or fears.

It's time to set that voice free.

Because the world is waiting to hear you.

Moving Abroad, and How My Voice Got Louder

I knew I wanted to live abroad since I was twelve. I tried more than once, but it never worked out. Migration requirements, money, health—there was always something standing in the way. And each time, it hurt. After doing everything "right," I still couldn't make it happen.

Between attempts, the dream went dormant. Buried under discouragement, it sank so deep I sometimes pretended it was gone. I told myself I was just "building my life," but it always returned. Again and again, I found myself checking visas, savings, and requirements, hoping this time would finally be my time.

In 2023, I researched options for Europe, narrowing in on Germany and Spain. Still, the timing wasn't right, and I thought the dream would fade again. But it didn't. This time was different. I felt it in my bones. My inner voice grew louder, refusing to be ignored.

What changed everything was asking a different question: *How can I make this work?*

Statements close doors. Questions open them. A good question creates space for answers—inside yourself and from others. That's when your voice, your true voice, finally has room to speak.

I listened, and I acted, one step at a time. I believe in manifestation, and part of manifesting your desires is following what I call "energetic nodes": those small, aligned actions that together create the path to your future.

Initially, I considered Germany and even began learning German. Later, a coach helped me explore both Germany and Spain, and I chose Spain. Around the same time, I almost bought an apartment in my home country, El Salvador. My savings weren't quite enough, but there were ways to make it work, and I loved that flat. Still, a quiet voice asked, "Is this really what you want? What about your dream of living in Europe?"

Logic said take the mortgage. My heart said go, and this time, I listened.

In September 2024, I moved to Spain. Those savings and months of planning became the foundation of a new life. Now, a year later, I'm writing these words from Córdoba, in Andalusia, Southern Spain.

Listening to your inner voice is not always easy. Acting on it can be even harder, especially when others don't understand your choices. Some relatives asked, "Why leave? You have everything here." And they were right in a way. But something inside me wouldn't let go. I'm grateful I listened, because following my desire has allowed me to create a life that feels truly mine.

When I shifted from focusing on limitations to asking *what's possible*, everything changed. Now I am building a new chapter on the other side of the Atlantic.

Traveling has taught me that cities and countries connect with us much like people do. With some, there's an instant spark—sometimes it feels like home, other times like the thrill of a holiday. And with others, there's simply no match, without any clear reason why.

After visiting ten cities across this beautiful country, I still choose Córdoba. Strange words, perhaps, from someone who never believed in love at first sight.

Spain—and especially Córdoba—was love at first visit. I had never set foot in Spain before, and I barely knew anything about Córdoba. Yet the moment I arrived, I felt at home. More than that, Spain rekindled my deep desire to write. The dream I carried since childhood, when I'd invent stories in my head, hoping one day they'd become a book. And now here I am, writing the very first chapter of my very first published book.

Do you feel a desire that strong within you? Maybe it's not about moving abroad. Maybe your path looks different—or maybe not so different. Only you can know.

So I ask: Where is your voice taking you? What is it whispering to you?

I'll end with the words of Oriana Fallaci:

"There are times in life when keeping silent becomes a guilt and speaking becomes an obligation."

This isn't only true in the collective sense. It's true in your own life. Your desires matter. Your voice matters. And only you can speak it, in the way only you can.

Your voice is meant to be heard. And the world is waiting.

So now, it's time to get clear on what you want and get loud to go for it.

Stephanie Graziano

Founder of Stephanie Graziano Coaching & Consulting
Coach

https://www.linkedin.com/in/stephanie-graziano-coo/
https://www.facebook.com/stephanie.graziano.10/
stephaniegraziano.commindhousemedia.com
www.stephaniegraziano.com
www.mindhousemedia.com

Stephanie Graziano is a life and business coach who helps women entrepreneurs overcome self-doubt, embrace their strengths, and step confidently into their power. With over 30 years as a C-suite executive, 15+ years of coaching experience, and a philosophy rooted in Taoist principles, Stephanie combines practical strategy with spiritual wisdom. She has been featured by CNN, the Los Angeles Times, Hollywood Reporter, and LA Start-Ups Magazine, and is dedicated to helping women refine their voices and lead with authenticity.

Awakening Her Voice

By Stephanie Graziano

Dedication

For every woman who has ever been told to be quiet, to stay small, or to dim her light—this is for you.

May you remember that your voice was never meant to be hidden.

It was meant to guide, to heal, to inspire, and to change lives beginning with your own.

As you turn these pages, I invite you to enter gently, with compassion for yourself. My story is just one path, but within it, you may find reflections of your own journey. For years, I believed that being "good" meant being silent, invisible, and unnoticed. It took me decades to realize that my quietness was not weakness but preparation.

This chapter is about finding, refining, and finally releasing the voice that was always inside me. My hope is that it will remind you of your own and that you'll give yourself permission to listen for it, honor it, and share it with the world in your own way.

The Moment That Changed Everything

It was a crisp day in September in Los Angeles. A young girl, her younger sister, and her parents were walking to dinner. The girls wore new dresses their grandmother had lovingly made, full skirts perfect for twirling, with heart-shaped buttons stitched into place like little reminders of love.

As they rounded a corner, the girls began spinning, delighting in the movement of fabric, giggling as they admired their reflections in the store windows. For a fleeting moment, it was pure joy.

And then, without warning, came the words that cut through the innocence of it all:

"Don't look at yourselves in the window like that! Only bad girls do that! Don't be so vain!"

The words landed like a knife. Spoken by their father, a man admired and powerful in their young eyes, they carried a weight far heavier than the moment itself. What might have been a passing comment instead became an imprint—etched into memory, shaping choices, confidence, and visibility for years to come.

The Good Girl Imprint

Years later, after a painful divorce, that same little girl—now a couple of years older—found herself helping her mother to hold life together with sheer grit. Her mother worked two jobs and did everything she could to keep food on the table, the car running, after-school care paid, and clothes on growing bodies. And yet, it wasn't enough.

There came a point when home was no longer an option. There simply wasn't money for rent. Survival became the only plan.

By the grace and kindness of others, she and her girls were taken in by a friend. She was given a spare room, while her daughters made a bed on the sofa in the den. It was safe but it came with unspoken rules. And the mother, weary and humbled, turned to her girls with words that echoed through their lives:

"Please girls, we need to be able to stay for a while. That means you must be good. Stay very quiet, don't get in the way, and don't let anyone know you're here. The quieter you can be, the better. Be good girls."

And so it was. The definition of "good" became tied to silence, invisibility, and not taking up space. Being "good" meant not being noticed.

This became another imprint, one that would influence the decades ahead.

Living in the Shadows

For dozens of years—through school, through the early parts of my career—I carried these definitions with me. To be a good girl meant excelling but not shining too brightly. Working hard, but not demanding recognition. Learning deeply, but not always sharing my voice.

I dug in and worked harder than anyone else. I became known for being intentional, curious, and willing to try new things when opportunities arose. And in my quietness, I discovered an unexpected gift: invisibility.

Invisibility can be a cloak, a protection, but it can also be a classroom. While I wasn't a threat to anyone, I could watch and observe. I studied how successful people interacted, how they influenced others, and how they navigated both conflict and opportunity. I became a student of human behavior, deciphering body language, tone, motivations, and unspoken alignments.

Looking back now, I realize this was an extraordinary education. I learned empathy by listening. I developed intuition by noticing the subtleties others missed. I sharpened discernment in silence.

And yet, a voice inside me whispered, "There's more." *You're meant to step forward.*

When the Whisper Became a Call

When I moved into leadership roles, I began to see more clearly where I needed to step up, where silence was no longer serving me. Speaking up was not natural for me. It went against everything I had been taught—be good, be quiet, don't draw attention.

But something in me was tired of living in the shadows. I began to ask myself: *Why must I stay silent? Why must my presence be hidden?*

And when I finally began to step forward, even tentatively, something remarkable happened.

I was noticed. Not for being loud or forceful, but for my work, my steadiness, and my intuitive responses. My perspective was sought out. I was asked to lead, to share my insights, and to help others grow. My voice, once carefully guarded, began to emerge in ways that felt aligned with who I truly was.

The Gifts of Silence

Here is what I've come to understand:

Being in the shadows is not always a bad thing. It isn't simply about being held back. Sometimes it is the soil where growth happens, the quiet space where skills take root. My years of silence were not wasted. They cultivated empathy, intuition, deep listening, and discernment—tools that would serve me well.

When I did step forward, I was not an empty voice trying to be heard. I was a voice shaped by experience, a voice carrying depth and authenticity.

And I discovered something powerful: A voice doesn't have to be loud to be strong.

Discovering the Power of My Voice

As I began using my voice, I realized it did not need to mirror anyone else's. It didn't need to be commanding or heavy-handed. My power came in gentleness, in deep intuition, and in choosing words with care.

In meetings with other leaders, I was able to enter the conversation gently, with questions and insights in a way that caused others to pause and think. They were persuaded to rethink the issue at hand in a way that was thoughtful instead of competitive and argumentative. It didn't challenge the perspectives; it opened everyone to consider alternative ideas.

Because I had learned to listen deeply, I could respond with intention. Because I had cultivated sensitivity to people's energy, I could sense what needed to be said and what did not. Because I had observed for so long, I could communicate with clarity.

A well-developed voice does not speak constantly. It speaks when it matters.

That has become my way. My voice now carries the strength of restraint, the wisdom of waiting, and the courage to speak when the moment is right.

Living in Authentic Alignment

Today, I feel blessed by the journey, even the painful imprints of childhood, even the hardships of single motherhood, even the years of silence. They all formed the woman I am now.

I no longer feel the need to rush in or to seek validation from others. My life is not about proving myself. It is about living authentically, speaking when my words can make a difference, and guiding others to discover the same freedom.

As a life coach and entrepreneur, I now hold space for people who struggle with their own voice. I understand what it feels like to be silenced by circumstance, by conditioning, by fear. And I know what it takes to gently reclaim that voice, to trust it, to let it guide you forward.

This is the gift I get to offer—a path of empowerment that is both relatable and deeply spiritual.

Unleashing Her Voice

"UnleashHER Voice" is more than a title. For me, it is a lifelong process. It is about peeling back the layers of "be quiet, be good, don't be seen" and stepping into the truth that our voices are not accidents. They are instruments of change.

Unleashing my voice did not mean becoming someone I'm not. It meant becoming more fully myself. It meant honoring my nature as an observer, an empath, and a seeker and allowing those qualities to flow into how I speak and lead.

I've discovered that the voice I once thought was too quiet was, in fact, perfectly suited for the work I was meant to do.

And I believe this is true for every woman: Your voice, however it sounds, however it comes through, carries wisdom and power. It doesn't have to match the world's expectations to matter. In fact, its authenticity is what makes it transformative.

An Invitation for You

If you are reading this and wondering how to find your own voice, let me say this: It is already within you. It may be layered with old stories, with cultural messages, and with fear. But it is there.

Start by listening to yourself, not the noise around you, not the echoes of old imprints, but the quiet knowing inside. That is where your true voice lives.

And when you are ready, let it out, gently at first if you must. Trust that it carries the exact strength it was meant to. Trust that your voice, just as it is, can make ripples that reach farther than you imagine.

Because when a woman unleashes her voice, she not only frees herself, she gives permission for others to do the same.

Reflection: Listening for Your Own Voice

Take a quiet moment, just for you. Settle in with a notebook or journal. Breathe deeply and let your mind soften.

1. **Remember the imprint.**
   Think back to a moment in your life when you were told—directly or indirectly—to be quiet, to stay small, or to hold back. Write down what was said or what you felt. Notice how that message may still echo in your choices today.

2. **Reframe the silence.**
   Ask yourself: *What gifts did my silence bring me?* Did it help you listen more deeply, observe others, or understand yourself in new ways? Write down at least three strengths you developed because of it.

3. **Claim your voice.**
   Now, place your hand over your heart and ask: *What is my voice longing to say?* Write whatever comes, without judgment. It doesn't need to be polished—let it flow freely.

4. **Choose one step.**
   Close by writing down one small way you can honor your voice this week. It could be speaking up in a conversation, journaling daily, or simply noticing when you silence yourself and gently choosing otherwise.

✨ **Remember:** Your voice doesn't have to be loud to be powerful. It only has to be yours.

Erica Elliott

WarriorHeart Healing Hearts
Speaker, Brain Code Strategist, Author & Consultant

https://www.facebook.com/warriorheartxo
https://www.instagram.com/warriorheartxo
https://msha.ke/warriorheartxo
https://linktr.ee/WarriorHeartxo

Erica Elliott holds a Master's Degree in Counseling Psychology and brings over 30 years of dedicated service to the field as a Licensed Counselor, Certified Brain Health Coach, and Certified Health Integrative Medicine Professional. With diverse expertise in various therapeutic modalities, Erica is specialized in Neurobiology, ADHD and Neurodiversity, Somatic Therapy, Energy Medicine, NLP, CBT, RET, EFT, TFT, Theology, EMDR, and the Gottman Method, all enriched by practices of Mindfulness and Meditation with an emphasis on spirituality. She is a mental health advocate heading a mission to equip individuals with brain health tools to master life. As the founder of WarriorHeart Healing Hearts, Erica serves as a Brain Code Strategist, guiding individuals on a holistic healing journey that integrates mind, body, and spirit. Her mission is to empower clients to navigate challenges and uncover their true potential. By employing multiple healing modalities, she facilitates rapid rewiring for success, assisting clients in transforming their struggles into personal masterpieces. Throughout her career, Erica has had the privilege of guiding thousands on their paths to healing, viewing this work not merely as a profession but as a profound calling. With a deep passion for nurturing growth, resilience, and vitality, Erica is dedicated to helping individuals unlock the extraordinary life that divine intention holds for each individual. Having faced personal trials, she understands that healing flourishes in compassionate relationships. Together with clients, Erica cultivates the belief iron sharpens iron with strength and transformation, helping to forge legacies that inspire. For those seeking support or wishing to connect, Erica reminds us all: we are destined for greatness. Her motto is always- Be Blessed and Be a Blessing!

Finding My Voice—A Story of Change and Possibility

By Erica Elliott

I was in fourth grade and already a mess. Something in me seemed to break after my great-grandmother moved away when I was in second grade. She was the one who believed in me, who loved me without question. When she moved, it felt like I lost my compass. I remember lying in bed one night after she left, crying out to God and asking Him why He wouldn't just take me to heaven instead of leaving me in the mess I was living in. Though I felt a whisper in my soul, God was answering and telling me, *"I will be your father. I love you and I have good plans for you,"* it didn't remove me from the chaos I was in.

Maybe that sounds dramatic for an eight-year-old, but pain doesn't care about age. Back then, people didn't talk about kids being depressed, anxious, or suicidal. Now, even with more awareness, we still see young kids talking about wanting to die. Abuse—emotional, verbal, physical—wasn't something adults openly addressed then. And yet, for some of us, it shaped our whole childhood. Though talked about so much more today, it is still an epidemic to be aware of.

After my great-grandmother left, I clung to little moments of escape. One of those moments was when my best friend had a birthday party. I was so excited to go. It was a rare chance to feel normal, to laugh, and to be away from the chaos and hurt at home. The party was wonderful. We played, we giggled, and we ate cake. For a few hours, I could just be a kid.

Then came the morning after.

Her older sister—just a year older than us—told everyone I bit her. I hadn't. I pleaded and cried, saying I would never do such a thing. But she had a bite mark, and in a small school of just twenty-three kids in my grade and in a small town in Paden, Oklahoma, the rumor spread like wildfire. My best friend believed her sister. I went from having one safe place outside my home to feeling like everywhere was dark and heavy. I've done enough healing work now, including EMDR therapy, to see that her sister was often jealous of our friendship. But knowing that now doesn't erase the damage then.

After that, I withdrew and hardened. If people were going to say I was bad, maybe I'd just act like it. I didn't know it at the time, but looking back, I can see the signs of ADHD—impulsive, restless, talkative, always in trouble.

One day in fourth grade, another boy and I decided to see who could get the most "licks" from the paddle. I got eleven that day. I don't even remember who "won," but I remember the principal calling me into his office. Mr. Hamilton looked me in the eye with a rather disappointed look and said, *"Erica, I know the kind of family you're growing up in, but you don't have to be a product of them."*

I didn't fully understand what he meant, but something in that moment lodged in my heart. I thought, *Wait... I don't have to be like my family? What does that mean?* The wheels of my mind began to turn.

Not long after, my teacher, Miss Tatum, signed me up for 4-H. I never asked my family for money to join, so looking back I'm sure she or the principal paid for it themselves. That act alone planted a seed—someone believed enough in me.

4-H had all kinds of activities, including speaking competitions. That's where my teacher put me, and I felt excited because there were prizes too. If you placed first, you got a Susan B. Anthony coin, and I wanted one. I didn't know where my sudden confidence came from, but maybe it was just that little whisper from my principal's words: *You can be different.* One thing was for sure: looking back, God was directing my path.

I chose my speech topic—well, actually, my first choice was taken—so I ended up with "How to Set the Table." Mind you, in my house, "setting the table" meant plopping down a plate and maybe a fork, definitely not a formal, proper setting. But I learned. I practiced. I memorized every word. I rehearsed until I could do it without a mistake.

And when the day came, I nailed it. First place. Blue ribbon. Susan B. Anthony coin. You'd have thought I'd just won a million dollars. That one moment cracked open a door in my brain: *If I could do this, what else could I do?*

I went on to do more 4-H speeches in the next continuing years with several other first-place wins and coins. Plus, I competed in other similar things as well.

That's the thing about someone believing in you. It can change everything. One moment, one sentence, and one open door can set a new trajectory.

I went on to finish my master's degree, and along the way had many opportunities to speak and sing on stages, to lead workshops, and to coach others to speak and sing on stage. But it all traces back to that principal's belief, that teacher's encouragement, God opening doors, and that one rare coin and first-place ribbon.

If you're reading this and you're in the middle of the mess—whether it's a painful past, a hard present, or fear about the future—hear me now: You are not a product of your family, your mistakes, or your circumstances. God can help you rewrite your story.

One Scripture that carried me through is this:

"For I know the plans I have for you," declares the Lord, "plans to prosper you and not to harm you, plans to give you hope and a future" (Jeremiah 29:11, NIV).

That promise is for you, too.

Brain Science Insight

When my principal told me I didn't have to be a product of my family, it wasn't just kind words—it was a neurological shift. In that instant, my **prefrontal cortex**—the part of the brain responsible for decision-making, planning, and envisioning the future—lit up with possibility. A single encouraging idea can rewire a brain's narrative, moving it from a fixed mindset ("I'm stuck like this") to a growth mindset ("I can change").

Neuroscience calls this *neuroplasticity*—your brain's ability to create new pathways based on new experiences and beliefs. That shift changed the filter through which I saw myself. From then on, I didn't just react to life; I began imagining what life could be. And every time I practiced that speech, I was reinforcing those new pathways, making the belief "I can succeed" stronger and more automatic. Every time I said yes to something new, it led me to another opportunity to shift and grow.

You might feel like your life is nothing but a mess right now. But under all of it, there's a masterpiece. You just need the right spark, the right person, or the right step to begin revealing it. The other side is better than a pot of gold. You see, "Beauty is in the Becoming" (Erica Elliott).

That spark might come from someone else, or it might be you deciding today to believe in yourself even if no one else does. Try something new. Join a group. Take a class. Write the first page of the book you've been thinking about. Speak your truth out loud.

Because sometimes, all it takes is one step to change your life forever.

And if I could find my voice at age eleven, you can find yours right now.

I pray this book has blessed you and that you use and share the tools you've learned. I have a book that expands on these areas and so much more that will be released by 2026 called **“Brain Coding - *We Repeat What We Don’t Rewire – It’s a Program.*”** This book will walk you through the deeper science of your thought patterns, habits, emotional coding, and how to build a daily system to live in the fullness of God’s design.

If you found this book helpful, may I ask you a favor to please leave a review on Amazon. Thank you!

As a Brain Code Strategist, I help people rewire with evidence-based tools to rapidly clear the mess and transform your life into the Masterpiece you were always created to be! People also love me speaking to their groups and organizations, teaching them tools in a fun, interactive, and transformative way. Excited to connect with you plus find free resources on the link below. I am always adding new tools and links. Be Blessed and Be a Blessing!

Leona Monfee

DIY with Leona Jo
Natural Health & Wellness Coach

www.linkedin.com/in/DIYLeonaJo
https://www.facebook.com/DIYwithLeonaJo/
https://instagram.com/diyleonajo
https://Leonajo.com
https://www.fuministry.com/

Ever since I can remember, I have always loved bringing joy to others; whether it was lending a hand, making them something to help them feel better, playing cards/games, or just listening. This is what lead me to the gratifying path that I am on. Along this journey, I have gained the education to help others in many ways, including family, friends, and co workers coming to me for support. I am a passionate healer with an alternative natural approach, helping women to reduce stress and anxiety, empower their lives and create positive change, and embrace a health and wellness lifestyle, using simple, self-directed, natural solutions. In all my years of acquiring my skills, I learned that having faith, no matter what, is how you move forward. Have faith in yourself and know that you are serving for a higher purpose, you will be guided to your next right step.

A Happier, Healthier Me—Overcoming Stress and Anxiety

By Leona Monfee

I lived on a beautiful acreage in a small town that you could drive around and see the whole town in about 10 to 15 minutes. Living in a little town meant that we did a lot of driving out of town. It was nothing to drive an hour or two for shopping or longer to visit family and friends, and we had all four seasons with long winters, so we drove in all kinds of weather. Somewhere along the way, I became afraid not only of driving but also of being the passenger. It got to the point where I was only driving in town, and only when I had to. I would become overwhelmed and panicked in any weather that wasn't clear and sunny. I couldn't control the fear, panic, and overwhelm every time I got into the vehicle. If we had to go some place and the weather wasn't clear and sunny, I would offer to sit in the back so that I could close my eyes and pray that the storm wouldn't come.

One time when we drove, over twelve hours, to the Island to spend Christmas with our oldest son. We were at the top of one of the passes. I looked up from the backseat and all I could see wasLeona Jo Monfee snow. I'm sure everyone in the vehicle felt my panic because my youngest son told me, "It's ok, Mom, just go back to sleep." I thought, "Really! Just go back to sleep! Now we are heading down this steep mountain in this blizzard!" Oh my gosh, I felt like I was dying. I closed my eyes—my heart was pounding, I couldn't breathe, my stomach was in knots, and my whole body was shaking; with every corner and breaking as we descended the summit, the pain, the fear, the overwhelm, and the humiliation consumed me. I had no control over it. As soon as we got to the bottom, my husband immediately found a place to pull over and let me out of the truck. I felt horrible and embarrassed. Why is this happening to me? I used to love travelling and seeing all the sights in any weather.

The storm came from out of nowhere, filling her very soul. What was this entity relentlessly growing stronger and darker inside of her with each overwhelming assault?

The storm continued to come and consume her life. Soon, she became the innocent spectator witnessing the destruction as the storm took charge. It became an uncontrollable trembling in her body and soul, inflicting more fear and darkness each time it came to strike her down. The fear and humiliation grew with each attack. She appeared to be okay on the outside, but she was slowly dying on the inside and didn't know how to revive herself.

Day after day, month after month, the storm became unyielding. She cowered alone in her darkness, shattered and consumed with indescribable fear and numbness, listening to the echoes of the people in her life, over and over again, "Why are you acting like this? Just stop it. It isn't that bad. Quit faking. There is something wrong with you. You are too much. Grow up..."

They just don't understand! *I can't stop the storm! I don't even know where it came from!! Why is this happening to me? Is there really something wrong with me? Am I going crazy?*

I had to fight harder. My family depends on me! No more! This can't be how my life ends, slowly dying inside! God, why are you doing this to me?! I know I have so much more to give! Someone! Anyone! PLEASE MAKE THE STORM STOP!!

Do you know this feeling, this feeling that is foreign to others? Well then, you are here for a reason—let me tell you how I know.

I showed up in the middle of a mini workshop for becoming an Intuitive Life Coach and running your own coaching business. I had no plans or thoughts of ever becoming a life coach. I already have my own business and I'm a Reiki master and natural herbalist, but a friend mentioned it and something she said caught my attention. I showed up for the rest of the days, and then it came time to purchase the program. I couldn't believe how expensive it was to become a Certified Intuitive Life Coach, and being Canadian, that meant it would be close to double the cost, which is way too much money that I didn't have to just throw away.

The woman hosting the workshop invited anyone who had questions to set up a personal interview to talk to her privately, so I thought, "Sure, why not?" I do have some questions, thinking the whole time, "There is no way I can afford to pay that much for a course, and I never would!"

There was a reason for me to be there and become a certified life coach. It turns out it was the help that I asked for. I learned how to naturally release fear, overwhelm, stress, and anxiety. I learned how to conquer the storm! I not only revived myself, but I also rose up stronger than before. I found my Inner Goddess, I found peace, and I found that I really do have so much more to give. Now I help other amazing women conquer the storm by releasing the obstacles that are holding them back from living their best life and becoming The Goddess they truly are! Becoming A Happier, Healthier Me! Here's what one of my clients said, "*Therapists get you to talk about thoughts, but they don't show you what to do with them. With Leona I learned how to process my thoughts. After just one session with Leona I learned how to bring my thoughts back into joy when I am down. This has been very helpful.*"

We may not know how or why we got to this point, but I do know that it is possible to move past it—past the fear, the panic, the stress, the anxiety, the overwhelm... We don't have to live with the storm. We move forward by empowering ourselves and tapping into our emotions and using our own insight and wisdom to empower ourselves. By asking the correct questions at the correct time and becoming clear on what we want and who we are; observing what emotions, concerns, or struggles come up and releasing the ones that are not serving us enables us to release the storm.

Shortly after starting the coaching course, my daughter had a doctor's appointment an hour and a half out of town, and it was winter. My husband was away working, and there was no one to drive her except for me, and I hadn't driven on the highway for ages. I had been using all the techniques that I was learning every day. The night before, I did a few extra sessions and prayed that the roads would be good.

We headed out early just in case the weather was bad. To our surprise, the roads were clear. We made it to her appointment with no issues, no panic, no overwhelm, and no fear. The drive was actually relaxing and enjoyable. Her appointment, however, was taking forever, and it doesn't stay light out that long in the winter. Her appointment ended up running three hours late; we didn't know why until we started heading back home. In the time that we sat waiting, it had snowed quite a bit, but by the time her appointment ended, all the snow had been cleaned or melted off the road. It turned out to be a lovely drive.

I believe that we end up where we are supposed to be in perfect Divine timing. If my daughter's appointment had come and I had never taken or heard about the coaching course, I would never have been able to go on this drive without total overwhelm—it was winter! And to actually be the driver?? Never would have happened!! When we got home, my daughter told me how proud she was of me. It made me feel proud of myself too, and it gave me a sense of peace and accomplishment. This is when I realized that the coaching course I was taking was the help that I had asked for, and I knew that I had to help other women to free themselves from the storm.

Now I have the honor and pleasure to teach amazing women to find their Inner Goddess, release the storm that is consuming them, and find their peace.

So, what is a health and wellness life coach?

I'm not a therapist and I don't diagnose!

You know how you hire a fitness coach to help you with the outer look of your body?

Well, hire a health and wellness life coach to help you with the inner work.

I will teach you and guide you through coaching, energy work, intuitive work, and more to identify the obstacles holding you back, the emotions attached to those obstacles, and how to release them so you can begin creating positive change.

Things don't have to stay the way they are. You can actually start releasing some of the obstacles by releasing the emotions.

There is nothing that we cannot overcome. We can become whoever we want to be. We don't have to shrink from society. By learning how to release the fear, the darkness, the panic, and the overwhelm, I took control of my life. I learned to breathe and take one day at a time. You can, too. God never gives you more than you can handle.

Are you ready to conquer the storm and become *A Happier, Healthier Me?*

It's time to find your Inner Goddess and Unleash Your Voice! I look forward to being your guide on this journey. See you on the inside.

I wish you peace, love, happiness, prosperity, kindness, and positivity.

With Gratitude,
Leona Jo

Thank you for purchasing this book. I have added a few bonuses and a discount on my *A Happier, Healthier Me* online course: https://leonajo.com/Unleash-Her-Voice-Bonus

Susan Tatem

Founder and CEO of Bright Path Coaching
Coach, Author

www.facebook/SusanMTatem
https://brightpath4autism.org

Bio for Susan Tatem, CEO of Bright Path Coaching, Author, Healthcare Provider, and Managing Partner for She Wins Women's NetworkSusan Tatem, the founder of Bright Path Coaching, is dedicated to empowering families of children with autism 12 years and older to navigate school and the transition into independent adulthood. Inspired by her own journey as a single mom raising a daughter with autism, Susan combines personal experience, professional expertise from 30 years in healthcare, and a deep passion to guide families with compassion and clarity. Her coaching provides parents with the tools to create a clear path for their children's future, addressing challenges like workforce readiness, independent living, and social skills. Susan's ultimate vision is to establish supported living communities worldwide, where young adults with autism can thrive. With honesty, integrity, and a heart for service, Bright Path Coaching equips families to transform worry into confidence, ensuring every individual with autism has the opportunity to lead a fulfilled, independent life. Additionally, Susan is the Managing Partner of the Tidewater Virginia Chapter of the She Wins Women's Network. She Wins is all about empowering women entrepreneurs and small business owners to connect, collaborate, and grow. It's a space where we can build meaningful relationships, elevate our businesses, and truly thrive shoulder to shoulder.

Unleash the Mother, Unleash the Mission

By Susan Tatem

I didn't find my voice on stage. I found it at a kitchen table at 2 a.m., surrounded by IEP paperwork and fear. I prayed, "God, show me the next right step." Not the next hundred—just one. My voice began not as a roar, but as a steady yes to the next step.

After a long IEP meeting, I sat in my car crying. My ex-husband neither participated in nor understood these meetings but had actually shown up for once. Instead of being helpful, he was a disaster, swearing up and down that my daughter didn't need it. I spent two hours being verbally bartered. All my insecurities flooded inside me: molestation, sexual assault, and discovering my first fiancé was a pedophile. My strength, confidence, and voice dissipated until I totally shut down, signing away my daughter's IEP. Ultimately, in the middle of third grade, I'd pulled her out of school and homeschooled her for the next seven years as a single mom who worked full-time.

The Season of Whispering

For years, I was the woman who got things done quietly. As a home-health physical therapist assistant, I learned patience, process, and what consistent effort can do. At home, I was a single mom raising a remarkable daughter with autism. We learned systems together—therapies, routines, visual schedules, social strategies, and the acronyms no one teaches you until you're already drowning.

When the time came to put her back into public school, I was NOT going to let them bully me again! I freaked the school out by showing up with two advocates and a lawyer. During our meeting, they insisted my daughter be placed in 10th grade since she was 15. I insisted she be placed in the 7th grade because that's where she was scholastically and developmentally. Ultimately, I said that they couldn't do anything without my signature being on that piece of paper, and until it said what ***I*** wanted it to say, I would **NOT** sign it! It was my first taste of victory, and I wanted more.

I had an advocate then—an angel in sneakers who translated the maze. She sat beside me in meetings, led with fierce grace I needed to understand, and asked the questions I didn't know I was allowed to ask. When she passed away, grief dragged me under. But it left something on the shore: She hadn't just carried me. She'd trained me.

It wasn't "being strong." It was being faithful: keeping my daughter safe today and preparing her for tomorrow, even when tomorrow felt like a cliff.

Speaking Up, Stepping Out

I cofounded a support group and shared my story. I told parents what I wish I'd known: You're not failing because you're overwhelmed; you're overwhelmed because you're doing the work of three people with the heart of one mother. I showed how I treated the school and IEP like they work for me instead of a yearly negotiation. It was all about three words: function, function, and function!

- I eliminated classes that served no purpose towards my daughter's future independence. What functional life skill does this class promote? Can we substitute a better fit?
- Which daily living skills matter most? Managing money? Then she needs math all year round, not half a year. Getting a job? Then she needs to learn to write a resume or do a job interview, not creative writing or another class where her learning disabilities would impede her ability to process and retain. I homeschooled her for seven years and knew her abilities better than anyone else on the planet!

- How do we build safety, communication, and community? I knew she would do well at a place called Wilson Workforce, a job training and life skill training organization, where students lived in dorms and would receive job training specific to the individual's needs. I started planning this before she went back into public school. I knew exactly who I needed to talk to and when. I knew what community agency would pay for it and had connected with them two years in advance.

Because I had networked and done the research, my daughter's post-graduation path to independence was crystal clear. When the day of her high school graduation came, my eyes filled with tears of overwhelming joy and pride, just like they did the moment she was born. She did it! No one else understood what a monumental moment that was for the two of us. Despite her GPA not showing it, I knew how difficult it was and how hard she had to work every single day just to function in that environment...but she did it. The next fall, she moved into her own apartment with all the supports in place she needed, including her driver's license. I had been working on this since she was first diagnosed at age 10. Now, 12 years later, it finally happened.

Bright Path 4 Autism: Because Every Piece Matters

When I opened *Bright Path 4 Autism,* I wasn't just opening a business; I launched my vision. I wanted to carry on my advocate's legacy by helping parents of children with autism transform from overwhelm, worry, and isolation to clarity, confidence, and support.

My journey is taking me to places I never dreamed I'd go. I write for books and magazines like *Autism Parenting Magazine*, speak on stages, and consult with churches and employers who want to welcome people with autism into their communities—not as charity, but as neighbors and contributors. My faith anchors me, and my daughter keeps teaching me.

"Because Every Piece Matters" isn't a tagline; it's a worldview. Every small skill, every small win, and every small step forward matters. The *IEP Power Hour* teaches them to take their power back. It's where parents dictate school goals with real life: laundry as functional math and grocery trips as community participation and money management.

On my TV show **Puzzled Parents** and my YouTube channel , I share stories that are raw, authentic, and honest.

The Courage to Own Your Narrative

Confidence isn't born from performing; it's born from truth. My truth includes chronic pain that limits what my body can do some days, the grief of losing the advocate who shaped me, the grit of working two jobs as a single mother, and the grace I lean on daily.

It also includes joy: an appointment my daughter handles independently, the quiet triumph of a paycheck earned, a meal cooked, and a friendship tended.

I used to think my voice had to sound like someone else's to matter. Now I know it matters *because* it's mine: seasoned by real life, softened by faith, and focused on service.

Not only do I have ***my*** voice, but I have also *become* the voice for those who cannot speak for themselves. I'm God's instrument for the special needs community.

What Unleashing My Voice Looks Like Now

- **On paper:** I teach families to connect IEP goals to adult life—job readiness, daily living, safety, and community participation—so "services" become steps toward independence.

- **On camera and stage:** Through *Puzzled Parents* and live talks, I name the hard subjects: the cliff after high school, the fear of "what happens if something happens to me," and the myth that independence only looks one way.
- **In community and for the future:** I build circles where parents don't have to be everything, help employers value reliability and pattern recognition, partner with churches to create true welcome, and work toward supported living communities where independence is personalized and dignity non-negotiable.

If You Need a Starting Point

Here's a simple framework I give families:

- **Name the North Star.** In two sentences, describe an ordinary, beautiful adulthood for your child.
- **Choose the Big Three.** Pick three skills to practice this quarter—prepare one meal, time a shower, use a debit card, and ask for help using a script.
- **Build the Team.** List who can help—teacher, job coach, neighbor, youth leader, small-group friend, aunt, bus driver, employer—and assign one micro-task to each.
- **Translate the Paper.** For every IEP goal, write an after plan: What does this look like after school? On Saturday? At church? At work?
- **Measure What Matters.** Count reps in real life. Track tries, not just wins. Celebrate attempts. Adjust supports. In autism, one size might not even fit the same person for two days in a row. Be fluid.

My Unapologetic Why

My daughter taught me that independence isn't a finish line; it's a journey. Some days it's smooth; other days it's loud and messy. But it's hers, and it's good.

I write for the mother who's staring at a form thinking, *I can't do this.* I want her to hear my voice and think, *I can. Yes, I can.* I also write for the girl I used to be: the one who believed she had to whisper forever. She didn't. Neither do you.

When a mother finds her voice, a family finds its future. And when families find their future, communities change.

Educate. Empower. Elevate. Because Every Piece Matters.

Priya Tandon

The Soul Sutras
Self-discovery to Personal Reinvention Transformational Coach and Empowerment Mentor

www.facebook.com/thesoulsutras
https://www.instagram.com/priyatandon/

As a Self-Discovery to Personal Reinvention Transformational Coach and Empowerment Mentor, I guide individuals—especially women—through profound life transitions, helping them rediscover their authentic selves and step into their fullest potential. Through a holistic approach blending mindset shifts, emotional healing, and strategic goal-setting, I empower clients to break free from limiting beliefs, build confidence, and create fulfilling lives. Whether navigating heartbreak, divorce, career shifts, or personal growth, my coaching fosters resilience, self-love, and clarity. I integrate proven techniques in emotional intelligence, mindfulness, and individual empowerment to help clients align with their true purpose. My mission is to transform challenges into opportunities for growth, providing the tools and support needed for lasting change. By bridging self-discovery with actionable reinvention strategies, I help individuals heal and thrive, creating a life of confidence, fulfillment, and empowerment. I am also a writer and editor, publishing articles in Coaching Perspectives, Elephant Journal, and Medium.

Becoming of a Butterfly

By Priya Tandon

A time comes when the caterpillar must break the cocoon walls, and a butterfly must spread its wings to fly into the unknown of the vast sky. The butterfly doesn't know the colors of her wings or the heights of the flight she will have to make to survive. She only hears the heartbeat of her heart and feels the fire of courage and grit burning in her to fly. And so she does.

For many years, I, too, was buried in a cocoon that looked like a haven from outside, but inside was a tumultuous picture. I was suffocating and was longing to breathe. As I continue to awaken and grow spiritually, emotionally, and mentally, the space inside the cocoon became tighter and tighter. I had to break the cocoon. And so I did and flew into the callings of the azure sky.

Love or a relationship can go wrong in many different ways. The changes to a human heart are in ways incomprehensible and sometimes forever. For me, I ended up locking the doors to my heart and throwing the key away, only to realize that one cannot contain love. Once we feed on the love, we become love. The sweet emotion of love is like the force of water that can break a dam's walls. I had so much love to give as a human to my family, friends, neighbors, and anyone, not just one significant relationship. I have no right to suppress what I feel and own in my veins, blood, and spirit. Love did not fail me; it was the relationship that failed me.

"It is better to live your own destiny imperfectly than to live an imitation of somebody else's life with perfection." ~ Bhagavad Gita

I had been at a place that was not authentic to my inner being- a relationship and a space that did not align with my true self.

I had assumed the role of a 'rescuer' being the 'stronger' one who had a solution to every problem we faced. I was left behind in my desire to progress, career, ambitions, and even well-being. I became the giver who sacrificed to fulfill expectations. Now excluded from the joint success as a couple, non-appreciated, overworked, I was alone as a mother to a child on the autism spectrum. As I write this, I may not be proud of what I did for myself, but I had made a commitment to love, and there was nothing bigger to me than that resolve then.

Yes, an empath and a rescuer with narrow boundaries, I am guilty of creating a destiny that was not mine but somebody else's. In the end, I had nothing left to give, and I refused to continue with the solo dance of giving and fulfilling others' expectations. What I gained when I left behind my past and an assumed relationship was priceless. I embraced myself wholly and set out on the path to living life authentically and honoring myself every day, no matter what!

Healing is not linear, though I was soon to find out. If one day I felt great, then the next was dreadful as it could be. Since healing does not come with a manual, I had to customize it according to my inner work's pace, with no deadlines to hang onto. My spiritual practice in solitude pestered me to go deep within. I saw where and what was still triggering my emotions related to the past. One by one, I could sit with those uncomfortable emotions and look at these upheavals in the eye. I knew how to calm my storm by addressing my trauma one moment at a time.

Many of us are stuck in the cocoon of circumstances and relationships. Many of us live not in alignment with our true selves or a higher purpose. Many of us do not know how to break open the shell constructed around us as a barrier to our wellness and authentic life. Each of us in our lifetime will have to awaken to take personal responsibility and be accountable for our lives — health, wealth, job, relationship, or personal development and growth. Our past may have brought us to the current, but it does not define the future for us. The ultimate realization is that we are the creators of our destiny and lives. To evolve, to be the person we always aspire to be, we have to keep on peeling back the onion layers to allow the hidden parts of ourselves to emerge. When we shed the masks of self-doubt, self-belief, limitations, and insecurities, we break through the barriers in our conscious and unconscious minds to create and express our destiny.

I had to learn how to trust my path, even though laid out with thorns, but it was still my path. We have to trust our path and have faith in the workings of the cosmos that we are where we are meant to be at any given moment, and respect the painful lessons for our inner growth and stability.

Everyone's path is different, and that is okay. Start by knowing who you are and chart your path. Maybe you want to rest your head under the shade of the tree along the river, live atop a mountain, and call it a life. Or perhaps you want to be an executive — do what empowers you and puts a smile on your face. Living a life built for and on others' expectations is a fake life, and you are playing a character who will one day rebel.

Moment by moment, life comes alive in our body, mind, and emotions- some moments are fleeting, and some we hold on to in our memory box. When we open the memory box and play its tunes, it becomes our past. When we participate in creating a moment, it becomes our 'now,' and when we start decorating and building a box for our moments to come, it becomes the future.

Afterall, we are the creators of our destiny, and we are the main characters of this play that we call 'life.' Why not be the hero of our lives too?

I am at uncanny content since I unleashed my voice to hear myself. This voice is more for me than the world because if I don't hear my own voice, then who will? This voice is my voice, and I know not to let it drown again in the noise of the world. I am creating my life, finding myself not in cubicles and corporate jobs but in the lap of nature, art, poetry, travels, writings, spirituality, community, purpose-driven work, and the laughter of my children. Sure, days are hard, but I own the days and nights now and am not ready to give up for anyone or anything in this world.

Know your true self, honor your path, and live life genuinely by shattering the cocoons of narratives that we keep telling ourselves over and over again.

Before the walls of beliefs, cultural conditioning, and limitations — self-imposed and circumstantial — close in, fly out of the cocoon. The butterfly does not know it yet, but the sky eagerly awaits a butterfly to spread its colorful, empowered wings.

Hannah Darby GMBPsP SMACCPH

Healing with Hannah
Holistic Healer

https://www.linkedin.com/in/hannahdarbyhealingwithhannah/
https://www.facebook.com/healingwithhannahdarby
https://www.instagram.com/healingwithhannahd/
https://www.healingwithhannah.co.uk/
https://www.accph.org.uk/united-kingdom/martley/therapists-and-coaches/hannah-darby

Hannah Darby GMBPsP SMACCPH is an award-winning holistic healer who helps guide individuals through their personal grief journeys with her unique H.E.A.L.® method. Hannah is a General Member of the British Psychological Society, a Senior Member of Accredited Counsellors, Coaches, Psychotherapists and Hypnotherapists, a Reiki Master Teacher, a Master HeartHealing® practitioner, a Masseuse, as well as a global bestselling Author. Hannah founded Healing with Hannah, a unique therapy practice based on her professional and personal wisdom, guided by science and spirituality. Hannah works with your mind, heart, and body to help you find deep healing with soulful integration, learning to live in peace with your grief. She has been featured in multiple international magazines. Hannah resides in the British countryside with her husband, four cats, and two chihuahuas. She enjoys country walks, music, and movies. Hannah is a woman of faith.

The Power of Confidence Lies in Your Voice

By Hannah Darby GMBPsP SMACCPH

Confidence is an inside game. I have spent so much time in my life searching for confidence, only to finally realize it's something that comes from within, not from outside. The confidence to use your voice, to hold your head high, and to stick to what you believe, no matter what others may think. Sounds easy in theory, but much harder in practice.

Our voice holds so much power. Far more power than we realize. Harnessing that power takes skill, courage, and resilience. Our voice is how we communicate our inner world and with the outside world. Our voice is how we communicate with ourselves. How we speak not only to others but also to ourselves is so important. My voice was taken from me, and it took me many years to get it back. I want to share part of this story with you today.

Women are quick to put each other down, but imagine how much we could achieve if we actually worked together. Only now am I starting to find women in my life who want to help pick you up, not bring you down. Don't be the woman who destroys other women; be the woman who helps other women rise.

For years, I have been an easy target, allowing others to pick on me, break me down, and change the voice in my mind to one full of darkness and despair, taking away my power. I was quiet; I hated confrontation and would do anything to get away from it. They not only used their words but also changed my words to break me. If all you hear about yourself is negative, it's hard not to let that enter your subconscious mind and change the way you speak to yourself, affecting the way you present yourself in the world. Our confidence is intrinsically linked to our voice. If you want to unlock your confidence, it all begins with your voice.

After years of being bullied by others, the voice in my mind was completely negative. I had given away all of my power. This worry and hurt for myself was carried with me for years to come. Rewriting that narrative and changing your inner voice takes courage, resilience, and determination. It takes grit and strength. More often than not, some of the hardest battles we face are within ourselves. The deepest scars we have are unseen. Remember this.

Learning to talk to myself positively has been one of the hardest things I have ever had to learn. The effects of the trauma I faced in my childhood turned my mind into a dark place, a place I couldn't hide from, as it was always with me. A dark cloud of doom surrounded my mind, a fog I could not see through, and a cord wrapped around my neck, stopping my voice and strangling my power. My voice was full of negativity for myself, with no self-belief, self-worth, or self-confidence. The cup was always half empty, and everything was turning into something to worry about. I masked this with smiles and laughter, never letting anyone see how much pain I was facing on the inside. The anxiety and depression reached a peak that I almost didn't make it past. Yet throughout all the trauma, I had a handful of people who always had my back, and for that I am extremely thankful. Most importantly, I didn't give up on myself, because I was worth it, and you are too.

Working on my voice and confidence wounds has changed my life completely. It allowed me to go back to the time my voice was first taken from me and set my voice free. Back to when the seeds of doubt we first sown in my mind by the bullies I faced, who slyly shot their comments at me when they thought I couldn't hear them. It has allowed me to speak to myself with grace and positivity, a voice I deserved to hear. I no longer put myself down. I used to always used to think things like - 'You're stupid' or 'If you weren't so useless, you could...' By stopping myself from putting myself down, it has helped me gain the confidence to share my story and finally feel worthy of just being me as I am. You can have this, too. The confidence you need is already there, just waiting for you to claim it. I would love to share this with you. If this resonates, get in touch.

Healing my heart has transformed my life, and it can transform yours, too, if you allow it. Opening myself up to levels of happiness, confidence, and clarity I never thought would be possible, and you can have this, too. For when we start to treat ourselves the way we wish others would treat us, the whole world starts to shift. It all begins on the inside, with our own thoughts, our inner voice. Once we start to change our inner voice, this is reflected in our outer voice.

Sharing these stories is so important to help others find their own strength. As I've said, some of the deepest scars we carry can never be seen. Sharing these scars allows us to heal on a deeper level, not only for ourselves but also to help others heal, too.

Even now, I still catch myself speaking to myself in a way I would never dream of talking to another. This is a good way to think about your voice, for more often than not, we are our own worst critics. But now I'm able to catch those thoughts and not allow myself to get hooked on them as I have before. Learning how to catch and unhook your voice from this negative train of thought is such an important skill to have, and one I would like to share with you today.

It's so important to notice the patterns of your thoughts, to catch them before they turn dark. So next time you catch yourself calling yourself stupid or ugly, or feel like you're pulling yourself down and speaking in a way you would never speak to others, stop and turn it around. Notice yourself falling down the rabbit holes of despair in your mind and catch yourself before you fall. A simple way to achieve this is by finding a statement to unhook your thought process with. Something easy to remember, something you can say out loud. Saying it out loud is the important part. It doesn't matter what the phrase is, but by saying it aloud, it interrupts the thought process and stops them in their tracks. I like simple phrases like 'whoops' or 'not right now.' By saying this to yourselves out loud, you interrupt the thought process and can stop negative thoughts in their tracks. Allowing you to catch yourself before you fall into the rabbit holes of negative thinking.

So next time you find yourself using your voice against yourself, remember the power of words, the power your voice holds. Stop, breathe, and ground yourself. Use your unhook phrase and turn those thoughts around. Your confidence is your power; your power lies in your voice.

Your voice is your power, your secret weapon to unleash upon the world. It's your choice whether you use this for good or bad. So be kind to others and be kind to yourself. After all, words are far mightier than the sword.

You can choose how to use your voice, to spread words of kindness rather than words full of pain. You have a power within you. It's your time to rise, be strong, courageous, and confident. You deserve to be treated how you treat others, you deserve to be listened to, and you deserve to feel confident using your voice and unleashing your power.

If you want to work on your confidence with me, I would love to hear from you. Allow me to give you the tools to unlock your inner goddess, your inner confidence, and allow your voice to shine brightly with the power to be heard. For your voice holds more power than you realize.

One of the greatest gifts you can give yourself is the gift of confidence. Yes, confidence is inside us. But sometimes we need to be guided by others to set it free to allow us to see how beautiful we truly are.

Now is your time to rise. It's your time to use your voice with all the power God gave you. Your inner voice should be your greatest ally, not your greatest critic. Finding the power in your voice will transform your life in more ways than you realize.

It's your time to unleash her.
It's your time to unleash your voice.
It's your time to unleash your confidence.
And it's your time to unleash your power.

Ariel Balfour

CEO of Trauma 2 Triumph Coaching Inc.
Mentor

https://www.linkkedin.com/in/ariel-balfour-07341b319
https://www.facebook.com/ariel.sommers/
https://www.instagram.com/thearielbalfour
www.thearielbalfour.com

Ariel Balfour is a trauma alchemist and emotional wellness mentor known as The Reclamation Warrior and Viking Queen. She helps high-performing entrepreneurs and industry disruptors heal their hidden wounds, regulate their nervous systems, and access fierce clarity to break through plateaus and step into seven-figure success. Through raw, real talk and powerful somatic methods, she dismantles the myths of mental health and teaches clients how to lead from embodied power—without bypassing the truth of their pain. With an edge forged in personal battles and professional mastery, Ariel doesn't do surface-level. Her work is deep, transformational, and built for those who are ready to reclaim everything they were told to suppress. When she's not mentoring CEOs or running her programs like Epic Effect or Release & Reclaim, she's chasing her two wild boys, training like a warrior, and reminding the world that true leadership starts from the inside out.

Unshackled: Finding My Voice Beyond the Diagnosis

By Ariel Balfour

For years, I lived inside a box. It wasn't made of wood or steel, but it was just as confining. It was labeled *bipolar disorder*, stamped in bold letters by a medical system that promised help but delivered a cage instead.

The day I got my diagnosis, I was told it was permanent. That my brain was broken or, as they said, "different." That the only way to live was to medicate, forever. There was no talk of healing, no curiosity about my past, and no acknowledgment of the trauma I had survived. Just a clinical pronouncement followed by a prescription... many prescriptions.

I was thirteen years old, terrified, and willing to believe anyone who promised relief. So, I swallowed the pills. Every day. Dutifully. I told myself I was doing what was necessary, that maybe this was just the life I had to accept unless I wanted to end up in the ground like the rest of the females in my family, handed the same life sentence.

At first, the medication dulled the chaos in my mind but it also dulled me. My laughter was quieter. My anger was muted. My creativity, the fire that once burned in my bones, flickered weakly in the shadows. I wasn't "well." I was sedated. Disconnected. Flatlined in the name of stability.

No one told me that "symptom management" could also mean "self-erasure." I was a mere shell of the person I once was. But that was the point, wasn't it?

The silence started in my mind but soon wrapped around my entire life. When I questioned my treatment, I was told I was being "noncompliant." When I asked if there were other ways to heal, I was warned of the "inevitable relapse," the doom of self-harm being inevitable if I ever stopped the meds. I was young, so I believed them without question... at least at first.

But deep down, there was a voice that refused to die. My voice. My truth. It was faint, muffled by pharmaceuticals and professional authority, but it was there: *There's more to you than this. You are not broken. You are not just a diagnosis.*

I didn't dare speak that voice out loud. In the mental health system, questioning the prescribed narrative can make you an instant target for suspicion. They call it "denial" or "lack of insight." They imply you're too unwell to know what's good for you. And I had seen how they treated people who resisted. I knew the power they held.

So, I stayed quiet for years. Outwardly compliant. Inwardly suffocating.

My turning point didn't happen in some dramatic rebellion. It happened in the quiet devastation of realizing that I didn't recognize myself anymore. I looked in the mirror and saw a hollowed-out version of me, a person who was existing but not living. I saw a woman sick, but not because of her diagnosis, but because of the medicine meant to mute it.

The truth was undeniable: The very system that promised to help me had kept me sick. Not sick in the sense of active symptoms, but sick in the sense of being trapped, powerless, and conditioned to believe I could never truly heal.

I was done. Done with numbing. Done with the shame. Done with accepting a life that wasn't mine.

It wasn't an easy decision to step away from medication. In fact, it was terrifying. Every warning from every psychiatrist echoed in my head. Every judgment from anyone ever using the phrases "crazy" or "she was sooo bipolar" rang as reminders. But I also knew that if I didn't try, if I didn't at least attempt to reclaim my mind, I would spend the rest of my life as a ghost in my own story.

So, I began the slow, deliberate process of tapering off. And in perfect timing, my body naturally sided with me and began rejecting it as well. I didn't do it recklessly. I educated myself, listened to my body, and sought support outside the traditional system. And as the fog began to lift, I felt something I hadn't felt in years: clarity.

Without the meds, my emotions came back in full force. It was messy for a while. There were days I thought I'd made a mistake. But I also realized something crucial... my emotions were not my enemy. They were my compass to my identity.

Instead of silencing my feelings, I learned to work with them. I explored trauma-informed therapy, somatic practices, breathwork, and energy healing. I stopped seeing myself as a "bipolar patient" and started seeing myself as a human with a history, a nervous system, and a story worth understanding.

I learned how my childhood experiences shaped my mental health. I learned that what psychiatry called "symptoms" were often survival responses, which were my body's way of navigating a world that had not been safe. And I learned that real healing wasn't about suppressing those responses but helping my body and mind feel safe enough to transmute them into something else entirely.

This wasn't about rejecting all medicine or demonizing people who choose medication. It was about reclaiming my right to decide what healing looked like for me, without fear, shame, or coercion.

Today, I've been medication-free for twenty years. An impossible outcome. That doesn't mean my life has been perfect or symptom-free. I still face challenges. I still have days when my mind feels like a storm. But I know how to navigate those storms now without handing over the steering wheel to someone who insists they know my waters better than I do.

My healing has been a combination of science and soul, grounded in understanding my nervous system and daring to explore beyond the rigid walls of conventional mental health treatment. It's been a journey of peeling back layers of trauma, learning to regulate my body, and building a life where I am no longer defined by a label.

Most importantly, I found my voice. My truth. My identity.

When I finally began to speak openly about my experience, I expected resistance. I expected people to accuse me of being reckless or irresponsible. And yes, as expected, many did. But what I didn't expect was the flood of messages from people who whispered, *Me too.*

People who had been told they would need medication forever. People who had been shamed for wanting to explore alternative healing. People who had been silenced by fear. They weren't just reaching out to thank me... they were reaching out to reclaim themselves.

That's when I realized my story wasn't just mine. It was part of a much larger conversation that needed to happen. One about choice, about trauma, and about the many paths to healing that have nothing to do with a prescription pad.

I speak out now because I refuse to let others be swallowed by the same system that nearly erased me. I fight for a future where mental health treatment is not a one-size-fits-all model. Where trauma is not a footnote but a starting point. Where healing means more than just symptom suppression.

We need to revolutionize how we view mental health. That means shifting from "managing disorders" to creating the conditions for the mind and body to heal. It means understanding that medication can be a tool but it is not the *only* tool. And it means honoring the voices of those who have lived the reality, not just studied it.

I believe in a world where mental health care is collaborative, not coercive. Where we are given options, education, and respect for our autonomy. Where asking questions is not a threat but a necessity.

For a long time, my voice was a whisper in a locked room. Now, it is a battle cry.

To those still inside the box, still afraid to speak, I say this: You are not broken. You are not just your diagnosis. And you are allowed to define what healing looks like for you.

I am living proof that it is possible to step outside the walls built for you, to reclaim your mind, your body, and your life. Not because it's easy but because your voice is worth hearing, and your life is worth living on your own terms.

It took me two decades to come this far, but I wouldn't trade this freedom for anything. I am unshackled. Unleashed.

I AM RECLAIMED.

And I will keep speaking, not just for me, but for the thousands still waiting for the courage or the permission to speak for themselves.

This is my story. But it is also ***our*** movement.

Nikki Hillhouse

nikkihillhouse.com

https://www.linkedin.com/in/nikki-hillhouse-a6b25529b/
https://www.facebook.com/nikki.hillhouse.1
https://www.instagram.com/nikkihillhouse/
https://www.nikkihillhouse.com/

Nikki is an experienced Mind Detox Practitioner, Meditation Teacher, Well-being Coach, Speaker, Writer and Wellness Retreat Facilitator. With a rich background in holistic health and therapeutic techniques, Nikki is dedicated to helping others unlock their full potential. Her mission is to empower others to overcome their greatest challenges, transcend fears, and step into a life of freedom, happiness, health, and fulfillment. With a great passion to help clients reconnect with their intuition, heal past wounds, and embrace their worthiness. Through her holistic approach, Nikki guides individuals toward self-discovery, resilience, and personal transformation, inspiring them to create a life without limits. Nikki has transformed her life from chronic pain and struggle to radiant health and resilience. Her journey led her from adversity to the tranquil shores of Turkey, where she now hosts transformational wellness retreats and runs a thriving coaching business, guiding others toward empowerment, transformation, and lasting well-being.

From Silence to Sovereignty

By Nikki Hillhouse

The Moment Everything Changed

A woman's legacy isn't just what she leaves behind; it's how she chooses to rise, heal, and inspire. A true legacy grows from transformation, courage, and breaking free from limitations. It means, in each moment, deciding that pain and struggle don't define the final chapter.

I learned this the hard way through a journey that began with what felt like an ending.

For years I was stuck in survival mode. A life-altering stroke left me in chronic pain, exhausted, and overwhelmed by loss. My body felt betrayed, and the woman staring back in the mirror was a stranger. She carried not just physical wounds but also unspoken fears, self-doubt, and the crushing belief that my best years were already behind me.

Doctors offered little comfort. Their voices felt like a life sentence: Accept a life limited by constraints. Their words echoed in sterile exam rooms, reinforcing a narrative I felt trapped by.

Yet, deep within me, I refused to believe that was the end of my story. Something—maybe intuition, stubbornness, or the human spirit—whispered that another way existed.

Waiting for a Savior That Never Came

At first, like so many of us do when faced with overwhelming circumstances, I waited for someone to save me. I put my faith in external forces: the next doctor, a breakthrough treatment, or a miracle that would restore what I had lost. Each appointment carried the weight of desperate hope, and each disappointment felt like another door closing on my future.

But no one was coming to rescue me. The realization hit me: I was waiting for salvation from sources that, while well-intentioned, could only address part of my healing. The doctors could treat my physical symptoms, but they couldn't heal the deeper wounds, the ones that existed in my mind, my spirit, and my sense of self-worth.

It was in this moment of profound disappointment that I discovered something extraordinary:

The power had been within me all along. I realized that healing wasn't just about my body. It was about my mind, my emotions, and my willingness to reclaim my power. The choice was mine, and mine alone, to make.

I made the decision to become the CEO of my health and my life. It was time to reclaim my power.

The Courage to Begin Again

This decision marked the beginning of what would become the most challenging and rewarding journey of my life. It wasn't easy; in fact, it was brutally difficult. Healing, I discovered, is not a straight path lined with steady progress and predictable milestones. It's a winding road filled with setbacks, breakthroughs, moments of doubt, and flashes of incredible strength you never knew you possessed.

There were days I wanted to give up, moments when the weight of it all felt too much to bear. The physical pain would flare, or the emotional exhaustion would overwhelm me, and I'd find myself questioning whether this journey toward healing was worth the effort. During these dark moments, the old patterns of thinking would resurface, whispering that perhaps the doctors were right; perhaps this limited existence was all I could expect.

But something remarkable began to happen as I committed to this path of self-directed healing. Each small step forward created momentum. Like a snowball rolling down a hill, my efforts began to pay off. Slowly, I started to feel stronger, not just physically, but emotionally and spiritually as well.

The transformation wasn't just in my body. It was in my entire relationship with myself and my circumstances. I stopped seeing myself as a victim of my circumstances and began to understand myself as the author of my own story. This shift in perspective was perhaps the most powerful medicine I could have prescribed for myself.

The Ripple Effect of Personal Transformation

As my healing journey progressed, I began to understand something profound: Healing isn't just personal—it's generational. When one woman chooses to heal, she doesn't just change her own life. She creates a ripple effect that touches everyone around her, expanding outward in ways she may never fully comprehend.

She becomes the living proof that transformation is possible. In a world that often tells us to accept our limitations and settle for less than we deserve, a woman who chooses to heal becomes a beacon of hope. She shows other women—her daughters, sisters, and friends—that they too can rewrite their stories. She demonstrates that the narrative of limitation and resignation is not the only option available to us.

This realization transformed my understanding of what legacy truly means.

A legacy, I learned, is built in the small, everyday choices we make. It's found in choosing self-worth over fear, speaking truth instead of staying silent, and breaking free from limiting beliefs rather than settling for a life that doesn't align with our soul's deepest knowing.

Legacy is not about waiting until the end of life to make an impact; it is about living in a way that inspires change now, in this moment, with every decision we make and every action we take.

The Universal Story of Women's Resilience

My story, while deeply personal, is not unique. So many women carry untold stories—narratives of pain and resilience, of dreams buried beneath the weight of responsibilities and expectations. We carry the burden of being everything for everyone, often losing ourselves in the process of caring for others. We become experts at self-sacrifice while remaining novices at self-care.

But every woman reaches a critical moment, a crossroad where she must make a fundamental choice: *Will she continue to live according to the limitations of her past, or will she rise into the life she was meant to live?* This moment of decision is both terrifying and exhilarating, representing nothing less than the choice between existing and truly living.

Women who choose to overcome adversity don't just transform their own lives. They inspire generations to come. They remind the world that strength is not about avoiding hardship but about using it as fuel for something greater. They demonstrate that our struggles don't define us. Our ability to rise from them does.

The True Meaning of Legacy

When you choose healing, you reclaim your power. When you prioritize your well-being, you challenge the narrative that women must always give to others while neglecting themselves. When you step into your purpose with courage and conviction, you inspire those around you to do the same. This is what legacy is truly about.

It's not about perfection. None of us are perfect, and the pursuit of perfection can become another form of self-imposed limitation.

Instead, it's about transformation. It's about choosing to heal, not just for ourselves, but for the women who will come after us. It's about showing that struggle does not define us; our ability to rise from it does.

"I transformed my pain into purpose, my struggle into personal growth, and my wounds into wisdom."

This transformation became my mission: to help other women do the same. To show them that no matter where they've been, no matter what they've endured, they have the power to create a life of meaning, freedom, and impact.

Your Legacy Starts Now

What legacy are you creating? This question demands honest self-reflection. Will you pass down fear, self-doubt, and the belief that life just happens to you? Or will you pass down resilience, courage, and the deep knowing that you are capable of anything you set your mind to?

A legacy is not measured by material success or external achievements, but by the impact you leave on others. It's found in the lessons you share, the support you offer, and the love you give freely. It's in the way you choose to live, to stand in your truth, and to empower those around you.

The world doesn't just need more women who survive—it needs more women who rise. Women who reclaim their power, embrace their worth, and leave behind a legacy of healing, wisdom, and strength. Women who declare with unwavering conviction.

Your story is still being written. Your legacy is being created in every decision you make, every boundary you set, and every dream you pursue. Every time you choose growth over comfort, every time you refuse to let fear hold you back, and every time you believe in your own power, you are actively shaping your legacy.

You were never meant to stay small. You were meant to step into your greatness, to heal not just yourself but the generations that will follow, to inspire, and to lead. The world is waiting for the unique impact that only you can make.

This is your time. Rewrite your story. Own your legacy. Rise.

Reflection

- What limiting beliefs have you accepted about yourself that may not actually be true?
- How might your healing journey inspire the women in your life?
- What small step can you take today to reclaim your power?
- What legacy do you want to leave for the next generation of women?

Sarah-Jane Layton

Soul Freedom
Spiritual Mum, 3 x International Best Selling Author, Soul Coach and Tao Healing Practitioner

www.linkedin.com/in/sarah-janelayton
https://www.facebook.com/sarecare
https://www.instagram.com/sarahjane_layton
Soul Freedom Page https://www.facebook.com/sarahsoulfreedom
Create Love Peace and Harmony on the New Motherhood Journey
https://m.facebook.com/groups/397137864640300/?ref=share

I empower and support Women and Mums to connect to the power of their souls. To love themselves and lead their families to embody a happy and healthy life. Support spiritual single mums to transform self doubt and overwhelm to trust themselves and be courageous. To heal their relationships with money and business so they have loving and abundant relationships. To release ancestral trauma and beliefs that do not serve them and their families. To be fully self expressed and achieve their goals/dreams. To live an authentic and integrous life. To create true health, unlimited wealth and time to live their best life To create soul aligned online business that financially supports them and their families. To serve others and leave a legacy their families would be proud of. To live a life of truth and soul freedom. To create love, peace and harmony for Women and their families.

The Power of Speaking Up

By Sarah-Jane Layton

While preparing to write my chapter in this book, I realized how often I've felt blocked in using my voice.

During school I was the quiet, conscientious student, not putting my hand up to ask questions or ask for help.

I remember telling my mom that I felt depressed; however, I never told another soul. I felt ashamed and didn't want anyone to know so told Mom not to tell anyone.

I also went to a doctor to inform them how I was feeling and agreed to take antidepressants, as I just wanted to feel better. I didn't want to be on tablets long-term; however, for now it was OK for temporary relief.

Another reason I didn't tell anyone was I didn't think anyone could help me and that I needed to work it out on my own, which forced me to become a very independent person. I think the reason I had depression was because I held things in and didn't express myself.

At around 16, I had my first boyfriend, who was 7 years older than me and was my mom's friend's son.

He invited me out one day to play tennis while I was working as a Kmart checkout chick. Of course, I didn't tell Mom the truth that he was my boyfriend and said that we were just friends; however, she found out the truth.

Mom and Dad separated when I was around 14 years old. My dad got remarried when I was around 17 years old, which was a lot to take in as a teenager. I also had 2 younger sisters that were 1 & 1/2years and 4 years younger. I'm sure we were all affected, even though we didn't talk about how we were feeling.

I didn't have the skills to support my sisters with the breakup of our family.

I remember Dad sitting me and my sisters down at McDonald's then telling us he'd met another lady. I burst into tears as I knew Mom and Dad probably wouldn't get back together.

Mom and Dad didn't communicate with each other after they divorced many years ago until my middle sister got married and had her first baby.

Then they decided it was better to get along, as they'd probably see each other at grandchildren's birthdays, etc.

Now, more than 30 years later, Mom and Dad and their partners happily meet up at family events, are friendly, and talk to each other, which is wonderful. I feel that my parents had a communication breakdown during their marriage and couldn't talk about things openly to resolve the issues before. I remember them giving each other the silent treatment, which was difficult for all involved, especially for the children, as they are not aware of the value of healthy and open communication.

One night the cops turned up to the house as Mom and Dad had a dispute and I felt stuck in the middle. Again I burst out crying because there was nothing I could do.

I didn't tell anyone at school about my parents breakup so had no support from teachers or kids that might have been going through similar family challenges.

In the 1990s, depression wasn't really spoken about much so it was difficult to know how to get help and support other than confiding in your doctor and prescriptions for relief. I'm glad I did that, as my depression lifted after going on antidepressants; however, it came back again several times over the years so I was on and off medication.

I think people feel so much shame from the negative feelings that we have, especially when we are not taught about emotional regulation and don't feel safe to express them in our homes and schools. So it can feel very isolating when we go through challenges and we don't feel we can share them with anyone or have a safe space to go to to be understood and loved.

Now as a mother to a 5-year-old boy, I never want him to feel that he can't share his thoughts, feelings, and challenges. I want him to feel safe and comfortable coming to me and discussing anything and would be grateful to love and support him with whatever he wants and needs.

Becoming a mother for the first time 5 years ago has filled my heart and soul with so much love and joy and is one of the most fulfilling jobs I have ever had. I love spending time with my son and next year he is starting school; however, I am planning to do part-time school combined with homeschooling. That way I can educate him about the most important subjects in life and support him to explore his interests and strengthen his abilities. I will encourage his uniqueness and creativity and be open to what he wants to learn as he grows. I also want the freedom to be able to travel whenever we choose and not be limited by school 5 days a week.

I believe travelling can expose children to so much learning and give them valuable life skills. Last night, Azali and I got home from a 2-week road trip from Mornington Peninsula, VIC, to Brisbane, QLD, during school holidays.

We both had an amazing time and lots of adventures and Azali enjoyed lots of "sleepovers," and we even slept in the car a couple of nights, unexpectedly. After our road trip I realized how much I love travel and how I'd love to be able to do it again, whenever I choose. I noticed that Azali really thrived also and that he is now more expressive, talking a lot more. We got to see so many animals and wildlife while travelling interstate, which is great as Azali loves animals. He cried on our last day when we were leaving a park, as he was having too much fun chasing the ducks.

Travelling teaches kids valuable life skills and expands their minds to see more of the world, not just home, family, and their local community.

I'm looking forward to opportunities where I can support mothers and families to live a happy, healthy, and free lifestyle where everyone can be supported and flourish to be their best self.

What instigated the road trip was an invite to a family festival called "Dream Day" at a property in NSW from an online male business mentor who I respect and who has a very successful business.

He's a family man and has recently started homeschooling his son and I've recently been following his journey online and been inspired by what he's creating for him and his community.

I'm keen to learn about what he and his family are doing to create their dream life so I can live mine and support others to do the same.

I'm also connected to a spiritual divine mother, Jacqui, who started homeschooling her kids 2.5 years ago. She has collaborated with an ex-Montessori teacher, Carli, who supports homeschooling parents and children.

They have launched various homeschooling programs together so I'm looking forward to investing in that to gain the skills and knowledge required to lead my son on this exciting journey.

I'm now getting better at creating and following through on goals and trusting they will be achieved in divine timing and letting go of the how.

Financially it can be very challenging as a stay-at-home mom who chooses not to be employed so I can be available for my son.

It has been difficult to always have courage and faith that I will be supported financially to live a life on my and my family's terms; I receive a parenting payment from the government and Azali's dad, Aaron, is a casual worker. However, I believe I am unconditionally supported as long as I am open and connected to the Tao, the creator and source of all souls.

I am committed to being responsible for my experience of life, as I am the creator and manifestor of everything in my life.

I am currently using Timeline Therapy on myself, which is an NLP tool I received last year when I became a certified Master NLP Practitioner.

This Emotional Release Technique clears emotions, including anger, sadness, fear, hurt, and guilt, plus more that hold us back in life.

As I went through a challenging time during my teenage years and into my 20s feeling shy and self-conscious of my body, alone, depressed, and unsupported during and after my parents' divorce, I don't want others to feel this way.

Now I am particularly motivated to work with teenagers who need support at this time, to help them move forward and overcome the challenges that hold them back.

For more information, book a free call at
https://calendly.com/sarahjanelayton3396815/discoverycall.

Kimberly Laverdure

Kimberly Laverdure, The Virtual Life Alchemisst
The Virtual Life Alchemist

https://www.linkedin.com/in/kimberly-laverdure-the-virtual-life-alchemist/
https://www.facebook.com/kimberly.smith72
https://www.instagram.com/kimberly_laverdure/
https://virtuallifealchemist.com
https://yourneighborhoodwitch.com

Kimberly Laverdure, The Virtual Life Alchemist, is a spiritual guide and business operations specialist who helps spiritually-minded, intuitive individuals align with their soul's purpose and create thriving, purpose-driven businesses. Combining personal transformation with practical business strategy, Kimberly empowers clients to heal limiting beliefs, trust their intuition, and design a life and business that reflects their deepest desires. Having faced her own challenges, Kimberly understands the importance of blending spiritual growth with actionable steps. Her holistic approach guides clients through defining their vision, setting boundaries, and taking inspired action. Whether deepening a personal journey or growing a soul-aligned business, Kimberly helps clients move from overwhelm to confidently stepping into their full potential. With her support, clients experience lasting transformation and confidently share their unique gifts with the world. Kimberly's work creates a balance between inner work and strategy, empowering clients to build businesses that nourish their soul and support their dreams.

A Voice Reclaimed: Merging Systems with Soul

By Kimberly Laverdure

For years, I knew how to be efficient. How to be strategic. How to help others grow. But efficiency did not mean being heard. I had become an expert at helping others find their voice while mine gathered dust. I did not know how to truly let myself be seen. Not until I stopped hiding the part of me I thought people would not understand, the intuitive, creative, soul-led part. The part that had been silenced for too long. This is the story of how I found my voice again, first in business, then in my life.

There Was a Time I Forgot My Voice

There was a time when I did not just lose my voice. I forgot I ever had one. I did not wake up one day without a voice. I lost it slowly, piece by piece.

Every time I swallowed the truth to keep the peace.
Every time I made myself small so someone else could feel big.
Every time I chose productivity over expression.

Silence became survival. I learned how to stay small, how to stay useful, how to stay unseen. I could build systems, lead teams, and help everyone else rise, but my own words stayed buried. Not because I did not have anything to say, but because I stopped believing anyone wanted to hear it. I had silenced my own truth so thoroughly, I forgot it could roar.

I became exceptional at helping others grow, but I forgot how to speak for myself. My strategy was sharp, my work was strong, but my voice, silenced under years of responsibility, trauma, and survival. And then one day, something in me refused to stay quiet.

Reclaiming my voice did not happen all at once. It began the moment

I stopped hiding the part of me I thought people would not understand, the intuitive, creative, soul-led woman who had been waiting her turn to speak. This is the story of how I stopped hiding and started speaking again, first in business, then in my life.

The Voice I Lost

My love for writing began at six years old. I always envisioned a career in storytelling, believing my words would shape my future. In high school, I explored different forms of writing: newspaper journalism, TV segment writing, poetry, and even songwriting. My English teachers were incredibly supportive, giving me extra attention and encouragement that left a lasting impact.

But life took a different turn. Marrying young and starting a family put my writing dreams on the back burner. As my relationships became more abusive, my creativity was stifled. Journaling, my outlet for self-expression and healing, stopped. My words, once a source of strength, faded into silence. My voice, my words, and my power became absent to keep me safe.

Over time, I became a master of logistics, operations, and systems. But deep down, the voice that had once felt so alive remained buried under years of survival. Every system I built reminded me what I could do, but not who I was. My voice was buried, but never gone. I had forgotten what it felt like to write for myself.

The Mask of Strategy

My career began in the corporate world, where I thrived in administrative roles, managing departments, and running other people's businesses. I moved into entrepreneurship out of necessity after a health crisis and an abusive relationship forced me to choose a new path. I started as a virtual assistant, then stepped into roles as an online business manager and eventually operations director.

I was building workflows that turned chaos into calm. I was the fixer, the builder, the strategist. And I was good at it. It allowed me to support myself and not be on Social Security Disability.

The systems I built worked. They brought structure, automation, and ease to countless businesses. But there was one system I had not figured out yet: how to stop compartmentalizing myself. I kept my business brain on one side and my inner voice, creative, intuitive, spiritual, on the other. I knew how to help others shine, but I had not allowed myself the same light.

People knew me for what I could do: build, lead, organize, create, but not for who I was. My voice did not disappear overnight. It was trained out of me. Conditioned into silence. I learned to speak only when it was safe, only when it served others, never when it revealed me. I had learned to perform, but I had not learned to speak for myself. My words had become strangers to me.

But the part of me I hid the longest, the intuitive, spiritual, wildly creative part, that was the voice that ended up saving me. I did not just reclaim my voice. I reclaimed the woman it belonged to.

A Moment of Awakening

It was not until I was behind the scenes of a 3-day virtual event, hired to run the tech, troubleshoot, and keep everything flowing, that something inside me cracked open.

As I listened to the speakers, something stirred. They were not just teaching strategies; they were sharing from a place of deep purpose, spiritual alignment, and emotional clarity. I had heard business advice before, but this was different.

For the first time in years, I remembered the sound of my own voice and that it deserved to be heard. Their words mirrored something I had been trying to ignore: that I, too, had something deeper to offer.

That event was not just another gig. It was a wake-up call.

Reclaiming My Voice

Right before this event, I contributed to a collaborative book project. When the book, *She Defies: Powerful Stories of Overcoming*, became a bestseller, it was not just a publishing win, it was personal reclamation. My story of how I overcame my past and current challenges to become a thriving business owner and woman was finally spoken out loud. My words were in print. My story was out in the world. My voice had finally returned.

Holding that book, I felt my voice expand, filling spaces I had long left empty. Every word I had held back had finally found a home. It was validation and healing in one. It reminded me that storytelling was not a chapter I had closed; it was a part of who I was all along.

That moment reignited my love for writing, and I started finding ways to weave it into my business. I started writing blogs, social media posts, and articles to support clients with copywriting and content, and began telling my own stories again. Slowly, the separation between my business self and my true self began to dissolve.

Integration as Liberation

I have been a psychic intuitive and medium since childhood. I had always tried to keep that side of me separate, fearing it would be misunderstood, dismissed, or seen as too out there for the business world.

But the more I reclaimed my voice, the more impossible it became to keep things separate. I realized that reclaiming my voice meant reclaiming the entire woman I had tucked away for safety.

Instead of resisting integration, I began to lean into it. I started asking my clients deeper questions:

- Where are you feeling blocked in your business?
- What personal patterns are holding you back from scaling?
- How can you integrate your healing with your strategy?

I brought intuition into strategy sessions. I blended energy alignment with business planning. I held space not just for growth, but for healing. And the results were undeniable.

One client shared: *"One of the biggest breakthroughs for me was learning to voice my emotions out loud instead of swallowing them. Kimberly showed me how to release the tension in my body by speaking the truth I had kept hidden. She also helped me restructure how I ground myself energetically, reversing the flow so that wisdom leads before time, which created a new sense of clarity and stability."*

A Turning Point in My Own Business

Clients were not just improving their workflows and operations, they were finally moving through the fears, burnout, and self-doubt that had silently sabotaged them for years.

They were healing their fear of success. They were releasing over-hustling and perfectionism. They were redefining worthiness in ways that let them finally receive.

And so was I. I was scaling too, not just businesses, but my own voice, courage, and presence.

This was not just about helping clients scale anymore. It was about guiding them home to themselves. It was about aligning their outer actions with their inner truth. It was about giving them permission to do business their way and giving myself the same.

Merging Two Worlds

Today, my work is the marriage of both worlds.

I still create systems. I still optimize processes. I still help businesses run like well-oiled machines. But now, I also hold space for transformation, for intuition, for deep inner work.

I am the Virtual Life Alchemist, a blend of structure and soul. I am no longer choosing between strategy and spirit. I am choosing to speak fully, boldly, and unapologetically.

Business does not have to be either/or. It can be both/and. Systems and soul. Strategy and spirit. Voice and truth. You do not have to pick a lane. You just have to claim all of who you are.

Unleashing HER Voice

Maybe you have been silent too. Maybe you have mastered survival so well, you forgot what thriving sounds like.

Your voice is waiting. It is time to stop whispering and start roaring.

Unleashing your voice is not a one-time act, it is a devotion. And the more of yourself you bring to the table, the more powerful your work becomes.

This is my voice.
Fully reclaimed.
And I hope it gives you the courage to unleash yours.

~ Kimberly Laverdure
The Virtual Life Alchemist
VirtualLifeAlchemist.com

Paula C Lamb

Health and Personal Growth Coach, Podcaster

https://www.linkedin.com/in/paulalamb/
https://www.facebook.com/BeyondtoFreedom/
https://linktr.ee/podcasterpaula
https://www.youtube.com/@knowingmeknowingyouwithpaula

Meet Paula Lamb, a South African expat now living in Vancouver, Canada. With a background in the service industry, fitness, nutrition, health, and personal growth coaching, Paula has dedicated her life to empowering individuals on their journey toward holistic well-being spiritually, mentally, and physically. A committed volunteer, she believes giving back is part of our greater purpose on Earth. Through her podcasts, Beyond to Freedom and Knowing Me, Knowing You with Paula, she entertains, empowers, and inspires transformation through conversations that encourage growth and connection. Paula is a regular contributor to HANNA Magazine and co-author of She Stands Strong: 30 Personal Stories of Strength & Resilience, She Glows: Empowering Women through Wellness and Self-Care, and Becoming an Unstoppable Woman: Rise of the Phoenix. In her writing, she weaves personal stories that share lessons of courage, resilience, and faith. Her mission: to inspire lasting peace, joy, and transformation, reminding us that we are stronger than we think.

Scars of Gold: My Kintsugi Journey

By Paula C Lamb

Every woman carries within her body silent stories. Some we celebrate, some we fear, and some we ignore until it's too late. When an alarming medical report landed in my hands, I learned just how quickly life can change. And it did for me. I've always been a health fanatic, diligent about check-ups, blood work, and paying close attention to my physical well-being. I understand the importance of vigilance.

So how did I end up here? I was forced to confront a truth I had always known: Health is not vanity; it is stewardship. What I didn't realize then was that this moment would not only demand a sharper focus on what I was putting into my body but would also test my faith and ultimately draw me closer to both my faith community and the power of prayer.

The Report That Changed Everything

In August 2025, I received the news: Abnormal cells had been found in my body. Within weeks, I was lying on a clinic table. The doctor was about to perform a procedure I hadn't needed in almost two decades. Back then, it had been smooth sailing, but this time, the second part of the procedure sent waves of stabbing pain through my body. I hadn't been offered any medication to prepare me.

"Don't hold your breath. Try to breathe through it," the doctor instructed as I quietly cried out.

But the pain was unbearable. My body went into spasm, my blood pressure plummeted, and I fought not to scream or faint. Worship music echoed in my mind as I tried to stay conscious, distract myself, and steady the spinning room. A nurse stood nearby, her masked face unreadable, her presence cold. When she reached out her hand for me to grasp, I felt no comfort.

"I can't take this anymore!" I cried.

"Just a few more minutes," the doctor replied.

Minutes stretched into eternity. By the time the procedure ended, nausea surged through me like a tidal wave. I was dizzy, weak, and in pain, barely able to sit up. What had just happened? I wondered, clutching my abdomen as I hobbled out of the room. They seated me in a recliner for monitoring. The nurse gave me water, then apple juice, as she checked my blood pressure.

One thought consumed me: *Why, God, did you allow this to happen to me?* In that moment, I felt abandoned.

The Aftermath

My husband was sitting just meters away in the waiting room, unaware of the trauma unfolding behind those closed doors. When I finally hobbled out to him, I felt as though I were floating, detached from my body, wondering if it had all been a bad dream. He looked helpless, unsure how to comfort me.

For days, the heaviness lingered. My body carried the trauma; my heart carried fear and sadness.

That Sunday, still fragile and shaken, I went to church. The pastor opened the service differently:

"There are people here who need prayer—for healing, for comfort, for strength. I would like to begin with prayer and invite those who need it to come forward."

God's presence doesn't show as a roar. It comes as a gentle nudge.

I moved with others to the front. As prayer warriors laid hands on those in need, a woman came to me and asked softly, "How can I support you?" Tears rolled down my cheeks. I felt so vulnerable, the enormity of what had happened finally unfolding.

As she prayed, I felt God's presence. Peace began to wash over me, not the end of the trauma, but the beginning of a deeper spiritual healing and a surety that God was with me that day. Looking back weeks later, I now see that healing on a much larger scale had begun in that clinic and continued through the prayers whispered over me.

An awakening had begun—a new journey, though I wasn't yet sure where it would lead.

Full Circle

Looking back, I see how the present and past seasons of my life are connected in a lifelong journey of renewal and transformation.

In my chapter for the anthology, *She Stands Strong: 30 Personal Stories of Strength and Resilience*, I wrote about my lifelong dance with fear and doubt. Life had taken me through dark and uncomfortable places, but confronting those challenges offered invaluable lessons, shaping my character in profound ways.

Later, in *She Glows: Empowering Women through Wellness and Self-Care*, I shared a simple yet profound revelation: True well-being begins within. It is not only about physical health but also about tending to the spiritual and emotional self, a step often neglected. Health is not just the absence of sickness; it is the presence of peace, clarity, joy, and faith. Self-care is not a single act; it is a way of living, a multi-faceted practice that makes us truly "Fit for Life."

And in *Becoming an Unstoppable Woman: Rise of the Phoenix*, I wrote about an awakening moment that transformed my life, one I never imagined would come full circle in this current season.

Part of my journey of salvation and surrender to Christ still had me resisting the church community until this profoundly traumatic moment. Then, God's Word came alive: *"Through prayer and supplication, with thanksgiving, present your requests to God"* and *"Where two or three are gathered in My name, there I am among them."*

For the first time, I saw what God was showing me: I could no longer walk my Christian faith journey alone. I needed my faith-filled community, even though I had long resisted drawing close to them. And this moment presented the perfect opportunity for me to reach out. Strength is not found in standing alone but in allowing others to hold you when you cannot stand. This is vulnerability at its finest—a quality I have often struggled to embrace.

A New Commitment

In this new season, I continue to pray and declare healing over my body each day. I visualize wholeness, giving thanks for God's promise to restore and renew. As my pastor reminded us: Jesus always seeks to bring peace, clarity, and sanctuary.

And as I wait, I have made a decision: Fear and doubt will no longer have the final say in my life. God is my strength. As Philippians 4:13 reminds me, *"I can do all things through Him who strengthens me."*

I have reclaimed my health with greater conviction. My morning rituals remain, but I have deepened and expanded my commitment to nourishing my body. Detoxing and renewing the physical self is one pursuit; detoxing and renewing my life is another. I will fight with everything God has entrusted to me—spirit, mind, and body—while trusting Him with the ending of my story.

The Turning Point

This experience has shown me that each scar we carry teaches us something. Storms will come not as detours, but as maps guiding us to our most authentic selves.

Whatever happens, however hard, must be embraced, for in it lies truth and awakening if we are ready to open our hearts and eyes. Our storms lead us to *Her*—the authentic self waiting to be unleashed. Only when we embrace the past and present—pain, mistakes, victories, all of it—can we begin to heal, release the old, and begin anew. Only then can we step into true transformation.

My life's trials and triumphs have gifted me wisdom, bringing me to the realization that our true power is eternal, steady, and unshaken by circumstance. When we anchor and align in God's truth—nourishing mind, body, and spirit—we don't just survive; we thrive. And in doing so, we *UnleashHer.*

Writing has become part of my healing journey. It has opened my heart, peeled back layers I once kept hidden, and revealed what still waits to be healed. With every word, every challenge faced with peace and unfathomable strength from God, I step closer to wholeness. Every step, no matter how small, is a victory worth celebrating.

This is the essence of Kintsugi, the Japanese art of mending broken pottery with lacquer and gold. The cracks are not erased; they are illuminated. Our scars are not proof of brokenness; they are proof of survival. In the same way, your scars are not something to hide. They are proof of strength, resilience, and the person you are becoming. Awakening to self is deeply linked to *UnleashingHer*, and my journey toward it feels much like a piece of pottery being mended, piece by piece, into a light for others.

I do not yet know what lies ahead. By the time you read this chapter, I will have received my medical results. But I know this: Uncertainty in God's hands becomes transformation. Just like Kintsugi, each crack can be gilded with gold, transforming our fractures into luminous lines of purpose. Pain can become a compass. Brokenness can bloom into beauty. Every step we take toward UnleashingHer strengthens us, uncovering resilience, authenticity, and beauty in the very places that feel broken. I am filled with anticipation for the future, growing in faith, and allowing the Holy Spirit to illuminate my path in life and in writing.

As I close, I invite you to explore my contributions to *Hanna Magazine* in 2025 and my co-authored anthologies, as mentioned in this piece. Each work offers a puzzle piece, a building block, a stepping stone. I hope my story sparks your curiosity to explore, unravel, and reveal the power within so that you, too, may *UnleashHer.*

Let my story also serve as a reminder to every woman: Honor your body and listen to its signals. Don't wait for a crisis to awaken you. Claim your health today. Schedule your checkups, complete your blood work, and nourish your body from the inside out. Guard your spiritual, mental, and physical health, because our health is a gift. Prevention is power.

Now, imagine the cracks and scars in your life glowing with gold. How have these golden lines shaped your story? What strength, beauty, or insight has emerged from them?

Remember, you are beautifully and wonderfully made. *UnleashHer.* #yougotthis

Jessica Gabriel

Divine Women Institute
Women's Empowerment Coach

www.facebook.com/thedivinewomeninstitute
www.instagram.com/wearedivinewomen
www.divinewomeninstitute.com

Jessica Gabriel, affectionately known as GourJess, is a Christian Women's Empowerment Coach, motivational speaker, and best-selling author passionate about helping women heal, rise, and walk in their divine identity. As founder of the Divine Women Institute, she equips women to overcome trauma, break limiting beliefs, and step boldly into their God-given purpose. Her own story of transformation from brokenness, low self-worth, and toxic relationships to wholeness, healing, and victory in Christ fuels her mission to inspire women worldwide. Through Spirit-led coaching, powerful keynote talks, and her writings, Jessica teaches the importance of renewing the mind with God's Word, reclaiming one's crown, and reigning fearlessly with Christ. She is a prophetic voice for healing, identity, and divine purpose, blending authenticity with biblical truth to ignite lasting transformation. Her message is clear: You are chosen, you are crowned, and through Christ, you are unstoppable.

Transformed By Truth: Unleashing My Voice of Victory

By Jessica Gabriel

Dedication

This chapter is dedicated to every woman who has ever lost her voice in the noise of the world to the ones who have smiled through pain, carried silent battles, and wondered if they would ever feel whole again.

May you know this truth: you are not broken — you are becoming.

May the Word of God awaken the fire within you, restore your identity, and remind you that your voice carries Heaven's sound.

You were never meant to stay silent; you were meant to speak life.

Your story is not over; it's being rewritten by grace.

Romans 12:2 (NLT) says,

"Let God transform you into a new person by changing the way you think. Then you will learn to know God's will for you, which is good and pleasing and perfect."

Have you ever looked in the mirror and realized you didn't recognize the woman staring back?

Not because her face had changed—but because her soul was buried beneath years of pain, fear, and pretending.

I know that woman well. I was her.

I was the one who smiled on the outside while silently screaming on the inside.

The one who showed up for everyone else while secretly wondering if she would ever feel whole again.

But the truth is—God doesn't heal who we pretend to be.

He heals who we truly are.

And when His Word collided with my brokenness, everything began to change.

The lies that once defined me started to crumble.

The shame that silenced me began to lose its grip.

That's when I realized: Transformation isn't about becoming someone different.

It's about awakening to who you were always meant to be.

John 14:6 (NIV):

"Jesus answered, 'I am the way and the truth and the life. No one comes to the Father except through me.'"

Truth has a name, and His name is Jesus.

For years, I chased healing through people, possessions, and performance but nothing worked until I met Him.

Not the Sunday-morning version of Jesus, but the living, breathing Truth who meets you right in your mess.

One night, at my lowest point, I cried out to God from a place of total surrender and He answered.

I didn't just find religion; I found resurrection.

That was the night Jesus came alive inside of me.

His presence filled the room, and it was as if the scales fell from my eyes.

The girl who had been drowning in shame met the Savior who walked on water and He pulled me up.

That moment didn't just save my life; it changed the entire trajectory of it.

My first chapter, in Becoming an Unstoppable Woman of Faith, told that story of how grace found me in the dark.

My second, in Rise of the Phoenix, spoke of rebirth, of rising from the ashes when everything around me burned.

But this one—Transformed by Truth—is about what comes next: restoration.

Joel 2:25 (NKJV):

> *"So I will restore to you the years that the swarming locust has eaten..."*

God has restored so much in my life—my peace, my confidence, my identity, and most powerfully, my voice.

The same voice the enemy once tried to silence is now the instrument God uses to bring healing.

I no longer whisper out of fear; I speak with fire.

My words, once soaked in pain, now carry power.

John 8:32 (NIV):

> *"Then you will know the truth, and the truth will set you free."*

When truth sets you free, it doesn't just free you—it frees everyone connected to your testimony.

That's why I believe our stories matter.

The world doesn't need more perfection; it needs more proof that God still redeems.

Every time we speak the truth of what He's done, we release light into dark places.

It's not just our breakthrough—it becomes someone else's.

Every time I tell my story, I imagine chains breaking somewhere in the spirit realm.

Because I know what Revelation 12:11 means when it says we overcome "by the blood of the Lamb and by the word of our testimony."

Your voice carries weight in Heaven.

When you speak truth, demons tremble, and destinies unlock.

Isaiah 61:1 (NLT):

"The Spirit of the Sovereign Lord is upon me, for the Lord has anointed me to bring good news to the poor.

He has sent me to comfort the brokenhearted and to proclaim that captives will be released and prisoners will be freed."

That is my why.

I write, speak, and coach because I know what it feels like to live bound and I know the freedom that comes through truth.

Through the Divine Women Institute, I now help women renew their minds, reclaim their voices, and rediscover their royal identity in Christ.

When a woman knows who she is in God, hell loses its grip on her.

This transformation didn't happen overnight.

It happened daily—every morning that I chose faith over fear, every time I opened my Bible instead of my phone, every moment I decided to believe what God said over what the world shouted.

It happened through tears, through worship, through surrender.

Ephesians 4:23–24 (NLT):

> *"Let the Spirit renew your thoughts and attitudes. Put on your new nature, created to be like God—truly righteous and holy."*

Transformation is a lifelong process of renewal.

It's not glamorous—it's holy.

It's the slow, steady work of becoming who God already sees.

And in that process, He's taught me this:

The same truth that transformed me will transform the world when I speak it.

So I will keep speaking.

I will keep writing.

I will keep unleashing my voice of victory until every daughter of God knows she was never meant to whisper her worth—she was meant to declare it.

Declaration

"Lord, thank You for transforming me by Your truth.

Thank You for restoring my mind, my heart, and my voice.

I will use my voice to glorify You, to speak life, and to empower others to do the same.

My story is not my shame—it is my testimony.

I am living proof that Your truth transforms. Amen."

Marissa Rowles

The Chrysalis Coach
Holistic Health and Wellness Coach

www.facebook.com/the.chrysalis.coach
www.instagram.com/the.chrysalis.coach
www.thechrysaliscoach.com

Marissa is a Certified Health and Wellness Coach who walks beside women in seasons of transformation. She guides her clients on their path to empowerment and teaches that it begins the moment we choose to return to ourselves. Through her work as The Chrysalis Coach, she works with women who are ready to step into a life of alignment and are feeling the call to embody their most authentic selves. Marissa's work lands where strategy meets soul. With tools that bridge science and spirituality, Marissa invites women to turn their sensitivity into strength, to set boundaries without guilt, and to claim self-care as a birthright. With those she works with, she shares the importance of coming home to your truth and healing through radical self-acceptance. Her writing has been featured in She Glows by She Rises Studios, and she is a frequent contributor to the magazine Wellness On Time.

Breaking Open: The Strength in Vulnerability

By Marissa Rowles

I remember the first time I fell apart in public.

It wasn't a dramatic breakdown onstage or a spectacular collapse at work. It was something that came from within me, and therefore, when it manifested, it felt all the more terrifying. I was sitting in a coffee shop on a weekday afternoon (can't focus writing from home) and was stressed, trying to make a deadline set in a few hours. I remember the hum of strangers all around me, my phone buzzing with messages I felt I should answer immediately, all while trying to breathe through the underlying panic I was suppressing underneath my ribs. After taking a quick look around and feeling like I was the only person in a state of desperation, I put my head in my hands and felt the room contract until all I could hear was the thump of my own breath. Someone passed by, and I heard the soft voice of a woman saying, "She will be alright." Snapping back to reality, I looked up to see that as she was leaving, her daughter was still looking back in my direction with a sincere look of concern. Her daughter knew that to me, at that exact moment, it felt like quite the opposite.

I am usually the one who thrives under pressure. The one who keeps her composure, even when things get difficult. I am the calm in the storm, the steady one, the one whose reliability never falters. That's why this moment of pressure, the feeling of wanting to escape, felt so foreign. It was so unfamiliar to me, the feeling of wanting to give up.

This wasn't who I believed myself to be. The girl that I knew myself to be never would.

At the time, everything in my life seemed to be colliding all at once—deadlines, responsibilities, and expectations weighing on my shoulders until it felt like too much to carry. And yet, what unsettled me most wasn't the stress of that itself. It was the quiet knowing that, in so many spaces—especially at work—I wasn't being myself. I was trying so hard to conceal my insecurities that I was formulating stories about my life for everyone I would meet. Covering my truth for fear of experiencing feelings of rejection, when the real truth was that I was hiding behind the fear of being truly seen.

What I didn't know back then, but I know now, is that those moments, those behaviors, aren't just about signs of someone with deep insecurities; they really mean so much more. They are indications that unhealed trauma is quietly pulling the strings, deciding it's safer to shrink, to hide, and to perform. The part of you designed to keep you safe has decided it's important not to be the true, authentic version of you, and it's better to put on a facade for your own protection.

But the longer you silence yourself, the longer the disconnection you have with yourself lasts, the heavier the weight of it all becomes. And that day in the café, with my head in my hands, I realized I couldn't hold it together anymore.

For years, I had worn different identities like costumes: the eager-to-please performer, the dependable volunteer, the successful sales rep, and the busy founder hustling to make an impact. Each role came with a script written by other people's expectations. I learned how to move through life doing what was necessary to look good, to be liked, and to be useful. On paper, the life looked enviable. Behind the scenes, I was exhausted and hollowed out in ways I couldn't name.

When things finally cracked—when grief, burnout, and the weight of other people's expectations—I saw what I had been unwilling to face: I hadn't been living as me at all. The real me, inside, felt broken. Sitting at the table by myself, trying to pull myself together, I knew I had to decide. I could hide my breakdown (like how I hid everything else), or I could let it be the doorway.

I chose the doorway.

And what I walked into was not an instant transformation, but an unraveling. Once you realize you've been sharing only fragments of your best self, the healing doesn't come from trying to choose the "right" identity–it comes from allowing all of who you are to come forward.

I spent so much time wanting to find the *one version* of me that would finally feel "enough," the perfect identity that would hold all the pieces of my life together, and would align me with the frequency of success.

But here's the truth I didn't want to admit: There is no perfect version. There is only you. All of you.

When I finally stopped trying to become her—the flawless woman, the polished woman, the untouchable woma —I met someone better. I met the woman who was willing to tell the truth. The woman who could admit she wasn't happy. Who could look at the façade of her life and whisper, *This isn't it.*

That whisper was terrifying, but it was also freeing. Because when you can finally tell yourself the truth about where you are, you also unlock the possibility of change. Denial keeps you stuck. Honesty cracks you open. And once you are open, you can begin again.

That was the beginning of my transformation. Not in a loud, public way, but in quiet, private choices. I began spending time alone. I began listening to myself instead of everyone else. I began nurturing the parts of me I had abandoned, like the little girl inside my heart who had learned long ago that hiding was safer than being seen.

I had to meet her. I had to love her. I had to show her it was safe now to come out of hiding. That she didn't have to keep carrying the fear of rejection. That she could put down the masks and still be loved.

And with every wall I let go of, I discovered something extraordinary: My future self had been waiting for me all along. She wasn't far away. She wasn't hidden in some distant success or milestone. She was here, inside me, the entire time. And she wasn't afraid. She wasn't shrinking. She wasn't hiding. She was free.

I started asking myself daily, *What would she do?*

The woman who doesn't silence her truth. The woman who doesn't dilute herself to fit in. The woman who is unapologetically whole.

And then I began doing those things, even when they terrified me. Especially when they terrified me. Speaking up when I wanted to stay silent. Saying no when my old patterns begged me to say yes. Choosing rest when the world told me to hustle.

It didn't happen overnight, but little by little, the distance between who I was and who I was becoming began to close.

I learned that belonging is never found in blending in. It is found in standing out. That alignment is not achieved by silencing your voice, but by letting it rise. And that the fastest way to connect to your truest, most powerful life is to speak your personal truth fearlessly, from the heart.

The more I expressed myself, the more I realized how much I had been carrying that was never mine to hold. Expectations, old stories, outdated roles—all of it began to fall away. And in releasing what wasn't mine, I finally made space for what was.

That is the paradox of becoming: The more you let go, the more you discover. The more you reveal, the more you belong. The more you break open, the more whole you become.

Looking back now, I can see that the woman in the café was never falling apart. She was breaking open to become who she really was. That moment of collapse was the doorway. And walking through it,

I discovered the truth that changed everything:

Your power doesn't come from choosing one identity. It comes from owning all of you, without apology.

And maybe, just maybe, that's what breaking open really is. Not the end, but the beginning. The moment when you finally put down the masks and let yourself be seen. Not as the person you thought you had to be, but as the whole, unapologetic next, best version of you.

Jennifer Jenkins

CEO of Rooted Holistic Health Coaching, Inc

https://www.linkedin.com/in/jennifer-jenkins-rn-chc-fns-ryt-nlp-practitioner-1103825/
https://www.instagram.com/jen_jenkins_health_coach/
www.rootedholistichealth.com

Jennifer Jenkins is a Holistic Registered Nurse, Certified Holistic Health Coach, and Master NLP Practitioner. She is the founder of Rooted Holistic Health Coaching and the Metabolic Mastery Academy, holding more than 20 advanced certifications in nutrition, neuroscience, behavioral change, energetics, and holistic healing. After overcoming multiple health conditions once deemed "incurable," Jennifer discovered that prioritizing health is the key that unlocks transformation in every area of life. She now helps individuals and business owners tap into their higher self, break free from limiting beliefs, and step into their role as the leader of their health, life, and business. Her vision is to impact over one million lives by showing people the truth: when you heal at the root and align body, mind, and purpose, you unlock the vitality, confidence, and results you've been searching for—proving transformation within always creates transformation in the world around you.

From Rejection to Radiance: Reclaiming the Power Within

By Jennifer Jenkins

From the very beginning, my life carried a message I didn't yet have the words to understand: *You don't belong.* My father had wanted a son, not a daughter. When my mother brought me home from the hospital, my sister, only four years old at the time, asked if I could be taken back because she had wanted a brother instead.

That moment became a family story—retold over the years as a kind of joke. Each time it came up, we all laughed at the thought of my sister's innocent request, and I even learned to laugh along. Yet each time I heard it, I unconsciously gave that story more power. I didn't realize that by repeatedly imagining and rehearsing it, I was reinforcing the belief that I wasn't wanted and did not realize how much rejection would show up as a fear in my life.

What I now understand through years of studying neuroscience is that the unconscious mind doesn't distinguish between a joke and reality. Repeated stories, even those told in laughter, wire themselves into our subconscious. Over time, they become the background script that shapes how we see ourselves and what we believe we deserve. For me, this script was clear: *I don't belong.*

As I grew older, I began to unconsciously collect evidence to confirm the belief that I didn't belong. I saw it in the bullying I endured at school, in the clubs and activities I was never chosen for, and in always being one of the last to be picked for a team. Each moment seemed to reinforce the idea that I was unwanted and unworthy. Later, in my late teens and early twenties, that belief found its strongest confirmation in an abusive relationship where the words *"No one else is going to want you"* were spoken so often they became a soundtrack in my mind. Over time, I stopped questioning them and began to accept them as truth. Without realizing it, I was building a case against myself—layer by layer, moment by moment—until the story of not belonging felt like the only story I had. Those words became my inner script, and the longer I lived by them, the more they defined my reality. Chronic health conditions emerged. My self-worth shrank. I lived in a prison built by old thoughts and beliefs, unable to see that I held the key to the door all along.

The Moment of Decision

There always comes a moment when we are invited to choose differently.

For me, that moment came when I finally walked away from the relationship that had stolen so many years of my life. But I didn't walk away strong or confident. I walked away broken. I had no self-confidence, no sense of who I truly was. I felt lost in the world, unsure of where I belonged. For so long, I had molded myself to fit into other people's expectations that I no longer knew where I ended and where others began.

I struggled to find my place. I carried the weight of feeling like an outsider, never truly fitting in—whether in my family, at school, or even in my own skin. And when I looked in the mirror, I saw not only the physical symptoms of my health struggles but also the reflection of someone who had forgotten her own worth.

That was the woman who made the decision: not polished, not confident, but tired of living small. I knew something had to change. If I continued living from the same story, I would remain trapped in the same patterns. If I wanted a different future, I would have to rebuild myself from the inside out.

And so, I chose. I chose to no longer be a victim of my past. I chose to stop believing the lies that had been spoken over me. I chose to step onto a path I didn't yet understand, but one I knew was my only way forward.

It wasn't glamorous. It wasn't easy. Rebuilding myself meant starting from the ground up. I had to relearn how to think, how to believe, and even how to love myself. I invested in courses, certifications, retreats, mentors, and coaches not because I wanted more accolades, but because I needed to become someone new.

And as I did, something extraordinary happened: Piece by piece, I began to find myself.

The Neuroscience of Becoming

One of the most profound lessons I've learned is this: Our personality creates our personal reality.

Our personality is made up of what we think, how we act, and how we feel each day. When we think the same thoughts, act the same way, and feel the same emotions over and over, we stay locked in the past. Even when we say we want change, nothing shifts because we're using the same mind that created the old reality to try to build a new one.

To create a new future, we must literally become someone new. That means thinking differently, acting differently, and feeling differently. Neuroscience calls this neuroplasticity—the brain's ability to form new connections and rewire itself. The moment we choose a new thought, take a new action, or feel a new emotion, we begin the process of rewriting our subconscious programming and creating a new story.

The Freedom of Forgiveness

The most powerful shift came to me through forgiveness.

For years, I held on to anger toward those who had hurt me. I thought that clinging to my pain kept me safe. But I learned that holding on only kept me bound to the very people and memories I wanted to escape.

Forgiveness is not about excusing what happened. It is not about saying the pain didn't matter. Forgiveness is about choosing freedom. It is about declaring, *I refuse to let the past dictate my future.*

The moment I forgave, I was released. I was no longer carrying the weight of other people's actions. I was free to step fully into the woman I was always meant to be.

From Healing to Leading

As I healed my inner world, my outer world began to transform. The illnesses that once consumed me lost their hold. My energy returned. My confidence grew. Most importantly, I began to see myself not as a victim of my past but as the creator of my future.

That transformation ignited my calling. Today, I coach and mentor women who are ready to break free from old stories and step into their higher selves. Together, we don't just focus on health. We transform lives from the inside out.

When a woman shifts her inner story, everything in her outer world begins to change. She releases the weight of limiting beliefs. Her body heals. She rediscovers her confidence. She steps boldly into the higher version of herself she always knew was waiting.

I have witnessed this transformation in hundreds of women. And each time I do, I am reminded that healing and empowerment are not only possible. They are our birthright.

Seven Steps to Rewrite Your Story

If you feel stuck in the past, longing for change, know that you are not alone. The same path that set me free is available to you.

1. **Become Consciously Aware of Your Story**
   Change begins with awareness. Most of our lives are lived on autopilot, running old unconscious programs. To change, we must first bring them into the light. Reflect on the earliest memories, the stories that have been repeated to you, and the beliefs you've carried. Write them down. Awareness is what allows you to make new choices.

2. **Challenge the Old Beliefs**
   Ask yourself: Is this belief absolutely true? Or is it simply a program I've been carrying? Questioning the validity of old beliefs creates space for new truths to emerge.

3. **Rehearse a New Truth**
   The brain learns through repetition. Choose new, empowering thoughts and practice them daily. Over time, your mind will accept them as your new reality.

4. **Act in Alignment**
   New thoughts require new behaviors. If you are stepping into the belief "I am worthy," then live in ways that reflect that worth. Set boundaries. Prioritize self-care. Say yes to opportunities that align with the future you are creating.

5. **Feel the Future Now**
   The unconscious mind does not distinguish between real and vividly imagined experiences. When you practice feeling the emotions of your desired future—joy, freedom, confidence—you teach your body to live in that reality now.

6. **Release Through Forgiveness**
   Forgiveness is the key to freedom. Write letters of release to

those who hurt you. Whether or not you send them, the act itself severs the ties of anger and resentment.

7. **Surround Yourself With Support**
   We rise faster in community. Seek out mentors, coaches, and women who will remind you of your worth and hold you accountable to the higher version of yourself. Transformation is magnified when we walk the journey together.

These steps are not quick fixes—they are practices. Each time you repeat them, you strengthen new neural pathways, rewrite old programs, and create momentum toward the life you truly desire.

Tolulope Olaniyan

Founder of Eventaal

https://www.linkedin.com/in/tolulope-suzanne-olaniyan-qfa-mbs-apa-gi-4b4ba41b/
https://www.facebook.com/profile.php?id=100015001145314
https://www.instagram.com/tolulope775
www.eventaal.com

Tolulope S. Olaniyan is a qualified financial adviser, transformational coach, author, and community leader dedicated to empowering women, migrants, and minority communities. With executive-level experience in community leadership, professional expertise in insurance and finance, and advanced qualifications including a master's in business Innovation and enterprise, she combines financial literacy with personal transformation coaching to help individuals thrive beyond borders. She is the founder of EVENTAAL and The Magnificent U Awards, initiatives that empowers, celebrate excellence, leadership, and diversity. An Amazon best-selling author of The Magnificent You: A 21-Day Guide to the Ultimate Life, Tolulope is passionate about helping women—particularly Black migrant women—reclaim their voice, build wealth, and live with freedom and purpose.

Breaking Free, Building Wealth

By Tolulope Olaniyan

"Her voice, her wealth, her freedom—when a woman rises, generations rise with her."

I looked at my aunt through the eyes of a fifteen-year-old girl and saw a woman who seemed unshaken by life's storms. She was radiant, full of life, carrying herself with quiet confidence. Yet behind her smile were stories of struggle—several marriages, seven children, and no formal education. At the time, I didn't fully grasp what that meant, but I knew something vital was missing. Something essential.

Later, my father shared stories of his own father. My grandfather was a man of influence, successful, with multiple wives and twenty-one children. Yet he believed educating girls was a waste. Only the boys went to school. He also shared stories about his mother, who would leave the house and travel for a week to a bigger town for business, preparing most of their meals and leaving them so they could manage while she was away. While this scenario does not apply to all families, it was very common at the time.

Back to my aunt—I was told I looked like her, and she particularly liked me as a child, naming me "Adufe." I knew if she had had some form of formal education, she could have settled well and turned out much better. But it was not just that. I also discovered that the decision not to educate the girls passed on a mindset about formal education being less important. Otherwise, how do you explain that I was the first grandchild to graduate? As I speak, you can count the graduates with your fingers in that large family. That mindset echoed through generations, shaping the lives of the women—and even the men—raised by these women. As Dr. Anan Kofi says, "If you educate a man, you educate an individual. But if you educate a woman, you educate a whole nation."

I was lucky, at least. My father got an education as an accountant, and my mother had a career with the government. However, my mother's upbringing reflected the belief that men were the superior heads of the home. While this was not inherently bad, some men abused this idea as a tool for manipulation and control.

When I married, I believed that complete submission was non-negotiable. I had been taught this from childhood. It echoed in churches, in communities, and in family whispers: "A woman's place is in the kitchen." I carried that belief quietly. I supported my husband's dreams. I buried my own. I kept the home together because that was my role. I was comfortable and cared for, yet a sense of purpose eluded me.

Migration added another layer: caring for our children alone while my husband pursued his career freely, choosing not to relocate. I overcompensated, trying to create stability for the children while ignoring the imbalance in my own life. My days revolved around family, church, and unending responsibilities. I was the unpaid minder, cook, teacher, counsellor, psychologist, accountant, PA, and, of course, the prayer intercessor. If anything went wrong—his job, his mood, his decisions—it was my fault. I had not prayed enough. I had not done enough. I did not understand the gaslighting, the manipulative power of using financial dominance as a tool for control. I did not understand how my voice could start to fade in the background and how my purpose started to fade in the background.

I have always felt I had a voice to silence injustice, to change stereotypes. I remember my first time speaking in front of a large audience of about 300 people. I was just a child of around 11, representing my school in a literary and debating competition. We won, as my voice projected far and clear. Faces dimmed as I faced my opponents and tore down their counterarguments. I went on to become the known voice of my secondary school, representing us in competitions and winning many times. But this voice became faint and almost unrecognizable as I was labeled unfriendly, difficult, oppressive, non-submissive, and unaccommodating. I started to change so much that I eventually broke down. I had no voice again, and my purpose was unrecognizable.

Some of my stories are shared in my Amazon best-selling book, The Magnificent You: A 21-Day Guide to the Ultimate Life. When I started reclaiming my identity as a Black migrant woman, I thought I was doing okay. I had started coaching and empowering others, but I did not yet see that complete financial independence and wealth building were crucial. I believed that as long as I was working in partnership at home, it did not matter.

The turning point came when I realized the truth: It was my life, not "ours." We were not working toward a common vision. When I confronted him about his affairs, he said, "How dare you challenge me? You can't even give monetary support to your parents unless I give you money."

Another time, he held a meeting with the children. I thought of apologizing, of seeking solutions. Instead, he said, "Everything you see, I bought with my money. Your mother can't even turn one cent into two." I froze. Here I was, holding a master's degree and professional diplomas, yet none of it mattered. My worth was measured solely by my financial dependence. My children were told their mother was ungrateful and incapable. Something inside me snapped. I realized I had been living a lie. I was sold a narrative that silenced me. I decided I would not be silenced again.

I found my voice again but felt like a free woman with an invisible rope limiting her ability to speak the truth. Societal expectations and family obligations—they were still there. Even with the betrayal, I was told to pray more. My life revolved around praying for someone who did not see me as an equal and continued to remind me that this marriage was not an equal partnership. I was told, "I am the man, the alpha male, and I do what I want." There was no sense of accountability. My pain, my struggle, my lack of freedom—these didn't matter. People only see visible scars, not the invisible ones.

I knew my freedom was non-negotiable and I needed a plan to become the woman I was born to be. I retrained and started from the beginning, taking a job that I could barely survive on and yet still caring for my family like I had a lot. My children could not tell. Sometimes, we have to start from the beginning to create that path to freedom. It may be difficult, but it is often the best decision we could ever make.

I retrained to become a qualified financial adviser and an accredited product adviser for general insurance. I expanded my coaching reach, wrote two books, and accomplished so many other things that I cannot even mention here.

Through my community outreach and empowerment initiatives, I realized my story was not unique. Many women, particularly Black migrant women, are silenced, made to feel small, and conditioned to serve the dreams of others at the cost of their own. I discovered that cross-culturally and across borders, women face similar struggles. Their voices are suppressed, ambitions minimized, and independence controlled using money as a tool. Stress, anxiety, and overwhelm are often intertwined with financial realities. Many women juggle careers, family responsibilities, and societal expectations, yet feel unseen, underappreciated, and trapped.

The numbers confirm this truth. Women earn less, save less, and invest less. In Western countries, women retire with an average of 35% less money than men. Companies founded by women receive less than 2% of venture funding. Research by BNY Mellon found that globally, only 1 in 10 women feel confident in understanding investing. These statistics are not just numbers—they are barriers that continue to silence women's potential and delay their freedom.

At this rate, closing the financial gender gap could take over 200 years.

This reality fueled my mission. I dedicated myself to financial empowerment and education for women—teaching them to break the silence, take control of their finances, and reclaim their worth. Money is not just numbers. Money is freedom, power, and choice. Financial dependence mutes a woman's voice, trapping her in circumstances that suppress her dreams. Financial literacy changes that. It equips women with the confidence to say "no," the tools to plan and build, and the freedom to thrive on their own terms. For migrant women, financial knowledge becomes a bridge—connecting them to stability, independence, and empowerment.

Through coaching, workshops, and community initiatives, I show women that their dreams matter, their voices matter, and their worth is undeniable. I remind them often: The way you handle money is the way you handle life. Every step toward financial empowerment is a step toward freedom.

To every woman reading this: Your voice is important. Your dreams are valid. Your worth is undeniable. Silence has stolen enough from women. It is time to speak, plan, and rise.

When a woman finds her financial voice, she doesn't just change her life—she transforms generations. She inspires others to rise alongside her. I began this journey because something inside me refused to be silenced. Today, I continue it because I know the truth: When women unleash their voices in wealth, they unleash futures.

May you never silence your dreams. May you never diminish your worth. And may your voice—in life, in love, and in finances—be heard, honored, and celebrated.

Jane Butler

Founder and CEO of Individually You Coaching
MSc, RN (Ret.), Health & Wellness Coach

https://www.facebook.com/share/p/1DEMwkWsEw/
https://www.instagram.com/individually.you

Jane Butler is a retired UK Registered Nurse with over 30 years of experience specializing in cardiology. Holding a master's degree in cardiology from Brighton University, she has contributed to peer-reviewed journals, books, and UK government policy. Today, Jane is the founder of Individually You Coaching, where she supports women—especially those navigating menopause—in restoring energy, improving sleep, and thriving through natural, back-to-basics approaches. Having personally experienced sleep challenges during menopause, Jane is passionate about helping women reclaim vitality through simple, sustainable strategies. She coaches clients 1:1 and in groups, both online and in person, and leads her supportive community, Love Your Menopause with Jane. A published author and international lecturer, Jane blends deep clinical expertise with compassionate coaching to help women step into their most confident, energized chapter of life.

From Silence to the Stage

By Jane Butler

The classroom smelled faintly of pencil shavings and floor polish, but all I could notice was the pounding in my chest. My name had been called. It was my turn. For weeks, I had dodged this moment, offering excuse after excuse, hoping my English teacher would forget that I still hadn't delivered my two-minute talk. But today, she didn't let me escape.

"Jane, it's time," she said firmly, pointing to the front of the class.

The room suddenly felt enormous, every desk lined up like a row of judges' benches. My friends were leaning on their elbows, whispering to each other, some looking at me with curiosity, others with mischief in their eyes. My palms were damp, my throat was dry, and my legs felt like lead as I dragged myself forward. I could hear my shoes squeaking on the polished floor, the sound echoing louder than it should have.

I had no notes, no plan, nothing prepared. All I had was fear.

"Fashion," I croaked when asked my topic. And then came the nonsense. Something about vertical stripesmaking you taller and horizontal ones making you wider. My voice shook as I rambled about how tall people should avoid vertical stripes and how overweight people should avoid horizontal ones. It was desperate, jumbled, and made little sense, something I think I had heard elsewhere and just regurgitated, desperate for something to say.

A ripple of giggles spread across the room. The girls in the back row covered their mouths, trying not to laugh, but I saw them. I felt them. The heat rushed to my face until I was certain I was glowing red. My hands fumbled with the edge of my jumper as I stood there, frozen.

I wanted the floor to open up and swallow me whole. In that moment, I promised myself one thing: never again. Never again would I put myself in a position where I had to speak in front of others.

What I didn't know then was that this humiliating two-minute disaster would become the seed of one of the greatest ironies of my life: the girl who couldn't speak would one day stand on international stages, using her voice to empower women across the world.

The Weight of Silence

That day cemented something deep inside me: the belief that I was not a speaker. My voice didn't belong in front of people. If I opened my mouth, I would be ridiculed.

The human brain is funny that way. One moment of embarrassment can echo for years, growing louder with time. Every time I thought about speaking up, whether in class, at gatherings, or even around people I didn't know well, the memory came rushing back. The giggles, the hot flush of shame, the garbled words.

So, I stayed quiet. I became skilled at listening, nodding, and letting others take the stage. My words stayed locked inside, safe from judgment but also stripped of power.

Yet even in my silence, there was a part of me that longed to speak, to share, to be heard. But I didn't know how.

Nursing: Finding a Different Kind of Voice

Life, however, has a way of nudging us in directions we don't expect. I became a nurse, a decision born out of compassion, practicality, and a desire to care for others. Nursing demanded skills I never thought I'd have to develop. Suddenly, I was talking every day: with patients, with families, with doctors, and with colleagues.

And here's the thing: I wasn't afraid. When I was advocating for a patient, explaining a diagnosis to a family, or reassuring someone who was frightened, it wasn't about me anymore. It wasn't about my voice being judged. It was about them.

That realization changed everything.

For over thirty years, I specialized in cardiology, working in the NHS. I was there for people on the hardest days of their lives. I held hands. I gave explanations. I translated medical jargon into human language. And slowly, without even realizing it, I was learning to speak again.

There were moments when my voice carried enormous weight. I remember one night shift when a patient's condition suddenly deteriorated, and the doctors were debating next steps. My instincts screamed something was wrong. I spoke up clearly, firmly, and without hesitation. My words cut through the discussion and led to a swift intervention that saved his life. That was the night I realized my voice could make the difference between life and death.

This wasn't public speaking. It wasn't a stage. But it was communication at its most raw and important level. And it was the beginning of me reclaiming my voice.

The Shift to Teaching and Speaking

As my experience grew, so did the opportunities. I began training junior nurses. I lectured at universities. I contributed to government policy on cardiac care. Suddenly, I found myself standing in front of rooms again, not classrooms of giggling teenagers this time, but lecture halls full of professionals.

At first, the nerves returned. I'd stand at the front, palms sweaty, the old memory of that English class whispering in my ear. But there was a difference now: I was prepared. I knew my subject. And most importantly, it wasn't about me. It was about what others needed to learn, understand, and take away.

The more I spoke, the more confident I became. My voice, once silenced by shame, started to grow strong.

From Nurse to Women's Health Coach

Years later, my path evolved again. After retiring from nursing, I felt called to support women in a different way as a women's health coach, specializing in menopause and sleep.

At first, I thought coaching would be one-on-one conversations, intimate and personal. And it was. But I quickly realized that if I wanted to truly make a difference, if I wanted to reach women globally, I would need to speak. On podcasts. At events. On stages. In front of cameras.

The irony wasn't lost on me. That girl who once stammered about stripes was now a woman being asked to deliver keynote talks. Me, the non-speaker, now invited to speak internationally.

And the most beautiful part? I love it. I love standing in front of audiences; however, I do still get nerves and butterflies (who doesn't) but now from excitement and what is possible. I love seeing women's eyes light up when something I say resonates. I love sparking conversations that ripple outward.

Public speaking is no longer my enemy; it's my ally, my tool, my joy.

The Power of Reframing

Looking back, I realize the shift happened when I stopped speaking about me. As a teenager, I was terrified because I thought it was all about how *I* would look, how *I* would sound, and whether *I* would be laughed at.

But when I reframed it when I spoke about the people I was serving, it transformed everything. Speaking became an act of service, not performance.

I wasn't there to impress. I was there to connect.

This lesson has carried me through every stage, every lecture, every keynote, and every workshop. And it's the message I share with every woman who tells me, "But I'm not confident enough" or "I could never do that."

Confidence doesn't come first. Courage does. Confidence grows from the act of showing up, even when your voice shakes.

The Irony and the Gift

Sometimes I imagine that 14-year-old girl standing at the front of her classroom, her cheeks burning with shame as laughter fills the room. I want to step beside her, place a hand on her shoulder, and whisper:

"Don't worry. One day, you'll stand on stages bigger than this. One day, people will lean forward to hear your words. One day, your voice will change lives."

She would never believe me. But I believe it now.

That two-minute disaster, as painful as it was, became part of my story. And without it, perhaps I would never have discovered the true power of my voice.

Your Voice Matters

If there's one thing I want women to take away from my story, it's this: Your voice matters. Even if it shakes. Even if it stumbles. Even if, in the beginning, it comes out as nonsense about stripes.

You don't need to wait until you feel "ready" or "perfect." Perfection isn't the point. Connection is.

And speaking up doesn't always mean microphones and spotlights. Sometimes it means telling your doctor you need answers. Sometimes it means saying "no" to something that drains you.

Sometimes it means raising your hand in a meeting or sharing your story with a friend. Every time you use your voice, you are taking up space in the world and that is powerful.

The world doesn't need flawless speakers. It needs authentic ones.

I went from silence to the stage, from fear to freedom. And if I can do it, so can you.

Unleash your voice. Because your story exactly as it is has the power to inspire, to heal, and to create change.

Debra A. Brewer

Founder and CEO of Sunshine Creations by DB
Certified Life Coach, Art Therapy Coach, Mixed Media Artist,
Graphic and Web Designer

www.sunshinecreationsdb.com
www.debrabrewer.com

Debra A. Brewer is a passionate Author, Graphic Designer, Web Designer, Art Therapy Coach ,Creative Branding Coach, and Mixed Media Artist. With a deep love for creativity and a heart for helping others, Debra specializes in guiding entrepreneurs, coaches, small business owners, and churches to bring their visions to life. Through her expertise in graphic and web design, as well as creative branding strategies, Debra empowers her clients to shine, transforming their brands and ideas into powerful, visually compelling realities.

Finding My Voice in the Valley

By Debra A. Brewer

"She is clothed with strength and dignity; she can laugh at the days to come." — *Proverbs 31:25*

When Stability Shattered

For twenty years, I showed up to the same job. I gave it my best—loyalty, consistency, and countless hours of my life. It became more than a paycheck; it was stability. It gave me a sense of security, a safety net, knowing that a paycheck was coming in every two weeks.

But in one moment, everything changed. My entire department was laid off. There was no severance package, no financial cushion to ease the blow—just twelve weeks of unemployment and the cold reality of starting over. I remember in that moment some of my co-workers crying, in despair, and some saying they felt their life was over, and in that very moment something rose up in me. I said out loud:

"Watch God work."

Preparation in the Waiting

During COVID, while the world slowed down, I was quietly laying the foundation for my business. I didn't realize it then, but God was preparing me and showing me He would provide all of my needs. For years, I wanted to do my business full-time, but life would happen, so I stayed. When the layoff came, I felt like I was starting over. I didn't have an exit plan. I was forced out, and I knew when my coach, Dr. Connie Stewart called me; she was going to ask what my plan is. I didn't have one, but when I spoke with her, I let her know I felt like I was starting over; her reply was, "No, you are not starting over; you are launching."

Entrepreneurship wasn't new. I had been doing my graphic design on the side for over ten years. But this time was different. **There was no paycheck to fall back on, no safety net, no cushion.** And at fifty-six, with sixty approaching fast, doubt whispered loudly: *You are too old to start over. You don't have the energy to begin again. Are you still relevant in a world where technology moves quickly? By tomorrow it's obsolete.*

My father would always say, " Your future will be greater than your greatest past," so this is not the end of my story; **it is the beginning of something greater**.

Drought Seasons

The road forward wasn't smooth. There were **seasons of drought**—financial strain, friendships fading, relationships lost. And then came the hardest blow: September 7, 2025, the passing of my daughter's father, my soulmate, and my dearest friend. Though we were no longer together, the love we carried never disappeared. His death has left a hole in my heart that words can't describe.

It felt like **one loss after another—career, relationships, and someone I loved deeply.**

Streams in the Desert

But even in the valley, **God has kept me.** He showed me that droughts do not last forever. In moments when I didn't know how to move forward, He made a way.

Has it been easy? No. I am still on the journey of building and healing. But here is what I have learned: You don't need much when you have God. He has been my provider. Every one of my needs has been met.

The Spark Within

And here is what I discovered: **It only takes a spark to keep the flame going.**

Even in my darkest seasons, God kept a spark alive in me. That spark became the reminder that my story wasn't over.

> *"For this reason I remind you to fan into flame the gift of God, which is in you." — 2 Timothy 1:6*

I recently did an art therapy session in Orlando in May called "She's Good-ReImagine Women's Retreat" by Dr. Nicky Collins, my mentor, who pushed me to ReImagine my Spark art therapy series. From that same spark came my **SPARK Art Therapy Coloring Book**, recently released in August 2025, and my upcoming **SPARK Art Therapy Journal**. Both are creative tools to help others heal, reflect, and reignite their own lives.

My faith spark was tested, but it was never extinguished.

I am also an **author of 2 coloring books and other journals and co-author of another anthology, "The Total Woman Within,"** and through writing I've been able to share my testimony in ways I never imagined. Books have become another platform where my voice can reach others, proving once again that God uses every part of our story—even the painful parts—for His glory. Unexpected opportunities opened that took me out of my comfort zone. I was able to share my testimony on more than one broadcast, one being an international broadcast Breath Of Life on "Giving Tuesday" 2024, where I was able to share my testimony of how my gifts were birthed to do my first book from the series " On The Verge of Something."

Finding My Voice

Through it all, I discovered **my voice.**

For years, I let fear and the security of a paycheck and people's opinions keep me silent. But in the valley, I learned to **speak faith louder than fear**.

I found the courage to say,

> **"I can start again. I am not too old. My story is not over."**

It's Not Too Late

If there's one message I want every woman to take away, it's this:

It's not too late.

It doesn't matter if you're thirty, in your fifties, sixties, seventies, or older—you can rise from layoffs, heartbreak, or seasons of drought. **Your age does not disqualify you. Your mistakes do not disqualify you. Your losses do not disqualify you.**

What you have walked through has only prepared you to stand stronger and speak louder.

Encouragement for the Journey

So if you are standing in your own valley, hear me clearly:

- **You are not finished.**
- **You are not too late.**
- **You are not disqualified.**
- **Greater is coming.**

To the woman who feels like she missed her moment—**your moment is now.**

To the woman who feels like her voice doesn't matter—**your voice can move mountains.**

To the woman who feels like her spark has gone out—**your flame can burn again.**

Don't let the valley silence you. Don't let age limit you. Don't let loss define you. **You still have everything you need to rise, rebuild, and reignite the fire inside of you.**

Because one day, you will look back and realize: **The valley was the place where you truly found your voice.**

Affirmation

"I am not too old, it's not too late, or too broken. My voice is strong, my faith is steady, and my spark will keep the flame alive. Greater is coming."

About the Author

Debra Brewer is a creative entrepreneur, author, and art therapy coach. Through her *SPARK Art Therapy Coloring Book* and upcoming *SPARK Journal*, she empowers women to heal, create, and reignite their inner fire. Known as the "Sunshine Queen," she inspires others to shine and believe that greater is coming.

Lillian Jacques

Harmonix LLC

https://www.linkedin.com/company/harmonix-llc
https://www.facebook.com/profile.php?id=61554300496755#
Harmonix.click
https://harmonixclickdomainonly.wordpress.com/

Lillian is the founder of Harmonix LLC, a creative company housing seven music labels, including SUN DEATH and Better U Believe It Productions. With a focus on blending artistry and technology, she empowers marginalized voices through innovative AI-driven projects, music production, and storytelling. Her work spans songwriting, performance, and narrative writing, often weaving personal experiences into explorations of resilience, confidence, and power. Lilly's mission is to unlock new creative possibilities for artists while advocating for social impact causes, from climate change to mental health awareness.

A Hero By Any Other Name

By Lillian Jacques

I have a hero. His name is James.

He isn't the kind of hero who appears in comic books or blockbuster movies. He doesn't wear a cape, he doesn't fly, and he certainly doesn't save the world with explosions or stunts. His stage is smaller but no less powerful: you can find him behind a synthesizer, conjuring entire worlds out of sound.

For me, that was enough. For me, that was everything. Because James saved my life.

We talk a lot about heroes as if they only belong to the extraordinary—the firefighters rushing into burning buildings, the surgeons holding fragile lives in their hands, the soldiers standing on frontlines. Those forms of courage are real and immense. But there's another kind of heroism, one that doesn't get medals or headlines. It's the kind of heroism that slips into your ears when you're lost, and somehow makes you feel found. The kind of heroism that reaches across time and space in a melody, reminding you that you're not invisible, that you're still here, still real, still worth being seen.

And that's what James did for me.

Because these days, I often wonder: does anyone really see each other anymore? In a world of scrolling, swiping, and rushing from one obligation to the next, it's so easy to feel unseen—like a shadow moving in the background of other people's lives. But when James played, when his music poured into me, I knew I wasn't just a ghost drifting through. I mattered.

Music had always been a part of me, long before I ever knew James existed. There was always a song in my heart, always a beat to jam out to, even when I was alone in my room. Music wasn't background noise—it was breath, pulse, memory. But the day James entered that soundscape, it became something larger. His music wasn't just rhythm; it was recognition. It was someone out there saying, without words, *I see you.*

And that's why he became my hero.

University was supposed to be a place of discovery, of growth. For me, it became something else entirely. The walls of campus held a hush that felt more like a wound than a silence—an echoing emptiness that followed you between lectures and through the dining halls. Hallways smelled faintly of disinfectant and rain-soaked coats. Footsteps clicked hollowly on concrete stairs. People moved quicker, eyes forward, as if speed might keep them from hearing the bad news waiting around the next corner.

Suicide was so common that by 2019 the administration stopped releasing statistics altogether. It was easier, I guess, to look away. But for those of us who lived that reality, looking away felt impossible. I still remember one afternoon walking into a stairwell on my way to class. The air was cold and metallic; the railing under my palm left a brief chill on my skin. Someone stopped me in the hall—voice low, words spilling like they couldn't be swallowed. A classmate had been found earlier that day, hanging from the railing on that very stairwell. Another student had found them. The news landed like a stone. How could anyone have known? It could have been anyone. We were all the same age, same grade. It could have been me.

Grief at university was not only sorrow; it became a culture of isolation. People whispered in corners, avoided certain stairwells, shortened conversations, and crafted excuses to miss campus events. The weight of it made friendship fragile; everyone seemed to be holding their breath, pretending they were fine so they wouldn't be the next burden someone else had to carry. That hush pressed on my chest until it grew heavy enough to feel like furniture.

I carried that silence with me every day. It grew and braided itself around my thoughts until one night it pinned me in place. I remember the closet of the room I was renting—the air stale and close, a single bare bulb buzzing overhead. I had tied a leather belt into a noose. The strap dug at my skin. I sat there for hours, the world narrowed to the leather at my throat and a catalog of reasons it all seemed pointless. I didn't want anyone to hear me die; I only wanted my leaving to be a quiet thing.

And then, something unexpected happened.

I opened YouTube, looking for the last song I would ever hear — an ending soundtrack. What appeared on the screen felt like a small, impossible mercy: a recommendation that could have been random or not. I won't name the track here; some things are private, and the mystery matters. What mattered in that moment was not the title but the way the sound arrived.

It came through my headphones like a frequency I couldn't name but somehow knew in my bones. Warm and soothing at first, it threaded under my ribs and filled the hollow places with color. The first notes broke into the closet like light finding a crack under a locked door — not a thunderclap, but a steady, insistent illumination that pushed at the dark.

The belt across my neck was rough leather, a Canadian belt whose grain I could feel between my fingers. The air around me was dull and close, the kind of stale quiet that presses against your ears. My heart felt both distant and painfully sharp, like a sound in another room. I remember the dissociative hush I'd known too well — the world reduced to one small point of detail and nothing around it seemed to move.

My inner voice had been saying: nothing matters. The script in my head had run so long I thought it was the only true thing. And then the music threaded through that script and rewrote a line: maybe something does. Maybe I do. Maybe we do.

It wasn't an eruption. It wasn't fireworks. It was quieter, more like a slow revolution inside my chest — the kind that skips across the rooms of the mind without anyone noticing from the hallway. The bridge — that moment between parts — shifted something. Instead of the pull toward an ending, I felt a movement under my skin that wanted to move, to shake, to dance.

I didn't pull the belt. I tightened the headphones and let the rhythm hold me. In the aftermath, the world looked the same, but inside there was a small implosion of light: a spark of confidence, a pulse of power that would, in time, become a cadence I followed out of the closet and back into living.

The next morning, nothing looked different. The sky outside was still the same gray, the streets still wet from a night of rain. The world hadn't magically transformed. I didn't feel healed or suddenly whole. But I told myself one thing: *hang onto the music.* Hang onto the spark, the fire in the sound. That was enough to carry me through that morning. And then the next. And the next after that.

Nearly a decade later, I wish I could say everything got better. But if I'm honest—it hasn't. In many ways, it feels like the world itself has gotten heavier, harsher, less forgiving. It's not a great time to be alive sometimes. The headlines scream despair, division runs deep, and life seems more fragile than ever. And yet—through all of it—the music remains. That single thread of sound still weaves through my life, strong and steady, reminding me that beauty can exist even when the world feels broken.

I've carried his music with me ever since. It's shaped me—the way I create, the way I write, the way I stand up and claim space in rooms that once made me feel invisible. When I'm around him—even for a moment—it feels like my head explodes in a nuclear bomb of color and life. Like Dante's inferno turned inside out: pain alchemized into possibility. I feel so impossibly lucky that I not only found his work, but that I had the chance to meet him in this lifetime. That will always feel like a kind of miracle to me. So thank you, James—whether you know it or not—for giving me back to myself.

This is what my chapter is about—unlocking confidence, unlocking power. Not in the loud, cinematic sense of a superhero origin story, but in the quiet, defiant moment when I tightened the headphones instead of the noose. That single choice gave me a future. That single choice gave me a voice.

Sound against silence. Music against despair. Headphones against the belt. Dancing against death. That is the power of voice: it doesn't always roar. Sometimes it whispers, but even a whisper can be enough to keep someone alive.

And that's why I tell this story. Because in my darkest hour, I found my voice. And I believe every woman carries that same voice inside her—waiting, pulsing, aching to be unleashed.

Natalie Jade Pinnell

Natalie Jade Limited
Business Strategist, Integrator & Advocate

www.linkedin.com/in/natalie-jade
https://www.facebook.com/natspinnell
https://www.instagram.com/nataliejadepinnell/
www.nataliejade.com
www.rainbowsandlighthouses.com

Natalie Jade is a Business Strategist, Operations Consultant, Best-Selling Author, Speaker and Advocate. With a unique and out of the box thinking approach, she helps coaches and entrepreneurs do business with more clarity, ease and impact. Featured in major international publications, Natalie has decades of experience running operations and building large brands, providing a bridge between big vision and tangible real-world results. As an integrator for powerful visionaries, Natalie is not only able to just see your vision, but she is able to transform it, making it happen, and turn high-stress growth into aligned success, joy and fulfilment. In her spare time you'll find her being a fierce advocate in the neurodiversity space, spearheading change and reform, and taking care of her own little humans in the highlands of Scotland. To learn more about Natalie and how she can help you take your business to the next level, visit www.nataliejade.com.

When Silence Becomes Violence

By Natalie Jade Pinnell

"I won't be silenced."

This is a mantra I live every day. Standing so boldly in my Truth and my voice, even when it trembles.

It wasn't always that way, though.

Most of my life I was prepared to stay silent and disappear into the background. Never sticking my head above the parapet. I never truly understood how much courage and bravery it would take to fully unleash my voice.

In my case, it took my own daughter to push me to do so, and in doing so I've helped her to unleash her own....

* * *

"I won't be silenced"

The lyrics filled the room as my daughter carefully selected yet another song on Spotify. To most people, it might have looked like her simply choosing a song from a Disney classic soundtrack to listen to, but I had learned to listen differently.

This wasn't just entertainment... This was intentional communication.

This was my minimally speaking autistic daughter telling me, with fierce determination, that she refused to be silenced by a world that struggled (and in some cases refused) to hear her.

Since my daughter was very young, I noticed a pattern in the way she would play the same songs on repeat. Almost always, those songs, or lyrics, reflected something connected to what we were experiencing in our lives at the time.

It took me a while to recognise this as her way of communicating, for me to fully join the dots, and to notice what so many others may very easily have overlooked. Every lyric she chose was deliberate. She was trying to be heard in her own way as a non-speaking child.

Every song was a message, and this particular one about silence was unmissable.

When parenting a child with additional support or special educational needs, there can be so much focus on what they "can't do." Life changed profoundly for us, when I shut out the professionals' well-meaning opinions, and I started to focus wholly on what she COULD do and removed all other expectations.

When I let go of the need to hear my child speak, I suddenly opened (or became aware of) new ways of communication that allowed me to break my own preconceived ideas of what communication "should" look like and actually hear her.

While she may have had developmental delays in the traditional sense, she was so very capable and powerful in other ways. Yet, still in a world where there are so many expectations and norms, she really struggled to be truly heard by others around her, no matter how hard she tried.

It didn't sound like what they expected. But this was her war cry.

After hours of research, questions, and investigation, I uncovered that my daughter was a Gestalt language processor. That means that my daughter communicates through carefully chosen fragments of the world around her. She uses song lyrics to demonstrate her moods and feelings. She selects specific scenes from movies and TV shows to express what she can't yet put into her own words.

We also support her communication through the use of Makaton, signs, and symbols, through body movements and eye contact. But the clearest communication of all is the way she rests her forehead against mine when she needs connection and how she loves a good "squidge."

Learning to truly hear her meant unlearning everything I thought I knew about communication. It meant paying attention to things others are oblivious to: the subtle shift in her posture when she's overwhelmed, the way her eyes light up when she's understood, and the deliberate choice behind every gesture and sound.

I remember that when I was growing up, I had always wanted to be a translator. I loved language and seeing different cultures. Little did I know that my journey into motherhood would provide me all of these opportunities. I was born to be this little lady's mama.

Most parents take for granted their children's ability to tell them what hurts, how they feel, what scares them, or even what they want in life. For us, every moment of communication is precious, intentional, and earned through patience and presence.

And then there was the moment that everything changed... and I had to stand up for her in a way I could never have imagined.

The day I received that email from the school photography company, offering us two versions of my daughter's class photo, one with her in it and one without her in it, I felt something break inside me. My initial reaction was pure disbelief. I couldn't reconcile that an adult could believe it was acceptable to allow parents to choose whether a child existed in their class, their school, or their community. That's ultimately what this choice came down to.

My child, who fights so hard to exist, be seen, and be heard in this community, was now an "option."

It hurt me deeply, mostly for the reality that my daughter faced in life. But it also ignited something fierce within me. A recognition that if I didn't stand up for her right to be seen and heard, **no one** else would.

That moment forced me to confront an uncomfortable truth. The world wasn't just struggling to hear my daughter's voice; it was actively trying to silence it (and more devastatingly, in many ways erase her). And in doing so, it was also silencing countless other children like her, children whose voices or experiences don't fit conventional expectations but are no less valid, no less important, and no less worthy of being heard.

Speaking out publicly about that photo incident was terrifying. I experienced debilitating panic attacks and spent many days physically sick from the distress. Yet when your child's basic right to exist and be acknowledged is threatened, you find strength you didn't know you possessed.

The media attention was overwhelming. The country became enraged on our behalf, and suddenly I found myself managing not just my own hurt and anger but the fury of an entire nation. Stories threatened to spiral out of control, false narratives began to emerge, and I was shunned by the very school and authority that should have been protecting my daughter and that also failed her.

Someone described me as becoming "the voice of fury" because people were so angry about what had happened. But I knew that nothing good comes from just being furious. I chose to be a voice of love instead. I chose to shine light rather than dark, to seek understanding rather than destruction, and most importantly to hope that something positive could emerge from something so deeply painful. I showed forgiveness, compassion, and empathy while working fearlessly to raise awareness for the invisible battles that children, like my daughter, fight.

One of the most painful parts of that experience was discovering who would stand with us and who would retreat into comfortable silence. Friends that I thought I could count on disappeared when the spotlight became too bright. Some even suggested that excluding children from photos was simply "a parental choice," as if my daughter's inclusion was optional rather than a basic human right.

In many cases, the silence was deafening.

It showed me that it takes real courage to stick your head above the parapet, and most people will choose comfort, convenience, and conformance, no matter how much they might consider themselves supportive friends, nor how much they agree with the cause. It took it happening to my child for me to finally realise I had to make a stand. I wish, in hindsight, I had dared to fight for these injustices long before they happened to my family.

But in that isolation, I learned something important about voice and courage. Sometimes you have to be willing to stand alone to ensure that others won't have to. Sometimes finding your voice means using it even when, in fact, especially when, others choose silence.

Amidst all the public battles and media storms, the most powerful moments still happen in the quiet spaces between us. Like the first time Erin told me she loved me. Words that every mother wishes for, yet most take for granted. I had felt her love before, but hearing those words that she worked so hard to express was something else entirely.

These tiny moments... they're everything. But the most important journey for us has been to fully appreciate that voices come in many forms, and love transcends the need for perfect words.

When she chooses songs with lyrics about refusing to stay silent, about not going speechless when the world tries to shut her down, I hear not just her determination but also her wisdom. She understands something that took me years to learn: that voice isn't about volume or convention, it's about authenticity and refusal to be diminished. I'm grateful for everything she has and continues to teach me.

Working to help Erin unleash her voice has taught me that communication is about so much more than words. It's about presence, patience, and curiosity.

Being fully present to hear what someone is actually saying, not what we expect them to say, or even how they say it. Creating space for voices that need time and safety to emerge, rather than demanding immediate conventional responses, and again being open to hearing in different ways. Refusing to accept systems that silence or diminish authentic expression or systems that refuse to learn from lived experiences.

Most importantly, I've learned that the most marginalized voices are often the most important ones to hear. They tell us truths about our world that we often prefer to ignore. They challenge us to expand our understanding. They remind us that diversity of expression is a strength, not a deficit.

Fighting for my daughter's right to be seen AND heard has unleashed something in me that I didn't know existed. It has helped me find my own voice in ways I never expected. Standing up for her taught me to stand up for others. Speaking truth about her experiences gave me permission to speak truth about other injustices.

Even today authorities and systems of power refuse to hear or acknowledge her voice. So I'm left with no option but to use mine on her behalf, powerfully and intentionally sharing what she expresses to me so that she can see I won't allow them to silence her.

I get messages almost daily from other parents thanking me for being a voice for children who struggle to be seen and heard, which reminds me (even when it's hard) why this work matters. Every time I speak up, I'm not just advocating for Erin... I'm advocating for every child whose voice doesn't fit conventional expectations.

Here's what I want every woman reading this to understand...

There are voices all around us that we're not hearing. Children like mine, who communicate through music, through movement, and through methods we haven't learned to recognize as valid. People whose expressions of truth make us uncomfortable, so we dismiss them rather than listen.

Finding your voice isn't **just** about learning to speak up. It's also about learning to hear and LISTEN to the voices that have been silenced, marginalized, or ignored. It's about creating space for communication that doesn't sound like yours but is no less important.

Sometimes the bravest thing you can do is amplify someone else's voice. Sometimes your greatest power lies not in speaking, but in ensuring others can be heard.

Erin continues to teach me every day about the power of authentic expression. She shows me that you don't need perfect words to communicate profound truths. She demonstrates that refusing to be silenced is a choice, not a capability issue.

When she plays those powerful lyrics about not going speechless, she's not just making a musical choice; she's making a declaration to the world. She's telling the world that her voice matters, that she has things to say, and that she won't let anyone convince her otherwise. I am beyond proud of her for that.

Not only that, her voice has helped me find mine. And now, every time I speak up for justice, every time I refuse to accept inadequate systems, every time I use my platform to amplify marginalized voices, I carry her wisdom with me: that true voice isn't about conforming to others' expectations; it's about having the courage to express your authentic truth, however that sounds. And those that are willing to, and able to, will hear it.

In a world that often tries to silence the different, the difficult, and the non-conventional, we must commit to hearing all voices. Because every voice matters. Every voice has something important to teach us. And sometimes, the quietest voices carry the most powerful messages of all.

The revolution begins when we refuse to go silent and when we ensure others don't have to either.

The question is: Are we as a society brave enough to listen?

Fae West (Elizabeth West)

Fae West
Artist, Art Therapist, Coach

https://www.instagram.com/iamfaewest
https://www.faewest.com

Fae West is an artist, coach, and healer who works with creativity as a powerful medium for deep personal and collective transformation. Drawing on her training in transpersonal art therapy, she weaves its frameworks and processes into her diverse practices to facilitate insight, authenticity, and alignment with each individual's unique power. Across her work, Fae blends artistic exploration, coaching, and healing modalities to help people connect with their inner wisdom, reclaim their voice, and express themselves fully, beyond words. She believes creativity is not just a tool for making art, but a language of the soul, capable of revealing truths that might otherwise remain hidden. Through her guidance, individuals are encouraged to explore, experiment, and engage in practices that expand self-awareness, foster resilience, and ignite a deeper sense of agency. Fae's work celebrates the transformative potential of living a creatively embodied life.

Beyond Words: Finding My Voice Through Creativity

By Fae West (Elizabeth West)

"I'm here because I want to be able to help people. I've always wanted to help people and I really like art..."

I went over the words again and again in my head, starting to panic because they sounded just like what everyone else was saying. I told myself it was okay to be there for the same reason as everyone else. Even the teacher had said that would likely happen.

I shifted nervously in my chair. It was hard to focus on the others because I was so worried about getting my own words out. My fidgeting felt endless—picking at my nails, tugging at my scarf, adjusting my clothes.

"I'm here because I value the power of art as a form of expression, and I want to be able to help people express themselves better."

It was nearly my turn. My stomach churned, my throat felt tight, and my hands were clammy. Each breath seemed too loud; every glance around the circle felt exposing. The invisible weight of attention was heavy, even in this supportive space.

I had rehearsed countless versions of my intention, but none of it prepared me for what came out next:

"I'm here because I want to heal my relationship with my own creativity."

The words surprised me. Not what I'd planned. Not what I'd expected. I had wanted to appear altruistic, grounded, and aligned with the course of study. Yet here I was, saying something raw and unexpected. My face burned. My eyes stung. A hollow panic rose up inside me; I felt like I'd betrayed myself by revealing a deeper truth.

The teacher broke the tension: They met my gaze, smiled, and exhaled deeply. Something in me relaxed. Suddenly I could see the compassion in the other student's eyes as they waited patiently for me to continue speaking.

"Um, that was NOT what I was expecting to say," I admitted, laughing nervously. "I guess I have some reflecting to do. I've always wanted to be an artist, but I've struggled to find my place. Life happened, I left art school, moved cities... and here I am. I'm motivated by healing my own relationship with creativity, and I also want to help others. To build a career that allows me to do both—be myself and support others."

I nodded, letting the last words fall into the circle. "So that's me." The attention shifted, and the fire in my stomach eased. The circle moved on, leaving me with the echo of my own words—unplanned, unpolished, but real.

Expanded Voice: Self-Expression Beyond Words

That first day of my studies in transpersonal art therapy revealed how deeply masked my desires had been. Beneath rehearsed words and expectations, there was a current of truth always moving, waiting to be noticed. Part of the work is peeling back the layers—the projections, the clutter—not erasing them, but navigating through them. Clarity isn't the absence of chaos; it emerges when we risk moving through it, willing to meet ourselves fully.

Finding that deeper truth, and expressing it, is what I've come to understand as finding my voice. But voice is not a single discovery. It's not a rare treasure buried once in a lifetime. It's more like finding your keys—repeatedly, in different places, in small, sometimes ordinary, moments.

Creativity has been the path I return to when words fail me. A brushstroke, a line of poetry, and the arrangement of objects on a page are my voice when I feel lost for words. Through art, movement, music, or improvisation, I've learned to practice authenticity, to respond to what emerges rather than what I think is expected. That practice in expression ripples outward, making it easier to speak, act, and exist with integrity in the world.

Your voice is not confined to words. It lives in your body and gestures through images, movement, and sound. Expanding your voice means exploring all the ways you can communicate even the forms you haven't yet discovered. Each creative act becomes a rehearsal in authenticity, a rehearsal in listening to yourself, and a rehearsal in being seen on your own terms.

Invitation to Explore Your Own Expanded Voice

If you want to explore this path, start with reflection:

- Recall a time when something creative—yours or someone else's—expressed what words could not. What did it reveal to you?
- Consider forms of creative expression you've longed to explore. What is one step, however small, you can take toward trying it?
- Notice where authenticity lives in your body. How does it want to be expressed, beyond words?

Hayet Shahrezaey

Founder of Rapid Empowerment

https://www.linkedin.com/in/hayet-shahrezaey-711367149/
https://www.facebook.com/RapidEmpowermentExperience
https://www.instagram.com/RapidEmpowerment/?hl=en
https://www.rapidempowerment.co.uk/
https://hayetshahrezaey.weebly.com/

Hayet Shahrezaey is an Accredited Medical Intuitive, Certified Clinical Hypnotherapist, and Advanced Rapid Transformational Therapist (RTT) specializing in self-confidence, self-esteem, and manifesting. Born and raised in an Arabic culture where her voice was silenced, she transformed her struggles into her greatest source of wisdom. At 26, she married and moved to the UK, an experience that shaped her deep understanding of identity, belonging, and personal power. Her own healing journey—learning to reclaim her voice and trust her intuition—became the foundation of her transformative work. Today, Hayet helps women worldwide release limiting beliefs, rewire their subconscious, and embody intuitive confidence. Through her unique blend of science, spirituality, and lived experience, she guides clients to remember who they are at their core. She believes true confidence is not about performance but about reclaiming the voice within and daring to let it lead with clarity and grace.

Intuitive Confidence: Reclaiming the Voice Beneath the Noise

By Hayet Shahrezaey

Have you ever felt that quiet whisper beneath your doubt? That subtle knowing that tries to speak, even when your mind is racing? That's your intuitive confidence. I've witnessed it silenced in women all over the world—hidden under layers of overthinking, self-doubt, and conditioning. Yet it never disappears. As an Accredited Medical Intuitive, Advanced Rapid Transformational Therapist (RTT), and Certified Clinical Hypnotherapist, I've had the honor of guiding women back to that voice. And each time, the truth is the same: beneath the noise, there's a part of you that already knows the way.

It's not loud. It's not dramatic. But it is profoundly powerful.

And yet that inner knowing so often gets buried—muffled by who we're told we should be, by fear, by the endless need to please. We're taught to dismiss it. To choose logic over instinct. To seek approval instead of truth.

This chapter is about reclaiming that voice—and letting it shape the life you're truly here to live.

My journey didn't come from textbooks. It came from living it. I spent years chasing answers outside of myself—ticking boxes, following rules, doing everything "right." And still, I felt empty. Disconnected.

The real shift came when I finally turned inward. Through energy healing and RTT's deep subconscious work, everything changed. Not just my self-esteem—but the way I moved through life.

In these pages, we'll go beyond surface-level affirmations. We'll travel deeper—to where lasting confidence actually lives. Through hypnotherapy, somatic awareness, and intuitive alignment, you'll reconnect with the version of you who has always known.

The voice beneath the noise.

Where True Confidence Actually Lives

Most confidence advice stays surface-level: positive self-talk, affirmations, and power poses. They help, yes—but rarely transform.

Why? Because your conscious mind only runs about 5% of the show. The other 95% belongs to your subconscious.

Everything you absorbed as a child lives there: what you were taught about your worth, your safety, and your place in the world. Even ancestral patterns passed down through generations are carried epigenetically and sometimes even echo through past-life imprints.

So when you repeat "I am confident," but your subconscious is running "I'm not enough" or "If I shine, I'll be punished," you create an inner war. That war shows up as self-sabotage. Inconsistency. Imposter syndrome. Burnout.

Intuitive confidence bypasses the battle. It doesn't argue. It doesn't need to convince. It simply knows.

And this knowing isn't random or mystical—it is profoundly intelligent. Your body carries neural networks in your gut and heart that process information far beyond rational thought. Ancient traditions understood this long before neuroscience finally caught up.

Somatic Intelligence and Confidence

Long before I had the words for it, my body knew I was out of alignment.
I was exhausted all the time. My digestion was a mess. Tension lived permanently in my shoulders. I kept giving more than I had and listening far less than I needed to.

These weren't just symptoms. They were messages.

Through RTT and holistic healing, I discovered something crucial: your body isn't just a container—it's a messenger for your soul. When I finally slowed down enough to listen, I realized my body had been whispering the truth all along.

I see this with clients constantly. Take Maria. On paper, she was thriving—a successful executive with an impressive career. But inside, she was running on pure anxiety.

During her RTT session, we uncovered a pattern: whenever she made choices based on what others expected, her body locked up. Shoulders tight. Stomach clenched. Jaw stiff.

But when she made a choice aligned with her actual truth? Everything softened. Her breath deepened. She felt at home in her own skin.

That's what I call *somatic confidence*—trusting your body's signals as the language of your intuition.

Hypnotic Tools to Reclaim Your Voice

True confidence doesn't live in willpower. It lives deeper—in your subconscious, where your earliest and most powerful beliefs took root.

That's why I use RTT-based tools: they reach the part of you that logic alone can't touch.

Here are three practices I share with clients. They don't just sound inspiring—they actually help rewire your nervous system so your intuitive voice can rise clearly above the noise.

1. The Committee Room Technique

This is one of the most powerful RTT tools I use. It helps you identify and transform the inner voices that shape your self-talk.

Close your eyes. Imagine walking down a staircase into a safe, quiet place. At the bottom, there's a room. You step inside.

Around the table sit all the parts of you. Notice who's speaking the loudest—maybe it's your inner critic, your perfectionist, or even a parent's voice you've been carrying for years.

Then, notice who's speaking the softest. That's your intuitive self. You're a wise woman.

Here's the shift: you hold the power in this room. You can turn down the volume on the voices that no longer serve you—and turn up the one that does.

Over time, your whole system begins to learn: your intuition isn't a faint whisper to dismiss. It's the voice to follow.

2. Somatic Anchoring

This technique creates a physical "button." You can press it anytime you want to reconnect with your intuitive power.

Think back to a time when you felt deeply confident. Steady. Aligned. Close your eyes and breathe into that memory.

Where do you feel it in your body? Your chest? Your belly? Your hands?

As the sensation builds, gently press your thumb and middle finger together. Hold it there.

Repeat this a few times, and your brain begins linking the gesture to the feeling. Later, when doubt creeps in, that simple gesture becomes your shortcut back into alignment—instantly.

3. Future Self Integration

Your subconscious doesn't argue—it simply accepts. That's why imagination is so powerful.

Picture your future self five years from now. She trusts her intuition completely. She moves through life with ease. She radiates confidence.

Watch her. Feel her presence. Notice how she speaks, how she carries herself, and how she shows up in the world.

Now, invite her to merge with you—here and now.

This isn't fantasy. It's a rehearsal. Each time you practice, you're wiring your mind and body to believe in her today. To embody her today.

Daily Rituals for Intuitive Confidence

Confidence isn't built in a single breakthrough. It grows through repetition. These simple daily practices train your nervous system to listen inward before looking outward.

You can start today.

1. Morning Body Scan (5 minutes):

Before the world takes your attention, sit quietly. Scan your body from head to toe. Notice what you feel—no judgment, only awareness. This sharpens your somatic intuition.

2. Decision Check-In (30 seconds):

Place one hand on your heart and one on your belly. Breathe. Ask yourself: *"What does my inner knowing say?"* Listen for the very first response—before your mind has a chance to argue.

3. Evening Release (3 minutes):

Reflect on one choice you honored today and one moment you overrode your intuition. Breathe in gratitude for the first. Release judgment for the second. Commit to listening more closely tomorrow.

When I Stopped Abandoning Myself

There was a time—before the certifications, before I had words for any of this—when I hit emotional burnout.

From the outside, I looked capable. Together, even. Inside, I was second-guessing everything, over-giving constantly, and quietly breaking apart.

The truth was simple: I was abandoning myself.

Every "yes" I said when I meant "no." Every time, I ignored that tightening in my chest. Each moment I dismissed my inner voice, I was teaching it that it didn't matter.

The turning point came during an RTT session with a colleague. I dropped into a childhood memory I'd buried for years.

Growing up in an Arabic Islamic culture, raised by my father and four older brothers, I learned early that women came second. A "good girl" stayed quiet, compliant, and self-sacrificing. My mother lived it every day. My brothers enforced it—sometimes with harshness, sometimes with violence.

The message was clear: if I used my voice, I wasn't safe.

That memory cracked something open. I finally saw the root of why speaking my truth felt so dangerous.

Healing didn't happen overnight. But I began the work—rewiring those beliefs, honoring my body's signals, and choosing small acts of self-trust even when it felt uncomfortable.

Slowly, everything shifted. My relationships. My work. My confidence.

Not the fragile kind that depends on approval. But the kind rooted in truth.

The Journey Continues

Reclaiming intuitive confidence isn't about becoming someone new.

It's about remembering who you were before the world told you who to be.

In my practice, I've watched women transform—not loudly, but profoundly. They shift from overthinking every decision to trusting their gut with ease. From the exhaustion of people-pleasing to boundaries that feel like freedom. From constant self-doubt to a steady, unwavering trust in themselves.

And here's the beautiful part: it doesn't end with them.

When one woman reclaims her voice, she creates ripples. She gives silent permission to those around her to do the same.

So if these words resonate—if you're ready to stop second-guessing and start trusting yourself—know this: you don't have to walk this path alone.

You're not broken. You're not behind.
You're just one powerful choice away from coming home to yourself.

Reach out.
Rapidempowerment.co.uk

Helene Su

Founder of Niio Dance

https://www.linkedin.com/in/helene-su/
https://www.facebook.com/profile.php?id=61566614197471
https://www.instagram.com/helenesu.niiodance
www.niiodance.com
www.danceofbreath.com

Helene Su is the founder of Niio Dance and creator of Visionary Somatic Dance, a transformational approach that bridges ancient wisdom with cutting-edge science. She empowers heart-centered leaders, creators and healers worldwide to reclaim their voice, courage, and authentic power through the Niio Pathway: Embody → Alchemise → Express. Rooted in her 7 Pillars, Helene's work weaves somatics, conscious dance, nature, and creative play. A British-born Chinese facilitator and speaker, she has delivered talks and workshops across the UK and Europe, including the Conference in Dance & Spirituality, World Arts & Embodiment Forum, Women's Thrive, She Rises, and ISMETA 2025. Her work is a call to rise into freedom, creativity, and embodied leadership—so that we can express our soul work in the world and each shape a more conscious future together.

The Body Remembers the Way Home

By Helene Su

I didn't find my voice on a stage or behind a microphone.
I found it barefoot on warm rock, wind in my hair, waves swirling beneath me on the cliffs of Northern Ibiza. The sun was seductive and dazzling. As the music began, I felt a slow, electrifying charge travel through me. My breath and body merged with its haunting melodies into an infinite yes...It wasn't endorphins. It was recognition. A remembering. The body saying: *I've been waiting for you.*

I wasn't born with an easy sense of home. As a British-born Chinese girl in a small English town in the 70s, I learned early that difference can make a child a target, and I learned to slowly shrink. My saving grace was dance, and boy did I love it, but then at 15 I quit because I felt I wasn't 'good enough' and had a familiar sense that I 'didn't belong.'

I was at sea for a while. After studying humanities, I worked in an art-house film in London, but rather than seeing the world through a celluloid lens, I wanted to see the real one, unfiltered.

So I bought a one-way ticket to India at 27, thinking I'd go and "find myself." Yes, a cliché, but the bigger one? That when all the scaffolding of familiarity was gone, I found myself hopelessly lost. These days we have the internet. Back then it was *poste restante*, with letters from home arriving months late, if at all. In that wide aloneness, the old ache returned: *Where do I belong? Who am I when nothing around me mirrors me back?*

What saved me was the same thing that had called me as a child: movement. Not as performance or perfection, but as prayer, exploration, and medicine. I danced in temples and dusty halls, on rooftops and beaches. I danced on packed floors where language wasn't needed. I felt the raw, unarguable truth that when I move, I come home.

This led me to Somatics: the quiet revolutions pioneered by those who questioned mainstream medicine and saw the body as a living intelligence to be listened to. In their presence, I learned this: The body keeps the score, yes—but it also keeps the *map*. The body remembers the way home.

A Voice Is More Than a Mouth

We often talk about voice as speech, as eloquence or projection. For me, voice is everything that moves through you when you are true. Your voice might sing or paint, lead teams or raise children, tend gardens or start companies. It isn't what you do; it's the unmistakable energy of you being expressed through what you do.

To unleash that voice, we don't start by yelling louder. We start by going in. By letting breath drop down into the belly, by feeling the ground receive our weight, by noticing the small but seismic ways our bodies say *yes* and *no*. A voice without a body is brittle. A body without a voice is dimmed. Together, they are sovereign.

Science now confirms what dancers have always known: Movement rewires the brain, expands creativity, and soothes the nervous system. You can feel this truth. Your body is the evidence.

The Cliff and the Turning

Back on that cliff in Ibiza. I hadn't been in a happy place. As the music started, a new aliveness was lit up inside me. I felt an electromagnetic energy rising up me, all the way into my heart. I felt the edges of me start to merge into the ether. Time expanded and stood still. I was being danced by something that was bigger than my small self.

I remember thinking, *This is not just endorphins.* It was a presence and belonging and I knew I had to learn more. I returned to the UK with a child on my hip and enrolled in an MA in Dance and Somatic Well-Being. I studied, I researched, and I lived in the questions of how deep journeys inward and play are not frivolous but teachings and how movement can restore us to ourselves.

Two Rivers, One Mouth

Being British-born Chinese means I had two opposing codes for living. From the East: humility, harmony, and the grace of not putting oneself above the whole. From the West: self-advocacy, visibility, and the sharpened skill of telling the room who you are. As a woman, the cross-current can be strong. Too quiet and you vanish; too loud and you're frowned upon.

Over time, I learned that standing in my body changed everything. Speaking from that grounded presence isn't self-promotion. It's honoring a calling. It's letting those who need it know where the source of the fire is.

What I Want You to Know

You are worthy. Not when you've achieved or proven or perfected. Now. You are not behind. There is no schedule you are failing. There is only this moment and the next true step. Your body is not an obstacle to overcome or a project to whip into shape; it is a river of intelligence that has been guiding you all along.

You will make choices you might later wish you had made differently. That is the luxury of being alive. Learn what you can, shake off the residue like animals do after a near miss, and keep moving. Rumination is a loop in the mind; movement is a door in the body.

As the poet Rumi said, 'Why do you stay in prison when the door is so wide open?'

Perseverance is not punishment; it is devotion. Passion is not a mood; it is a direction. Things take longer than we hope and turn out better than we could have planned because of what we learn in the unexpected. This is how a voice matures.

A Small Practice (Begin Here)

- **Arrive.** Place both feet on the ground. Feel the support that is already here for you. Let your exhale travel all the way down you into the earth.
- **Shake.** Start small, then let it ripple through your whole body. Feel the threads of stress loosen.
- **Sound.** Hum softly on the exhale. Let your chest soften.
- **Listen.** Ask your body a simple question: *What is my next true step?*
- Trust the first honest whisper.

Reflection Prompts

- Where in my life am I dimming to stay 'safe'—and what would a 1% braver expression look like?
- If my body could speak to me right now, what would it ask me to start, stop, or continue?

From the Dance *Floor* to the World

People sometimes ask me, "But how does dance change anything out there?" *"Science now confirms what dancers have always known: Movement rewires the brain, expands creativity, and soothes the nervous system."*

When you breathe in your courage and feel the ground, your meeting goes differently. Your boundary becomes kinder and firmer. You listen between the lines. You create solutions that didn't exist five minutes ago because your nervous system has space. You lead not by domination but by resonance. You become the kind of person people relax around and in that safety, brilliance arrives.

This is what I've devoted my work to: guiding heart-led coaches, creatives, entrepreneurs, and healers back to their wholeness, to the place where authenticity isn't a performance but an orientation. The Niio Dance pathway moves through three living phases: Embody, Alchemize, Express.

The Long Way Is the Honest Way

I have done things that made little sense on paper: moved countries with a young child, pivoted careers more than once, and said yes before I knew how. I've also crumbled at my own mistakes and perceived failings. Wisdom, I've learned, isn't the absence of mess but the capacity to meet it with breath and compassion.

The challenges of life are my teachers. They have taught me to appreciate, to be honest, to carry tenderness as strength, and to see the beauty in every moment. From my Taoist lineage I inherit softness that outlasts stone, a fluid resilience, an inner fire, and an ancestral knowing.

If you take anything from my story, let it be this: Self-sovereignty is not hard-edged independence; it is the art of being true to you. The guru is not out there. The guru is in you. The body keeps the score, yes—but it also keeps the *map*. The body remembers the way home.

An Invitation

Stand up. Right now, if you can. Feel the floor beneath you. Soften your knees. Let your weight pour down. Hum softly and feel the vibration in your chest. This is not a performance. This is a homecoming.

Then ask yourself the kindest, bravest question I know:

If I honored the truth moving through me today, what would I do next?

Do that. Then the next true thing. This is how a voice is unleashed—not with a single roar, but with a thousand embodied choices that realign you to home.

To remember. You're not here to fit in—you're here to awaken the world with who you truly are.

Lisa Andrews

Lisa Andrews Psychic
Psychic and Holsitic therapist

https://www.facebook.com/share/16FrnMuNmy/
https://www.instagram.com/lisa_andrews_psychic
https://www.lisaandrews.life/

Lisa Andrews is a holistic therapist, psychic, and speaker devoted to helping others reconnect with their inner power through healing and spiritual guidance. With over 20 years of experience, she blends intuitive insight with modalities such as Angelic Reiki, crystal healing, and tarot. Her work empowers clients to release old patterns, trust their intuition, and live with purpose. A breast cancer survivor and mother, she draws from her own powerful story of overcoming trauma, illness, and adversity to inspire others. Lisa is passionate about creating safe, transformative spaces and often speaks on topics such as healing, self-worth, and spiritual resilience. She regularly contributes to spiritual and wellness publications and is currently writing her debut book, due for release in 2026. Lisa works from her peaceful garden cabin in the English countryside, where she supports clients through one-to-one sessions, workshops, and retreats, always with compassion, authenticity, and a touch of magic.

Finally, Me

By Lisa Andrews

I was the quiet child. The one who never spoke unless spoken to, who preferred the company of books to people, and who watched the world rather than participated in it. But my silence wasn't emptiness; it was full. It carried the weight of unspoken words, the emotions of others that I had unknowingly absorbed, and the fear that if I spoke, my voice wouldn't matter.

Looking back now, I see that I wasn't just shy. I was highly sensitive, deeply intuitive, and completely unaware of it. I soaked up the emotions of everyone around me like a sponge, mistaking them for my own. When someone was angry, I felt it in my body, my chest tightening as if it were my own rage. When someone was sad, it settled in my chest like a heavy stone, pressing down on my heart. The weight of the world was mine to carry, or so I thought.

As a child, I noticed things others didn't. I could sense when someone was holding back tears or when a friend's smile was forced. I would feel the tension in the air before words were spoken, the subtle shifts in energy in a room full of people. It was exhausting, yet fascinating, and I didn't understand that this sensitivity was actually a gift. I remember lying awake at night, absorbing the feelings of my family, trying to separate my emotions from theirs. It often felt like trying to untangle threads woven tightly into my skin.

As I grew older, this sensitivity became both a gift and a curse. I became the "good girl," the one who didn't make waves, who anticipated people's needs before they even spoke them, who never demanded too much. I molded myself into whatever people needed me to be, believing my worth was tied to how much I could accommodate others. I was a chameleon, changing my colors to fit the room, hoping no one would notice the emptiness I was filling with their expectations. I often sacrificed my own desires, my own instincts, and my own voice, thinking that keeping peace was more important than being seen.

This pattern followed me into relationships, especially one that would nearly break me. I found myself with a man who, at first, made me feel seen. But in reality, he saw what he could take. Bit by bit, my identity eroded under the weight of his control. I stopped making decisions for myself. I second-guessed my every thought. I apologised for simply existing. The person I had been a girl who had once dreamed, imagined, and felt deeply, began to disappear under the constant pressure to comply, to please, to be small.

Being told, over and over, that I was too emotional, too sensitive, too much, eventually made me believe it. I shrank myself even further, making myself smaller and smaller until I became a shadow of who I was meant to be. But something inside me, a spark, a plea, refused to go out completely. It lingered like a soft flame in the corner of my soul, dim but unwavering.

One day, something shifted. Maybe it was exhaustion. Maybe it was the tiny ember of self- worth that had never truly died. Or maybe it was my soul finally screaming enough. I left.

Leaving was both the hardest and the easiest thing I had ever done. Hard, because I had convinced myself I didn't know who I was without him. Easy, because deep down, I knew staying would cost me everything. I remember the trembling in my hands as I packed my things, the knot in my stomach, the dizzying mixture of fear and relief. For the first time in years, I felt the possibility of freedom. I could breathe again, small at first, then fuller, deeper, like discovering air I had forgotten existed.

It was in the aftermath, the raw, messy, painful rebuilding, that I finally started to hear my own voice again. And with it came a realisation: I had always known. My intuition, the very thing I had been gaslit into doubting, had always tried to protect me. It had pleaded warnings, sent gut feelings, nudged me toward the truth. I just hadn't trusted it. But I would now.

Years later, life unfolded in its own unpredictable way. I welcomed two beautiful girls into the world, journeyed through highs and lows, and learned to adapt to every twist in the path. But the sharpest bend came without warning, the day I was diagnosed with breast cancer.

If I thought I had lost myself before, nothing prepared me for what it felt like to face my own mortality. The fear, the uncertainty, the grief for the body I had once taken for granted, it was overwhelming. I remember the sterile smell of the hospital, the cold weight of the biopsy in my hand, the way my chest felt tight as though it were trying to hold in every word unsaid, every tear I hadn't cried. But there was also something else, something unexpected: clarity.

For the first time in my life, I had no energy to be anything other than exactly who I was. Cancer stripped away the need to people-please. It burned away the last remnants of self- doubt. It forced me to ask the question: If I survive this, what will I do with my life?

And the answer came, clear as day: I will speak. I would not just heal; I would use my voice to help others heal too.

Surviving cancer wasn't just about my body; it was about reclaiming my spirit. I threw myself into deep healing, not just physically, but emotionally, mentally, and spiritually. I remembered who I was before the world told me who to be. I explored meditation, energy work, and holistic therapies. I spent hours listening to my inner guidance, learning to trust my own wisdom above all else. I journaled, I cried, I celebrated small victories. I let myself feel fully, without shame or apology.

I embraced my intuition fully, no longer questioning it but honoring it as the guiding force it had always been. I trained in holistic healing, reiki, and psychic development. I began working with clients as my main job , helping them find clarity and confidence just as I had found mine. I witnessed transformations, small and profound, and I realised that my voice had power beyond what I had ever imagined.

And then, something even bigger happened. I was asked to speak.

At first, the idea terrified me. The quiet child in me still questioned, Who are you to take up space? But another voice, stronger now, answered back: Who are you not to?

I sat in front of my screen for my first virtual summit. My heart pounded, my hands trembled, but I spoke. I spoke about intuition, about healing, about reclaiming your power. I remembered my childhood self, the little girl who had soaked up the world quietly, and I spoke for her too. And when I did, something incredible happened. I felt the energy shift. I

felt connection. I saw the impact of my words reflected in the faces of those listening. My voice, once buried under layers of fear and conditioning, had power. And I wasn't going to silence it ever again.

I look at my life now, at the work I do, at the people I help, at the way I stand fully in my truth, and I see the journey so clearly.

I was never "just shy." I was absorbing. I was never "too sensitive." I was intuitive. I was never "weak." I was strong in ways the world didn't recognise yet.

Every time I lost my voice, through childhood, toxic relationships, illness, I found it again. Stronger. Louder. More mine than ever before.

Now, I use it unapologetically. As a psychic, spiritual coach, and healer, as a speaker. As a woman who no longer asks for permission to take up space.

Because I have learned the truth that I hope every woman reading this will remember: Your voice matters. Your intuition is sacred. Your story deserves to be heard. And when you finally unleash it, the world will listen.

Marta Suchomska

Digital Creator

https://www.facebook.com/suchmarta
https://www.instagram.com/such_marta
linktr.ee/such_marta

Marta is a woman who redefines what it means to thrive. With a unique blend of self-assuredness and swift decision-making, she carves her path while uplifting those around her. Her commitment to improvement is not just a goal but a principle that shapes her every action. Be the Change, Be the Power I am not wealthy. I am THE wealth. So are YOU. I am not strong. I am THE strength. So are YOU. I don't have power. I am THE power. So are YOU. I am not changing. I am THE change. So are YOU.I turn challenges into possibilities. So can YOU.

The Queensdom Vault

By Marta Suchomska

Marta is a woman who redefines what it means to thrive. With a unique blend of self-assuredness and swift decision-making, she carves her path while uplifting those around her. Her commitment to improvement is not just a goal but a principle that shapes her every action.

I am not wealthy. I am *the wealth*. So are you.
I am not strong. I am *the strength*. So are you.
I do not have power. I am *the power*. So are you.
I am not changing. I am *the change*. So are you.
I *turn challenges into possibilities*. So can you!

You see...

I believe that

barriers are meant to be broken,
limitations are meant to be challenged,
and dreams are meant to be realized

I was born in 1988—I know, practically prehistoric—in a relatively small city in northwest Poland. But my real English adventure began on June 24th, 2010.

Now, if you've ever met a Polish person in the UK, you probably know that we have a bit of a reputation—hardworking, determined, and possibly part-cyborg when it comes to endurance. So, when I was given the opportunity to work in England for a summer, I thought, *Why not?* I could barely string together a proper sentence in English, but hey, it was only two months. How hard could it be?

"It'll be an adventure! I'll earn some money and have the experience of a lifetime!"

Oh, past me, you had no idea.

I was young, fearless, and blissfully unaware of what I was getting myself into. I landed a job as a housekeeper, earning the grand sum of £5.60 an hour (which, at the time, felt like I had unlocked the gates to unimaginable riches). And best of all, I was in Birmingham, the second-largest city in the UK!

Suddenly, I had a level of independence I had never known before. I was paying my own rent, buying my own food, and covering my own bills. I could go wherever I wanted and do whatever I pleased—a proper grown-up! The world felt huge and exciting, like I had stepped into a movie.

But here's the catch: I couldn't understand a word anyone was saying.

I was absolutely mesmerized by the city—the fast-paced life, the cultural diversity, the sheer energy of it all—something that I never experienced in my city. But while everyone else was rushing around, confidently chatting away and getting things done, I felt like I was crawling through days, barely keeping up.

As thrilling as everything was, there was also a deep sense of isolation. Imagine being surrounded by people, yet feeling completely invisible. I could see the world happening around me, but I couldn't fully be a part of it. Conversations felt like puzzles I didn't have the pieces for. It was frustrating. It was lonely.

And yet... deep down, something inside me wasn't ready to give up.

I had a choice:

- Stick to the plan, grit my teeth, endure the next few weeks, and go home, back to my comfort zone, my family, and the life I knew.

or

- Jump ALL IN. Learn the language, adapt, make connections, and actually become a part of this new world.

Now, I'd love to say I made the decision after deep self-reflection, but in reality, it was more like,
"Screw it. Let's see what happens!"

I decided to stay for a year. One whole year to learn English in college, explore the city, and see what this new life had to offer.

Of course, making the decision was one thing. Breaking the news to my family? A whole different challenge.

I might have been an adult (on paper, at least), but in our close-knit family, my parents' opinion mattered. I wanted their blessing—not just their approval, but their genuine support. If they had said no, I would have packed my bags and gone home as planned. But instead, they did something amazing.

Despite the heartache of having me so far away, they encouraged me. They supported my dreams, even though it meant missing me every single day. My parents and sister let me go, even when it hurt, because they believed in me.

Looking back now, I can see how that decision changed everything. It was the first of many bold moves I would make—the first step in a journey of discovering my strength, adaptability, and sheer stubborn determination to create a life on my own terms.

* * *

I eagerly enrolled in college, blissfully convinced that from this point on, everything would be smooth sailing.

Ah, sweet, innocent past me... bless her heart.

Looking back now, I can't help but smile at my naïve optimism. Because if life were actually that easy,

We'd all be sipping cocktails on a beach without a care in the world.

It's hard to explain to someone who has never left everything behind just how bittersweet an opportunity like this can be. Yes, it was my choice. Yes, it was an amazing adventure. But it also came with an emotional price tag that no one warns you about.

The loneliness hit first, you know, two months versus one year... makes the difference. Navigating life solo in a country where I sometimes felt like an uninvited guest. While most people welcomed me with kindness, not everyone was thrilled to have me around. And let's not forget the financial reality check.

Earning money for a summer holiday? Fun, exciting, extra cash for shopping and nights out!
Earning money to actually build a new life? A whole different ballgame.

I became an expert in penny-pinching survival tactics. I walked miles to college to save on bus fare, rain or shine (but mostly rain, because, well... England). My diet consisted largely of the cheapest bread and the cheapest strawberry jam imaginable—a combination I have never been able to enjoy since. And, of course, I kept all of this hidden from my family because the last thing I wanted was to worry them.

Was it hard? Oh, absolutely.
Was it worth it? Without a doubt.

I still remember that first day of college—nervous, excited, and completely terrified. I walked in expecting to learn English.

What I didn't expect... was to meet someone who would completely change the way I saw the world.

My teacher, Ahmed Shahrour, was from Syria, and he didn't just teach; he understood. He knew the struggles we faced and the silent battles we fought each day. He wasn't just patient; he was unwaveringly kind. He wasn't just encouraging; he made us believe in ourselves when we doubted our place in this new world.

He had this rare ability to see people—not just students, but individuals with dreams, fears, and untold stories. He tailored his lessons to fit us, not the other way around. In a time when I often felt invisible, he made me feel seen, worthy, and important. And for that, I will be forever grateful.

Years after finishing college, I found myself writing to him, wanting to express what I hadn't fully realized at the time. I thanked him for the difference he made, for the hope he had given me when I needed it most.

His response?

It was something so simple, yet so profound, that I have carried it in my heart ever since:

"You know, Marta, people are more likely to succeed if you believe in them. I had faith in your abilities, and you delivered.

We have a brain, and we must use it or risk losing it. You have used your brain skillfully, and the credit is due to you in part and to me in part.

Almost everyone can succeed if they use their brains properly. I also believe everyone should be a good manager of their brain, and in this way, we can control our problems, worries, and any difficulties in life.

Being positive is always best at the end."

* * *

In the meantime, life went on.

One moment, I was getting my life together—better house share, a luxury of taking the bus instead of walking miles every morning. The next? I was developing a full-blown crush on a handsome stranger I saw on my daily commute.

The first time I stepped onto the bus and saw him, he smiled. Oh, that smile. From that moment on, my mornings had a brand-new purpose—catching a glimpse of Mr. Handsome. Monday to Friday. Week after week. Month after month. Eight months!

And then one fateful morning in October, disaster struck. His smile was gone. In its place? A grumpy, miserable expression that made my heart sink. How dare life rob me of my daily serotonin boost?!

Before I could stop myself, I did something bold, recklessly impulsive, even, as for me (You know, I am a serious person. Stick up my butt kinda). I scribbled a little note that "You look better when you smile" style, handed it to him with my heart pounding in my chest, and dramatically exited the bus like some kind of rom-com heroine.

The next morning, he handed me a note back.

"Hope I smiled good enough for you. – Liam"

Oh, and he casually included his phone number.

I stormed into work, grabbed my colleague, and had a full-on crisis meeting about the appropriate response time. Should I play it cool and wait a day? Act busy and uninterested?

Spoiler alert: I caved and texted him the same day.

And just like that, my life took another turn. We started dating, and suddenly, everything felt lighter, brighter, and more possible. My confidence soared. I pushed myself further, enrolled in more courses, and kept growing.

But life has a funny way of balancing joy with unexpected challenges.

Because then... I became a mom.

And nothing—NOTHING—could have prepared me for the emotional rollercoaster that followed.

I had been thriving, adapting, and finding my place in the UK. But motherhood? That was a whole new level. A level that required more of me than I had to give. And for the first time in years, I felt like I was drowning.

There was no village to help raise my child. No parents to pop in for baby cuddles. No one to say, *"Here, let me take him for an hour while you sleep."* My parents, my sister—they were all on the other side of a screen, offering advice I couldn't fully use. And as much as some of Liam's family tried to be there, they had their own lives, their own responsibilities.

It was exhausting.
It was lonely.
And honestly? It was brutal.

A few years ago, finding affordable playgroups, local communities, or just places where I could meet other parents wasn't easy. The isolation hit hard. I had fought so hard to build a life in the UK, yet here I was—struggling, frustrated, constantly running on fumes.

Then came the next wave of stress—moving house. Again. And that's when the downward spiral truly began. I was exhausted, unsupported, snapping at everyone, and feeling like I was doing this entire parenting journey alone.

I flew back to Poland whenever I could. Even just for a week. There, my child was surrounded by family, soaking up his heritage, thriving in ways that broke my heart. Because instead of recharging, every visit made me wonder—was I making a mistake?

I kept dreaming about what life would be like if I moved back for good. The support, the ease, the relief of not carrying it all alone. It felt like my heart was being pulled in two different directions.

And just when I thought I couldn't take any more mentally... life sent me an unexpected light.

It all started with a spring closet clear-out. I was selling clothes online when I received a message from a buyer—a man purchasing clothes for his terminally ill wife, Julie. He couldn't pick them up, so we arranged to have them shipped instead. One small, simple decision.

And that decision changed everything.

Julie messaged me to say thank you, and one message turned into another... and another. Before I knew it, we were talking daily. She became the anchor I didn't even realize I needed.

Julie has a way of seeing straight into my soul. She taught me how to express what I was feeling—honestly, openly, without fear.

Since May 2015, she has been there—for the highs, for the lows, and for everything in between. Our deep, meaningful conversations opened my mind in ways I never expected.

She helped me understand myself. She made me stronger.

And just like that, when I needed it the most, the universe reminded me—even in the darkest moments, the right people will find you.

And just like that, I found my voice.

Life finally felt stable, solid—mine. I wasn't just surviving anymore; I was thriving. In my own way.

I had carved out a place for myself in the hospitality industry, something I had always been passionate about. I worked my way up, from cleaning hotel rooms to landing a good position at Carrs Lane Conference Centre. I loved the job, the people, and the buzz of the industry. It felt like I was exactly where I was meant to be.

And then... life, being the unpredictable rollercoaster it is, threw in another plot twist.

Surprise! Baby number two is on the way!

Oh, and just to keep things extra interesting, I also decided that pregnancy + full-time university studies were a perfectly reasonable combination. So, there I was—pregnant, exhausted, but determined, studying MA International Hospitality Management full-time at University College Birmingham.

Somehow, amidst the chaos, we made it work. We settled into a beautiful rhythm—days out, visiting friends, catching up with family. Life felt... good. Really good.

I felt strong. Capable. In control.

Until I didn't.

Or rather—until no one did.

Because March 2020 happened. And suddenly, the world stopped.

The pandemic stole everything we thought was secure.
Our freedom. Our routines. Our jobs. Our sense of safety.

No one was prepared. Not emotionally. Not financially. Not socially. In *any* way.

I found myself in a situation I never imagined:

- Raising a wild toddler who seemed to have endless energy.
- Homeschooling my older child with absolutely zero experience (shoutout to proper, passionate teachers—you ROCK!).
- Jobless, as the hospitality industry crumbled overnight.

At first, it was adrenaline-fueled chaos. The world was confused, panicked, and stuck inside. Suddenly, we were all baking banana bread, downloading Zoom, and nodding along to people saying *"let's just pivot!"* as if that made any sense.

And then, a few days into the first lockdown, just when I thought we had enough to handle, our world shattered.

My children's grandad was rushed to the hospital. Ten days later, we were grieving.

It was devastating. There was no proper goodbye. No gathering of loved ones. Just this overwhelming sense of loss on top of an already broken world.

While everyone was scrambling for some sense of stability and reassurance, all we had were new buzzwords being thrown around—

"Pivot!"
"New normal!"
"Take care, stay safe!" (which basically became the new *"See you later"*)

But somehow, I had to rise.

Because through all the grief, uncertainty, and fear, one thing became crystal clear: We are stronger than we think. When we chose to.

And after everything I had already been through—all the challenges, the setbacks, the resilience I had built up—I knew that if I could survive that, I could survive anything.

I made a choice.
Every challenge would be an opportunity.
Every setback, a lesson.

And for the first time in a long time, I felt something surprising.

Gratitude.

Because as hard as it was,

I realized that everything I had been through had prepared me for this.

And if I could keep going, I could come out of this stronger than ever.

I somehow figured out how to homeschool without completely losing my sanity. (Barely.)

We found joy in the small things—our tiny garden, the unusually nice weather (seriously, was that even the UK?), and just being together as a family.

Of course, there were some not-so-great days too. Days where the kids were bouncing off the walls, I was contemplating running away (only half-joking), and our home felt way too small for the chaos inside it.

But at night, after the kids were finally asleep (or at least pretending to be), I would grab my laptop and get to work. I had the skills. I "just" needed to figure out how to bring them all together in a way that worked for me and helped others.

So, I did what many lost souls in 2020 did...
I turned to Facebook.

And that's where I met Jagdeep Hayre—a woman who would change my life.

Now, let me be clear—I was never the kind of person to say things like "soul sister." I mean, come on. But then, Jagdeep happened. And suddenly, I understood exactly what that meant.

We connected instantly, and before I knew it, I was spilling my thoughts, fears, and past regrets to a total stranger. But she wasn't just any stranger. She was exactly what I needed.

She challenged me. Inspired me. She made me believe that I could do anything.

And through our deep conversations, a lightbulb went off in my head.

I started noticing a pattern. So many brilliant, passionate businesswomen were out there—phenomenal coaches with a wealth of talent, experience, and wisdom.

But there was one big problem...

They absolutely hated the tech side of things.
And branding? Website setup? Creating resources? That was their worst nightmare.

Lucky for them, I LOVED that stuff.

Suddenly, I was the answer to their problems!

I built my membership and services around helping them thrive:

- Designing memberships and courses
- Creating PDFs, workbooks, and marketing materials
- Bringing their branding and vision to life
- Relieving their stress so they could focus on their passion

And then, because apparently, I love a challenge, I also launched my own digital magazine showcasing thriving women in business.

I was running a membership AND a digital magazine at the same time.

Which, in hindsight, was an absolutely insane idea.

At first, it was exciting—connecting with incredible women, creating resources, and building something from scratch.

But then... reality hit.

The membership required constant engagement—posting content, replying to messages, and marketing. Some days, I simply wasn't in the mood. Other days, I was too exhausted to respond to another message. And sometimes, I just had way too much going on.

The magazine, on the other hand, was a labor of love that consumed hours of my life—forms, writing, editing, designing, and distribution.

I was passionate about both, but the sheer volume of work was crushing me.

Most days, I felt like I was sprinting from one task to the next, never quite finishing anything to the level of perfection I wanted.

And yes, I know *perfection* is *technically* "impossible," but, let's be real, it's still my goal.

There was always something more to do.
More people to connect with.
More deadlines creeping up on me.

I had built a business I loved—but at what cost?

And that's when I knew... something had to change.

* * *

And then—as if the universe finally decided to cut me some slack—the perfect job opportunity landed in my lap!

And all thanks to my incredible general manager, who somehow saw potential in me that I wasn't even fully aware of myself. (Honestly, I think she might be a wizard.)

To this day, I am forever grateful that she took a chance on me.

Because this job? It is everything.

- Aligns with my skills, knowledge, and experience
- Fuels my passion for the industry
- Allows me to spread my wings and grow

But most importantly, it gave me a gift that I desperately needed—peace of mind.

For the first time in a long time, I could breathe.
I could take a step back, reassess, and figure out where my energy would be best spent.

And the first thing I did?
I took a long, hard look at my two digital ventures.

I had to face a brutal truth—something had to give.

Between the membership community and the digital magazine, I was juggling more than I could realistically handle. I had less time, more responsibilities, and I was stretched thin.

So, after a lot of soul-searching (and probably an unhealthy amount of coffee), I made the big decision.

I closed both.

Letting go? Bittersweet.

But also? The best decision I could have made.

By shifting my focus, I allowed myself to step into a new chapter where I could channel my energy into something even greater.

* * *

And guess what?
I still hustle—just differently.
Smarter. More intentionally. And with WAY more balance.

And that's how *The Queensdom Vault* was born.

- A community for female entrepreneurs and professionals.
- A space dedicated to supporting, uplifting, and empowering women.
- My passion, my mission, and a way to make a real difference in the lives of ambitious women chasing their dreams.

This is so much more than just a group.

This is me, showing up fully for myself, for others, and for a future that feels right.

And honestly?

It's the best decision I ever made.

Within this nurturing space, I have created a home for women who dream big, who push past obstacles, and who seek not just success but also fulfillment in both their personal and professional lives. I understand their journeys intimately—their aspirations, challenges, and daily struggles—because I have walked a similar path. More importantly, I have discovered and developed a wealth of solutions that help them navigate these challenges with confidence and ease.

At *The Queensdom Vault* (Skool and FB), I have built an expansive network of resources designed to educate, empower, and uplift. I provide the knowledge and support necessary to help women grow their businesses and careers strategically. I recognize that every woman's journey is unique, which is why we don't believe in one-size-fits-all approaches. Instead, we focus on customized and tailored solutions to address individual needs.

More than just offering education and resources, I have cultivated an environment of security, trust, and collaboration—a place where women feel truly seen and heard. This is a safe space, a sisterhood, a collective force of ambitious women determined to succeed. Whether someone is just starting their entrepreneurial journey or is already established and looking for further growth, she will find invaluable guidance, encouragement, and a strong support system here.

My role extends beyond just providing tools and strategies. I help women rediscover balance in their lives. So many women feel overwhelmed, constantly juggling responsibilities, and struggling to find time for themselves. I show them how to work smarter, not harder, freeing up their time so they can focus on what they love, whether it's spending time with family, growing their passions, or simply enjoying life.

Along the way, I have also shared my own journey through book collaborations, contributing chapters that reflect my experiences, lessons, and transformations as a businesswoman. While some of the services I provided at the time of writing those chapters are no longer part of my offerings, each book stands as a testament to my willingness to evolve, embrace change, and pivot fearlessly. These books don't just showcase my expertise; they highlight the many turns I have taken, the risks I have embraced, and my unwavering commitment to growth.

At the heart of it all, I believe in them. I believe in their dreams, their abilities, and their potential to achieve greatness. And as they climb the ladder of success, I stand proudly beside them—not as the hero of their story, but as a steadfast supporter, a guide, and a small but meaningful part of their incredible journey.

The Queensdom Vault is more than just a group. It is a movement, a revolution, and a celebration of empowered women paving their own paths to success.

There's so much more ahead!

So much potential, so much thriving still to come. And I can't wait to see where this journey takes me next.

I hope that you will always remember that moving forward is a choice, and even the smallest of baby steps will eventually get you where you want to be, and often quicker than what you might think.

Know that my door is open, should you want to connect, and have someone in your corner to help you move forward.

Every day, you have chance encounters, and you never know which of these will have the biggest impacts on your life.

Everyone you meet can be a part of your story—allow it!

Get out of your comfort zone, be open to connection, and learn from every interaction.

But most of all, remember that every challenge is an opportunity.

Jacqueline Crider

PBJ Mortgage and Financial Mastery Simplified
CEO, Author, Coach

https://www.linkedin.com/in/pbj-mortgage-jacqueline-crider/
https://www.facebook.com/jax.crider
https://www.instagram.com/jax_crider/
www.pbjteam.comurals.co/jax-crider

Jax Crider is a dynamic force in financial education, mortgage lending, and entrepreneurial innovation. As the founder of PBJ Mortgage and Financial Mastery Simplified, Jax has helped thousands achieve homeownership while simplifying complex financial concepts into clear, actionable strategies. A best-selling author, podcast host, and recognized thought leader, Jax's expertise has been featured on magazine covers and major platforms. With a law degree and multiple accolades, Jax blends traditional financial principles with non-traditional methods to help people break free from outdated financial "rules" and create success on their own terms. Their Financial Instinct Framework and HouseU course empower individuals to take control of their financial futures with confidence and ease. A passionate educator and innovator, Jax's mission is to revolutionize financial literacy, making it accessible, personalized, and empowering—impacting 100,000 lives by 2035 and redefining what financial success truly means.

Finding My Voice: From Whisper to Roar

By Jacqueline Crider

The Whisper Before the Roar

My only real desire in life has always been simple: to help others achieve what they want. I've been a teacher at heart since I can remember. So when I started working in mortgages, people were surprised. To me, it wasn't strange at all. It was just teaching in a different language: the language of money.

I had zero desire to make headlines. No urge to stand on stages. No craving for the spotlight. What I wanted was something quieter but deeper—the validation of knowing I had helped someone. That I'd sat with them in the chaos of their finances and helped them see the way through.

But deep down, even as a little girl of five or six, I knew I was meant for something *big*. World-changing big. That knowing was always there, humming beneath the surface. And still—I shied away from the limelight. I convinced myself that impact could only come from behind the curtain, never in front of it.

Then came the nudge. My very first podcast guest spot. I didn't think much of it at first, but afterward, someone looked me straight in the eye and said, *"You need to lean into this. You have a voice."*

At the time, I laughed it off. I hated being on video. Hated it. The thought of showing up on camera made my stomach churn. But he insisted, "You'd love podcasting." I promised I'd think about it.

A year and a half later, I found myself wide awake at 2 a.m., typing a desperate Facebook message to him: *What if I really did start a podcast?* By 5 a.m., he replied, urging me to do it the very next week.

That was the crack in the dam. Another coach had nudged too and had finally convinced me that my voice mattered. And in that moment, I realized something terrifying and freeing all at once: If I didn't lean into my voice, I would never accomplish what God had placed on my heart.

Worse, if I kept hiding, I'd fail my daughters. I'd fail the women watching me, silently wondering if their voices were worth anything at all. I'd confirm the same lie I'd swallowed for years—that our voices don't need to be heard. That they don't matter as much as they do.

That was the night I decided: My whisper had to become a roar.

The Cost of Silence

So often I kept quiet when I knew I should be speaking up. That's the sneaky thing about silence—It doesn't just happen once; it becomes a habit. A reflex.

For women, I think it's almost baked into us. We're raised to question ourselves. To weigh every word. To fight an internal battle about whether what we have to say is valuable enough. My own version of that came from people-pleasing and a deep craving for validation. On the outside, I looked outgoing and confident. But on the inside? I was constantly second-guessing, running my words through an endless filter of *what-ifs.*

That started young. I remember sitting in classrooms, knowing the answer but refusing to raise my hand. The fear of being wrong, of being criticized, kept me small. And honestly? That fear never really left.

When I began selling subprime mortgages, the silence looked different. I was selling one of the hardest products in the hardest possible way—calling old leads, people who had already heard "no" dozens of times. They hung up on me. They called me names. Some said awful, cutting things. And yet, in that storm of rejection, something shifted. I decided the only way forward was to ask questions, to listen, and to use my voice—not to sell, but to educate. Client by client, one-on-one, I started learning that my voice could be a tool.

But using your voice across a desk with one client is a far cry from stepping into the public, vocal space I was being called toward. And every time I didn't, the cost was real.

The frustration. The shame. The gnawing feeling that I was failing at something I knew I was supposed to do. It only got worse when I heard others speaking with absolute authority, as if their version of financial advice was gospel. I would sit there, quiet, simmering inside, knowing I had a perspective that mattered, often quite opposing traditional wisdom—but not the courage to share it.

I told myself I wasn't enough. Not experienced enough. Not credible enough. Which is laughable, really. I hold a law degree. I've sold more financial products than most professionals will in their lifetime. I devour books, constantly learning. Lack of knowledge was never my issue. Lack of trust in myself was.

And the hardest realization came later: I wasn't the only one. I began to see the same story play out in women all around me—brilliant, capable, insightful women shrinking themselves. I saw it most clearly in my youngest daughter. She went from bounding confidence, the kind all kids have, to whispering things like, *"I can't do that."*

That was my breaking point. I knew the cost of silence wasn't just mine to bear anymore. If I didn't break the pattern, if I didn't step up and use my voice, my daughters—and women watching me—might believe the same lie I did. That our voices don't matter. That our voices aren't enough.

And I refuse to let that lie take root.

The Echo That Woke Me Up

The truth is, I never woke up one morning magically confident. It was a slow unfolding and the voices of other women (and a few men who believed in me) were the ones who cracked me open.

Let's circle back to that first podcast guest spot. I'll never forget it. The host looked me straight in the eye and said, "You have a voice. You should be doing this."

I wanted to roll my eyes. Me? A podcaster? I hated video, hated hearing my own voice recorded, and hated the idea of being that visible. But his words lodged in the back of my mind, and no matter how much I tried to ignore them, they kept echoing.

Fast forward a year and a half, and I'm lying awake at 2 a.m., staring at the ceiling. That quiet nudge had grown into a weight on my chest I couldn't shake. I finally grabbed my phone and messaged him: What if I really did start a podcast?

By 5 a.m., he had answered, and he didn't give me the months I wanted to plan and polish and make everything perfect. He said, "I'll be your first guest. We're recording next week."

I wanted to fight him. Every part of me screamed, No! I'm not ready. I need more time. I wanted my voice to sound like it belonged. I wanted the branding dialed in, the equipment flawless, and the topics bulletproof. I wanted to be perfect.

But something in me knew that if I kept waiting for perfect, I'd never start. So I leaned in. Shaky, unprepared, terrified—but I leaned in.

That was the moment the echo became a roar.

It wasn't polished. It wasn't perfect. I stumbled over my words, obsessed over whether anyone would even care. But each episode felt like cracking open a door that had been locked for years. And each time I used my voice, shaky as it was, I felt other women leaning in. Saying, "Me too."

That's when it clicked: My voice wasn't just about me. It was about the women sitting in silence, carrying the same doubts, and waiting for someone else to go first. My courage became their permission. Their voices, in turn, became my fuel. It was a chorus and it reminded me that none of us were ever meant to do this alone.

Owning My Voice, Creating Space for Yours

Finding my voice didn't mean I suddenly stopped being afraid. I still get nervous before hitting "record." I still second-guess myself when I publish something raw. The difference now is that I no longer let the fear be the final word.

My voice has become less about me and more about the women I'm speaking to—the ones quietly wrestling with the same doubts I carried. Each time I speak up, I imagine them leaning in, hearing the thing they've been waiting to hear: *"You're not alone. Your story matters. Your voice matters."*

I see it in my daughters too. They watch me now, not shrinking, not silencing myself, but stepping into what I know I'm called to. They see the messy bravery and the wobbly courage, and they're learning that confidence isn't about being perfect—it's about being willing.

And that's the power of owning your voice. It gives others permission to find theirs. It creates a ripple, one whisper becoming a chorus, until silence is no longer the default.

So I keep speaking, not because I love the spotlight, but because my silence once cost too much. And because I know that somewhere, another woman is waiting for her own moment at 2 a.m., when she decides to finally stop hiding and let her voice be heard.

My voice was once a whisper. Now it's a roar. And it's your turn—step into the woman you were always meant to be and let the world hear you.

Sara Evelyne

Founder of Echoes Rising

https://www.linkedin.com/in/sara-evelyne
echoes.of.hope
www.saraevelyne.com
https://twloha.com/blog/author/sara-evelyne/

Sara Evelyne is a mother scholar, poet, and brain injury survivor who cultivates hope at the intersections of mental health, resilience, and social justice. Through her work in advocacy and education, she transforms lived experience into collective understanding, proving that personal narratives carry profound power. Her work has appeared multiple times on the To Write Love on Her Arms (TWLOHA) blog and in PBA Voices, where she co-authored survivor narratives for the Brain Injury Association of America. Her forthcoming poetry will appear in Letting Grief Speak: Writing Portals for Life After Loss (Columbia University Press) and A Mother(hood)fucking Arsenal of Poetry (Demeter Press). Sara is currently writing her memoir Wolfpit while developing Echoes Rising, an emerging social impact initiative that amplifies marginalized voices at the intersection of storytelling and connection. Her work creates spaces where healing meets advocacy, always reminding others to never forget how far you've come just by waking up today.

Echoes Rising: Beyond Silence and Persistence

By Sara Evelyne

What began as my single voice became a chorus, an echo shared by many.

I had started college right out of high school, still carrying the heavy shadow of grief and trauma from my mother's death, and left before I ever felt like I belonged. I tried again at twenty-three, this time with a toddler by my side and a marriage already cracking beneath me. Over the years, I would start and stop more times than I can count, carrying books and children, debt and doubt, until I finally walked across the stage with my bachelor's degree twenty-two years later. The statistics say women like me—single mothers, heads of household, living with disability and instability—rarely finish. But my journey has always been about what lives beyond the statistics: persistence, survival, and the conviction that my children's futures were closely linked with mine.

Twenty-two years, three children, and countless interruptions later, I carried my degree across the stage. But what mattered most wasn't just the diploma. It was that my children saw me finish what once felt impossible. They witnessed failure, recovery, struggle, and rising. That is the quiet legacy of student-parents: showing in real time that education and resilience are intertwined.

Few saw the years in between—the muddy middle where survival was counting breaths, pennies, and minutes between crises. Semesters shaped as much by doctor's appointments as lectures, nights when my son's meltdowns drowned out study sessions, mornings blurred by neurofatigue that stole words from the page, housing insecurity, custody fears, and the unseen weight of concussions bruising my resolve.

My lived experience as a student-parent fueled a deeper commitment to understand the challenges that women like me face behind the scenes. This led to me applying for an undergraduate research fellowship, uncovering systemic barriers confronting student-parents—housing insecurity, mental health struggles, financial instability, and the sheer complexity of juggling academic and caregiving roles. This research not only validated my own story but also became a foundation for my leadership and advocacy, informing how I shape the *Live Your Dream Award* process and build community through *Echoes Rising*. It became clear that my personal persistence echoed a larger chorus of resilience and need, calling for structural change and compassionate support for those walking this difficult path.

When I applied for the Soroptimist Live Your Dream Award, my voice was fragile.

Winning that scholarship, a program designed to support women like me who are primary financial providers for their families, was transformative. When I was named a Live Your Dream Award winner, I stood at a podium and spoke words forged in years of quiet survival: "Whether it's one step, half a step, or just waking up—that counts." That wasn't a polished line for applause. It was the truth I had carried through eviction notices, custody battles, concussions, and nights when finishing an assignment felt as impossible as breathing. Housing insecurity, custody fears, and the invisible aftermath of concussions pressed against me until even hope felt fragile.

But still, I carried on—not because it was easy, but because stopping was unthinkable. It was the mantra my children had seen me live out in real time—that persistence does not always look like progress, but it still matters.

When I advanced to the regional level, my voice became an echo. I spoke anew, my story expanding from survival into justice and belonging. My fight was part of a larger call to visibility and worth.

The Soroptimist Live Your Dream Award became evidence of my becoming. One stage reminded me and others that waking up counts. Another marked my shift from surviving to fighting for justice.

* * *

Those words traveled into classrooms, into my children's memories, and into the ears of women needing to hear their own hidden struggles and determination reflected back. They became echoes of living proof that survival, once voiced, ripples outward.

An echo is what happens when a voice doesn't stop at the self. An echo says: You are not alone here. Your voice is not swallowed nor does it fall into a pit. It carries. In my life, that echo became more than recognition. It became the responsibility to hold open space for other women to step into their own light, to know that their stories matter, too.

My words reverberated: My children heard them and other women recognized their stories in mine. An echo transformed my individual declaration into collective belonging, inviting others to respond, share voices, and build shared strength. That is what an echo does. It repeats, it expands, and it circles back in ways the first sound could never predict.

From applicant to recipient to judge to program chair of the Live Your Dream Award at my local Soroptimist club, I now support ...

That is why I rise, and why I will keep rising. Not because the path was smooth, but because echoes remind me I was never alone. To every woman wondering if she belongs—in school, in recovery, or in life—keep going one more day, then one more. That is how a voice becomes an echo, how persistence becomes belonging, and invisibility turns into light.

Together, our stories carry the power to transform silence into strength and hope into lasting change.

Angélica María Andújar De Jesús

Registered Nurse, R.N.

https://facebook.com/angelica.andujar.9809/

Graduated with a bachelor's degree in Journalism and with a second bachelor's degree in science in Nursing. Recently works as a Registered Nurse in a Rehab Center of the Oncology Hospital Dr. Isaac Gonzalez Martinez. She loves to write poetry, paint and sing in her free time. She wants to pursue graduate studies and write books in her future.

Nursing: An Act of Love

By Angélica María Andújar De Jesús

Bringing comfort to the patients is the ultimate goal of my mission as a registered nurse. Paying close attention to any change in their condition and health is essential. I provide the correct medication to help improve their condition, assist with body transfers, perform bed baths, and help with shower baths. I also measure vital signs, record them, and notify the team if any abnormalities are detected. I monitor and record the patient's intake and output. In addition, I measure blood sugar levels to be stable. I also provide bedside rounding to verify everything is fine and assist with any needs. I change clothes or diapers when necessary, reposition patients to prevent ulcers, and change wound dressings as needed. I take blood samples and administer oral and intravenous medication.

My purpose is to see patients who have been bedridden for a long time finally walking down the hall of the center with a smile on their faces. That moment makes me feel that everything I've done was worth it. What I love about my job is that there's always something different to do and something new to learn. It is very rewarding to see people happy and healthy again. Giving your time to others is invaluable; it shows commitment, passion to help others, a sense of justice for everyone and love for those who are disadvantaged.

Working as a registered nurse has also made me more awake to taking care of myself. I see the doctors, take medication, and engage in activities that keep me physically and mentally stable. For example, painting helps me reflect on the valuable and remarkable moments in life, relieves my stress, and challenges me to step out of my comfort zone.

On the other hand, bathing the patients is a moment when I forget I'm doing a job and instead focus on connecting with them. We listen to music together, sing songs by our favorite Puerto Rican singers, and talk about their needs, their backgrounds, and their life experiences. For a moment, I forget about my own problems and concentrate on the task at hand. We need more people who understand the importance of doing their job and serving others, rather than constantly thinking about their personal ambitions and needs. It is essential that every patient can achieve their goal of becoming and walking like they did before surgery. I want my patients to regain independence and be able to do things physically and mentally.

As the first person in my family to graduate with a bachelor's degree, it is important to be a role model and do things the right way. I've always struggled with type 2 diabetes and anxiety, but those challenges have made me more selective, detail-oriented, and focused on life. For me, it is important to choose love through serving and caring for my family and friends.

I believe that we all come from the same God—a God of love, care, and giving. It is important to create a safe and secure environment for each patient. I do my best to respond to any call or request they have. I wash my hands frequently, use gloves in any intervention and conduct bedside rounds to ensure that everything is in order and that nothing could harm or cause a fall.

Working as a registered nurse in Puerto Rico is a challenging job that requires patience, empathy, and the ability to multitask. It demands love and devotion to caring for others. It is both one of the most difficult and rewarding jobs, as we must take care of many patients simultaneously, with time always working against us. Taking care of others teaches us the real priorities in life: good health and having a family and friends to love. It reminds me of the love I have received from my grandmother, mother, and all the powerful women around me who saw it not as an obligation or responsibility but as a purpose—something they did for their families and communities without asking anything in return.

Joan Soto Melendez

Rumbo Al Bienestar LLC
Licensed Professional Counselor

https://www.linkedin.com/in/joansoto
https://www.facebook.com/rumboalbienestarllc
https://www.instagram.com/rumboalbienestarllc
www.rumboalbienestar.org
https://www.youtube.com/@rumboalbienestarllc

Joan Soto is a Bilingual Licensed Professional Counselor (LPC) and DBT-certified coach who helps individuals break free from burnout and emotional overwhelm—guiding them toward healing, clarity, and purpose. She is the Founder and CEO of Rumbo Al Bienestar, LLC, a mental health practice offering holistic, trauma-informed, and culturally responsive care. For nearly a decade, Joan has supported professionals, caregivers, students, and individuals living with chronic conditions through life transitions and deep emotional healing. Her work is especially rooted in empowering professional Latinas to reclaim their joy, balance, and personal agency. Whether you're navigating grief, recovering from narcissistic abuse, or working to prevent caregiver burnout—you deserve support that honors your whole story. ✨

Ready to grow with intention and feel truly seen?

Let's connect. 🎧 Listen to my new podcast (in Spanish): @rumboalbienestarllcServices:

- Virtual Therapy (CT residents)
- Trauma-Responsive Coaching (U.S. & International)
- Workshops & Speaking Engagements

Becoming Her—The Woman I Refused to Give Up On

By Joan Soto Melendez

Introduction

In my previous chapter, *"Steps to Become an Entrepreneur After Facing Adversity,"* in the book *Becoming an Unstoppable Woman Entrepreneur: Part II*, I shared how I began as a promising young girl with very few resources. I was raised in Puerto Rico by hard-working family members who modeled loyalty to employment, even when it came at the cost of their dignity. I remember witnessing my grandmother being verbally attacked by her boss—and even then, she stayed. I knew early on: I didn't want that to be my story.

In Puerto Rico, it's not uncommon to graduate from college and still struggle to find stable employment. And while I excelled in school and dreamed of creating a better world, opportunity felt out of reach. I was not born into wealth, privilege, or connections. But I had vision, faith, and a quiet fire inside me.

That fire carried me through domestic violence, single motherhood, chronic illness, cultural transition, and starting over in a new country. Today, I stand proudly as a bilingual licensed professional counselor, trauma-responsive clinician, and DBT-certified coach. I've worked in the mental health field for nearly a decade, and I am the founder and CEO of *Rumbo Al Bienestar, LLC*, a practice rooted in culturally responsive, holistic care.

My life is a tapestry woven with hardship, hope, and healing—and I refused to give up on the woman I was becoming, even when the world tried to count me out.

Acknowledging the Barriers

Being a therapist, business owner, and mother to a child with behavioral health challenges—all while living with a chronic illness like IBS (Irritable Bowel Syndrome)—is not for the faint of heart. There were times I felt like I was walking a tightrope with no safety net, caught between survival and purpose. The systemic barriers stacked against me—from healthcare gaps to racism to cultural bias—could have broken me. But I chose not to be defined by them.

What made it even more painful was the emotional toll of navigating it all alone. As an Afro-Latina, I faced implicit bias and discouragement from employers who didn't believe someone like me could lead, manage, or rise. That's when I knew: I had to write my own story. I began to "cook a new recipe," as I say—one filled with the ingredients of faith, resilience, and self-love.

Becoming My Own Therapist: Using My Skills to Heal Myself

People often assume that therapists have it all figured out. But healing is an ongoing, intimate process. I've used the very tools I teach others—mindfulness, boundaries, radical acceptance, and cognitive restructuring—to hold myself through some of the darkest seasons of my life.

Therapy became both my profession and my personal salvation. In fact, it was through writing, journaling, and reflecting during my own therapy that I started to rebuild my confidence, process my trauma, and reclaim my voice.

Even therapists need therapy. And that doesn't make us weak. It makes us wise. Every session I've had, both as a clinician and as a client, has brought me closer to the woman I knew I could become.

Faith & Hope: The Foundation of My Transformation

My spiritual journey has been the cornerstone of my healing. When I faced domestic violence, betrayal, and disillusionment, it was my faith in God that carried me. I clung to the promise in Romans 5:1-5, especially the reminder that suffering produces perseverance, character, and hope.

I stopped asking, "Why is this happening to me?" and started trusting that God was building something within me.

I realized that every storm I survived was strengthening the fruit of the Spirit in me—love, joy, peace, patience, kindness, goodness, faithfulness, gentleness, and self-control.

Hope became my daily practice. Faith became my fuel.

UNLEASH: 7 Keys That Helped Me Thrive and Transform My Life

To become the woman I refused to give up on, I had to UNLEASH what was already inside me—bit by bit, moment by moment. Healing and transformation didn't happen overnight. It took consistent effort, compassion, strategy, faith, and courage.

Here is what UNLEASH looks like in my life and how it can transform yours, too:

U — Understand Your Limits
(Spoon Theory & Self-Compassion)

As someone living with a chronic illness (IBS), I had to learn to respect my energy. The Spoon Theory taught me that I only have so many "spoons" (units of energy) per day and that spending them wisely is self-love, not weakness.

Instead of pushing through exhaustion or burnout, I learned to listen to my body and offer myself grace. This shift required unlearning toxic productivity and embracing radical self-compassion.

Tip: *Start by tracking your energy, not just your time. Ask yourself each morning, "How many spoons do I have today—and how can I use them wisely?"*

N — Navigate with Faith and Hope

Faith has always been the compass guiding me through life's storms. When I left an abusive relationship and had to rebuild from nothing, my faith in God was the only light in a very dark tunnel.

Romans 5:1-5 became my anchor: *"Suffering produces perseverance; perseverance, character; and character, hope."*

Even when I couldn't see the next step, I kept walking. Hope was not just a feeling. It was my daily decision.

Tip: *Choose one verse, affirmation, or spiritual truth to carry with you each day. Let it shape your mindset and remind you you're not alone.*

L — Let Go of Perfection (Celebrate Wins & Learn from Mistakes)

I used to believe I had to be perfect to be worthy—perfect as a mother, therapist, and businesswoman. That belief nearly broke me.

But healing taught me to celebrate small wins: making a phone call I was anxious about, saying "no" when I needed rest, and finishing a goal I once feared. I also learned to see mistakes as feedback, not failure.

Tip: *Start a "small wins" journal. At the end of each day or week, write down one thing—no matter how small—that you're proud of.*

E — Embrace the Power of Small Steps (SMART Goals & Dinosaur Analogy 🦕)

A big dream used to feel like a scary dinosaur—I couldn't see the whole picture, and it felt overwhelming. But when I broke it into tiny, actionable SMART goals, things started to move.

Example: Instead of saying, "Launch my business," I wrote:

- Research business license in my state.
- Create a simple logo.
- Write my mission statement

🌿 ***Tip:*** *Take one big goal and break it down into 3-5 micro-steps. Focus only on the next right action.*

A — Align With Joy

I used to think success had to look serious, like grinding 24/7. But true abundance is rooted in joy, creativity, and play. I intentionally wove fun and rest into my routine—dance breaks in between sessions, gratitude walks, and time with my son.

Life is not a race. Joy makes the journey sustainable.

🌿 ***Tip:*** *What brings you joy outside of your goals? Make space for that every week. It's not indulgent; it's essential.*

S — Surround Yourself With the Right People

My healing was never a solo act. I had a village—therapists, pastors, mentors, and friends—who saw me, uplifted me, and believed in me when I forgot how.

After surviving domestic violence, I had to rebuild trust, not just in others, but in myself. Being part of communities that honored my healing reminded me I was never alone.

Tip: Identify your support circle. If you don't have one yet, start with one safe person or join a supportive group (online or local).

H — Hold Your Boundaries & Prioritize Peace

Peace is not passive—it's an active, intentional choice. I learned to organize my life using tools like "urgent vs. important," to say no without guilt, and to stop fighting every battle. Not everything deserves your energy.

Some days, my win was choosing peace over productivity. Other days, it was speaking up when I used to stay silent.

***Tip:** Try the "3Ds Rule": Do it, Delegate it, or Drop it. Not everything belongs on your plate.*

UnleashHER: The Woman You're Becoming

When I began to UNLEASH these practices in my life, I became softer—but also stronger. I became more present, more peaceful, and more powerful.

It wasn't a straight line. Healing rarely is. But each step was a return to myself, to the woman I always knew I could become.

You don't have to wait for permission to become her.
You don't need to be perfect to begin.
You simply need to believe that she's already within you—and she's worth the effort.

Transforming Pain into Purpose

I didn't just survive abuse. I rebuilt a life worth living. I didn't just migrate. I planted roots. I didn't just become a therapist. I became a healer, a coach, and a voice for women who feel unseen.

And though my healing is still in progress, I know this for sure: My imperfections do not disqualify me. They qualify me to walk with others through their own transformation.

Everything I've endured has led me to this sacred work of helping others rise. And I'm not done. There's still so much to build, create, and give.

Conclusion: A Bold Declaration

I am bold. I am capable. I am resilient.

I am the woman I refused to give up on.

With God's guidance, I will continue to break generational patterns, build a legacy, and walk boldly in my purpose. I no longer carry the voices of shame or doubt. I've unpacked the old suitcases.

I stand here today as a Latina entrepreneur, a therapist, a survivor, and a mother—not despite my story, but because of it.

And if you're reading this and see yourself in any part of my journey, I want you to know:

You are not too broken.
You are not too far gone.
And you are never, ever alone.

The woman you're becoming is already within you.

And she's worth fighting for.

Tiffany Tyler-Garner, PhD

Dr. Tyler Inspires
Psychologist

www.linkedin.com/in/dr-tiffany-tyler-garner-a603431b
https://facebook.com/drtgtyler
https://www.instagram.com/drtgtyler/
https://www.sherisesstudios.com/tiffanytyler
www.drtylerinspires.com

Dr. Tiffany Tyler-Garner is an educational psychologist, published researcher, and thought leader. Her personal and professional achievements reveal a servant leader committed to transforming the conditions that impact children, families and communities. Currently, Dr. Tyler-Garner spearheads workforce development and social initiatives for the City of Las Vegas. Moreover, Dr. Tyler-Garner has a rich history of service that includes serving on an array of governmental and nonprofit boards and commissions. Dr. Tyler-Garner's commendations include the Urban Chamber of Commerce's Women Business Advocate award, Vegas Inc.'s Humanitarian of the Year award, Workforce Connections' Workforce Development Champion of the Year award, and UNLV College of Education Alumna of the Year award. Dr. Tyler holds a Doctorate in Educational

Psychology for the University of Nevada- Las Vegas, a Master of Science in Counseling from California State University- Northridge, and Bachelor of Arts in Psychology and Sociology from the University of Southern California.

A Voice Coming into View

By Tiffany Tyler-Garner, PhD

"This woman, this woman here, this woman is something else," I said as I pondered what I had found in my exhale.

After years of holding my breath, watching my step, and waiting for the other shoe to drop, I had finally decided that I was through, through:

- The worst of it.
- Waiting my turn.
- Hoping the past was different.
- Stalling my future.
- Asking for permission.
- Apologizing.
- Explaining.

The decision to declare that I was through the worst of it brought more of my voice into view because it took the anxiety of wondering how bad it could get away. It was not a lofty prediction that nothing else would happen. Rather, it was a declaration that my resilience, learning, and perseverance had positioned me to be more equipped than the little girl silently molested. Now I was the woman that survived it. I could defend myself. I had weathered divorce and successfully raised my children. Things would never be as bad as being a defenseless little girl and not knowing why he molested me.

Similarly, deciding not to wait my turn brought more of my voice into view because it placed me in the driver's seat of my own life. My destiny no longer hung in the balance waiting for others. I had decided that "my turn" was independent of anyone's turn, turning, or tune. For the first time in my life, my turn was contingent upon me taking it.

My voice also became clearer when I released the expectation that my past could be any different than it had been. Logically, I knew that I could not change the past, but for years I lamented that it had not unfolded as I expected. I was angered by my father's absence, the presence of trauma, and cyclical instability. I was angry about most things, including being poor, Black, and sad. I now know these dimensions were the foundation of my resilience and can be celebrated.

Another voice-defining milestone was overcoming my struggle with perfectionism. My need to be perfect or belief that I could perform myself into worth had stalled my future. I had spent most of my twenties waiting to be good enough to have the future or change I desired. So much so that I had delayed starting things by waiting for the perfect time or conditions. I now know these timings do not exist. There is no such thing as perfect timing or the perfect conditions. Generally, there is only the decision to start. This awareness has freed me to start no matter what is happening around me or in me. Now, I yell to myself, "Go!"

My voice also began coming into view once I was through apologizing and explaining. I was through apologizing for being the only Tiffany I could be. I was done explaining why I had boundaries. It is incredibly empowering to decide you will no longer apologize or explain the things you have no control over. I had spent years apologizing or explaining things like my race, upbringing, personality, and preferences. Once I decided I would no longer apologize for being myself, I was finally able to inhabit an authenticity that is transformative.

There is power in unapologetically being yourself. As a result, my voice came into view when I was done with blame, perfectionism, imposter syndrome, and wishing:

- I was somebody else.

- I had somebody else's anything.
- I was a different kind of beautiful.

Being done with blame allowed me to move on when no one took responsibility. When I stopped comparing my journey and myself to others, I was able to celebrate my becoming. I fell in love with myself! I now know what it is to say that beauty is in the eye of the beholder and be your own beholder. It has been a powerful unveiling, an enthusiastic "behold." I now say, "I am the only me" instead of "I am only me."

As my voice has finally come into view, I am accepting:

- Me.
- My past.
- My purpose.
- Opportunities.
- Forgiveness.
- Change.
- Hope.

Imagine spending most of your life wanting to be someone or something else. Imagine believing that some other future is waiting to be born if only you can change your past. Consider not seeing the purpose to which you have been called or the opportunities that lie ahead because you have spent years allowing shame, guilt, abuse, or trauma to silence you or close your eyes. These toxic emotions cloud, minimize, and dare to choke out your voice! So, each day I challenge myself to embrace my past, purpose, opportunities, and self. Equally important, I challenge myself to fully accept forgiveness, change, and hope. I no longer allow my acceptance, forgiveness, change, or hope to be constrained. I have chosen to heal. In doing so, my voice has come into view.

Moreover, every day more of my voice comes into view with the gentle acceptance that I survived for a reason. This acceptance heralds the possibilities. It is a deliverance that has freed me from expectation, exception, and the most egregious acts of dehumanization. The most powerful aspect of this acceptance is accepting that:

- I have the right to have expectations for myself and others.
- I do not have to fall prey to exceptionalism.
- The ways in which others wronged me did not make me wrong or bad.

My voice is finally coming into view because I can see:

- My expectations, dreams, and hopes.
- Other people's expectations, agendas, and intentions.
- Where having boundaries could serve me.
- The value in saying no.
- The blessing of saying yes to the right things.
- The peace that comes with acceptance.
- The way is good.
- How truths can coexist.

I am finding my voice because I now have a vision for myself. I also have boundaries now. These refinements have enabled me to use my voice for my best interest, needs, and goals. Confidently, I now say, "No!" With excitement, I now say, "Yes!" I allow myself to be okay or contented, particularly when I am reminded that the only person I can change is me. I also give myself permission to change my mind. Moreover, I no longer require myself to find the truth. Rather, I live by and embrace my truth.

My voice is finally coming into view as I visit every part and every version of me. Each visitation brings a new awareness, acceptance, or truth. As if weaving a new rug with old threads, I am untying the things that had me bound and retying them in ways that allow me to climb. With these finely braided old threads, I am climbing out of:

- The hole.

- My past.
- My place.
- My perception.
- My persecution.
- My guilt.
- My shame.
- My inability.
- Apathy.

I am climbing out of anything that no longer serves me. I am climbing into things like peace, joy, health, love, and transformation. What once was a noose has become a rope to freedom.

My voice is coming into view because I refuse to carry:

- On.
- Around.
- Over.

I refuse to carry on when folks foster confusion or bring conflict. I do not even say my peace. Rather, I maintain my peace. I also don't carry around things anymore, especially trauma, hurts, or grudges. Not only do I let bygones be bygones, but I also say bye and let people go on as soon as I realize they are not for me. I trust my intuition without a reference. Lastly, I do not carry over anything past its season, including old approaches, faulty thinking, or unhealthy relationships.

Because my voice has finally come into view, I see me, others see me, and I can finally hear myself.

Michele Gunn

Founder of Cultivate and Thrive
Self-Actualization Coach

https://www.linkedin.com/in/michelegunn/
https://www.facebook.com/michele.jonasgunn/
https://www.instagram.com/michelegunn1
https://www.michelegunn.com/
https://linqapp.com/profile

Michele Gunn is a Gallup-Certified Strengths Coach, author, and speaker dedicated to helping women discover who God created them to be. Drawing on her experience as a wife, mother, grandmother, and professional leader, Michele blends practical wisdom with faith-based guidance to inspire women to embrace their strengths, cultivate clarity, and live with confidence. Through her coaching practice, Cultivate and Thrive, and her online column, Graceful Awakening on Patheos, Michele encourages Christian women to rise above fear, align with their God-given purpose, and shine with lasting joy. She speaks and writes on topics of faith, personal growth, and empowerment, equipping women to live authentically and leave a legacy of light. When she's not writing or coaching, Michele enjoys time with her family and finding joy in life's simple, God-given moments.

Whispers of Worth: Discovering the Voice Within

By Michele Gunn

The Quiet That Wasn't Mine

There is an incident that still somewhat haunts me today. It happened back in the first or second grade. I think it was the first grade because I really loved my second-grade teacher. It haunts me because I know what it did to me. I often think about how my actions and words may have affected my children. Anyway, I was a talker. Nonstop. I remember that in the comments on my report cards, I would often receive a seven. Seven meant "talks too much." It's funny what memories stick with you. Well, not really funny; more like interesting. This teacher put tape on my mouth to make me stop talking. That would not be tolerated today. Well, it worked. She stifled me. As a six-year-old little girl, an adult whom I respected and was taught to listen to made it very clear to me that my voice should not be heard.

The truth is, I was taught by many adults that I should be seen and not heard. I should do what I was told instead of figuring out what I wanted to do. I was told who to become instead of embracing who I was created to be. I pray that what I share with you in this chapter will inspire you to find your voice (or reclaim it) through faith and personal growth.

Silenced in My Youth

As I shared above, my experiences were not just limited to school. It was the way I was raised. I was taught to do what I was told, how to think, and what to want. I was not my own person. I didn't even know who I was. I didn't know who I could be. I was not told I was a person who had value. I had no self-esteem and I was not encouraged to be anything more. Yes, I was encouraged to get good grades and to go to college. I am talking about more. I am talking about the foundation of a human being.

I had a natural curiosity for learning. I was often labeled as nosy by classmates as well as family. That caused me to retreat and it stifled my natural curiosity. Since I was not encouraged to have opinions or to speak out at all, I essentially lost my voice. Later in my adult years, I learned that these two characteristics are an important part of who I am. They make me, me. Socially, I had limited opportunities to choose and grow friendships. This further led to my retreating into my shell. I do remember one special friend I made in the eighth grade. Our friendship was special. She encouraged me to be me. We had so much fun together. She moved away that same year, leaving me to feel alone again. Silent. Voiceless.

The Invisible College Girl

I was blessed that my parents paid for most of my college. I wish I could have done that for my children. It did come at a cost. I had to negotiate my major to something that was acceptable. I also had to attend a college I could commute to. It was a good college and I received a great education. The problem was that I was not permitted to get involved at school or socialize. I had to come right home after classes. College life did not help me really grow as a person. I was unable to make those lifelong friends that many people talk about. I was not able to grow my professional network to help start a career.

I longed for deep, meaningful friendships. I missed out on learning how to create lasting friendships. I needed connection, growth, and sisterhood. This reinforced my feelings of isolation. It compounded self-doubt, as I never really knew what I could do beyond college classes. I missed out on joining clubs and taking on leadership roles.

I did learn that I still had no voice. They say college is where you find yourself. I was still lost. The quote, *"You may not control all the events that happen to you, but you can decide not to be reduced by them,"* by Maya Angelou, is something I needed to hear but never did.

The Mirror and the Message

One major turning point in my life was discovering affirmations without even knowing the term. Growing up, I never heard of personal development or personal growth, let alone the term affirmations. But that is exactly what I did. As a teenager who felt ugly, unloved, and worthless, I made a decision. Something had to change, and it was me. I needed to value myself. *But how?* In the mornings when getting ready for school, junior high, and high school, I would look at myself in the mirror and tell myself what was good about me. Even if I didn't believe it, I did it anyway. I spoke love to myself. Love that no one else shared with me. It challenged my negative beliefs. I stomped them down to make room for love, love of self.

This marked the beginning of healing, step by step, from within. There was a lot of work to do. I had no idea. As I grew into adulthood, I found my faith. God loved me. He loves me just the way I am because He made me. I was not familiar with scriptures growing up. As an adult, I am embracing God's Word. I find great love in Jeremiah 1:5, which says, *"Before I formed you in the womb I knew you, before you were born I dedicated you, a prophet to the nations I appointed you."* Not only does that Scripture show me great love, but it also tells me I was created for a purpose.

The Faith that Freed Me

I found love in my husband and in my children. They gave me some value, self-worth, and a purpose. They did not give me my identity and true value. They did not make me feel worthy on my own. It was growing in my faith and developing a personal relationship with God that has provided insight into who I am. I had to learn what Psalm 139:14 tells us: *"I praise you, because I am wonderfully made; wonderful are your works! My very self, you know."* I am valued because I was created by God. You are too!!

The Scripture that has guided my growth and self-worth continually is Matthew 28:18-20, which says, *"Then Jesus approached and said to them, 'All power in heaven and on earth has been given to me. Go, therefore, and make disciples of all nations, baptizing them in the name of the Father, and of the Son, and of the Holy Spirit, teaching them to observe all that I have commanded you. And behold, I am with you always, until the end of the age."* (usccb.org)

This Scripture, although not as self-validating as others, guides me to continually shift from seeking external validation to walking in divine purpose. It is on this journey that I have found both tools and people to help me discover my value and to bring back my voice. I now focus my value and my voice on helping other women embrace their own value and voice.

Let Her Speak: The Message for Others

Embrace your voice and story. There is no other person like you. You were created as an individual for a specific purpose, a purpose all your own. Remember the words of Melissa Etheridge: *"You are more powerful than you know; you are beautiful just as you are."*

If you are having difficulty finding and living your value, try these things:

- **Affirmations**: Say them in front of a mirror, preferably morning and evening, and say them like you believe them.
- **Journaling**: Put your feelings on paper, look for patterns, and see your strengths at work.
- **Pray**: Pray in gratitude for who you are.

- **Community**: Find support and encouragement.
- **Scripture**: Choose something that speaks to you and pray it in times of doubt (Proverbs 31:25, *"She is clothed with strength and dignity, and laughs at the days to come."*
- **Permission**: Give yourself permission to shine.

Struggles do not define the end. They are the shape of the beginning. Remember 2 Timothy 1:7, *"For God did not give us a spirit of cowardice but rather of power and love and self-control."*

The Power of a Woman Unleashed

Although my story is not over, I am making a difference one woman at a time. I still have growing to do and my voice still needs to be heard. I now have the confidence to share it. I will not be stifled. There is beauty in every woman's voice, especially those who were once silent.

Believe. Speak. Shine. Be heard.

Corinne Brown

Corinne Brown Coaching
Leadership/Results Coach

www.linkedin.com/in/corinne-brown-36513673
https://www.facebook.com/corinnebrowncoaching/
www.instagram.com/corinne_brown_coaching
corinnebrowncoaching@gmail.com
www.corinnebrowncoaching.com

Corinne Brown is a leadership coach, writer, and speaker who empowers women to reclaim their voice, rise in confidence, and lead with purpose. With over 14 years of coaching experience across Australia and internationally, Corinne specialises in mindset, emotional intelligence, and transformational leadership. As the founder of a thriving coaching practice, Corinne supports individuals and teams to break through limiting beliefs, overcome self-doubt, and lead authentically. Corinne's journey, from self-silencing to self-ownership, inspires others to embrace their power and live with intention. A passionate advocate for psychosocial safety and inclusive leadership, Corinne believes every woman deserves to be heard, seen, and valued. She brings compassion, clarity, and fierce truth to her work, helping others find their voice and speak it boldly. Unleash Her Voice is a reflection of her mission: to guide women back to themselves—stronger, wiser, and ready to rise.

Breaking the Chains That Held Me Captive

By Corinne Brown

This chapter is my honest reflection on how deeply ingrained childhood trauma shaped who I was before I found my voice. For years, I lived silently under invisible chains forged by fear, silence, and the pressure to be "good" and agreeable. I hid my true feelings, muffled my voice, and wore a mask that kept me small and unseen. But there came a point when I could no longer ignore the restless whisper inside me telling me that this was not my truth. Breaking free wasn't easy—it meant confronting painful memories, setting boundaries, and learning to stand up for myself even when it scared me. Through this messy and sometimes painful process, I began to reclaim my voice, my worth, and my power. Now, I show up authentically, speak up boldly, and live as the woman I was always meant to be—free from the chains of my past.

For most of my life, I did not know I was living in a prison. There were no metal bars, no guards, and no locked doors. The prison was invisible, built from experiences I had endured long before I could understand them. It had been there since childhood—walls made of unspoken rules, ceilings made of fear, and floors paved with silence. I didn't know freedom because I had never tasted it.

My earliest memories are snapshots of moments that seemed small at the time but became the foundation for the beliefs that shaped me.

When I spoke up as a child, I was told I was "too loud," "too curious," or "too much." When I showed emotion, I was met with discomfort or dismissal: "Don't cry," "Stop making a fuss," or the cutting "You're overreacting." Over time, I learned the lesson that my needs were inconvenient and my feelings unsafe to share. It wasn't a single moment of pain—it was a slow layering of messages that taught me it was better, safer, to stay quiet.

This conditioning wove itself into my very identity. I became the agreeable one, the peacemaker, the pleaser. I learned to read the room before I spoke, to anticipate what others needed before they even asked, and to mould myself into whatever version of me would cause the least disruption. It was survival. And yet, while it protected me as a child, it suffocated me as an adult.

The truth is, childhood trauma does not politely step aside when you grow up. It follows you and shapes your relationships, your choices, your career, and your ability to trust. I walked into every situation carrying the unspoken belief that my value depended on keeping the peace and keeping myself small.

I wore my mask so well that even I forgot it was there. I smiled when I felt like screaming. I said "yes" when my soul begged me to say "no." I learned to suppress my own truth so completely that I could barely hear it anymore. The mask became my identity, and the chains—the invisible ones I had carried for decades—felt like they were part of my body.

But deep down, something inside me was restless. There were moments, fleeting at first, where I caught glimpses of another version of me—a woman who spoke with conviction, who didn't shrink to make others comfortable, and who trusted herself. I didn't know her yet, but I longed to.

The shift didn't happen overnight. It began as a whisper, a quiet knowing: "This is not who you truly are." At first, I ignored it. The whisper was inconvenient. It threatened the life I had built, the relationships I had maintained, and the image I had curated.

But the whisper refused to be silenced. Each time I betrayed myself with another forced smile or another swallowed truth, the voice grew louder.

Until one day, I could no longer pretend I didn't hear it.

The breaking of the chains was not dramatic, not a single burst of defiance, but a series of small, terrifying acts of courage. It was telling the truth, even when my voice faulted. It was setting boundaries, even when people didn't like it. It was allowing myself to grieve for the little girl who was never given the freedom to be fully herself.

The first time I spoke up for myself, I felt exposed, like standing under a harsh light. My hands trembled, my heart pounded, and my breath caught in my throat. But I survived it. And in surviving, I proved to myself that my voice would not destroy me. It would save me.

Each time I chose myself, a link in the chain broke. Some fell away easily; others clung tight, demanding more work, more healing, and more self-compassion. I had to relearn who I was without the weight of those chains. It was not an easy process—healing never is—but it was worth every painful step.

Today, I stand not as someone untouched by trauma, but as someone who has transformed it. Those chains? They are no longer my prison. They are the proof of my survival, forged into my strength. I am no longer silent. I am no longer small. I am the woman who shows up, stands up, and speaks up—not just for herself, but for the girl she once was, and for anyone still learning that their voice matters.

Because the truth is this: The chains that hold us captive are often the ones we believe we cannot break. But when you dare to rise, you learn that the lock was never on the outside—it was always within you. And the key? It was your voice, waiting to be used all along.

Self-Reflection: Owning My Story

Looking back now, I can see how every experience, every wound, and every silenced moment shaped the person I became. For years, I resented my past, wishing it could have been different, wishing someone had stepped in to protect me, to tell me I was enough just as I was. But I have come to understand that while those years left scars, they also forged my resilience. They forced me to develop strength, empathy, and a deep understanding of the human heart.

One of the hardest truths I had to face was that no one was coming to save me. I had spent so much time hoping that one day, someone would see the pain behind my smile and reach in to pull me out. But healing didn't come from someone else's intervention—it came from my own decision to stop abandoning myself.

Self-reflection is not about blaming the people who hurt me, nor is it about minimizing what happened. It is about owning my story in a way that empowers me rather than traps me. I have learned to look at my past without flinching, to acknowledge the hard truths, and to understand that my survival came at the cost of my authenticity for far too long.

Breaking free meant I had to redefine my worth. It meant letting go of the belief that I was only lovable when I was agreeable or useful to others. It meant understanding that my voice matters not because it will please everyone, but because it is mine, and it is the most authentic expression of who I am.

Now, when I feel the old urge to shrink back, I remind myself of what is at stake. If I silence myself, I betray the little girl I once was—the girl who desperately needed someone to tell her she could be exactly who she was without fear. So I speak up. I set boundaries. I let people see the real me, even when it feels vulnerable.

I have learned that healing is not a final destination. It is a daily choice.

Some days, I still feel the echoes of those old chains, the pull to retreat into silence or self-doubt. But now I have the awareness and the tools to choose differently. I can remind myself of the truth: that I am not that small, silenced child anymore. I am a woman who has rebuilt herself from the inside out.

My story is no longer one of captivity. It is one of reclamation.

I have taken back my voice, my worth, and my power. And I carry them with me, not just for myself, but as a beacon of hope for others who are still learning that they, too, can break free.

The journey is ongoing, but I walk it now with my head high, my heart open, and my voice strong.

Let me leave you with this:

Your voice is not just a sound—it's the key that unlocks the life you were always meant to live.

Breaking free isn't about forgetting your past; it's about refusing to let it define your future.

Every chain you break becomes proof of your strength and a beacon for others still finding their courage.

Corinne Brown

Krizel Rodriguez

CEO of Leading Lady Network

https://www.linkedin.com/in/krizelrodriguez/
https://www.facebook.com/leadingladynetwork
https://www.instagram.com/lareinaleader/
https://leadingladynetwork.com/
https://www.facebook.com/groups/leadingladynetwork

Krizel Rodriguez is the CEO and Founder of the Leading Lady Network®, a platform dedicated to empowering women of all shapes, shades, and sizes to step into leadership with confidence and purpose. Known as the "La Reina of Leadership," she is a pageant queen, a TEDx speaker, and an award-winning entrepreneur. Krizel created the signature TAILOR™ Method, inspired by her daughter, to guide women in building clarity, confidence, and visibility. Her story of resilience—overcoming divorce, illness, and invisibility—fuels her mission to help women embrace their queen energy and own their space. Through her programs, such as the Crown Society™, Reign and Shine Leadership Academy™, and Royal Reign Framework™, Krizel equips women with the tools to lead authentically in every area of life. She has been recognized as a Change Maker, inspiring women worldwide to reign and shine.

The Crown I Almost Lost

By Krizel Rodriguez

I wasn't raised to be quiet.

I was raised to be humble.

There's a difference.

Growing up in a Latino household, humility was a valued and integral part of our way of life. My parents taught me that no matter what I accomplished, I was no better than anyone else. They raised me to respect others, to lead with gratitude, and to let my character speak louder than my ego.

But here's the thing: Humility is not the same as invisibility. My parents didn't teach me to hide. They knew I had a voice... a very loud, bold, and passionate one! They never tried to take it away from me.

The world, though? The world had other plans.

From the start, I noticed how uncomfortable people became when I spoke up. They wanted my work ethic but not my ideas. They wanted my presence, but not my perspective. They wanted me to shine, but only just enough to light the room, not enough to take center stage.

And for a long time, I let them set the rules...until I didn't.

The Cost of Playing Small

I don't tell this part of my story to point fingers. I tell it because I know I'm not the only one who has ever chosen to play small in a world that didn't quite know what to do with them.

I held jobs where I consistently outperformed expectations, but I rarely received recognition for it. I gave 110% but let others take the credit. And deep down, I told myself it was okay. That humility meant letting my work speak for itself.

But humility and silence are not the same thing. Somewhere along the way, I got the two confused.

And it cost me years of my life.

At home, I lived through a fourteen-year marriage where my voice became softer and softer until I hardly recognized myself. At work, I saw my ideas walk out of the room in someone else's mouth. And inside, I felt the slow ache of erasure. You know, the kind where you begin to question if you even matter.

But here's the truth: I was never powerless. Even in the moments I stayed quiet, it wasn't because I didn't have a voice. It was because I chose, again and again, to value peace over presence.

Until one day, peace no longer felt like peace. It felt like disappearing.

The Moment Everything Changed

The turning point came the day I held my daughter for the first time. I had left my marriage and started a whole new life. One that allowed me to use my voice, but I wasn't quite ready. I was used to years of silence, so when the opportunities came, I didn't know what to do.

But then, looking at my daughter's little face, I thought about the kind of woman I wanted her to see when she looked at me. A mother who played small to make others comfortable? Or a mother who stood tall in her truth, even when it made people uncomfortable?

That was my wake-up call.

I couldn't tell her to chase her dreams if I wasn't brave enough to chase my own. I couldn't tell her she had a voice if I kept silencing mine.

I realized then that my story wasn't just mine. It was hers too. And if I wanted her to believe she was powerful, I had to start believing it for myself.

In that moment, I felt a surge of love and fear all at once. Love, because she was mine! My miracle, my purpose, and my reason. Fear, because I realized that everything I did from that moment on would shape the way she saw herself, her worth, and her place in the world.

I thought about the example I had been setting until then—a woman who worked hard but stayed in the background. A woman who let others speak louder, take credit, and take up space while she disappeared into humility—a woman who remained in places that dimmed her light because it felt easier than fighting to shine.

And I knew. I couldn't let that be the blueprint for her life.

That was the moment everything changed.

It wasn't about chasing crowns or accolades. It wasn't even about me anymore. It was about her.

My daughter became my why. She was the reason I pushed past fear to step onto the TEDx stage. She was the reason I walked into a pageant I never thought I'd enter. She was the reason I created the TAILOR Method. I wanted her name and her legacy to be tied to something transformational.

Every time I was tempted to shrink again, I remembered her face. Every time I thought about giving up, I remembered the promise I made to her.

And in fighting to be visible, I wasn't just saving myself. I was building a world where she and every daughter after her would know that their voices were crowns they never had to take off.

Learning to Take Up Space

My first act of rebellion against invisibility wasn't loud or dramatic. It was a choice—a decision to step out of the corner and onto a stage.

That stage was TEDx.

I remember standing there, hands trembling, heart pounding, wondering if anyone would care about my story. But I spoke anyway.

And that moment changed me.

It wasn't about applause or validation. It was about hearing my own voice echo back to me, reminding me of something I'd always known but had forgotten: *I was never invisible. I just stopped showing up fully.*

Not long after, I did something that would push me even further outside my comfort zone: I entered a pageant.

Now, I didn't walk into that pageant because I was chasing crowns or gowns. Well, who am I kidding? I definitely wanted a gown, but it symbolized so much more. I walked in because I was chasing visibility. I wanted to take up space in a way I had never allowed myself to before.

When they placed that crown on my head and named me Mrs. Texas Plus America 2024, it wasn't the crown that gave me power. It was the confirmation of what I had already decided: I belong here. I always have.

Building Something Bigger Than Me

That moment lit a fire inside me.

I didn't just want to reclaim my voice. I wanted to create a space where other women could reclaim theirs, too. Women who had been told they were too much, not enough, or simply didn't fit the mold of leadership. Women who had been overlooked, underestimated, or made to feel small.

That's why I built the *Leading Lady Network.*

What began as an idea evolved into a movement. A community where women could learn to lead, connect, and be celebrated for who they are, no matter their shape, shade, size, or age. From that, the *Crown Society* was born. A place where women aren't just reminded that they're queens, they're given the tools, the sisterhood, and the courage to live like it.

I even created my own coaching method—the TAILOR Method—named after my daughter. Because this isn't just about me reclaiming my voice, it's about building a legacy where every woman, regardless of her shape, shade, size, or age, knows her crown is already hers.

Taking Responsibility

Here's the part I need to say out loud: I don't blame anyone for the years I stayed quiet.

Yes, the world tried to silence me. Yes, I lived through systems, workplaces, and relationships that didn't value my voice. But at the end of the day, I was the one who chose to shrink.

And the same woman who chose to shrink is the same woman who decided to rise.

That's where the power lies.

Taking ownership of my story means I don't have to wait for anyone to hand me a crown, an opportunity, or a seat at the table. I create it for myself. And that is what unleashing your voice is really about.

Your Voice Matters

If you've ever felt invisible, I want you to hear this: You are not too late. You are not too small. You are not disqualified.

The very things you think make you unworthy—the struggles, the setbacks, the scars—those are the things that make you powerful.

Unleashing your voice isn't about being the loudest. It's about being the truest. It's about speaking your truth even when your voice shakes. It's about standing tall even when the world tries to box you in.

And when you do, you don't just unleash your own voice. You unlock the voices of every woman watching you, wondering if she can do it too.

The Crown I Almost Lost

Today, when my daughter looks at me, she doesn't see a woman who disappeared. She sees a woman who fought, who rose, who created something from nothing. She sees a woman who almost lost her crown but chose to reclaim it.

That's the legacy I want to leave. Not perfection. Not polished leadership. But authenticity, resilience, and truth.

Because the crown was never about the sparkle, it was about the story.

I almost lost mine when I thought being invisible was safer. But I found it again when I realized that my story—exactly as it is—was worth being told.

So now, I ask you:

What crown are you hiding?
What story are you silencing?
What would happen if you chose visibility today?

Because, Queen, your crown is waiting.

And the moment you choose to unleash your voice...

You've already won.

Sherry VINSON

Founder and Owner of Kendi Bella Bouquets & Things LLC

www.linkedin.com/in/sherry-vinson-ba9565ab
www.facebook.com/kendibellabouquets
www.instagram.com/kendibella
http://kendibella.com/

Sherry Vinson is a devoted wife, mother, and grandmother whose love for family fuels her passion for life. As the creator and founder of Kendi Bella Bouquets & Things LLC, she has turned her creativity into a thriving small business that brings joy and beauty to her community. Beyond her entrepreneurial spirit, Sherry is an aspiring author, seeking to share her journey and inspire others through the written word. She believes in honoring God in all aspects of her life and is dedicated to empowering women to recognize and embrace their own strength. Through her work and writing, she aims to uplift and encourage others, reminding them that they are capable of achieving greatness. With a heart full of love and a mission to inspire, Sherry continues to make a positive impact on those around her.

Embrace My Power

By Sherry VINSON

"Your latter days will be greater!"

That's what my grandmother told me when I was just a pre-teen. At the time, I didn't fully understand what she meant. But something about those words clung to me. They echoed inside me like a promise, like a secret treasure I couldn't yet unlock but knew I needed to hold onto.

When I asked her to explain, she said,
"You've had such a hard life in your young years, but when you get older, things will get better."

That promise became my secret weapon. Anytime life felt too heavy, I whispered it. When I felt unloved, I clung to it. When my heart hurt, I repeated it like a prayer. It became my first taste of faith, a flicker of hope that kept me moving forward when everything else told me to give up.

The funny thing is, I don't even think my grandmother remembered saying it. But her words rooted themselves deep inside me. And now, years later, I can see how that single sentence planted a seed in my soul—a seed that would grow into resilience, courage, and eventually, confidence.

A Childhood That Grew Me Too Fast

I was mature for my age because I had to be. Responsibility was placed on my shoulders early. I remember standing on a stool just to wash dishes or stir a pot of food for my siblings. I brushed their hair, tied their shoes, fixed their breakfast, and somehow made it to the bus stop for elementary school.

Those tasks weren't impossible. But they cost me something. I would have rather been reading a book, playing outside, or just being a carefree kid. Instead, I carried weight that didn't belong to me.

In my young mind, the hardship made sense: I wasn't with my mother. I believed that if she were there, my life would be softer, easier, and maybe even magical. I dreamed she would swoop in and save me, give me the spoiled-princess life I longed for. But that day never came.

So I grew up learning to carry what was given, to survive with what I had. My dad loved me, but my living situation forced me to grow up faster than I should have. It wasn't abuse. It was expectation. And expectation has a way of silencing a child's joy, forcing them into roles they aren't ready to play.

Learning the Wrong Lesson

Somewhere along the way, I absorbed a dangerous lesson:

Be quiet—that's what the world seemed to whisper. Stay small—that's what I told myself. Sit in the back, blend in, and don't you dare cause trouble. I convinced myself that invisibility was safer, even though it slowly starved my soul.

I tried to do that. I really did. But life has a way of pressing on the parts of you that refuse to stay hidden. Whenever something cut too deep or felt too unfair, I would burst out. Anger gave me courage, and my big mouth landed me in hot water more times than I can count.

As a teenager, this tension lived inside me. I wanted to be invisible, yet I couldn't ignore injustice. I'd speak up when I was mad, but in all other moments, I shrank back. I carried the label of "introvert" like a shield, using it as an excuse to silence myself.

But here's what I know now:
My voice has always mattered.

Not just when I'm angry.
Not just when I've been pushed too far.
Not just when I'm at my breaking point.

It mattered simply because it was mine.

Finding My Voice

For years, I believed anger was the only key to courage. I believed explosions were the only way to prove I had something worth saying. But now I know my voice carries power even in stillness, even before I reach my breaking point. My truth doesn't need fire to be fierce. It already is.

Over time, I noticed something: I was bold when it came to protecting my children. I was fearless when standing up for family members or those who couldn't defend themselves. But when it came to me, I only fought back when I couldn't take it anymore. And then, regret would follow.

But growth is a teacher. Slowly, I began to trust myself. Slowly, I learned to believe that what I had to say carried weight. Slowly, I learned that my voice didn't need to be the loudest in the room to matter. It just needed to be steady, authentic, and rooted in truth.

Some of the most powerful moments in my life came when I listened to that gentle nudge in my spirit and shared what God placed on my heart—a Bible verse, an encouraging word, a reminder of hope. I can't tell you how many times someone later told me that something I said helped them hold on a little longer. Some even wrote thank-you notes.

And while I always give God the glory, I won't lie. It felt good to know He used my voice to remind someone else of their worth.

The Lessons Hidden in Struggle

Life has tested me in ways I never expected. Sometimes storms came crashing down all at once; other times pain dripped slowly, wearing me down like water against stone.

Adversity has been both my wound and my classroom. It cut deep, left scars, and tried to convince me I was broken. But those scars became textbooks, teaching me lessons I never asked for but desperately needed. They taught me that survival itself is proof of strength. It reveals strength we didn't know we had, resilience we didn't know we could carry, and courage that rises up when everything else feels broken.

And because of my journey through heartache, responsibility, and seasons where confidence felt like a faraway dream, I know what it feels like to question your worth. To wonder if you'll ever rise above it all. To carry scars that whisper, "*You're not enough.*"

But I also know this: Those scars can tell a different story. They can become proof of survival. They can shine as marks of growth. They can remind you that you are still here, still standing, still becoming.

What Confidence Really Is

Confidence is not pretending life is perfect. It's not about masking pain behind a smile or performing strength you don't feel.

For me, confidence isn't about looking polished or pretending life is flawless. It's about standing tall on shaky knees, walking forward with tear-stained cheeks, and still daring to believe I am worthy. Confidence is messy, but it's mine.

It's daring to walk boldly into your future with your head held high because you've already proven you can survive what tried to break you.

An Invitation

So if you've ever struggled to find your voice like I did, hear me when I say: You are not alone.

Every stumble I've taken has carved a stronger step forward. The broken pieces of my past didn't just glue themselves back together. They rearranged into a mosaic more breathtaking than what was whole. That is the gift of rising: You don't come back the same; you come back transformed. Every trial you've endured can become the foundation for unshakable confidence.

Your silence does not serve you. Your shrinking does not honor the woman you are becoming. The world needs your voice, your wisdom, and your testimony.

This is your invitation to rise.
To rediscover your voice.
To embrace your power.
To step into the version of yourself that adversity has been preparing you for all along.

Because God did not allow your struggles for no reason. More often than not, the very thing you survived is the very thing someone else needs to hear to survive too.

My Vow

Today, I stand in my latter days—and yes, they are greater. Not because life is easy, but because I now know who I am.

I vow to use my voice so that other women don't have to wait as long as I did to unleash theirs.

I vow to speak life into the silent places.
I vow to amplify courage in the women who've been told to stay small.

I vow to remind you that your voice is not just worthy; it is necessary.

Because when one woman rises, she carries others with her.

Hear Me

So, if you've ever struggled to find your voice, lean in:

You are not alone.
Your broken pieces can become something beautiful.
Your pain can give birth to your power.
Your voice is enough. I've learned that power doesn't always roar. My courage is no longer fueled by fury. And my permission to speak? It never belonged to anyone else. It has been mine all along.

Sometimes the strongest voices are not the loudest ones. Sometimes they are the voices that speak with steady conviction, quiet courage, and unshakable faith.

So let today be the day you stop shrinking.
Let today be the day you rise.
Let today be the day you UnleashHER Voice.

Because your latter days will be greater.

Claribel Coreano

Empower Global Coaching
Coach

https://www.linkedin.com/in/claricor44/
https://www.facebook.com/claribel.coreano
https://www.instagram.com/empowergrowth_claribel_coreano
https://empowerglobalcoaching.com/

About Claribel Coreano, M.S. Claribel Coreano is a Transformational Christian Life Coach, writer, and intuitive artist with over 29 years of experience in the human services field. She holds a master's degree in human services with a concentration in Marriage & Family Therapy and Psychology from Capella University and is certified in multiple life coaching disciplines including NLP, Women's Empowerment, Trauma-Informed Coaching, and Health & Wellness Coaching with a focus on Diabetes Prevention.

Claribel began her career during the early HIV/AIDS epidemic and went on to serve diverse communities—homeless populations, individuals with mental health and substance use challenges, veterans, and justice-involved clients. These experiences, combined with her personal journey as a survivor of childhood trauma and domestic violence, shaped her passion to empower others through healing, mindset renewal, and resilience-building.

She is the founder of Empower Global Coaching, based in Spring Hill, FL, where she supports individuals, families, and groups with coaching services centered around trauma recovery, healthy relationships, spiritual growth, parenting, and health & wellness. Her approach blends Christian principles with evidence-based strategies, offering compassionate guidance that meets people where they are and equips them to thrive.

An accomplished author and contributing writer, Claribel has published A Butterfly Flies Towards the Wind and So, You Want to Be a Life Coach?, as well as contributions in international works from Dublin, Ireland on gratitude and resilience. In her creative work, she expresses herself through painting, using mixed media and intuitive methods as a form of relaxation and inspiration.

Through her books, coaching, workshops, and artistic expression, Claribel continues to serve as a light and encourager helping others reset their lives, find healing, and walk confidently in their God-given purpose.

Unpacking the Luggage of Shame: My Journey from Silence to Wholeness

By Claribel Coreano

> *"Therefore, if anyone is in Christ, he is new creature; old things have passed away; behold, all things have become new." KJV*

Healing from the Weight of Shame

For many years, I carried the weight of shame like heavy luggage on my back, weighing me down from the effects of past wounds caused by traumatic events from my childhood, adolescence, and young adulthood. I did not know what exactly shame was or how it was affecting my personality, decisions, and outcomes. Until I decided to start working on my trauma healing. And this is what I have learned so far: that shame is one of the most painful emotions we can carry as an unhealthy behavioral habit. Unlike guilt, which says, "I did something wrong," shame says, "I am something wrong." It strikes at the very core of our identity, whispering lies that we are unworthy, unlovable, or beyond redemption. It's a pesky condemning voice that is often overpowering but that can be healed once identified. Shame always tries to remind you of your past. But the truth is, you are not your past, and I am not my past. You are not your pain, and I am not my pain. Healing is possible, and you don't have to do it alone; you just have to take the first step. I assure you that you don't have to walk through this process alone.

The Link Between Trauma and Shame

Why is it important to identify if shame is present in your life? For one, anyone who has suffered from major traumatic events can agree that there is a connection between shame and trauma. Trauma is better identifiable by evidence of the emotional and psychological response to traumatic events, and shame is identifiable by evidence of the residual feeling that affects a person through feeling unworthy, unlovable, and undeserving and is often evident by stagnation, thus placing a standstill pause in your life because of the way that it makes you feel.

Brené Brown, renowned shame and vulnerability researcher, writes:

"Shame is the intensely painful feeling or experience of believing that we are flawed and therefore unworthy of love and belonging."

Those who have suffered traumatic events can attest to how this pesky little bug called "shame" can affect a person by inflicting a demoralizing and destructive pattern of emotions throughout their lives. And many experts agree that what makes shame stand out is that it is a unique disturbance that exists without any real purpose. And unlike guilt, shame is more than that; it tends to go deeper. It is the act of hurting ourselves by carrying it to an extent that it completely debilitates us daily. And if we are not careful, shame can become a state of being because it brings a deep-rooted feeling, emotion, or attachment as part of your identity. The effect of shame on the person causes more damage than low self-esteem.

To clarify, shame makes you believe that you are somehow flawed due to surviving the destructive patterns of your experience. And this is where it becomes most damaging, first by its toxic negative influence of devaluing your own humanity. The person who is stuck in shame tends to cover it up by masking their wounded self because of the shame it carries. The effect is profoundly damaging because, unlike guilt, which can inspire change, shame makes the person feel like there is no way out of the stagnation they find themselves in. It's not necessarily about what you did, but it is more about what you believe because of it. It creates a distorted state of being that fragments your identity and results in a state of emotional paralysis or inability to communicate those feelings.

For example, in my case, I became a master at masking my wounded self, and I overcompensated with perfectionism, hoping no one would see the shattered pieces behind my smile. I was afraid to speak up or communicate my feelings. I thought sharing my truth would bring me humiliation or attacks from others who would try to silence me. And then again, this same fear had made me a perfect target for domestic and narcissistic abuse. Not because I was weak, but because it was directly connected to the shame that I was carrying. A heavy shame that did not allow me to recognize these patterns or the ability to protect myself from those who overstepped my boundaries or caused me harm.

I became what I like to call a recovering shame addict, derived from a false belief that I was truly at fault or did something to have caused it. This was in part because no one has ever validated my pain or listened to my cry for help as a child, adolescent, or adult. It was a horrible state of being because I was doing everything to cover it up like nothing happened so no one would notice the damage it had caused me. I was too afraid to speak up or even share what I had gone through. I felt that I would be devalued, dehumanized, and belittled in the same way my abusers had made me feel. So, I adapted to pretending that everything was honky-dory, but on the inside, it was killing my soul slowly.

This toxic shame was one of the precipitating factors that led me to become the perfect victim for abuse and learned helplessness. You see, they saw right through me and probably must have said, "Wow, she is the perfect candidate; she does not know how to fight back, defend herself, or speak out." This made them feel confident that when they disrespect me, I would take them back. The sad reality is that I obeyed, I respected, and I forgave more than they ever deserved.

Another thing about this "pesky shame bug" is that it left me in a state of limbo, not knowing whether what appeared to me was reality or an illusion. In fact, it drags you down to the pit of despair, where settling for just a little bit of reciprocity seemed like enough, but in reality, even that was not enough to make me feel validated, loved, or understood. I still was lacking, hurting, and did not know any way to come out of this convoluted turmoil called "SHAME."

Shame: A Disability of the Soul

Shame can become a disability of the soul because it turned my soul into a silent battlefield. On the outside, I looked like I was managing just fine. On the inside, I was quietly breaking. Toxic shame taught me to settle for crumbs of affection and crumbs of acceptance, to confuse pain with love, and to believe that reciprocity, no matter how little, was enough. It wasn't. It created a disability in my soul. I didn't know how to heal because I didn't even have the words to name what was happening to me. I just knew I felt stuck, hurt, and disconnected from who I was meant to be.

You may ask, *"How did you overcome this disability?" "How did you learn to regulate the feelings attached to it?" "How did you learn to heal from it?"* It wasn't easy. It was a long road to my healing journey. I must say that it took tears upon tears of quiet nights accepting what it was, what happened to me, and why I let it happen. I realized that I could always blame shame if I wanted to, because I was not quite awakened to all of my trauma yet to be able to recognize it for what it was. It was a disability of the soul that kept me functioning with limitations—those invisible to the naked eye but living inside me, hurting me through the memories of the shame that blinded me into a state of pain. I can't believe that I can say this now without breaking down into pieces. Wow, that's progress!

My Awakening

My first awakening was that I learned that I am not a 'shame'; that was a remarkable moment of reckoning in an instant. *"Oh, so you mean to tell me that I am not my shame?"* Yes, beautiful soul, you are not your shame. That pesky bug was a BYPRODUCT OF MY TRAUMA that somehow continued to fester into woundedness and learned helplessness.

The second awakening came with the realization that it was not my fault to acknowledge that my innocence had been slowly stripped away by those who stripped it from me and to let go of the feeling of betrayal from those who were supposed to protect me, which came with a minute of numbness or frozen silence. And as I reflected on it, I got stronger, and I told my younger self, *"See girl, you were never at fault," "You are loved,"* and *"You deserve to be loved."* I felt much better knowing that she knew this. I felt gratitude, healing, and love for both of us.

The third awakening came when I learned how to self-regulate those unpleasant feelings that shame had brought to me. I learned to diffuse them, channel them out, name them, feel them, and embrace them, but the most liberating part was that I learned how to kick them out of my system. It wasn't easy, but with practice, I kept naming them one by one, step by step, reclaiming myself, accepting myself, owning my feelings, and embracing them to function normally but responding differently. You see, now I was fully in charge, not my shame and not what happened to me. I had become wiser, healed, and empowered to know the difference. Like, ok, this is "Trauma," and this is "Shame." I kicked them both out of the way and said, Good riddance! You are not allowed back; you are not welcome here in this space called my beautiful soul. No trespassing. I have become whole. I have healed, and I am ready for my next chapter of healing.

Fourth awakening, I had to clean sweep my mind of all the garbage clutter that shame and trauma left me with. Boy, did they have a party. The cleanup took time to evict those negative thoughts and to learn how to reprogram my mind with positive thoughts. I wasn't going to take any chance on staying the same, no way; I've come this far. So, I kept pushing! I had to continue with the cleanup by learning how to self-regulate my mind so that my feelings obey and not act out by punishing my body. You see, trauma has a way of tricking us by hiding and damaging our bodies through internalized trauma and shame. It was hard to identify where trauma was hiding but when I found it, that is where I began my fifth step: taking better self-care of my body.

Fifth awakening: Now it was time for damage control by conducting a thorough inventory of how trauma and shame caused dysfunction in my body. I had to relearn how to take care of myself, my feelings, my mind, and my body. Yes, it wasn't easy. I had to lose not only all the weight gained from the baggage that I was carrying but also the emotional and mental weight that triggered it. I began by accepting my weight, changing habits, and making lifestyle changes that helped me to heal my body one step at a time. The miracle happened when I learned that trauma and shame had nothing on me, not anymore, and I learned that I was in control of healing my body by changing myself and my thoughts, embracing my feelings, and responding accordingly by speaking my truth. Wow, I now understand what it means when they say, "The truth will set you free." In my life, the truth did set me free. It helped me heal and continues to heal me. Out of my five awakenings, I developed a tool to help others gain insight and healing from shame.

Final Encouragement

My final encouragement to you is from a quote by Ann Voskamp that goes:

"Shame dies when stories are told in safe places."

So share your story and let shame die. And always remember these truths:
You are worthy of healing.
You are worthy of being heard.
You are worthy of being whole.

As you are reading this story, I invite you to take your first step towards your healing today and start unpacking that luggage of shame. You can achieve healing. Share this story with others who may need to read it too.

Healing is calling, and when your soul is ready, shame is shaking in its boots.

Claribel Coreano

Simone Williams Young

CEO of Young at Heart Publishing LLC

https://www.facebook.com/ProphetSimone
https://www.instagram.com/your_kingdom_coach/
www.yahpublishingllc.com
https://linktr.ee/SimoneWilliamsYoung

Simone Williams Young is a best-selling author, prophet, publisher, coach, and visionary leader who has transformed personal tragedy into purpose. After the heartbreaking loss of her son to gun violence, Simone wrote I Choose to Live, a powerful book that birthed Young at Heart Publishing LLC, her faith-based company dedicated to helping authors bring their stories to life. A seasoned writer of multiple books, she is also a grief coach, life coach, and prophetic teacher whose work empowers others to embrace healing, find their voice, and walk boldly into their calling. Known as The Kingdom Writing Coach, Simone inspires authors and entrepreneurs to turn pain into platforms and create impact that lasts. She is also the founder of The Authors Lounge and Winners Circle Gazette. Simone's life and leadership remind others that resilience is possible, and every voice has the power to change lives.

I Didn't Save You to Keep Quiet

By Simone Williams Young

For most of my life, silence felt safer than sound. If I stayed quiet, no one could reject me. If I held back my words, no one could say I was too much. Shyness wrapped around me like a blanket, and fear kept me in the shadows. I thought silence was strength, but it wasn't. Silence looks like protection, but it is really a prison that keeps you from becoming who you are meant to be.

Then came the seasons that tested me beyond anything I thought I could handle. In 2016, I buried my father, my anchor and my covering. His absence left me drifting. In 2019, I walked away from a twenty-year marriage weighed down by addiction and disappointment. That ending felt like another kind of death, the kind that shakes who you think you are. And in August 2020, I faced the unthinkable when my son Ashton's life was taken by gun violence. He was a college student, an athlete, a young man with so much promise, and suddenly he was gone. I was on the road when I got the call. I never got to see him at the morgue, never got to hold him again, and never got to say goodbye. Within just a few years, I had endured the death of my father, the loss of a marriage, and the murder of my son. Each one pressed me deeper into silence, and I honestly wondered if I would ever come back.

Only weeks after Ashton's death, I stood to be ordained. My heart was shattered, yet I was called to carry a mantle. Can you imagine being handed divine responsibility in the same season where grief is trying to bury you alive? I wanted to crawl under a rock and hide and never come out, but I knew I had to choose to live past how I felt.

Life didn't end in that valley. In 2021, I remarried and found love that was whole, steady, and safe. In 2022, I wrote *I Choose to Live,* the book that told Ashton's story and birthed *Young at Heart Publishing.* Out of ashes, purpose was born. Out of devastation, direction emerged.

What started as me fighting to survive turned into a reason for others to believe they could survive too.

Then in 2025, I faced another battle when I underwent brain surgery. In the place of recovery and trying to get well, I heard God speak the words that shook me: "I didn't save you to keep quiet." At that moment I knew I had to get myself together, because God had use of me, and crawling back into my shell was not an option. Those words changed everything. They reminded me that silence had never been humility. It was fear. It was rejection disguised as safety. It was bondage pretending to be my comfort. And I knew I could not keep living that way.

Confidence, I discovered, is not about being loud or pretending you're never afraid. It is not the absence of fear. Confidence is the choice to rise even when you are scared like crazy and unsure. It is opening your mouth when your voice is shaking. It is showing up in places where you once felt invisible. Every time I pushed past silence, I realized my voice carried more weight than my fear ever could.

Just know confidence doesn't show up overnight. People sometimes see me now and think I never struggle, but I do. Fear still tries to creep in. Shyness still tries to quiet me. Rejection still reminds me of moments when I felt overlooked. Confidence isn't permanent. It's a choice I make daily. I wake up and I choose it. I remind myself of who I am and whose I am. My confidence doesn't come from pretending to have it all together. My confidence comes from knowing the One who holds me together.

Silence can be strength in the right moments. There is wisdom in knowing when to hold your peace, and silence has kept me out of situations where speaking would have only made things worse. But the silence I am talking about here was not wisdom. It was sabotage. It wasn't protecting me. It was slowly destroying me. It was fear dressed up as safety. It was rejection hiding under the mask of humility. It was self-sabotage trying to disguise itself as strength.

That kind of silence doesn't cover you; it cages you. And that is what it was doing to me.

You weren't created to live in that kind of silence. You weren't created to just get by. You were created to live fully, to take up space, to be heard, and to walk boldly in who you are. You don't have to shout to carry power. You don't have to be flawless to make an impact. But you do have to stop letting the wrong kind of silence speak louder than your destiny.

Maybe as you read this, you see yourself. Maybe you've stayed quiet when you should have spoken. Maybe you've swallowed dreams because you were afraid of being laughed at. Maybe you've carried truths that have weighed you down because you thought no one would listen. If that's you, let me say this plainly: The world needs your voice. Silence may have carried you this far, but it cannot carry you into the future that belongs to you.

Think about where you've been holding back. What truths have you hidden? What dreams have you buried? Now imagine what could happen if you gave yourself permission to be heard. Imagine how your courage to speak could unlock someone else's courage too.

When I look back over my journey—my father's passing, my divorce, my son's death, being ordained in the middle of grief, remarriage, writing my book, building a company, and that life-altering moment after surgery—I see one clear thread. Every loss that I had to endure tried to silence me, but my faith produced my comeback and proved my voice was never meant to die.

I was not created to live small in silence. I was called to live bold in sound. And so are you. You are not reading this by accident. This is your reminder that confidence does not come from perfection or ease. Confidence comes from persistence, from resilience, and from faith that refuses to bow to fear. My confidence flows from knowing whose I am, and it is a choice I continue to make every single day. Yours can too.

Monica Connolly

Founder of Monica Connolly Coaching
Coach

https://www.linkedin.com/in/mnconnolly/
https://www.facebook.com/monica.a.connolly.7
https://www.instagram.com/monicaconnollyandco/
https://monicaconnollycoaching.com/

Monica Connolly is a Certified Holistic Health and Master Life Coach, Transformation Expert, and trauma-informed practitioner who helps women reclaim their health, identity, and purpose. After surviving chronic illness, emotional eating, and the weight of caregiving, Monica transformed her own life—losing 150 pounds, healing from burnout, and rediscovering her voice. Her journey from silence to strength inspired her to create the THRIVE Blueprint, a framework that blends nervous system healing, gut health, mindset mastery, and purpose alignment. As the founder of Monica Connolly Coaching and host of the Unshakeable Belief podcast, she empowers women to rise from survival mode into soul-led living. Monica's story has been featured on stages, summits, and in multiple collaborative works, where she shares her signature blend of grit and grace. Known as the "Transformation Catalyst Coach," she reminds women everywhere: you are not broken—you are awakening, and you were made for more.

Ashes to Amplified: Finding My Voice in the Fire

By Monica Connolly

There was a time when my silence spoke louder than any words ever could.

On the outside, I was the strong one—the dependable mom, the faithful wife, the reliable employee who kept it all together no matter the cost. People admired my strength, but what they didn't see was the truth: I wasn't strong. I was disappearing.

I remember the day my doctor looked me in the eye and, without a shred of empathy, said, *"If you don't make changes, you're going to die."* His words hit like a gavel against my chest. Guilty. Condemned. Too far gone.

I left that office, drove home numb, and sat in the car gripping the steering wheel until my knuckles turned white. That's when the tears came—hot, angry, and relentless. Not just because of my failing health, but because I realized something even more devastating: I had lost my voice. Somewhere between caregiving, surviving chronic illness, and carrying the weight of everyone else's needs, I had stopped existing for myself. I was still breathing, but I wasn't alive. I had stopped speaking up. I stopped asking for help when I was drowning. I smiled when I wanted to scream. I agreed to things that broke me because saying "no" felt like betrayal. I lost the courage to say what I needed, what I felt, and who I truly was. My voice had been replaced by the version of me that only knows how to survive - and in that moment, I realized I was done surviving. I wanted to live again.

For years, silence had been my safety. I learned young that it was easier to smile, comply, and push through than to ask for help or admit I was breaking. That silence followed me into adulthood—

into my marriage, into motherhood, into every room where I showed up polished and put-together while quietly unraveling inside.

But here's the thing about silence: eventually, it cracks.

That day in my car was one of those cracks. My body was screaming, my spirit was crumbling, and the truth I had buried for so long could no longer be contained. Something in me whispered, *Enough. No more shrinking. No more disappearing. No more silence.*

I didn't know it then, but that was the moment my voice began to return.

Rising Through Fire

For a long time, I thought confidence meant volume. I believed the women who had it walked into rooms effortlessly, with polished smiles and unshakable poise. I didn't realize confidence could be quiet. That sometimes, confidence begins in the smallest whisper—*I matter. I'm still here.*

The truth is, my journey back to my voice wasn't dramatic. It didn't happen overnight. It happened in tiny moments that, at the time, felt insignificant. Standing in front of the mirror and daring to look myself in the eye. Taking a walk when my body screamed to stay on the couch. Choosing to nourish myself instead of punishing myself. Whispering prayers when the shame was so heavy I could hardly breathe.

Little by little, those whispers grew louder.

And then came the fire.

The fire of loss. The fire of chronic illness. The fire of grief that nearly consumed me. For years, I thought the flames meant destruction. Now I know they meant transformation.

Like the phoenix that has become my symbol, I didn't rise *in spite of* the fire—I rose *because of it.*

That rising wasn't about becoming someone new. It was about reclaiming the woman I had always been, buried beneath silence, survival, and shame.

And here's the part I want every woman to hear: The same fire that tried to take you out can become the very spark that ignites your voice.

The Invitation

Maybe your story looks different than mine. Maybe it's not illness or caregiving or grief that has silenced you, but something else—a broken dream, a relationship that left scars, or the weight of always being "the strong one."

Whatever the reason, I want you to know this: Silence is not your ending.

Your voice is still inside you, waiting to be released. It doesn't matter how many years you've been quiet, how heavy the shame feels, or how far gone you think you are. You are not broken—you are awakening.

Confidence doesn't begin when you have all the answers. It begins the moment you decide to stop disappearing. Power isn't found in being perfect. It's found in telling the truth.

Your fire hasn't destroyed you. It has refined you.

And now, it's your turn to rise.

Your story matters. Your voice matters. *You* matter.

A Step to Begin

If you've been quiet for so long that you don't know where to start, let me give you one small step.

Tonight, stand in front of a mirror. Not to judge your reflection. Not to pick apart what you see. But to *see yourself.*

Look into your own eyes and speak these words out loud:
"I am still here. My voice matters. I am worth being heard."

Say it once. Then again. Say it until the words stop feeling like a stranger's and start sinking into your soul.

If writing is more comfortable, take a journal and finish this sentence:

The truth I've been too afraid to say is...

Don't edit it. Don't polish it. Just let your voice flow onto the page.

Your confidence won't come all at once. But every time you practice truth—in the mirror, on the page, in a whisper—you reclaim a little more of yourself.

Generational & Faith-Rooted Impact

When I found my voice again, I thought it was only for me. What I didn't realize was how much it would ripple out.

My children began to see a mother who didn't just survive but lived with intention. They watched me choose health, speak honestly, and set boundaries I never had before. And in doing so, they learned that they, too, were allowed to take up space—that their voices mattered just as much as mine.

My clients, many of whom have carried the same lies of not being enough, now see that healing isn't theory for me. It's testimony. Every time I share my story, I give them permission to believe that change is possible for them too.

And for every woman who hears or reads these words, I want you to know this: Your healing is never just your own. When you rise, others rise with you. Your courage creates room for their courage. Your freedom becomes a map for someone else.

This is the beauty of God's design—that nothing we walk through is wasted. The verse that once cracked open hope in me, Jeremiah 29:11, still whispers truth: *"For I know the plans I have for you," declares the Lord, "plans to prosper you and not to harm you, plans to give you hope and a future."*

I clung to that promise in the dark. And now, standing on the other side of the fire, I see that God was faithful all along. My story, my voice, my rising—none of it was accidental. It was preparation for the women I was called to serve.

I stand here today not as a woman still buried in silence, but as someone who has shed 150 pounds, healed chronic pain that once kept me from climbing stairs, and rebuilt an identity rooted in truth. I became a certified coach, launched a podcast, and now speak on stages I once would have hidden from. None of these things happened overnight. They were the fruit of choosing, again and again, to believe that change was possible even when the lie screamed louder than the truth. If transformation was possible for me, it is possible for you, too.

* * *

I used to believe my silence was strength. I thought disappearing made me dependable, that shrinking myself made me lovable, and that sacrificing my needs made me worthy. But silence is not strength. It is surrender. And the day I decided to speak, to reclaim my body and my truth, was the day I finally came alive.

Your story may be different from mine, but the truth is the same: Your voice carries power. Not the polished version. Not the one wrapped in perfection or performance. The real one—the voice that has walked through fire, the one that trembles but still speaks, the one that refuses to be buried any longer.

When women unleash their voices, generations shift. Families heal. Chains break. Dreams awaken.

So let this be your moment. Step out of the silence. Speak your truth. Unleash your voice.

Because the world doesn't just need another story.
The world needs *yours.*

Carol Salvadori

Founder and CEO of LeadLoud Academy

https://www.leadloudacademy.com/

Carol Salvadori is the founder of LeadLoud Academy, a global platform dedicated to helping women speak with impact, lead with authority, and shape change in an AI-powered world. As a coach, speaker, and multi-book author, Carol has guided women from boardrooms to stages to everyday conversations where their voices needed to be heard. Her signature approach blends practical communication strategies with the kind of deep, inner confidence that transforms not just a career but a life. Her mission is clear: to ensure no woman ever feels she has to shrink herself to fit in. Carol believes that when one woman owns her voice, she creates space for countless others to do the same. Based in Brisbane, Australia, Carol draws daily inspiration from her daughter Lilli, who reminds her that the legacy of a loud, confident voice is one of the greatest gifts we can pass on to the next generation.

The Voice That Changes Rooms: From Silence to Spotlight

By Carol Salvadori

A woman's voice can change a room but only if she's brave enough to use it. I learned this the hard way.

The first time I realized a room could change because of my voice, I almost didn't speak. I was sitting at the end of a long table, surrounded by people older, louder, and more certain than I felt. My hands were clasped under the table, knuckles tight, my heart pounding so loudly I was sure someone could hear it. The conversation was moving quickly, opinions flying like arrows, and every instinct told me to stay quiet, to let the moment pass. But then, from somewhere deep in me, came a question: If I don't speak now, what am I teaching my daughter? That day, in that room, I learned that my silence would teach her far more than my words ever could and I wasn't willing to let the lesson be that her thoughts didn't matter.

I opened my mouth. It was not a speech, just a sentence. But the moment the words left my lips, something shifted. The energy in the room stilled. Heads turned. Eyes locked on me. And for the first time, I understood. voice, when rooted in conviction, doesn't just fill space. It commands it. It wasn't just the content of what I said, it was the presence behind it. The unshakable decision to be heard.

Every woman knows that moment. The one where you feel the words rising, only to swallow them back down. Maybe it's in a meeting where your idea is overlooked or a conversation where speaking your truth feels dangerous. We've all been there. But here's the truth I wish I'd known earlier: Every time we hold back, we teach the world how to treat our voice.

The truth is, I wasn't always this way. For years, my voice lived in the shadows of other people's confidence. I let opportunities slip past because I feared judgement. I played small in conversations that mattered. I told myself I was protecting harmony, but really, I was protecting myself from discomfort. And like so many women, I mistook silence for safety, not realizing that silence can be its own kind of danger.

But silence has a cost. It cost me opportunities I didn't take, ideas that went unheard, and the deep, unshakable belief that my voice mattered. Breaking that cycle wasn't easy. It took heartbreak, resilience, and a fierce promise to my daughter that we would never live small again. That promise became the compass that has guided me ever since.

The First Ripple: How My Voice Changed the Room

Not long after that first moment at the table, I found myself in another room, different people, different stakes, but the same flicker of hesitation before I spoke. This time it was a community meeting about a decision that would impact dozens of families. I wasn't the most experienced person there. I wasn't the one with the title or the years of influence. But I was the one with a perspective no one else had voiced, and I could feel the weight of that truth pressing on me.

I took a breath and spoke clearly, steadily, without rushing. At first, it felt like my words were suspended in the air, waiting for approval. But then something shifted. The tone of the conversation softened, the interruptions stopped, and people began to truly listen. It wasn't magic. I didn't suddenly have all the answers. But in that moment, my presence changed the temperature of the room. It went from noise to focus, from competing voices to one clear point of connection. The impact wasn't just in the decision that followed. It was in the way people started turning towards me when they spoke, signalling that my voice had earned its place.

That was when I understood: A woman's voice can change a room not because she's the loudest, but because she's anchored in purpose. When you speak with that kind of grounding, it resonates long after the words are gone.

The Anatomy of a Voice That Changes Rooms

Over the years, I learned that this ability isn't an accident. It's a skill every woman can develop, and it's made up of five key elements:

- **Intention**. Know why you're speaking before you open your mouth. Words land differently when they're rooted in clarity. Ask yourself: What do I want this room to think, feel, or do after I speak?
- **Presence**. Your posture, stillness, and eye contact signal confidence before a single word is spoken. Walk into a room as though you already belong there because you do.
- **Tone & Pacing**. Speak like you expect to be listened to, not like you're asking for permission. Use pauses to let your words breathe and to give your audience space to absorb your message.
- **Storytelling**. People remember stories, not bullet points. Anchor your message in emotion, using real-life examples that allow others to see themselves in your words.
- **Courage**. The willingness to be uncomfortable for the sake of truth is the mark of a real leader. Speak even when your voice shakes. That's often when it matters most.

When you master these elements, you don't just contribute to the conversation. You influence it. You stop competing for airtime and start commanding attention. The most powerful voices in history are rarely the ones that spoke the most, but the ones that spoke with unshakable conviction.

From My Voice to Yours

The beauty of this is that it's not just for leaders, speakers, or women in the public eye. It is for every woman who walks into a room, whether it is a boardroom, kitchen, classroom or courtroom, and chooses to own her presence. Owning your voice doesn't always mean making grand speeches. Sometimes it's saying 'no' when it's easier to say 'yes.' Sometimes it's sharing your idea even when you're not sure how it will be received. Sometimes it's asking the question no one else is brave enough to ask.

When you speak with intention, presence, tone, story, and courage, you don't just get heard. You change what happens next. And when one woman changes a room, she changes the rooms she'll walk into for the rest of her life and paves the way for others to do the same. That's the ripple effect of a voice that is fully owned. It creates waves in places you may never even see.

The Legacy of a Voice Unleashed

When I look back now, I see every moment of silence as a stepping stone, not a failure, but a necessary pause before the rise. Without those years of holding back, I wouldn't understand the liberation that comes from speaking forward. Without the rooms where I felt invisible, I wouldn't know the profound shift that happens when you make yourself seen.

And here's what I've learned: Your voice is not just for you. It's for the women who are watching, the ones still unsure if their words will matter. It's for the daughters who learn from how we stand, speak, and hold our space. It's for the women who have yet to step into their first room of power and need to know it's possible to be both kind and commanding, humble and unshakably sure.

When you unleash your voice, you don't just change your own life. You alter the landscape for every woman who comes after you. Every conversation, every meeting, every stage becomes a platform for possibility. This is how revolutions begin, not always with a roar, but often with one steady, unflinching voice that refuses to be silenced.

So here is my invitation to you: Walk into your next room with intention. Stand in your presence. Tell the story only you can tell. And speak not because you are fearless, but because you refuse to let fear have the final word.

This is my truth: I will not wait for permission to speak. I will take up space, tell my story, and own my presence. I will be the voice that changes rooms, and I will leave them better than I found them.

The world is full of rooms waiting for the voice that will shift their course. And maybe, just maybe, that voice is yours.

Kimberly Seabrooks

Kim's Health Coaching
Certified Health Coach

https://www.linkedin.com/in/kimberly-seabrooks-90086631/
https://www.facebook.com/kimberly.seabrooks
https://www.instagram.com/kimberlyseabroo/
https://procoach.app/kimberly-seabrooks-2@whatsnewwithkim

Kimberly SeabrooksKim's Health CoachKimberly Seabrooks is a Certified Health Coach, Quality Assurance Specialist, and passionate advocate for holistic well-being. With a Bachelor's Degree in Business and nearly five years of experience as a health coach, Kimberly has dedicated her career to empowering individuals—particularly women in their 40s and 50s—to navigate the challenges of aging with grace, vitality, and resilience. As the founder of Kim's Health Coaching, Kimberly combines her professional expertise with a compassionate, client-centered approach. Recognizing the unique challenges that midlife brings, she has developed strategies to help women manage hormonal shifts, menopause, and other transitions with confidence. In addition to her coaching practice, Kimberly is a published author, contributing to anthologies like Resilient: The Power to Get Back Up and Becoming an Unstoppable Woman in Health & Wellness Part 2.

Through her writing, YouTube channel, and one-on-one coaching, Kimberly inspires people to take control of their health journeys and live fulfilling lives.

The Courage to Be Heard

By Kimberly Seabrooks

The Silence That Shaped Me

For years, my voice was hidden beneath layers of silence, shame, and fear. As a child, my words were stolen before they even had a chance to form. Abuse silenced me, trauma taught me to shrink, and society reinforced the lie that a "good girl" should stay quiet and not ruffle feathers.

But here's the truth I've learned through the pain, the therapy, the tears, the prayers, and the triumphs: When a woman unleashes her voice, she unleashes her power. And once that power is awakened, nothing—and no one—can stop her.

This chapter is not just my story; it's an invitation to every woman reading these words. Your story, your truth, your voice—it matters. And when you unlock it, you don't just transform your own life; you light a path for generations of women to come.

Why Women Lose Their Voices

Women are born with powerful voices. Think about the cry of a newborn girl—loud, unapologetic, demanding to be heard. But somewhere along the way, many of us are taught to dim our volume.

We're told to:

- "Be nice."
- "Don't be too emotional."
- "Stay in your place."
- "Don't make people uncomfortable."

These subtle (and sometimes not-so-subtle) messages condition us to shrink. Some of us were silenced by abuse, some by rejection, some by workplaces that valued compliance over creativity, and others by families that couldn't handle the weight of our truth.

But here's the thing: Silence is not our natural state. Speaking, sharing, and declaring who we are—that is our birthright.

Finding My Voice Again

For me, regaining my voice started with a whisper. In therapy sessions where my truth spilled out for the first time. In late-night journal entries where I wrote the words I could never say out loud. In prayers where I asked God, "Why me? And how do I move forward?"

Each time I spoke—even in secret—I took back a piece of myself. And the more I spoke, the louder my voice became. Eventually, I realized that my silence had never protected me; it only imprisoned me. My voice, on the other hand, was the key to my freedom.

The Power of Owning Your Story

Here's what I know now: When a woman tells her story, she not only heals herself, she heals others.

I remember the first time I shared openly about my abuse. I was terrified. My heart raced, my hands shook, and I almost backed out. But after I spoke, women came up to me in tears, whispering, "That happened to me, too."

In that moment, I understood something profound: Our stories are not just for us. They are survival guides for the women walking behind us. When we unleash our voices, we break generational chains. We create new possibilities. We show other women that they are not alone, not crazy, and not powerless.

Steps to Unlock Your Voice

If you are reading this and wondering how to begin, here are steps that helped me, and I believe they can help you too:

1. Acknowledge Your Truth

Stop minimizing what you've been through. Your pain is real. Your experiences are valid. Healing begins the moment you stop dismissing your own story.

2. Find Safe Spaces

Not every room deserves your story. Start small. Write in your journal. Share with a trusted friend, mentor, or therapist. Safe spaces allow your voice to stretch without fear.

3. Challenge the Lies

Silence is fueled by lies: "No one will believe me." "It's my fault." "I'm too much." Replace them with truths: "My story matters." "I am worthy of being heard." "I am not too much. I am enough."

4. Practice Speaking Out

Confidence is built through practice. Say no when you mean no. Speak up in meetings. Share your opinion without apologizing. Every small act of courage builds a louder, stronger voice.

5. Turn Pain into Power

Your story does not define you as a victim—it defines you as a survivor, a thriver, a warrior. The very thing that was meant to silence you can become the source of your power.

When Women Speak, the World Shifts

History proves it: Women's voices spark revolutions. From Rosa Parks refusing to give up her seat, to Malala Yousafzai demanding education, to everyday women like you and me raising children, leading businesses, writing books, and running communities—our voices matter.

And here's something I've witnessed firsthand: When one woman finds her voice, it creates a ripple effect. Her daughter learns to speak boldly. Her friends start telling their truths. Her community grows stronger. Her workplace becomes more inclusive. Her marriage becomes more authentic.

The world is literally waiting for your voice.

The Lies That Keep Us Quiet

Even as we step into our power, old lies linger. Let's call them out:

- **"I don't want to be a burden."**
  Speaking your truth is not a burden—it's a blessing.
- **"No one will listen."**
  Your voice may not be for everyone, but it will always be for someone.
- **"It's safer to stay quiet."**
  Silence might feel safe, but it keeps you stuck. Growth and freedom live on the other side of speaking up.

My Turning Point

There was a day when I realized my silence was costing me too much. I was living small, playing safe, and letting fear dictate my choices. But deep down, I knew God had given me a purpose that required my full voice.

So I made a decision: I would no longer whisper. I would no longer water down my truth. I would no longer apologize for existing.

The first time I spoke boldly, it felt like fire leaving my chest. Scary, yes—but also freeing. I had finally given myself permission to be fully me. And I haven't looked back since.

Unleashing HER Voice—Together

Sister, I want you to know something: You don't have to do this alone. Part of unleashing your voice is surrounding yourself with women who remind you of your worth, who push you to speak louder, and who clap the loudest when you do.

That's why movements matter. Communities matter. Books like this matter. Because when women gather, we amplify each other's voices.

A Future of Bold Voices

Imagine a world where every woman feels free to speak. A world where girls grow up knowing that their voices can move mountains. A world where silence is no longer a survival strategy, but boldness is the norm.

That's the world we're building. And it begins with you.

A Prayer for the Woman Reading This

I pray you find the courage to speak. I pray your voice grows stronger every time you use it. I pray you no longer shrink, no longer apologize, and no longer hide.

I pray you remember that your voice is a gift from God—not just for you, but for everyone who needs the hope your story carries.

Final Word: Speak Anyway

Even if your voice shakes—speak.
Even if people doubt you—speak.
Even if you've been silenced before—speak.
Even if you're scared—speak.

Because your voice has the power to unlock your freedom, inspire another woman's healing, and change the world.

Sister, it's time.

It's time to **UnleashHER Voice.**

Glen Alex

LCSW, Author, Podcast Host, Marquis Who's Who, Wellth Counselor, Mental Health Educator of the Year 2025 (USA)

https://www.linkedin.com/in/glenalex
https://www.facebook.com/livingintotalhealth
https://www.instagram.com/glen_alex/
https://glenalex.com/
https://www.youtube.com/@LivingInTotalHealthGlenAlex

Glen Alex's life's work is about health, with careers in social work, writing, charity, therapeutic massage, and tennis. Her transformative mission is to help others be joyful, connected, confident, and complete, the life experience she calls Wellth, which is health + other riches. Glen's journey in health began with boundaries. So engaged in childhood by the nuance of interaction, she saw when people smiled, cringed, and when pain crossed their faces. Glen clearly remembers vowing to not be the one to cause another person pain, unnecessarily. She saw boundaries respected and boundaries violated, and it stuck. From there, Glen's work expanded to other areas of health and she developed a unique, no-nonsense approach to help others lead their healthiest, most joyful life. Glen Alex is Author of award-winning Living In Total Health, Licensed Clinical Social Worker, Speaker, Licensed Massage Therapist, Marquis Who's Who Inductee, The Glen Alex Show Podcast Host.

Voice is Power

By Glen Alex

For me, unleashing my voice is about healthy boundaries, which involve authentic self-expression and self-advocacy. As I described in my five-time award-winning book, *Living in Total Health,* boundaries are the innate alarm system we humans have that is monitored by our intuition 24 hours a day, 7 days a week. Intuition alerts us when we are in physical, mental, emotional, or spiritual danger through physical sensations and/or a sense of *knowing*.

My understanding and appreciation of healthy boundaries began in childhood. As the youngest of 10 children, I had ample opportunity to witness family and friends interact. I was so engaged by the nuance of their interactions. I saw when people smiled, cringed, and when pain crossed their faces. I clearly remember vowing to not be the one to cause another person pain unnecessarily, aside from self-defense. I saw boundaries respected and boundaries violated in real time, and it stuck.

I realized early on that living my healthiest and most joyful life requires me to speak and enforce my boundaries, using my voice backed up by my choices and actions. Thus, the unleashing of my voice has not been nor is now a one-off. Rather, it has been a gradual expansion of expressing my Truth. I'll share a few significant moments in my life when I unleashed my voice.

I first unleashed my voice at age 12. Growing up as the youngest of 10, I was a shy, quiet child and had many role models to learn from. In my mind, I committed to the behaviors I wanted to emulate and rejected the hurtful ones, even though at the time I didn't consciously know about boundaries specifically.

I was also a responsible kid who did what my parents said to do and I had a good sense of right and wrong. Thus, I was appointed babysitter.

My summers from ages 12 to 14 were all about caring for my nieces and nephews, the children of my older siblings. They were good kids overall, although they displayed the usual wants and defiance of children. I unleashed my 'mother voice,' which appeared out of nowhere when any one of them disobeyed me or acted out. My voice was clear, serious, firm, and intentional.

I witnessed mothers in stores, in the park, and even during my family's social events scream and yell and repeat themselves and threaten their children in order to get them to obey. Intuitively, I understood that there had to be a better way to teach cooperation to kids. Thus, my first act of setting boundaries, which I recall was a verbal one, was with my nieces and nephews. And my vocal sincerity garnered their attention enough to comply. While I didn't threaten to spank them, my voice communicated that their behavior was unacceptable. Consequently, they capitulated.

When I turned 15 and entered the 10th grade, I developed interest in extracurricular activities in high school. So that summer, I wanted to engage in those opportunities. My siblings had other priorities, however, that included my continuing to babysit for them for free. And when they informed me that their children would be on school break for the summer and asked me to confirm a start date to babysit, I mustered the courage to say "no"—the second unleashing of my voice.

I said *no* to free babysitting every day and *no* to my siblings deciding how I would commit my time and energy. As the shy, quiet child in the family, my speaking up with such conviction was so foreign to my siblings that my oldest sister dubbed me "Space Baby." Looking back, I suppose it did seem to her as if I was abducted by aliens, experimented on, and returned a different person. Even so, I welcomed the new nickname and silently wore it as a badge of empowerment.

In my early 20s, I was with a man in whom I had a romantic interest. We talked and laughed, then kissed. His hands grew more and more exploratory, and honestly, I enjoyed it to a point. However, it was not right for me to go further with him, not then and not there. I took hold of his hands and said, *"I don't wanna have sex."* Naturally, he attempted to persuade me to give in to his charms. I repeated myself once and withdrew my energy from him. He then drove me home.

It didn't occur to me then that he wouldn't like or be interested in me after that. Quite frankly, I didn't care because I was clear that I did not want to have sex with him at that time.

Five years into my first marriage, I realized that we were in trouble. The ex and I then went to marriage counseling and identified areas for improvement, individually and as a couple. Well, 6 years later and after a move to a new state where he and I had the opportunity to truly start over without family, friends, or other distractions, our relationship got worse. He became more distant emotionally and physically.

The loneliness I experienced in that marriage was unbearable for me. So after a good deal of self-reflection, I gained the understanding that as much as I didn't want to be a divorce statistic, I was diminishing and suffocating in that relationship. Being single again and enduring the inherent challenges represented more hope to me than remaining in my empty marriage. Thus, instead of having an affair for attention and false validation or indulging in food and/or alcohol to cope with the loneliness or ignoring my inner wisdom, I said *yes* to divorce.

After separating from my ex-husband, I moved to Las Vegas, Nevada. Once there, I was drawn to hemodialysis, which was open to me as a Social Worker. And as a Licensed Clinical Social Worker, I had a deeper understanding of human nature and psychological issues than Licensed Social Workers did, and more experience dealing with these issues. After 8 years of experience, my 3rd supervisor with one company, who was a former dialysis nurse, did not appreciate my approach to patients who presented problems in the clinic and with following doctor's orders.

After I intervened with a patient who was verbally abusing a nurse caring for her with my direct, no-non-sense approach, the supervisor basically reprimanded me for not being "soft" or "caring" enough to "empathize" with the patient. Her idea was that social workers are *touchy-feely* and sympathetic and don't challenge patient behaviors. I disagreed with her and continued with my approach. And by all accounts, patients in my clinic were less likely to act out during treatment and negatively impact the 30 or so other patients and staff members.

In another situation, the shift charge nurse complained that I wasn't attentive enough to a patient who was distressed. So, this supervisor met with me and her assistant to advise me about how to provide social work in a dialysis clinic. Again, I unleashed my voice.

This time, I clearly informed the supervisor that the nurse who complained about me allowed the patient in question to bring vodka in a travel mug into the clinic, and the patient refused to speak with me. I further explained that appropriate boundaries are required for the health and safety of everyone and that respecting the patient's declining to speak with me was the proper way for me to respond to the situation.

The supervisor later admitted to me that they gained a better understanding of boundaries and acknowledged the nurse's responsibility in allowing the patient to bring alcohol into the clinic, a licensed medical facility.

Throughout the years, I have chosen to unleash my voice with silence. There were a few people who were blatantly disrespectful to me. One of those individuals was a female relative who suddenly accused me of being mean to her. She loudly blurted out this accusation at a family function while I spoke with another attendee.

As I managed my anger that was triggered by this relative's boundary violation, another relative jumped between us and played peacemaker.

I calmly asked the relative what I did to offend her. She rambled a bit and then alleged that I said *xyz* and hurt her feelings. I took a deep breath and said, *"I don't speak like that."* This relative continued with her rant. So I detached from the situation and literally did not utter another sound to her. She then walked away.

The unleashing of my voice at age 12 has served me well in my life in affirming and setting healthy boundaries. From discovering my 'mother voice' with nieces and nephews, to first saying "no" to unlimited babysitting, to standing my ground against a relative's accusation, the power of my voice is evident. And my voice continues to communicate my personal Truth, enable me to self-advocate, and most importantly, protect my boundaries. Utilizing the power of my voice is an ongoing, proactive process, which is followed up with my congruent behavior. Health and wellness require effective self-expression, self-advocacy, constant diligence, monitoring of my boundaries, and unleashing of my voice.

Wendy Raven Johnson

Founder of Designed To Be HER

https://www.facebook.com/raven77143
https://www.instagram.com/wendyravenjohnson
https://designedtobeher.com/
https://designedtobeher.com/report

Wendy Johnson (Raven) is the founder of Designed to Be HER™, a soul-led space for high-achieving women who look successful on the outside but feel disconnected on the inside. A Registered Nurse with a background in corporate leadership, she brings clinical insight and soulful strategy to helping women see themselves clearly—often for the first time. She uses Human Design as the most precise method to make the invisible undeniable—bridging the seen and the unseen. Wendy doesn't fix identities—she unravels the lies they were built on. Her work helps women decode their true energetic blueprint, release outdated roles and rules, and remember who they've always been. She serves as a mirror for the woman who's done performing, pleasing, or pretending—and is finally ready to lead, speak, and live from the truth of who she is. This isn't reinvention. It's remembrance. She is HER.

Lost Her. Found Her. Became HER.

By Wendy Raven Johnson

"Your voice was never lost—just buried beneath who you thought you had to be." —Wendy "Raven" Johnson

The Cost of Being the "Good Girl"

I used to think my voice didn't matter.

Not because someone told me to be quiet.
But because the world gave me gold stars for staying small.

For being easy to be around.
For not making waves.
For being the "good girl" who didn't ask for too much, need too much, or feel too much.

I was praised for being accommodating.
Applauded for being selfless.
Celebrated for how well I kept things together.

And I confused that with being strong.

But behind the smiles and thank-yous, there was a silence I carried like armor.
A silence that protected everyone else's comfort... at the expense of my own truth.

And I wore it well.

I got good at saying "I'm fine" when I wasn't.
At making peace when I was actually heartbroken.
At biting my tongue even when everything inside me was screaming to be heard.

That silence didn't come from weakness. It came from survival.

But eventually, the cost got too high.
And I had to choose: keep being who everyone needed me to be—or finally become who I was always meant to be.

How I Found My Voice

I found my voice when my mother passed away.

It wasn't planned. It wasn't pretty. It was just necessary.

I had a grieving father and a 4-year-old daughter who needed me. Something in me rose—not a roar, but a steady strength. A knowing. A quiet, unwavering sense of *we're doing this.* That moment pulled something out of me that I didn't even realize I had buried: **my voice**.

It was the kind of voice that just *knew* what had to be done.

But many years later, I lost it again.

And this time... I didn't see it happening.

I silenced myself, little by little, in a relationship where keeping the peace meant betraying myself. I stopped asking for what I needed. I walked on eggshells to avoid rocking the boat. I thought if I could just love harder, try more, and be "better," things would be okay.

But things weren't okay.

And neither was I.

I was disappearing—and the worst part was, no one even noticed.

Because I had trained them not to.

And here's what I know now:

If you have to lose yourself to keep someone, you're not actually being kept—you're being caged.

The Truth About "Finding Your Voice"

People love to glamorize it—**"finding your voice."**
Like it's some big dramatic movie moment.
You stand up, shout your truth, and suddenly everything clicks.
You feel powerful, untouchable. Free.

But in real life?

It's messier than that.
It's quieter. Slower.
More raw than anyone warns you.

It doesn't feel like fireworks.
It feels like your heart racing as you type a message you're terrified to send.
It feels like your throat tightening when you finally say, *"I don't agree with that."*

It looks like whispering *"I'm not okay"* and wondering if that makes you too much.

It looks like rehearsing your boundaries in your head 10 times before saying them out loud.

Finding your voice isn't a moment—it's a **return**.
To your truth. To your needs. To your *knowing.*

It's not just about the words you speak.
It's about the *permission* you give yourself to exist fully even when it's inconvenient. Even when it's uncomfortable.

Because somewhere along the line, you learned to be likable instead of honest.
Polished instead of powerful.
And that survival strategy? It worked until it didn't.

Finding your voice is how you start undoing that.

And it rarely happens all at once.
It's not one breakthrough. It's a thousand tiny moments.
Each one a soft rebellion.

Each time you choose yourself, even when your voice shakes,
You're not just speaking.
You're remembering who you are.

Why I Went Quiet (And How I Came Back)

There's a part of my Human Design that makes me deeply attuned to emotions especially in relationships.

I can feel what's not being said.
I sense tension before it's acknowledged.
I read the room before anyone else even notices the shift.

It's like I've always had an internal tuning fork for other people's emotions which meant I became really good at adjusting myself to keep things calm.

So I held things in.
Not because I didn't know what I felt... but because I could feel what *they* felt too and it felt safer to make space for *them* than speak up for *me.*

I thought that was strength. I thought if I could be the calm one, the understanding one, the "easy" one, everything would be okay.

But here's what no one tells you:

Absorbing discomfort doesn't dissolve it. It just buries it deeper inside you.

And over time, I wasn't just managing emotions. I was erasing myself.

All in the name of keeping the peace.

But peace that comes at the cost of your truth?

That's not peace.
That's **performance**.

And I was done performing.

When I discovered Human Design, I wasn't only looking for answers—I was looking for a mirror, something that could reflect back the truth I'd buried. And that's what I found.

I learned I wasn't too much.
I wasn't too emotional.
I wasn't broken.
I was built for depth.
Wired for honesty.
Made to feel things deeply and speak them clearly.

Human Design didn't just help me "understand" myself.
It helped me **forgive** myself—for all the times I stayed silent to keep others comfortable.
For all the years I edited myself to fit the room.
For all the times I prioritized peace over my truth.

And little by little, I started coming back to my voice.
Not the one others expected.
Not the one I thought I "should" use.
But the one that was *mine* all along.

The one that just needed to be heard—by *me* first.

Your Voice Doesn't Need Permission

For some of us, reclaiming our voice looks like softness. Stillness. Precision. Speaking one true sentence and letting it stand.

If you've ever felt like the world only knows the edited version of you—the palatable, polished, easy version—I want you to know:

You can stop performing.

Your voice is not gone.
It's just waiting for you to let it be heard.

If you've spent years silencing yourself to be accepted, I want you to hear me:

There is nothing wrong with you.

You don't have to shout to be powerful.

You don't have to be fearless to be free.

You just have to be willing to tell yourself the truth.

That's where it starts.

This Is How You Unleash HER

You don't need a perfect plan. You just need to begin. Right here. Right now.

1. **Check your inner dialogue.**
   Are you speaking kindly to yourself? Or are you silencing yourself before others even get the chance? Start noticing.

2. **Feel before you filter.**
   Truth isn't always neat or convenient. Let yourself feel it anyway.

3. **Use your body as your compass.**
   If your throat tightens or your chest contracts, that's not drama—that's data. Listen.

4. **Speak even if you're shaking.**
   Clarity will meet you on the other side of courage.

5. **Start small, but start.**
   Say what's true. Say it out loud. To the mirror. To a journal. To someone safe. Let your voice practice being heard.

Your Voice Is a Portal—Not Just for You, But for Others

I use my voice today because silence is too heavy to carry.

I speak because I remember what it felt like to silence it and disappear.

To sit at dinner tables and feel invisible.
To lie next to someone and still feel alone.
To smile in photos while screaming on the inside.

And I now help other women do the same.
Using Human Design, I support women in unlocking the voice that was always there—buried under expectation, survival, and silence.

This isn't about becoming someone new.
It's about *remembering the version of you that never needed to be fixed.*

Unperformed. Unmuted. Unmistakably HER.

This isn't just a tagline.

It's the mission I live by and the invitation I'm passing to you.

I don't do this work because I've always known how to use my voice.
I do it because I know what it's like to hold it in.

To say the "right" thing while suppressing the *true* thing.
To keep everything running smoothly—by staying silent.

I know what it's like to show up for everyone but yourself.
To keep the peace, even when it costs you your power.

But I also know what it's like to come back—to remember.
To feel your voice rise again–to be stronger, wiser, and clearer than ever before.

To speak.

To rise.

So if you're ready to stop performing, stop shrinking, and start speaking with the kind of honesty that sets you free—

Let this be your moment.

Because it won't just be your voice that returns.

It'll be your clarity.
Your power.
Your presence.
And most of all... it'll be **HER.**

The part of you that was never broken—just buried.

And now?

Unleash HER voice.

Unperformed. Unmuted. Unmistakably HER.

Raven
xoxo

Anne-Marie Springer

CEO of Wise Moose Grinds

www.linkedin.com/in/anne-marie-springer-52958143
https://www.facebook.com/annemarie.springer98
https://wisemoosegrinds.com

Anne-Marie Springer is a retired Navy nurse, author, and entrepreneur whose life's work centers on compassion, resilience, and bold empowerment. With over 40 years of federal service, she began her nursing career in the U.S. Navy in 1984 and earned her BSN from the University of South Florida. After serving in diverse medical units, she transitioned to population health nursing, focusing on preventive care for families until retiring from the Veterans Health Administration in 2024. Anne-Marie is the author of Help, My Baby Won't Stop Crying: A Simple Guide for New Parents, and co-author of Becoming an Unstoppable Woman Entrepreneur II and She Defies: Powerful Stories of Overcoming. She leads Wise Moose Grinds, an online coffee brand, and co-owns Magic Gavel Auctions. A passionate mentor, Anne-Marie strives to inspire women to discover confidence and purpose through mindset and leadership development. She lives in Ohio with her husband and two dogs.

Scrubs, Duty, and the Making of a Leader

By Anne-Marie Springer

The Quiet Beginnings of Confidence

I didn't always recognize the woman in the mirror as a leader. In the early days of my military career, I often second-guessed my life choices. I entered the Navy as a junior enlisted member. I spent many hours peeling potatoes, scrubbing floors, and studying protocols—the true epitome of reaching for my highest potential from the ground up.

Confidence, for me, was forged in the first 12 years of my naval service. It grew quietly, like roots beneath the surface, nourished by every physical and mental challenge I faced and every test I passed. I used this confidence to follow my dream of a career in medicine, becoming a leader and a naval officer.

Have you ever looked in the mirror and wondered if the person staring back was ready to lead?

Developing and embracing confidence will elevate your leadership skills to their highest potential. Confidence rooted in authenticity becomes the gateway to meaningful influence.

Scrubs and Service

The first time I wore scrubs, I felt both exposed and empowered. They weren't just a uniform but a symbol of responsibility, of care, of healing. They reminded me how far I had come from those early days in boot camp, when I questioned whether I belonged in the military at all.

Wearing scrubs taught me humility, and reminded me that leadership isn't about titles, it's about service. I learned to listen deeply to patients, to advocate for their needs, and to navigate the delicate balance between clinical precision and human compassion.

One night on the surgical ward, a sailor arrived after a traumatic accident. His family was far away and his condition uncertain. As I stayed by his side, caring for him, I realized I wasn't just his nurse; I was his lifeline.

Leadership often begins when no one is watching, guided only by the heart. As Oprah Winfrey once said, "I was once afraid of people saying, 'Who does she think she is?" Now I have the courage to stand and say, This is who I am."

Duty and Discipline

In the military, duty is more than a concept, it's a code. It means showing up, even when you're exhausted, and that happens on most shifts. It means making decisions that affect lives and holding yourself to a standard that others rely on. I learned to lead teams, manage crises, and mentor younger nurses and sailors.

One of my most transformative experiences came during a humanitarian mission overseas. My unit was tasked with providing medical care in a remote village in Vietnam, where resources were limited. The conditions were challenging, the needs overwhelming, and I watched as those I had trained stepped into leadership roles, improvised solutions, comforted patients, and embodied the very essence of selfless service.

When you lead with authenticity, you empower others to rise. You become a mirror in which they can see their own potential.

The Making of a Leader

Leadership is not a destination, but a transformation that is shaped by every choice you make, every challenge you face, and every moment of doubt and courage you experience. When I became a commissioned naval officer, I underwent a profound identity shift as I stepped into the new role, carrying with me the lessons of my enlisted years: the humility of scrubbing floors, the discipline of duty, and the empathy of nursing.

You don't need to be perfect to be a leader but you do need to be present and have the courage to show up, scars and all. The making of a leader is not about arriving but evolving, embracing your past, honoring your growth, and stepping boldly into your future.

Unlocking Confidence and Power

Confidence is not a switch; it is more like a seed. It grows through experience, reflection, and the quiet victories that often go unnoticed. And power? Power is not dominance; it is influence and the ability to uplift, to inspire, and to create change.

For every woman reading this, I want you to know: Your story matters. Your journey, whether it begins in scrubs, in a classroom, in a boardroom, or at a kitchen table is worthy of leadership. You don't have to wait for permission. You don't have to silence your voice. You are already enough.

It's about unlocking the confidence that's been quietly growing within you all along. Look in the mirror again, and see the woman who has weathered storms, who has shown up, who has dared to dream. She is ready, she is powerful, she is you!

The Power of Permission

There's a moment in every woman's life when she realizes she doesn't need anyone else's permission to rise. That moment for me came in the middle of a deployment, surrounded by chaos, when I made a decision that saved a life and changed mine. We were short-staffed, under pressure, and facing a critical situation with a patient whose condition was deteriorating rapidly. I chose to trust my training, my instincts, and my voice to challenge a dangerous order.

The outcome was positive, but the real victory was internal. I had permitted myself to lead. That's the kind of permission I want every woman to claim. Not just in moments of crisis, but in everyday life. In boardrooms and break rooms. In PTA meetings and policy discussions. In creative pursuits and quiet reflections. You don't need to be granted authority to be powerful. You already are. If you're waiting for a sign, let this be it: You are allowed to take up space, to speak boldly, and to lead.

The Rise of Confidence

Confidence doesn't arrive all at once, it builds over time, shaped by the moments we choose courage over comfort. It grows when we speak up, take risks, and advocate for ourselves and others. I've seen it bloom in women who once doubted themselves: a young nurse finding her voice, a mother launching her dream, and survivors choosing joy.

Confidence isn't arrogance or perfection, it is the quiet knowing that you are capable and worthy. It's walking tall, speaking truth, and leading with grace. And the best part? Confidence is contagious. When you embody it, you light the way for others.

The Stories We Carry

Every woman carries a story, some etched in joy, some etched in sorrow, some whispered, others shouted, and some are still unfolding. Each one of them matters. I've learned that the most powerful leaders are not those with the loudest voices, but those who are willing to share their truth. Vulnerability is not weakness. It is a bridge that connects and heals us and reminds us that we are not alone.

Our stories are sacred and when we share them, we unlock something in others. We give them courage, hope, and a roadmap to follow on their journey. Tell, write, speak, sing, paint, and live your story. Let it be messy and magnificent and all yours.

The Power of Her Circle

No woman rises alone. Behind every confident leader is a circle of mentors, friends, and kindred spirits. I've been blessed with a global sisterhood, women who challenged, comforted, and celebrated me, especially when I forgot my own worth. When women support each other, we become unstoppable. We become the change.

Serena Williams reminds us, *"Every woman's success should be an inspiration to another. We are strongest when we cheer each other on."* Embrace the power of your circle.

The Legacy of Leadership

Leadership isn't about titles or achievements, it's about impact. It's the lives we touch, the voices we help rise, and the stories we dare to share. It's the ripple effect of our choices, courage, and compassion.

I want my legacy to be one of empowerment of women who found their voice because I used mine, of leaders who rose because I reached back, and of stories told because I dared to share mine. I want that for you, too.

Your legacy begins now with every word you speak, every hand you hold, and every risk you take. It's not something you build later; it's something you live today.

Legacy isn't just what we leave behind. It's what we live every day. Lead with love, courage, and intention, and know your legacy is already unfolding.

Closing Reflection: Mirror Moments

So I ask again: Have you ever looked in the mirror and wondered if the person staring back was ready to lead?

If you have, know that leadership doesn't require perfection. It requires presence, purpose, and, most of all, belief in yourself, your story, and your ability to rise. I didn't always recognize the leader in the mirror, but now, I see her clearly, not fearless, but fierce, not flawless but faithful, and she's ready. She doesn't have all the answers, but she's willing to keep asking the right questions.

Look in the mirror and see what I see—radiant power, unwavering confidence, and the divine spark of a woman born to lead with purpose!

Alison Lines

Alison's Soul Image
Coach

https://www.linkedin.com/in/alison-lines-mba
https://www.facebook.com/profile.php?id=100012376906736
https://www.instagram.com/the_datingqueen

Alison Lines is an empowerment coach, mental health advocate, and fashion enthusiast dedicated to helping others embrace their authentic selves. She is the founder of Alison's Soul Image and L&A Luxury Dating Society, two businesses designed to help individuals heal, grow, and connect through style, self-love, and conscious relationships. Passionate about empowering women, Alison volunteers with Dress for Success, where she helps others build confidence and step into their power. An MBA graduate, Alison is an international bestselling author, dynamic speaker, and co-author of Dream to Rise. She is currently pursuing her Trauma-Informed Coaching Certification to deepen her work with clients. Alison is also a proud member of the National Society of Leadership and Success, a sister of Sigma Kappa, and an active participant in the Reading Theater Project, where she expresses her creativity and love for the arts. She inspires others to lead boldly, live beautifully, and love unapologetically.

Finding My Power

By Alison Lines

Lights, Camera, Action. I remember standing there in the center of the stage, thinking to myself, *What am I doing? What will everyone think?* I have never done this before. I feel vulnerable and confident at the same time. Thinking back to that moment in time, it was the first time I showed how truly empowered and confident I was. This was back in high school when I performed for the first time in public at a coffee house with my rendition of "Someone Like You" from Jekyll and Hyde. I was wearing a purple velvet dress, much like royalty, as I stepped onto that stage. The fear was there, but much like everything in life so was the dichotomy of empowerment. Growing up I was the shy girl, but I always loved performing, so on this very special day, I had stepped out of my shell and shocked quite a few people. It was incredible. My shining moment—I didn't know at the time this was only the beginning for me, and over years I would have the same feelings and emotions in other experiences as I did when I first stepped on that stage.

Prior to this shining moment, I had been a woman of self-doubt, lacking in confidence and limited in self-love. I believed, based on others' opinions, mainly my parents, that I was too much. As much as I loved being on the stage and the center of attention, I shied away from it due to fear of not being accepted and judged. My very identity was being shaped by others, not by myself. Your identity, the very thing that makes you unique and becomes your life, is the very thing that people try to take from you. It was an inner battle for me to fight to stay the person I was and not the person everyone expected me to be. This is where empowerment comes into play. I knew that I had a big mission and vision for my life and there was a large gap between who I was and who I wanted to become. A major piece to this transformation for a woman or man is to become empowered in who they are and in everything they do. This is often met with pushback and criticism and many times I have wanted to give up, but I never have because I became empowered and started making some major changes in my life.

Discovery

So, you may say...how does one become empowered when they never were before? It takes a lot of strength, a deep inner dive into yourself and the will to transform both yourself and your life. In my case this included my love of helping others. I have experienced many empowering moments in my life, from me signing on the stage in high school, joining a sorority in college, a domestic violence survivor standing up to my parents, completing my master's degree, owning two businesses, writing a book, being a speaker on an international stage and finally losing the love of my life unexpectedly. These are just some of the pivotal moments in my life that came to fruition because of being empowered.

As an only child, I was thoroughly excited to go to college and be away from home. It was freedom in my mind and I could not wait for this new chapter in my life. I had never thought of being a sorority girl, but I came to love it. It all started when I met a woman after I had tried out for a play for the theater, and the director was in one sorority while another assistant was in a different sorority. I knew I desired a family away from home, but I still was lacking in confidence and power. I understood that I was not too much, but I still feared being judged. The Director was from Alpha Sigma Tau and the assistant was from Sigma Kappa. I was drawn to both of them for different reasons. One thing they had in common was power and confidence and I sought that in my life. Both women wanted me to spend time with their sororities; they saw the power I didn't see in me. They both saw a natural-born leader who just needed some guidance to get there. I remember having such a level of disbelief in the fact that both of these women wanted me in their sororities. Often, I thought to myself, *"What do they see that I don't?"* Each one of them knew I had the potential to be even greater than I already was. They saw my unlimited potential and they each wanted a piece of it. This was another moment of empowerment. I went from not believing in myself to having two sororities fighting over me. Ultimately, I gained power from their interest in me and I became empowered through my journey to becoming a sister. Ultimately, come bid day, I had to decide who I would choose. After spending time with both sororities, I felt drawn to one particular sorority and pledged for them.

Sigma Kappa was my home away from home. I loved my sisters and we had the best times together, with so many beautiful memories shared. As wonderful as Sigma Kappa was, I really had to earn my way to get through pledging. Pledging is a ritual of all sorority and fraternities, I cannot go into details, but it made me strong and it gave me power. I was given leadership positions and tasks that often were quite challenging, not only emotionally but also psychologically. The amount of strength a person needs to complete pledging is quite high. I remember not sleeping, not eating, staying up all night memorizing facts or being out all night doing a sisterly bonding activity. Pledging teaches you that you are much stronger than you believe and that you can achieve anything. During these times, I had to know myself; I had to empower myself to do the things that were necessary to succeed and join the sisterhood and become a sister. There were days when I wanted to cry, and there were moments when I couldn't see myself finishing, but underneath it all, I was never a quitter and no matter what, I would be a Sigma Kappa. Empowerment takes perseverance, resilience, and a strong sense of self, and Sigma Kappa was the catalyst that helped me to grow and develop those skills.

Growth and Development

All leaders experience many trials and tribulations. It's what makes a good leader. At the heart of a good leader is the power to move people and to help them to become better people and have better lives. Empowerment and confidence are at the core of everything. For the longest time I believed that I was not a leader but rather a follower. I had been groomed so to speak that I always felt, whenever I was put into leadership, that I would fail. Well, here is the number one thing that successful people do every day: They fail. How would any one of us know how to succeed if we didn't fail a bunch of times in the process? I was a survivor of rape and sexual assault. I had one too many toxic relationships. If anyone saw my track record with men, they might think I was doomed from the beginning. Behind every one of those instances was the power of a leader, who never knew or believed she was. For example, after my rape and then later sexual assault, I saw myself differently. I was not just a survivor, but I realized I thrived under pressure and my mission and vision were far bigger than I could have ever dreamed of.

During my growth and development stage, I spent a large amount of time with a therapist, who helped me to understand that none of this was my fault and I was finding ways to take my power back. Believe me when I say it took a lot of soul searching on my part to guide me to be a great leader and to feel truly empowered within myself. This is where my story takes a bit of a turn. After many years of just not liking men, experiencing poor dates, and starts of relationships, I took my power back in another way. A lot of women after being raped will go one of two ways: one is they will never enjoy sexual activity because they do not feel safe and secure, and they are unable to trust; or two, they will go the opposite way and find a way to love it again by being with someone who allows them to have the power. I remember reading books in college about erotica and BDSM and, most importantly to me, dominance and submission. One might argue that it is a way for men to abuse women, but I always desired it, and my body craved it.

Dominance and submission, when done properly, are a beautiful things. Unfortunately, it does receive a bad rap and at times is considered taboo. For a submissive, this is her safe place. She gives all of herself to her Dominant and in return, he takes care of her in all ways. Yes, I am a submissive and it has helped me to see myself as that natural-born leader and to push myself to new heights. You see, a good Dominant can read your needs, desires, wants, and he is responsible for bringing you pleasure, love, intimacy, and connection. I did not learn this until later in life when I met the most beautiful man, who worshipped me and pushed me to my limits. He always wanted the best for me because he knew that I was a changemaker. I was going to be a woman who changed the world, one person at a time. I fell in love with this man and we were what you would call written in the stars, until sadly he passed away. I cannot explain how devastating it is to lose not only your Dominant, but also the love of your life.

Lucas had given me so very much in the time that we were together; he doted on me and cherished the ground I walked on. We had this incredibly special connection and everyone around us could feel the energy between us. Now I am not saying go find a Dom and find your power, but what I am saying is it helped me to see things that I could not see and he could. He in a sense, lifted the veil that I had been living under and I blossomed under his guidance and control. During this time, I wrote my first anthology, *Dream to Rise*, was asked to be a speaker on an international stage, and had my first speaking appearance. I had finished my masters but went back for trauma-informed coaching. Finally, I already had one business and we were building a second business together. I also saw myself as the sexy and sensual goddess I was and once I did, I never turned back. I loved the attention and because I was being cherished, I felt beautiful every single day. Not a moment went by where my Lucas did not say how beautiful I was.

I truly believe that Lucas gave me a new start in life. After his passing, I was lost, heartbroken, angry, and sad—so many mixed emotions as to why he had been taken from me. The realization hits hard. Only God knows and it's time to start forming a closer relationship with him. Submission and surrender are equal to power and confidence. After about a week, I started to get myself together and be able to do typical daily things and it was difficult at first because he was here, and now, he wasn't. How do you explain to a woman who has lost the only man who truly loved and respected her that he is no longer on this earth? You don't; you just grieve. I was fortunate and had made some great connections and a grief counselor was in that mix. This fabulous woman made me realize that I may never have the answers to my questions and that there is no wrong way to grieve, only your way. I am very grateful to have her in my life. But I was the one who made the changes and the decisions to turn my grief into a new mission and vision where I bring more love into the world. Lucas and I had felt so strongly about how we experienced our love that we felt others would benefit from learning how we did it. I did not know at the time that God had been grooming me to be the leader of my own mission and vision, not others. Its why I was never truly in charge because this was a far greater mission than I could receive from another boss. I was my own boss and I began to have more conversations with God, and I would write to Lucas.

One day I was sitting in my chair and one download came and then another and another. I could not stop these downloads from coming. I knew right then and there that everything was going to be ok and I understood why I could never figure out what my purpose was on the planet. God had helped me to move from being devastated to taking that grief and turning it into something truly transformational to bring love to the world. Needless to say, what I have planned is a major undertaking but I work on it as much as I can and one day *L&A Luxury Dating Society* will be the most sought-after dating program around the world. As God is my witness, this is my purpose, and now I will never abandon it; rather I will nurture it into something beautiful. This is my legacy and it honors my love Lucas, who passed far too soon. Each part of the membership will go to mental health and addiction resources for those in need. Lucas empowered me, but not before I empowered myself. My life has been a series of both unfortunate and fortunate events and those times, especially when I relied on resilience and power, were the ones that empowered me the most.

Empowerment is finding yourself, and having the true belief that you are powerful. It is innate and often can be found within the most troubling or most exciting of times. Empowerment is often also paired with resilience and confidence because you need all three to unleash the power inside of you. Each and every one of us has the power within ourselves to be empowered, just as long as we believe, and our faith is stronger than our fear. Remember to always release your power from within and become the very best version of yourself you can be.

Julianne Williams

MPH, Certified Grief Educator

http://linkedin.com/in/julianne-williams-1aa76917
https://www.facebook.com/BraveEnoughCommunity
https://www.instagram.com/Brave_Enough_Community_/
https://juliannewilliams.com/

Born with a congenital heart defect requiring life-saving surgery, Julianne has always embodied tenacity. Those early health challenges prepared her for future hardships. Rising through administration in the skilled nursing sector, she developed a passion for caring for the elderly and infirm. As her career advanced, her husband faced mental health struggles, tragically taking his life when Julianne was 36 years old and their children ages 7 and 3. Undeterred, Julianne ascended to President of her starting company, the nation's second-largest skilled nursing provider with 320 locations across 21 states. After its 2016 sale, she co-founded her own company, selling it in 2022. Driven by her experiences, Julianne authored international best-selling books sharing insights on grief. Today, her children are young adults: one a medical professional, the other training as a private pilot.

Freedom Through Forgiveness

By Julianne Williams

We have been told "forgive and forget" since we were children.

By letting go of past pain, your voice becomes yours again, not hindered by negative emotions or regret.

What is forgiveness? The Merriam-Webster dictionary defines forgiveness as 1. to cease to feel resentment against (an offender) PARDON. 2a. to give up resentment or claim requital for 2b to grant relief from payment.

The Bible also guides us through many verses to forgive. Colossians 3:13 directs us to "bear with each other and forgive one another if any of you has a grievance against someone. Forgive as the Lord forgave you." Ephesians 4:32 says, "Be kind to one another, tenderhearted, forgiving one another as God in Christ forgave you."

The question I always come back to is, "How can I truly soften my heart to someone who has inflicted pain in my life?" After all, they made a choice to hurt me. Why is it incumbent upon me to show kindness in a situation when my heart is broken?

Sometimes, the most difficult person to forgive is yourself. The truth is, it IS all about you. Forgiveness is about your peace, your sorrows, and your future.

As I look back at my life, I realize forgiveness has been the path to taking back my life and moving forward purposefully to build the future, giving me success and significance. Forgiveness has been the key to reclaiming my power and releasing emotions that were holding me back from experiencing peace. You see, the people who have wronged me are not worth giving even more of the time I have here on earth. I realized each day is precious and my happiness is MY choice.

I have witnessed family members hold a grudge for years, to the point that years passed without speaking. I have had family members betray me in my most dire circumstances. I have also had my feelings hurt by people in the normal course of my day—by accident or intentionally.

As I write this chapter, I still have one loss I still must reconcile: the suicide of my husband. And I will continue to search for my path to peace. Healing for me does start with recognizing the block here; maybe that I need to start with forgiving myself for the regrets I hold, which really were not the genesis or cause of my husband's decision.

I have experienced intense feelings of sorrow, anger, disappointment, and heartache. I have been confused as to why another person would harm me or betray me. Sadly, I realized I have done the same to others.

The biggest lesson I have learned through forgiveness is not only do I not have to forget, but I also don't have to reconcile with the person who caused me pain.

Once I realized forgiveness does not require reconciliation and is really the decision to release myself and/or the person involved from intense feelings, lightness arrived. Carrying the emotions of resentment, anger, or regret is a heavy load to bear. Importantly, carrying the load is not always the solution to healing the pain. When you forgive, you are not releasing the other person from their responsibility in the hurt. When you forgive, you are releasing and/or accepting your role and emotions, which will allow healing.

How do we journey to forgiveness? First, we acknowledge it is a choice. As I just stated above, it is the decision to let go of negative emotions tethering you to the pain you are feeling. What are the strategies to consider on this difficult walk?

For me, one of the most helpful (not easy) places to start is to **try to understand the other person's side of the story** and why they may have done or reacted in this circumstance. One of the most painful betrayals I have experienced comes from my late husband's father attempting to take partial custody of my children after my husband's death. What he did felt unexplainable. My children were forced into a world of judges and court-appointed psychologists. Financially I was struggling due to the death of my husband and the additional expenses while trying to raise my children on my own, which made things even harder. And, while I did forgive, I did not engage in a relationship after the courts reinforced he overreached. As time passed, I realized a few things: e was grieving the death of his son, something he had not experienced. I was in control of my children and how they would be parented. They were the only piece he had left of his son. He did not necessarily agree with the schedules, permitted activities, or other "rules" I had for my small children. When I constantly said "no" or confronted him on not bringing them home on time or letting them do things I felt were unsafe, he could not see another option to resolve the problem other than taking the advice of one of his attorney friends to use the legal system. This was even after meeting with pastors and other family members for mediation. While I haven't forgotten the chaos and pain this created, I will no longer let it influence my future.

Establishing boundaries also helped me forgive because I understood not only did I not have to accept certain behaviors, but I was worth honoring my needs and emotions. Instead of holding the hurt, use the pain as an opportunity to learn. I learned how I would interact with others, what my dealbreakers were in a relationship, and steps I could take to insulate myself from situations that placed me at risk. I realized when a close friend of mine decided to deepen a relationship with a person who assaulted me in front of her that being able to trust another person to protect me was a necessary element I needed in a friendship. I am not upset with that person, as she did the best she could, and I made a choice around what mattered to me. Carrying resentment would not change what happened. Playing the victim would not change what happened. What did change is that I became clear about my needs and placed value on meeting them. This allowed me to reclaim my confidence.

In many ways, I see forgiveness as working through the grief process. One step in the grief process is to **identify and name your feelings so you can release them**. Until we know what is driving our emotions, it is hard to understand them. There are no right or wrong feelings. The way you feel is yours. Instead of defending your position to others or trying to get even, healing comes from acknowledgment of your pain, disappointment, anger, or whatever you are holding. It's then making a choice to accept your emotions and claim the power you have over feelings. Feelings are real; they are not permanent. It likely won't be pleasant to allow your feelings to emerge so you can experience them. Remind yourself there is purpose to the pain. Unleashing our voice means choosing to control what you do next.

The last thing I do is to **distinguish if you are the target or the source of the problem**. We have all heard about someone who is angry coming home and kicking their dog. The psychological term for that is projection. Others can hurt us by projecting their feelings of anger, low self-esteem, or failures through their words and actions. We have all said or done things we did not mean in anger or confusion. When I forgave the person who attacked me verbally, it became very clear the individual was yelling criticisms of herself, which had nothing to do with how I treated her in the past. She had a detailed ledger of what she felt I had done to wrong her. When I analyzed the words, the very things she so cruelly said were either jealousy of my friendship and/or behaviors of mine she didn't like about herself. While I was the target, I was not responsible for her behavior or feelings about me. Forgiveness prevented me from internalizing her opinion of me and staying on track with my goals and aspirations.

When I need to forgive myself, I apply the above to my behavior around the "why" coupled with kindness and compassion. Through that lens, it can allow you to fully take responsibility for the choices you have made in error. Depending on the situation, I may need to understand what I was feeling at the time so I can concentrate on making better decisions with myself or others. And an apology is an important part of making amends. When we are sorry, remorse shown can be healing for all involved. No one is perfect and acknowledging a mistake can do a world of good.

Forgiveness is a choice. When we forgive, we release ourselves from negative thoughts, low self-esteem, and continuing pain. Forgiveness does not mean you have to bring a person back into your life or forget what hurt you. Forgiveness is one tool to release guilt, anger, or sorrow. When we forgive, we unleash our ability to live our truth.

Jo Ann Nider

Jo Ann's Creations & Organizing with a Personal Touch
Entrepreneur | Writer

https://www.linkedin.com/in/joannnider/
https://www.facebook.com/jo.a.nider
https://www.instagram.com/livelifefullywithcancer/
www.JoAnnNider.com
www.ChalkCouture.com/JoAnnNider

Jo Ann Nider is a multi-faceted entrepreneur, author, and advocate whose life and work embody resilience and purpose. A cancer warrior, Jo Ann has transformed her challenges into opportunities to inspire others, showing that it is possible to thrive even in the face of adversity. She is the founder of Organizing with a Personal Touch and Jo Ann's Creations, where she blends professional organizing with high-end DIY décor to help people create order, beauty, and calm in their lives. As Managing Partner for the She Wins Women's Network in Netcong, NJ, Jo Ann empowers women to rise boldly into their fullest potential. Her story and insights are featured in multiple publications, including Becoming an Unstoppable Woman: Rise of the Phoenix, HA.N.N.A. magazine, SHEWINS magazine and SUCCESS magazine. Jo Ann continues to build a legacy of strength, vision, and impact through every project she undertakes. IT'S TIME TO LIVE ~jn

I Got Cancer. I'm Not Cancer

By Jo Ann Nider

I got cancer.
I'm beside myself.
I'm broken-hearted.
I'm confused.
I'm hurting.
I'm sad.
I'm scared.
I'm tired.
I'm uncertain.
I got cancer.

I have no words.
Yet I have so much to say.

I got cancer.
Biopsies
Chemotherapy
Apheresis
Stem Cell Transplant
I didn't pass the test.
I did not reach remission.
I continue to fight,
while recovering from a stem cell transplant
I got cancer.

I got cancer again.
Mammograms
MRIs
Ultrasounds

Biopsies
A partial mastectomy
I got cancer.

I got cancer.
Cancer in full relapse
Chemotherapy
Chemotherapy reaction
First year in relapse lost
Never to be seen or enjoyed
I had to rest.
I had to sleep.
I couldn't eat.
I couldn't walk.
I couldn't bathe myself.
I couldn't stay out of the hospital.
I got cancer.

I got cancer.
This is my fault.
Just as it was when I was a kid
I'm not doing my part.
I stopped being the breadwinner.
I lost myself in my diagnosis.
I lost myself in my treatments.
I lost my ability to parent.
I lost my ability to be a partner.
A wife
A mother
A friend
A sibling
My children no longer look at me as a capable woman, a successful woman.

I am no longer the caregiver.
I am the one in need of care.
I got cancer.

I got cancer.
I no longer support others as I once did.
Mentally
Emotionally
Physically
I no longer make you feel good about yourself.
I got cancer.

I got cancer.
Insecurities for a 56-year-old with cancer
Emotional
Financial
Mental
Physical
Medically drained
I got cancer.

I got cancer.
I've disappointed my children.
I've disappointed my husband.
I've disappointed my family.
I've disappointed my mother.
I've disappointed my father.
I've disappointed my community.
I've disappointed myself.
I got cancer.

I got cancer.
I no longer serve at my highest level.

I no longer pursue my ambition.
I can no longer find my purpose.
I can no longer find my passion.
I got cancer.

I got cancer.
I am insecure.
Adult insecurities unlock the box where childhood insecurities live.
They come flooding back.
As if it were earlier today
I must have misbehaved.
I failed my test.
I'm not smart enough.
I was not watching my sister when she fell.
I did not watch my brother when he ran off.
I did not make enough money to help pay our bills.
My father loved me but scolded me often.
I was a kid.
I did not have cancer then.
He must have known I would.
I got cancer.

I got cancer.
You have my cancer.
You are not living your life.
You have my cancer.
Your purpose and passion are no more.
I believed in you.
In your purpose
In your passion
So much so that I had enough for both of us.
I carried your purpose.
I carried your passion.

I carried you.
You do not have cancer.
You fear purpose and passion.
I held your purpose and passion.
In my hand
In my heart
In my soul
I knew you needed me to support you.
With all of my purpose
With all of my passion
With all of my support
With all of my love,
I got cancer.

I got cancer; you have my cancer.
My purpose and passion are here.
Waiting to be held with love
Support to pursue my purpose
As I had for you
I got cancer.

I got cancer; you have my cancer.
You stopped living.
Your purpose
Your passion
Your energy
Your will to live
Are locked in my heart
It is my fault.
It was me,
not you pursuing your purpose
Your dreams
Your will to be

Your will to live passionately
I pursued it for you when you couldn't.
With all the things I can no longer do
I cannot pursue for you.
I got cancer; you have my cancer.

You have my cancer.
You must unlock the box in my heart.
You must find the key to your passions.
You must find the key to your purpose.
You must find the key to unlock your will to live.
You must find the key to your dreams for you.
You must take the key with you.
I got cancer; you have my cancer.

I got cancer; you have my cancer.
I wish with everything inside of me.
I could do all the things I no longer do.
For you
Our kids
Our home
And if there would be room
I wish I could do and be me.
For myself
and for all of you
I got cancer; you have my cancer.

I got cancer; you have my cancer.
It is my fault.
We are about to be homeless.
I got cancer.
I have cancer.
I am not cancer!

I am not who I used to be.
I got cancer.

I have cancer.
I have suffered a stroke.
I had a heart attack.
I have rheumatoid disease.
I had a stem cell transplant.
I got cancer. You do not have cancer.

It's time to UnleashHER Voice.

I got cancer. You do not have my cancer.
You have sat back watching our life go by.
I have told you for years.
We need to live.
To enjoy our life
I have been passionate about living
especially since December 14, 2018
We are not living a fulfilling, joyful life.
I'm not sure we're living at all.
I got cancer; you do not have my cancer.

You do not have my cancer.
I have loved you.
Fiercely
Passionately
Joyfully
Romantically
Sensually
You do not have my cancer.

I got cancer; you do not have my cancer.

I have loved you unconditionally.
I have shown you great support.
I have cheered you on.
Whether you wanted me to or not,
You are worth far more.
Then you give yourself credit for
you do not deserve to be held back.
For anyone who ever told you
You weren't good enough.
To be who you are
To be what you wanted to be
For who you are now
Their opinion of you is none of your business!
You do not have my cancer.

You chose a path.
You have had a great relationship
with your chosen path,
If you no longer want to continue
On this path,
It's your decision.
But to stay on a path because you're afraid of the long-awaited
"Aha I told you, you weren't cut out for the path you chose!"
"As always, I am right!"
It's time for you to do what feels good to you.
If staying on this path feels right, stay.
If it no longer serves you, change your path.
I believe you were made for more.
Let go of the fear and live your life.
Live and love your path!
You do not have my cancer!

You do not have my cancer, you are living in ***FEAR.***

Fear is your cancer!
It's holding you back.
Fear sets boundaries.
Fear questions who you are.
Without the fear of just one phrase
Without the fear of just one person
You would be living a very different life.
One of self-confidence
enthusiasm
energy
the feeling of loving yourself and your life
without your cancer
You have a reason to wake up.
To continue your journey
To live without cancer
You do not have cancer.

Now ponder that for just a moment. Take 10 minutes and write it down. ***UnleashHER Voice!***
Write down how you would feel if you didn't worry about the noise in your ear or the opinions of anyone but yourself. What is it? What would you be doing?
Write it down no matter how big or small.
What is it that you're passionate about? How would your life be different?
Are you healthier?
Are you enjoying the little things, the big things, and the oh-so-important things in the middle?

What does your life look like following your heart, passions, and desires? The things that excite you. How do you identify yourself by doing the above? Where do you live? What do you drive? Are you financially free? Most importantly, how are your relationships?

With family, friends, and your partner. What would your successful self say to you?

Write it all down. If you do not ***UnleashYour Voice,*** you are letting ***Cancer*** and ***Fear*** win!
It's time to UnLeashHer Voice.
It's time to UnLeashHis Voice.
It's time to tell Cancer to go Fuck itself,
It's time to UnleashYour Voice onto anyone who is stopping you from being YOU!
UnleashYour Voice and follow your heart.

You may have allowed years to go by, not trying something new. Something you have desired, something that lights you on fire
I got Cancer, I AM NOT CANCER.
You do not have my Cancer. Your Cancer is Fear! YOU ARE NOT FEAR! IT'S TIME TO UNLEASHER VOICE! IT'S TIME TO UNLEASH YOUR VOICE.
As always and most importantly, "It's Time to Live."
jn

Debra Hillard

Founder and Owner of DK Hillard Art, LLC

https://www.linkedin.com/in/debra-hillard-93526913/
https://www.facebook.com/dkhillardwraptures/
https://www.instagram.com/dkhillard/
https://www.dkhillard.com
https://www.dkhillardart.com

DK Hillard is an artist and sacred guide whose path is one of remembrance. Her work is "Soul Woven" — a weaving of painting, fabric, and story into living prayers that awaken memory and truth. Each creation becomes a threshold, inviting others to step into their own soul's initiation. For over two decades she guided transformation through the body as a trainer and life coach. Now she carries that devotion into the sacred realm, where creativity is not art for art's sake, but ritual, medicine, and prophecy. Her offerings move through many forms: Soul Wraptures that hold and protect, Soul Portraits that mirror spirit, and immersive journeys shaped by archetypal exploration, ancestral healing, and embodied expression. Through these woven experiences, she guides others into the mystery — a journey of self-discovery, remembrance, and becoming. To encounter her work is to enter ceremony itself: a soul woven path of beauty, fire, and transformation.

The Path to Embodiment

By Debra Hillard

In the first volume of *Unleash Her Voice,* I wrote about an unleashing of monumental proportions—one that freed my spirit from lifetimes of bondage. In the wake of that sacred ceremony, I expected flight. Expansion. Joy.

Instead, my body began to break down. Rapidly. With no clear diagnosis, no treatment that helped, and no explanation that made sense.

The very vessel that carried my newly liberated spirit felt like it was collapsing under the weight of something I couldn't yet see. In a matter of months, I seemed to age a decade.

What no one tells you is that when the spirit breaks free, the body may not follow so easily.

A spirit of immense power cannot easily thrive in a body wracked with pain and the constraints of illness. I found myself spiraling into depression and curtailing my creative pursuits. The things I used to relish, look forward to, and thrive doing lost their color. I felt lost to myself, a shadow slipping in and out of my days without actually living them.

Without the physical wherewithal to go anywhere or engage with friends, I became more and more of a recluse. Not because I didn't want a connection, but because I simply didn't have the energy to reach out.

This was not the first time in my life that I had experienced such total debilitation. The memories lingered in the back of my mind—reminders of how easy it would be to lose everything again. The thought haunted me: *What if this is it? What if the collapse is permanent this time?*

It was after a sudden, mysterious symptom sent me to the doctor once again—with no clear answer—that something deeper began to stir. I realized this wasn't just about illness anymore. Something else was afoot. Something other than strange, inexplicable symptoms.

Could it be that I was actually dying, and I needed to accept the inevitable?

One sleepless night, tossing in my bed, I felt myself on the edge of resignation. Maybe I wouldn't be able to heal myself in this lifetime, despite all the work, all the rituals, and all the prophecies that had told me I was here to do just that. Perhaps illness would once again be my undoing, not because I hadn't tried, but because I had failed to find the one key that would unlock the healing I so deeply longed for.

I was almost there—at the edge of surrendering completely. Letting myself slip away.

But no.

Spirit hadn't brought me this far just to abandon me. Deep inside, some ancient knowing refused to go dark. I hadn't freed my spirit so completely only to give up now.

Still, the question echoed:

How do I unleash my voice in a body that refuses to hold me?

As an artist, painting has always been how I listen to Spirit. It's how I hear what lives beneath language. How I pray. How I channel memory into form. But after that ceremony, the one that cracked everything open, I hadn't painted. Not once.

My work had shifted into other sacred expressions: medicine bundles, soul wraptures, and ritual—but something was missing. Some part of me remained unmet, unexpressed. Waiting.

Then came a quiet invitation: a Soul Portrait commission. It asked me to return to the canvas, to daily ritual, to sacred silence. To presence. To let Spirit move through my hands again.

I hesitated.

I knew what it would require. A level of surrender I hadn't yet accessed. A willingness to be present in a body that still didn't feel like home.

But something stirred. A whisper in my bones: *This is the way back.*

And so I returned to the brush.

The first stroke on canvas was like a key in a lock I didn't know existed. My body responded before my mind. A sudden rush of sensation. A subtle opening. Not emotional—visceral. I felt something shift in my tissue, like an ancient door creaking open.

I wasn't remembering who I was in theory.

I was remembering in flesh.

This was an embodiment. Not the concept. Not the performance. The *actual* descent of Spirit into form.

And it was only just beginning.

Not long after, as my husband's birthday approached, I searched for a meaningful gift. Nothing came to mind—until I saw a flicker. Horses. An experience I'd seen days before was now calling loudly. I booked it for him, but I knew it was for me. My body responded before my mind did. The moment I saw them, my body lit up. Horses had always lived deep in my spirit, even if I had pushed them far away because of fear and injury. But they were calling me now. Not as memory, but as *medicine.*

The more I allowed myself to follow these subtle callings—brushstroke, horse breath, sacred silence—the more I began to see the thread that had always been there. Each day, small moments emerged like breadcrumbs from Spirit, leading me not backward, but into something older than memory. A re-membering. My soul was calling for a deeper healing—one that no doctor had been able to offer, because it wasn't only physical. It was soul-deep. Cellular. Ancestral.

I had been told during that first unleashing that I was a healer. But what I hadn't yet understood was that the first body I had to heal was my own.

And this healing was not about protocols or performance. It was about truth.

Unleashing my voice, I realized, was not about words. Not first.
It was about presence.
And presence requires embodiment.
And embodiment meant turning toward everything I had once tried to transcend. It meant facing every trauma my body had ever carried—this lifetime and beyond.

I had to stop overriding my body's signals. Stop chasing answers outside myself. Stop assuming that being "spiritual" meant being untouchable. I had to stop trying to ascend out of my pain.

This wasn't about finding the perfect protocol. It was about reclaiming the power I had given away—over and over again—by believing that someone else knew what was best for me. My body was the only one that had ever known. And it was time I listened.

All my years as a personal trainer have been spent guiding clients through transformation. All my years as an artist, in channeling Spirit onto canvas. All the sacred tools and rituals I had created to guide others home to themselves. Every step had been leading me here. To this moment. To this unraveling. To this reweaving.

The voice I wanted to find—the one I longed to reclaim—was not floating above me.
It was buried deep. In the bone. In scar. In grief.
In the places I had been told were too messy, too emotional, too much.

And so, I began the slow process of descent. Again.

My brush became a prayer. My medicine bundles became altars. My sacred tools became mirrors. My animals, my ancestors, my own trembling breath—these became my teachers.

And what I found is this:
The deeper I go into my body, the clearer my voice becomes. Not louder. Not more convincing. *Clearer.* Truer. Resonant in a way that can't be performed or faked.

This is what it means to unleash the voice of an embodied woman.

She doesn't shout to be heard.
She doesn't convince.
She doesn't perform.

She speaks from the marrow of her being.
And the world feels it.

I am still learning to trust her. Still learning to stay. My body still aches and falters. But I know now that this is not regression. This is the sacred rhythm of becoming.

I am no longer trying to return to who I once was.
I am becoming who I truly am.

This is not a journey of perfection.
This is a return to presence.

To inhabit myself fully.
To let Spirit not just move through me but live in me.

My voice is not something I conjure.
It is something I remember.

And now, I am letting her speak. Not just through words, but through canvas, through ritual, through every sacred breath. I am letting her speak through my hands, my bones, and my silence. Through presence.

If something in you is stirring as you read this—if your voice feels caught in your throat, or your body has been whispering through pain or exhaustion—I invite you to listen.

Not to me. To *her*.

To the voice in your bones. The one you've quieted to survive. The one who is still waiting for you to return.

This journey isn't easy. But it is sacred. And it is yours.

If you're ready to remember—through your body, not beyond it—I offer private Soul Portrait sessions and sacred tools to support your becoming.

This isn't for everyone. It's for those who know they can't go back, who are ready to come home—fully, fiercely, in the skin they're in.

Are you ready to meet the voice that lives in you?

Anna Barboza Lugo

Pure Tea Love, Pure CBD Love, Pure Love Travel, women Inspiring Women and Men Too.
Business Owner, Author, Mentor, & Child of God

https://www.linkedin.com/in/anna-lugo-62746219/
https://www.facebook.com/anna.barboza.lugo/
https://www.instagram.com/Alohalugo/
www.puretealove.com

Hello My Name is Anna Barboza Lugo, I am a successful business woman and owner of Pure Tea Love, pure CBD Love and will soon launch Pure Love Travel. I am a proud mother of a 46 year old daughter and live strong in my faith. I consider myself a Child of God. I manage several social media pages called UP2UGOD, THX2GOD, and Women Inspiring Women. I am a five time best selling Author and excited to release this sixth anthology. I'm a retired IT professional and recently relocated to a beach in Daytona Beach Shores in Florida. My new passion is Traveling the world. and my love language is praying for others.

My Quali-Tea' of Life Improved Once I Became a BOSS

By Anna Barboza Lugo

Growing up, we were taught to never talk back, to never speak back, or disrespect our elders. We were told to speak only when we were spoken to. I guess I interpret that as "don't ever use your voice to speak up or speak out" or make my voice heard. Sadly, I learned a limited belief about using my voice and I did not realize how powerful it was once I finally started to gain the confidence needed to speak up. It wasn't until I reached the age of 50 that I began to take a stand and speak up and stick up for myself. It's been 16 years since I gained my voice and I will no longer be silent or afraid to speak up and no longer hold back what needs to be said and heard. I no longer silence my thoughts, and my hurts, my desires, my passions, my beliefs, my boundaries, or my doubts. And especially will not hold back when using my voice to praise the Lord. The tongue is a powerful thing; when you use your voice, you become free. The Bible teaches that your voice is a powerful God-given gift that should be used to worship Him, to build and lift each other, to encourage and inspire, not to tear down and confess your faith and share God's message with the world.

Once I learned that my voice is indeed a powerful tool and a God-given gift, then I realized that I have the abili-Tea' to use what God gave me to speak up on my own behalf and share my beliefs. I realized it's time that I stop wasting another precious moment being silent.

I've always had mentors and coaches who believed in me but I also had bosses and naysayers who tried to silence my voice. Being a PBX technician in the early 80s was seen as a man's job; it was a time when women were not taken seriously or had their voices heard in an all-male-dominated field. I recall one time when I went to Japan to test our voicemail system with the telephone equipment. I was in a room with 20 chain-smoking men and when I went to plug in the equipment under the table, they all said, "No, no, get up from there; women don't do that here, it's a man's job." I think I shocked them when I said, "Well, it's my duty and job and this lady will do whatever it takes to get the integration tested." Even with my voice trembling, I had to say what I had to say. Things sure have come along way for women since working and leaving the corporate world.

Over the last 40 years, I've held a lot of positions and titles and received many promotions while working in the corporate world. I even earned a Distinguished Leadership Award while working at my last company. But it was never good enough for promotion, no matter how many leadership conferences or mentorship programs I was involved in and it was a lot; it was still not good enough in the eyes of my directors or superiors. I somehow always felt defeated and undeserving and unnoticed for all the hard work and self-development with no recognition. I had to learn that I work for the Lord and He is the ultimate boss. After all, He was the one who had plans for me all along. I'm thankful I can still hear His small, quiet, and gentle voice saying, "All you need is faith the size of a mustard seed."

Friday the 13th, 2020, was my last day at my corporate job and I believe it was one of the best days in my professional career. It felt as if all the weight of the world was lifted from my shoulders and I never felt so relieved. Of course, all the thoughts raced through my head on how I will survive. How do I go from making 6 figures to $420.00 a week? But let me tell you, when you "let go and you let God," supernatural change occurs. I believe God took me out of the corporate world for a reason. That reason was so that I would finally take fate into my own hands and become the boss of me.

On November 11, 2020, it was the year I decided to become my own boss and business owner. Leaving the corporate world actually forced me to find an alternative way to make money and start living as the entrepreneur that I've always been. It was the beginning of a wonderful journey of creating something from nothing, which was a new and challenging project for me.

See, I've been a project manager for many years and I learned that in order to launch a project, I would need to utilize the same skills I used for so many years being part of the PMO organization. Everything we did was around structured processes and phases and rules of engagement. It was following a framework of *Discovery & Exploring, Initiate & Kickoff, Plan, Design & Execute, Implement, Test & Monitor,* then mitigate risks and issues and document lessons learned and I must say this is a discipline that I still use to this day. I wanted to leverage my skills and somehow incorporate them into my new venture just so I had some method to my madness. Many, many years ago we incorporated TQI into the business. TQI stands for Total Quali-Tea' Improvement. We focused on quality and improvements. What worked, what didn't work and what could we do better.

Pure CBD Love

Pure CBD Love was born and launched on November 11, 2020, on my daddy's birthday. The reason I choose CBD is because I started using CBD products in 2018 after my daughter was in a horrific accident. It was the only relief I could find for my anxiety, inflammation, stress, insomnia, and so many other ailments. I thought to myself, if I can start my own business, then I could buy the product wholesale. So we started out and came up with a name, then a logo, found a domain, and created a website. Had a business license issued and opened an account with Chase Bank. We attended 100 episodes of the ABCs of CBD and educated ourselves about this new industry. The bank took a chance on us because we told the agent we are not a dispensary; we are healers, not dealers, because we believe CBD is hope, not dope! After all, it's a God-made plant. So this kind gentleman at the bank took a chance and let us open an account. We had cards issued with DBA Pure CBD Love.

A month later, we had to close the account because the governance team said it's derived from the cannabis plant and we are considered a dispensary. The misconception is real and a lot of people are confused with CBD vs. THC. But we didn't let that stop us from ultimately making our own special blend salve. A CBD salve with 20 essential oils. Our plan was to have CBD Par-Tea's until COVID shut everything down. We still didn't let that stop us. While we were learning about the industry and attending trade shows to find new distrbutors we learned how CBD is actually medicine. How we became healers is a blessing from above. I would create Immuni-Tea' packages for my family and friends who need it after their cancer treatments. The Lord knows I want nothing more than to help them to get the relief without worrying about the cost. So I basically gave the store away and discovered recently that this first company is more of a hobby than a business. We are passionate about helping others feel well.

Pure Tea Love

My second company was launched on my Papa Georgie's birthday on February 22, 2022; it was a two's day!! lol... All kidding aside. It really was on a Tuesday!!

I decided to open a second business, so I launched Pure Tea' Love and created a slogan "We Have A Tea' For That." I thought it was a perfect way to start having "Tea Par-Tea's" and share both company products. I had my good friend and artist Adriana Reynoso create my logos and artwork for all of my businesses. She created exactly what I had envisioned. Tea cups with affirmations. The first set of cups had Creativi-Tea, Integri-Tea, Tranquili-Tea, Simplici-Tea', Immuni-Tea, Sinceri-Tea, Serenit-Tea, Prosperi-Tea, and Possibili-Tea'.

This was the first piece of art she created for Pure Tea Love. She created so many great pieces of art and I can't wait to share them with you. Each drawing has a specific message and words of encouragement and inspiration. We are really more than just Bea-U'Tea and Brains. We have Clari-Tea now. We have operated with Hones-Tea' and Humili-Tea'. with Digni-Tea' and Diversi-Tea', and Equali-Tea'. We embrace our Femini-tea.

We offer six Tea's, that are more than just affirmations; they are good for you, which keeps us thriving in the wellness industry. Our Tea's consist of I am Love, I Am Peace, I Am Energy, I am Joy, I am Merry and I am Bliss.

Tea'V Host on Momma's Birthday

On my momma's birthday, February 17, 2023, I launched a podcast and became a Tea'V host on Everyday Woman's TV, a 24/7 inspirational channel. My show was called We Have a Tea' for That... Positivi-Tea'! I also have a solo book I'm working on called "We Have a Tea for That."

Became a Best-selling Author 7 Times

Between 2023 and 2025, I have released 7 anthologies:

1. Guide to living your best life—'Spirituali-Tea' is my Priori-Tea' for Eterni-Tea'
2. Pray Don't Panic—Everything is Up2uGod
3. Breaking the Glass Ceiling—My Ten Cent Raise
4. A Heart of a Mother—A Single Mother's Love is Endless
5. Letters to Him—It Takes Someone Special to Be a Daddy
6. Possibility to Prosperity—From Scarci-Tea' to Prosperi-Tea' to a Generosi-Tea' Rock Star
7. Unleash Her Voice—My Quali-Tea' of Life Improved Once I Became a Boss

Book #8 will be released in December 2025.

I was also featured several times on *Blossoms of My Life* that aired on *Elevation Worship* radio.

Pure Love Travel

Pure Love Travel was born and launched on my birthday, September 30, 2025. Since retiring, I have fallen in love with traveling. In fact, I have taken 12 trips in 9 months. And I have partnered with Travorium to offer a travel membership club that provides you up to 80% off traveling. Why pay retail when you can pay wholesale? I am not a travel agent or travel advisor. I am a travel consultant that offers a travel club membership with access to 7 different wholesale sites to choose from. The best part is the perks and rewards. I am guaranteed an all-inclusive vacation twice a year by just using my points earned on a monthly basis. This is the same reason I started my CBD business—to gain deep discounts for items I'm certain to purchase.

I no longer worked for bosses but rather I became a boss. And it feels great to say I'm the boss of me. I must say this journey in recreating myself and starting a few companies from the ground up has been an exhilarating feeling.

My true identi-Tea' is being in integri-Tea' with myself. Always put God first and be still enough to hear His voice. I know He heard my voice and my prayers and this is what prayer looks like. I'm *The Boss of Me* and it feels like Royal-Tea.' I've never felt more confident in saying this than I do now.

Remember *Voice Carry*; use your voice to carry you into the next season. Whisper if you must but don't remain silent.

It took me fifty years to learn how to use my voice and for the past five years I realized God's confidence is my true confidence. My secret weapon is putting God first in everything I do. He knows the plans he has for me.

Charel Morris

Founder of Stone Circle Productions

https://www.linkedin.com/in/charel/
https://www.facebook.com/charel.morris/
https://www.instagram.com/cybershaman/p/DIRYwemoM4c/
https://app.kartra.com/

Charel Morris is a shamanic visionary and elemental wisdom keeper bridging ancient feminine teachings with modern women's empowerment. Through deep visioning work and sacred dreaming, she channels stories and wisdom from the lineage of wise women who have walked this earth for over 5,000 years. As a practitioner of shamanic healing arts, she guides women to reconnect with their elemental nature—helping them ground in earth's truth, flow with water's intuition, ignite fire's passion, speak air's wisdom, and connect with spirit's eternal knowing. Her work focuses on helping women remember their ancestral power and plant seeds of healing for the next seven generations. Charel believes that every woman's voice carries ancient medicine, and her mission is to help women trust their visions, honor their dreams, and speak their truth as sacred transmission. Through her writing and healing work, she creates pathways for the divine feminine to awaken in modern hearts.

The Ancient Call Within

By Charel Morris

In the quiet moments before dawn, something stirs. It whispers through the wind, pulses in the earth beneath our feet, and flickers in the flames that have warmed humanity for millennia. It is the voice of the ancients—the wise women who walked this earth for five thousand years before us, who understood the sacred dance between spirit and soil, between fire and flow.

They knew what we are only beginning to remember: that within every woman lies an unbreakable connection to the elements that shape our world. Earth grounds us in truth. Water flows through us as intuition. Fire ignites our passion and purpose. Air carries our words across vast distances. And spirit binds it all together, reminding us that we are both ancient and eternal.

These women—our grandmothers' grandmothers, stretching back through countless generations—did not question their right to speak. They were the healers, the storytellers, and the keepers of wisdom. They understood that their voices were channels for something far greater. They knew that when a woman speaks her truth, she speaks not only for herself but for all the women who came before her and all who will come after.

Yet somewhere along the way, we learned to whisper when we should have roared. They knew that when a woman speaks her truth, she speaks not only for herself but for all the women who came before her and all who will come after. We forgot that our voices carry the wisdom of ages, that our stories hold the power to heal not just ourselves but the world around us.

The women whose stories fill these pages have heard the ancient call. They have remembered who they are—daughters of the earth, carriers of sacred fire, vessels of ancient wisdom made manifest in modern times. All found their way back to a truth that has never left us: that every woman's voice matters, every story has power, and every truth spoken aloud sends ripples across the waters of time.

Their stories are invitations—not just to witness their journeys, but to remember your own. For within you, too, lives the wisdom of the ancients. Within you burns the same fire that has guided women through darkness for countless generations.

The ancient women are not gone. They live in every moment you choose courage over comfort, truth over approval, and authenticity over perfection. They are the strength in your voice, the knowing in your belly, and the fire in your heart.

This is more than an anthology of personal stories. This is a rekindling—a remembering of who we have always been. Your voice—your true, unfiltered, unapologetic voice—is the bridge between ancient wisdom and modern transformation.

The elements are listening. The ancestors are waiting. Your voice—your true, unfiltered, unapologetic voice—is the bridge between ancient wisdom and modern transformation.

It is time to remember. It is time to speak. It is time to unleash her—the ancient woman within you who has never forgotten her power.

The earth is ready to receive your truth.
The waters are ready to carry your story.
The fire is ready to ignite your purpose.
The air is ready to amplify your voice.
Your spirit is ready to soar.

* * *

What ancient wisdom lives within your story? What elemental truth are you ready to speak? The women in these pages have shown us the way. Now it's your turn to step into the circle and add your voice to the eternal song.

My Journey into the Sacred Stories

In my time of shamanic visioning and dreaming, I have found stories and other women have shared stories with me. Now I share them with you—to light a fire within you for your own stories to flicker and fill you with light, or so you might hear something in the wind and know the words of power you need to speak.

Each time we step on our earth, it is moving energy and wisdom into you. We have known intuition flowing through us—now let the words speak through you. We open ourselves to the core of spirit and the oneness that as women we hold for the entire universe.

These visions come not as my own imaginings but as remembrances passed down through the sacred feminine lineage. They arrive in meditation, in dreams, in moments when the veil between worlds grows thin. The ancient teachers, oddesses, and crones have never stopped teaching. They simply teach through different channels now.

Five Voices, Five Elements

Air - The Whispered Wisdom

"I would climb the ancient oak behind our house, swaying between earth and sky, the wind whispering stories to me—tales of my grandmother, who held her tongue through decades of silence, and her grandmother before her, who spoke only in kitchen prayers. The leaves rustled with their unspoken words, and I knew that someday, I would speak the wisdom and power they had carried in their quiet hearts. Their voices live in mine now, carried on every breath I take, every truth I dare to speak aloud."

Earth - The Grounded Truth

"My mother taught me to press my palms into garden soil each morning, feeling for the pulse beneath. When I finally found the courage to leave the marriage that was burying me alive, I knelt in that same dirt and felt five thousand years of women's strength rising through my palms—women who had planted, harvested, and endured. In that moment, I knew my roots ran deeper than my fear."

Water - The Flowing Intuition

"Standing knee-deep in the river where my great-grandmother once washed clothes, I felt her knowing flow through me like current over stones. When I stopped fighting the current of my own life—stopped trying to swim upstream against my deepest knowing—her wisdom flowed through me. I learned that tears and rivers carry the same medicine: They both know exactly where they need to go."

Fire - The Sacred Spark

"In the candlelit vigil for my sister's passing, I understood why women had always been the keepers of flame. Each flickering light held a prayer, a memory, a piece of feminine sacred burning bright against the darkness. That night, I stopped hiding my light under baskets of should and ought. I let my fire burn as fierce and bright as the women before me had always known it could."

Spirit - The Eternal Connection

"In the desert silence where my ancestors once danced beneath endless stars, I finally heard it—the song that connects all women across all time. It wasn't words or melody, but something deeper: the rhythm of birth and death, creation and transformation, the eternal pulse of feminine spirit moving through every generation. I realized I had never been alone, never been the first to face what I was facing."

* * *

These are not just stories. They are remembrances. They are the ancient feminine awakening in modern hearts, the elemental wisdom rising in contemporary voices.

Our stories are seeds planted for the next seven generations. When we speak our truth, we create pathways for our daughters and their daughters to walk with greater confidence, deeper knowing, and stronger connection to their own elemental power.

The sacred women who guide us through visions and dreams weave a web of wisdom that will sustain generations to come. Every truth we speak today becomes a light in the darkness for a woman fifty years from now. Every story we share becomes medicine for healing we may never witness but will certainly help create.

This is the sacred responsibility and profound gift of unleashing our voices: We speak not only for ourselves but for all the women who come after us. We dream not only our own dreams but also the dreams that will guide future generations home to themselves.

What element calls to your story? What ancient wisdom is ready to speak through you? What truth are you ready to plant as a seed for the next seven generations?

The ancestors are waiting. Your voice matters. Your story is medicine.

It is time to speak.

J.J Mathieu

Author & Astrologer

https://www.facebook.com/jjmathieuauthor/
https://www.instagram.com/j.j.mathieu/
www.jjmathieuauthor.com

J.J. Mathieu is a writer, astrologer and full-time mom with a background in corporate and academic Communication. She earned a Master's Degree in Communication Studies from the University of Rhode Island and is a graduate of Debra Silverman's School of Applied Astrology. J.J. has been writing in a variety of contexts since she was a child crafting fiction books with pencil and spiral-bound notebook in hand. She has worn many hats during her career, but all have centered around or have been influenced by her love of writing. J.J.'s work has appeared on The Barre Blog and MomsIntoFitness.com. Her personal challenges serve as the foundation of her writing, which focuses on inspiring others to see their own lives through a lens of deep compassion and love for themselves and others. In addition to writing, J.J. loves reading, baking, mindful movement and anything chocolate and sparkly. Connect with J.J. at www.jjmathieuauthor.com or jjmathieuauthor@gmail.com.

My Heartbreaking Choice

By J.J Mathieu

The summer of 2008 was shaping up to be another busy one. I was in the second trimester of my second pregnancy after having lost my first to a very early miscarriage just a few months before. My younger sister was pregnant with her first child, due to be born in mid-July, and my husband, Taylor, and I were looking forward to a week-long vacation on Block Island, a small island just off the coast of our beloved home state of Rhode Island. Even though Block Island is still part of Rhode Island proper, it has always been my happy place—a place to escape the heat, humidity, and hustle of the mainland. I savor everything that the island has to offer, from the natural beauty of its beaches to its breathtaking sunsets to the sweetness of the ice cream shops that beckon you as soon as you step off the ferry. I couldn't wait to dip my toes into the white sand with a good book and the beginnings of the list for my Babies R Us registry. Shortly after returning from our local island getaway, Taylor and I would be having the much-anticipated ultrasound to find out the sex of our baby. Life was good for this mama-to-be.

Not long after we crossed Block Island Sound and settled into our rental house, things began to unravel. Less than 24 hours after our vacation began, I was out on a morning walk under crystal clear blue skies when I got a phone call from my parents saying that our condo had been robbed. My heart jumped into my throat as my thoughts, words, and legs immediately veered to the side of the road. "Are the cats okay?" I stammered into the phone. Our two cats, Piccadilly and Twinkles, had resumed their duties of keeping watch over our home while we were away for the week. "We don't know," my mom answered. "They're missing right now, but that doesn't mean they aren't hiding in the building somewhere."

Within minutes, Taylor and I were in line for the next ferry back to the mainland to look for our missing cats and assess the state of our property. My parents met us at the ferry, drove us back to our condo in Providence, and helped us locate our missing pets and secure our home so that we could finish out our vacation with cats in tow.

Thankfully, we were able to spend the rest of the week enjoying the best of Block Island at our rental home with our friends—both human and furry. I read through some of my pregnancy books and finished my baby registry list. Since Taylor and I were expecting our baby just a couple of days after Christmas that year, we made sure to take advantage of our time as a family of two before the reality of parenthood set in. On the ferry ride back home, I breathed in deeply as the salty sea air gently tousled my hair and the anticipated joy of my impending motherhood seeped into my soul.

Two weeks after returning from our babymoon, the big day arrived—ultrasound day! I couldn't wait to find out if the baby was a boy or a girl. Taylor was going to accompany me to the ultrasound and then we were going to celebrate the good news with a trip over to Babies R Us to set up our registry. My heart raced as the ultrasound technician smeared warm gel on my baby bump. I reached for Taylor's hand and we both looked at the screen as the image of our baby came into view. As the technician took images and measurements, I craned my neck to see if I could catch a glimpse of anything that would indicate the sex of the baby. A couple of minutes later, the technician confirmed that the baby was a boy. Taylor and I smiled at one another, completely oblivious to the additional images that were being brought up on the screen. At that point in time, we felt that we had no reason to question why the technician kept the wand focused on the baby's brain. After a moment or two, she finally disclosed that something didn't look quite right. I remember the sick feeling that instantly came over me when she explained that the baby's brain should be divided into two halves and it wasn't coming across that way on the ultrasound images. Of course, I immediately questioned if something was wrong. Since she wasn't at liberty to say what was really wrong with my baby, she assured me that I'd get all of the answers to my questions at my next ultrasound—a Level 3—scheduled for two days later at the Prenatal Diagnosis Center in Providence.

For two days, I imagined every possible scenario—good, bad, and otherwise—for why my baby's brain was showing as one whole mass instead of two distinct hemispheres. In between all of my research and a couple of sleepless nights, my sister gave birth to my first nephew. I remember visiting her in the hospital with half of my heart full of joy and the other half shattered into a million pieces. I just kept hoping for the best-case scenario, which was one that included my son playing with my new nephew several months into the future.

Two days later, my worst fears were confirmed when the doctor at the Prenatal Diagnosis Center came into the ultrasound room after reviewing all of the Level 3 images. My baby had a craniopharyngioma—a non-malignant brain tumor. He was already showing signs of struggle at this stage in the pregnancy. I sobbed as the doctor presented me with my options: I could wait and see if the baby would make it to term or I could end the pregnancy. If I decided to end the pregnancy, I could deliver the baby naturally, or I could opt to be put under anesthesia and have a Dilation and Evacuation (D&E), or a second-trimester abortion. The choice was mine and mine alone. The only caveat was that I had to make the decision fairly quickly, as I was almost into the 19th week of my pregnancy and if I didn't decide soon, my only option would be to deliver the baby. As I couldn't bear the thought of delivering, I opted to have the D&E as soon as possible. The surgery was scheduled for just five days later on August 4, 2008.

Even though I had arranged to have this unwanted surgery to end my son's life, I remember begging God to let him live, knowing that the chances of that prayer being answered were slim to none. I'm not sure why I even prayed; at that point, my faith in God was very small. I think I was just pulling out everything I could think of—everything inside of myself—to save that little boy's life and my sanity along with it. The night before the surgery, like clockwork, my son's gentle kicks, flip-flops, and flutters woke me in the early hours of the morning. Instead of willing myself to fall back to sleep right away, I lay in bed and tried to savor the last time this little boy would wake me up with his late-night antics. Tears began to fall as I wondered how everything could still look and feel the same from the outside, knowing that on the inside, all was certainly not well. I clutched my belly and sobbed myself back to sleep, hoping that I'd wake up from this nightmare and all would be as it should, or at least how I thought it should be.

After the D&E, I was in such a state of shock, disbelief, and pain that all I could do was lie in bed with Piccadilly and Twinkles, who never left my side, and cry. We had just been robbed, our home had been invaded and I felt so out of control and vulnerable. And to top it all off, my body had betrayed me. It wasn't doing its job and had allowed something to happen to my baby. Of course, I had no idea what I had done to deserve another devastating blow, but I imagined that it had to have been something I did, something I ate, something I drank, or some cleaning product that I had exposed myself to. Was it the fact that I exercised downstairs in a dingy basement for all of those months? These self-deprecating thoughts swirled around in my head as I tried to make sense of why I had lost my son and had been forced to make that choice myself. I was the one who signed the papers giving the doctor permission to end his life—to put a needle into his heart and to administer the medicine that would stop the beating. To allow his body to be taken from mine in pieces, which I would never see but would later be autopsied to confirm that he was, indeed, suffering from a non-malignant craniopharyngioma.

Over 17 years later, his death and the way I had initiated the end of his life still haunt me. I sometimes question if I made the right choice. But, when I think back to the ultrasound that revealed the trouble he was already experiencing in utero—his inability to properly swallow the amniotic fluid that was supposed to sustain him, protect him, and bring him life—I know that I did the right thing. As much as it still hurts to admit that to myself, it's true. But his death and the very little time that we did spend bonded together will forever be a part of my story—the story of how I became a mom before I had an actual baby in my arms.

I know that I'm not the only one who's suffered grief and loss and who has found herself slumped over her lap sobbing out every last tear in her body. I know that I'm not the only one who has pleaded with God for something that was never hers for the asking. But, I do know that once my tears dried and my vision became clear again, there was a reason why God didn't, or rather couldn't, answer my prayers. Perhaps it is because he already had. He knew that giving me the brief opportunity to spend time with the little boy that I never met, along with the grief of learning what it was like to experience a late-term abortion—and, yes, I'm going to use the proper term because that's what it was, that's what I had legally allowed to happen—would someday empower me to see the bigger picture and to experience motherhood through my own lens, in my own way and in my own time.

It is with this renewed faith that I finally feel comfortable revealing the true circumstances behind my pregnancy "loss." For almost two decades, I've let others believe that my son died in utero, when in fact, I was the one who made the heartbreaking choice to end his life. It's a decision that I didn't think I'd ever have to make and one that I wouldn't wish upon anyone. At the time, I felt selfish for taking what I felt was the easier route—being put to sleep so that I wouldn't have to live through the peak of the nightmare. I had said my goodbye during the wee hours of that morning, on my own time and in my own way. To this day, I carry his memory as well as the circumstances surrounding his death like a badge of honor. I am his mother and it is through our unique bond that I have grown into the strong, proud woman who writes these truth-filled words today.

Sonia Rodrigues

Transition to Wellness
Psychotherapist & Coach

https://www.linkedin.com/in/sonia-rodrigues-48b87149/
https://www.facebook.com/SoniaRodriguesLPC/
https://instagram.com/transition.to.wellness
www.transitiontowellness.com
https://soniarodrigues-marto.tribesites.com/

Sonia Rodrigues has been a licensed psychotherapist for over 20 years. She is the owner of a psychotherapy and coaching practice called Transition to Wellness. She has worked with people of all ages, helping them navigate various challenges in their life. She utilizes a holistic approach and provides a safe and supportive environment where her clients can feel supported on their path towards healing from their traumatic experiences and guided towards creating the life they desire. She provides individual therapy, coaching and also offers a variety of workshops on topics related to trauma, post-traumatic growth and fostering resilience.

Finding My Voice After Betrayal

By Sonia Rodrigues

There was a time in my life when I thought strength meant always being understanding, forgiving, and patient. I was not silent, but I was not standing fully in my power either. I often questioned myself, wondering if I was asking for too much, if I was too emotional, too direct, or too much of anything. I knew how to hold everything together: the role of therapist, mother, and professional, always composed, yet inside, I was exhausted from carrying the weight of everyone else's needs.

Like many women, I mistook self-sacrifice for love and endurance for strength. I believed that if I could just love harder, forgive more, or communicate better, things would change. But deep down, I knew I was abandoning myself. The betrayal that finally broke through my denial was not only the betrayal of another person; it was the betrayal of my own worth.

The Moment Everything Changed

There comes a moment in every woman's life when she realizes that the pain she has been carrying is no longer sustainable. For me, that moment came after uncovering layers of dishonesty in a relationship I believed was built on love and truth. Betrayal trauma cuts deep because it fractures your sense of safety and self. It makes you question everything—your reality, your intuition, your value.

As a psychotherapist, I had helped countless others navigate these very emotions, yet this time I was the one unraveling. I remember sitting in the quiet, feeling my chest ache, my mind spinning between disbelief and clarity. That was the night I made a quiet promise to myself. I would no longer settle for crumbs and call it connection. I would no longer give my peace away to prove my worth.

The Slow Rebuild

Healing after betrayal is not a single decision but a daily practice. It is the process of grieving not only the person who hurt you, but the version of yourself who tolerated what you did not deserve. I began to realize that the parts of me that over-gave and over-forgave were simply trying to feel loved and safe. When I met those parts with compassion instead of judgment, I began to heal.

I turned inward and started treating myself as tenderly as I would a client in pain. I journaled through the grief, cried when I needed to, and practiced staying with my feelings instead of rationalizing them away. Each time I honored what I felt, I reclaimed another piece of my power.

In therapy, we talk about self-betrayal, the moments we silence our truth, ignore our boundaries, or question our own intuition to preserve a relationship. I had lived that pattern for years. The moment I stopped betraying myself, I began healing from the betrayals of others.

Realizing My Worth

As my healing deepened, I redefined what worth meant. It was no longer tied to being chosen or needed. Worth was not about perfection, productivity, or pleasing others. Worth was inherent, unchanging, and mine to own.

I started asking myself the same questions I now ask my clients.
What am I tolerating that drains me?
What would my life look like if I stopped trying to earn love and began to receive it freely?
What would it feel like to be fully seen and valued?

The answers required me to let go of relationships that could not meet me where I was going. Some people were attached to the version of me who doubted herself. They were not ready for the woman who finally knew her worth. Letting go was painful, but it was also the most loving choice I could make for my own peace and for my family. I wanted my children to see strength and self-worth and know how to ask for it in their own relationships. That in itself was the motivation I needed to say, *No More.*

The Power of Boundaries

Boundaries became my language of self-respect. They were not walls to keep people out but structures that protected my peace. I learned that the more I honored my boundaries, the more I trusted myself.

I began saying no without apology.
I learned to rest without guilt.
I allowed space for only what felt aligned with my growth.

Every time I honored my own limits, I reminded myself that I was no longer living in survival mode. I was creating a life of emotional safety and integrity.

Helping Others Find Theirs

As I rose, I felt called to help other women do the same. In my work, I began noticing how many women were navigating similar patterns—overgiving, over-functioning, and living in quiet self-doubt. Many were successful on the outside but emotionally depleted on the inside.

That realization became the foundation for *Transition to Wellness*, a space I created for emotional, clinical, and spiritual healing. My mission became helping women rebuild their self-worth, find their voices, and remember that they never have to settle for less than they deserve.

Healing is not about becoming someone new. It is about remembering who you are beneath the conditioning, beneath the fear, and beneath the need to prove your worth.

The Therapeutic Truth About Betrayal

Betrayal trauma does not only break your heart; it dysregulates your nervous system. Your mind becomes caught in loops of confusion and hypervigilance. Your body forgets how to feel safe. Healing begins by restoring that sense of internal safety.

For me, that looked like:

- Grounding through deep breathing and mindfulness.
- Reconnecting with my body through gentle movement.
- Writing as a form of emotional release instead of self-criticism.
- Practicing affirmations rooted in truth: *I am worthy. I am safe. I am enough.*

Small consistent acts of self-care became the building blocks of my recovery. Healing is not about doing more. It is about doing less of what hurts your spirit.

The Shift Into Alignment

The more I honored my truth, the more aligned my life became. Opportunities appeared that reflected my growth—collaborations, friendships, and experiences that matched my energy rather than drained it. I stopped chasing what was not meant for me. I learned to trust timing, intuition, and the gentle voice of my higher self.

Alignment feels like peace, not chaos. It looks like mutual respect, not inconsistency. It sounds like honesty, not silence. Healing taught me that it is safe to outgrow the people and patterns that were never meant to hold my light.

Stepping into alignment is not a one-time awakening; it is a daily practice of choosing what feels true over what feels familiar. It requires faith, courage, and discernment. Some days alignment feels like flow—the right opportunities meeting you at the right time. Other days, it looks like standing alone in your truth while everything around you rearranges itself to match your new vibration. Alignment asks us to let go of control and trust that what is meant for us will never require us to shrink to keep it. It invites us to move through life with grace and grounded confidence, knowing that peace is the truest indicator that we are exactly where we are meant to be.

Reflection Prompts for Reclaiming Your Power

If you are on your own journey of healing, take a moment to reflect on these questions:

1. Where in your life have you questioned or minimized your needs to keep the peace?
2. What relationships leave you feeling drained instead of fulfilled?
3. What would change if you believed you were worthy of reciprocity and respect?
4. How can you begin honoring your emotions instead of rationalizing them away?
5. What does standing in your power look like for you today?

Awareness is where transformation begins.

Strategies for Rebuilding Self-Worth

1. **Practice emotional honesty.**
   Allow yourself to feel without judgment. Emotions are messengers. They show you what needs attention and healing.

2. **Reconnect with your body.**
   The body holds stories that words cannot. Move, stretch, breathe, and learn to listen to what your body is trying to tell you.

3. **Create an emotional wellness routine.**
   Just as you schedule physical checkups, create a rhythm for emotional self-care: time to reflect, release, and realign.

4. **Choose truth-telling relationships.**
   Surround yourself with people who encourage growth and mirror authenticity. Protect your energy from those who cannot meet you with respect.

5. **Rewrite your story.**
   You are not too much, and you are not asking for too much. Replace self-doubt with self-compassion. Reframe your narrative from victimhood to victory.

The New Chapter

Today, I no longer define myself by betrayal. I define myself by the courage it took to rise. My voice, once hesitant and unsure, now speaks with conviction and compassion. Through *Transition to Wellness*, I help women do the same—find their voices, reclaim their power, and step into the fullness of who they are.

Healing is not about forgetting the past. It is about integrating it, honoring it, and allowing it to shape a wiser, stronger version of yourself.

I often tell the women I work with, *You are not too much. You are not asking for too much.* You are learning what it means to stand in your worth, and that is something to be proud of.

If you take one thing from my story, let it be this:
Your healing will become someone else's hope.
Your voice will light the path for another woman still searching for hers.
And when you choose to stand in your truth, you not only change your life, but you also give others permission to rise with you.

Steps to Begin Honoring Yourself Today

Healing begins with small, intentional choices—the ones that whisper *I matter, I deserve peace, I am enough.*

Here are steps you can begin taking today to honor yourself and build a foundation of self-respect and emotional freedom.

1. **Start listening to your inner voice.**
   Spend a few quiet minutes each day checking in with yourself. Ask, *What do I need right now? What am I feeling?* Your intuition is your internal compass, and it becomes stronger each time you choose to listen instead of dismissing it.

2. **Stop apologizing for having needs.**
   Your needs do not make you difficult or demanding—they make you human. Begin to notice when you over-apologize or minimize what you feel, and replace it with self-validation.

3. **Set boundaries that protect your peace.**
   Boundaries are not punishments; they are acts of love for yourself and for others. Start small. Say no when something feels misaligned or when saying yes would drain you. Over time, boundaries become the scaffolding that supports your emotional freedom.

4. **Reclaim your time and energy.**
   Notice where your energy flows each day. Are you constantly giving without receiving? Are you saying yes to people or commitments that no longer serve you? Choose one area of your life where you can reclaim your time and invest it back into yourself.

5. **Surround yourself with truth-tellers.**
   Healing thrives in safe, authentic connection. Seek friendships and communities that celebrate your growth, challenge you

to rise, and remind you of your worth. Release those who only take from your spirit without giving in return.

6. **Speak to yourself with compassion.**
   Your inner dialogue sets the tone for your healing. When self-doubt creeps in, respond with gentleness. Replace "What's wrong with me?" with "What do I need to feel safe and loved right now?"

7. **Choose alignment over approval.**
   You do not need to prove your worth through someone else's acceptance. Alignment means choosing peace over people-pleasing, authenticity over performance, and integrity over comfort.

8. **Remember that you are not too much and you are not asking for too much.**
   You are simply learning to honor the fullness of who you are—emotionally, spiritually, and relationally. You are learning to expect the same depth of care that you so freely give.

Closing Reflections

Today, I stand in my truth with deep gratitude for the woman I have become—a woman who no longer doubts her worth, silences her intuition, or overextends herself for love that must be earned.

Through *Transition to Wellness*, my mission continues to grow: helping women find their voices, rebuild their confidence, and rediscover the joy of living in emotional alignment.

Healing is not a one-time decision; it is a lifelong practice of returning to yourself.
Each time you choose truth over fear, you honor the woman you are becoming.

Each time you set a boundary, you affirm your worth.
And each time you speak your truth, you create space for another woman to do the same.

You are not too much.
You are not asking for too much.
You are enough, exactly as you are.

Nana Adjoa Sifa Amponsah

Founder of Guzakuza

https://www.linkedin.com/in/nana-adjoa-sifa-amponsah-91099950/

www.nadjoasifa.orgwww.guzakuza.com

Nana Adjoa A. Sifa is a gender- lens entrepreneur and ecosystem builder committed to driving change in social investment, agrifood system and amplifying women's voices. As Founder of Guzakuza, she has ignited over 9,000 women across 36 countries, equipping them to build scalable, sustainable businesses through initiatives like Ignite Africa, MentorHer, WiFAI, and SheFarms.A World Economic Forum Global Shaper, UN Women UK Delegate, and NYU-GWSLP Fellow, Nana has shaped global conversations on women, entrepreneurship, and climate. She has spoken on high-level panels, including presenting the Berlin Charter at the G20.Recognised with awards like the UK's Inspiring Women Award and Africa 40 Under 40, her work has been featured in The New York Times, Spore Magazine, and DW TV. She also founded The FeMail, a platform championing women's voices in business. Nana is passionate about unlocking capital, reshaping systems, and creating opportunities for women to thrive in agrifood and beyond.

When a Whisper Becomes a Roar

By Nana Adjoa Sifa Amponsah

I did not set out to be "a voice." I set out to survive, to try, to build something small enough to matter to me and perhaps one or two others. But life has a way of testing how small you want to stay.

I remember standing in a room once, surrounded by men who had been celebrated for feeding the nation. It was Ghana's prestigious National Farmers' Day. Banners fluttered. Speeches echoed. Awards gleamed. Yet as names were called, faces applauded, and trophies handed out, I kept counting. One, two, ten, twenty. Where were the women?

In over two decades, only one woman had been recognized at the very top. One.

That silence cut deeper than the speeches. It told a story: women feed the nation but are invisible when the nation gives thanks. That day, something inside me broke open. I did not whisper my discomfort. I said it aloud: "This cannot continue. Women farmers deserve recognition too."

Was it comfortable? Not at all. The air grew heavier. Some frowned. Some murmured that I was being difficult, maybe even disrespectful. But I knew this: silence protects systems. And speaking shakes them.

The Weight of Silence

Every woman knows the weight of silence.

The moments we wanted to raise our hand but didn't. The meetings where we swallowed an idea and watched a man say it minutes later, greeted with applause. The times culture told us, "Stay quiet, you are enough only if you are invisible."

Silence is not neutral. It is heavy. It bends our backs. It squeezes our throats. It convinces us that playing small is safer.

But here is the truth I have learned: your silence serves no one—not you, not your daughters, not the world you dream of.

When we shrink, when we hide, when we let fear stitch our mouths shut, we deny the world the gift of our story.

Planting Seeds of Change

When I founded Guzakuza, I was not trying to be heroic. I was trying to solve a problem that haunted me: why are women—the backbone of African agriculture—so often treated as afterthoughts?

Women till the soil, carry food to markets, hold families together. Yet they are the least resourced, the least heard, the least celebrated.

So I decided to build a platform where women could learn, grow, and lead. It was not glamorous in the beginning. It was messy, lonely, sometimes terrifying. There were days I wondered how to pay the bills, days I questioned whether my vision was too ambitious, days I felt the hot breath of doubt whispering, "Who do you think you are? Why would anyone listen?"

Maybe you've heard that voice too.

But something remarkable happened. Women came. From Ghana. From across Africa. From across the ocean. They came with dreams tucked into the folds of their fears. They came with stories they thought were too small, too ordinary, too unworthy. And together, we began to speak.

Stories That Shook the Ground

I remember Ama, a young woman who joined our fellowship. She had been mocked for leaving a "real job" to farm. Her family doubted her. Neighbors laughed. She almost quit. But through our work together, she discovered not only better farming techniques but also her own worth. She started speaking boldly about her business. Today, she trains other women, multiplying courage wherever she goes.

Or Fatou from Senegal, who came in convinced she had nothing to offer. By the end of her program, she stood before hundreds, sharing her vision with such conviction that no one could look away.

These women are proof that confidence is not found—it is built. It grows in the soil of mentorship, knowledge, and community. And when one woman's confidence rises, others find permission to rise too.

Over time, I heard the words that fuel my work more than any title or trophy: "Because of you, I didn't give up."

That, dear reader, is what happens when a whisper becomes a roar.

Confidence Is a Practice

People often tell me, "You're so confident." I smile, but here's the secret: confidence is not a permanent state. It is not something you either have or don't have.

Confidence is a practice.

It is built brick by brick, by daring to show up even when your knees shake. By saying yes when your whole body screams no. By walking into rooms where you feel you don't belong—and staying until you realize you do.

It is failing publicly and choosing not to crawl into silence but to try again.

It is telling your story, not once but over and over, until the shame dissolves and your voice feels natural, strong, free.

Confidence is not the absence of fear. It is speaking anyway.

Power Reclaimed

The truth about power is this: it is rarely handed over freely. It must be claimed, reclaimed, and sometimes wrestled back from those who guard it jealously.

In agriculture, power is land. Power is money. Power is recognition. For too long, women have been denied all three. And yet, women remain in the fields, feeding nations, sustaining families, holding economies afloat.

This contradiction enrages me—and it should enrage you too.

But anger is not enough. Anger must be harnessed, directed, sharpened into strategy. That is why I continue to push for policies that deliberately include women, why I speak truth to power even when it is uncomfortable, and why I create spaces where women can practice power until it feels natural.

When one woman rises, others see it can be done. When a hundred rise, systems begin to shift. When thousands rise, cultures transform.

Your Story Is Not Too Ordinary

Here's what I want you to hear most: your story is not too ordinary.

Too many women disqualify themselves before the world even gets a chance. We think our struggles are too common, our victories too small, our voices too shaky.

But your story may be the exact light another woman needs to find her way.

Think of it this way: the first time I stood in front of an audience to share my vision, I was terrified. I stumbled. I doubted myself. But someone in that audience later came to me and said, “I needed to hear that. Because of you, I will try.”

Imagine if I had stayed silent. Imagine if you stay silent.

Reflection: From Whisper to Roar

So if you are reading this and doubting yourself, hear me clearly: the world is waiting for your voice. Not a perfect voice, not a practiced one, but your authentic one.

Because every time a woman dares to speak her truth, she does more than change her own life. She creates cracks in the wall of silence. And through those cracks, light pours in for the rest of us.

So I ask you:

Where are you whispering when you should be roaring?
Who benefits from your silence—and who suffers because of it?
What one story, if you told it, could unlock courage in another woman?

I began as a whisper. Today, I roar—not because I am fearless, but because I know fear is not my master. I roar because I have seen what happens when women find their voices: nations feed themselves, businesses flourish, families thrive, and little girls grow up believing they can be anything.

And so can you.

You may feel small now. You may think no one is listening. But let me tell you: a voice does not have to be loud to be powerful. It only has to be true.

So stand tall. Speak boldly. Dare to shake the room.

Because when a whisper becomes a roar, the world will never be the same again.

Martha Maria Smith

Founder of martiem.smith.com

http://linkedin.com/in/martie-smith-8b062025
https://www.facebook.com/martie.smith.37?mibextid=LQQJ4d
http://martiemsmith.com/

Martie M. SmithTop International Resilience Ambassador | Award-Winning Author | Inspirational SpeakerMartie M. Smith is a U.S. veteran, 4x best-selling author, and globally recognized resilience expert and ambassador. From mechanic to mentor, her journey reflects unwavering courage through adversity—transforming caregiving, surgeries, and reinvention into a purpose-driven mission. Her books, including Creative Chaos Warrior and She Wins, Beyond the Hurt share powerful stories of healing, leadership, and growth. With authenticity and heart, Martie inspires people of all ages to embrace their truth and rise stronger. 🏆 Honors & Awards• Certified Personal Trainer (2023)• ICWP International Woman Educator Award (2023)• Heart of Gold, Resilience, and Humanitarian Awards (2024)• Star Educator & Tenacious Educationist (2024)• SWUSA Global Leadership & Keynote Speaker (2024)• Top Resilience Ambassador & Inspirational Icon (2025)• Force Magazine Top 10 Entrepreneurs (2025)• Brainz 500 Global Leader & Senior Contributor ✨ "Writing is how I honor resilience." —Martie M. Smith

From Wreckage to Reinvention: A Mind, Body, and Soul Awakening

By Martha Maria Smith

The Day Everything Stopped

The day my life came to a screeching halt, I thought it was the end. What I didn't realize was that it was the beginning of everything I had been running from, everything I had been afraid to face, and everything God had been trying to whisper to me all along.

For years, my life felt like a pinball machine. I was bouncing from place to place, job to job, ricocheting between medical appointments for myself and emergency hospital visits for loved ones. My days blurred into endless motion, always doing, rarely being. From the outside, it might have looked like resilience. People said, "You're so strong." But inside, I was unraveling.

I was watching the slow erosion of bodies, minds, and souls all around me while my own life spun further out of control. And yet, I kept insisting to myself that I was managing, that if I just kept moving, eventually I would hit solid ground. But the truth was harder and harsher.

I was unbalanced.
I was unstable.
I was wrecked.

If you've ever lived in survival mode, you know this exhausting dance. You keep moving because if you stop, you fear you might collapse. You convince yourself that momentum equals safety. But deep inside, the truth gnaws at you: This is not living; this is barely existing.

And then, life forced me to stop.

Not a gentle slowdown. Not a polite tap on the shoulder. But a screeching, full-stop moment that demanded I face what I had been avoiding. In that stillness, the kind of quiet that feels heavy in your chest, God met me. Not with anger, not with disappointment, but with a whisper that wrapped around my brokenness like a balm:

You are still My work in progress.

Those words became oxygen to my suffocating spirit. They were not just words; they were a lifeline. They reminded me that brokenness does not cancel purpose. That endings can become beginnings. That healing starts not with perfection, but with permission. Permission to rest. Permission to feel. Permission to believe again.

Reflection and Action

Reflection: When was the last time you honestly stopped, not just physically, but mentally and emotionally? What did that moment reveal to you?

Action: Write down one area of your life where you need a pause, not as a weakness, but as a turning point.

The Mind: Rewriting the Story

The first place I had to heal was not my body. It was my mind.

For years, I had been living under a set of unspoken rules that governed every choice I made:

> My worth equals my productivity.
> Rest is laziness.
> My needs come last.
>
> Sound familiar?
>
> These beliefs had built walls around my potential. I wore exhaustion like a badge of honor, confusing burnout with

accomplishment. I silenced my own needs, believing that selflessness meant strength. But when God whispered, "You are still My work in progress," I realized those walls could come down.

Changing my mind did not happen overnight. It began with small, daily choices to replace lies with truth:
"I'm not enough." - "I am fearfully and wonderfully made."
"I'm too broken." - "I am becoming."
"I can't." - "With God, all things are possible."

Each shift was like reclaiming a piece of myself. Confidence did not explode overnight. It grew like a seed breaking through soil, fragile at first, but determined to reach the light. And each time I chose truth over fear, my mind rewired itself toward possibility instead of defeat.

Reflection and Action

Reflection: What is one recurring thought that leaves you drained or defeated?

Action: Write it down, then rewrite it as truth. Say it out loud every morning for the next 30 days.

The Body: Making Peace with My Vessel

When your body has been in survival mode for too long, it sends signals, urgent and unrelenting, until you finally pay attention. Mine had been speaking for years through fatigue, through pain, through illness. But I had become a master at silencing it with coffee, overwork, and the lie of "I'll rest later."

Later never came.

It wasn't until my health forced me to stop that I began to see my body differently—not as a burden to drag through life, but as an ally to honor. This was not an easy shift. For so long, I treated my body like an afterthought, like a machine that could keep going if I pushed it hard enough.

But reinvention meant listening. It meant learning to treat my body with the reverence it deserved. I started small, so small it almost felt insignificant at first:

> Gentle walks instead of punishing workouts.
> Foods that nourished rather than whatever was fast and convenient.
> Sleep, not as an optional luxury, but as a sacred appointment with renewal.
>
> Each act of care was an act of gratitude, not only for my body but also for the God who gave it to me. I began to see my reflection not as something to criticize but as evidence of survival, a vessel that had carried me through storms. My scars told stories. My weariness was proof of endurance. My breath, even on the hardest days, was a miracle.
>
> I also learned the language of my body's signals. Fatigue did not mean weakness; it meant rest was required. Pain was not an inconvenience; it was a message that something needed attention. The more I tuned in, the more I realized that honoring my body was inseparable from honoring my spirit.
>
> And slowly, as my body grew stronger, so did my hope. Movement became not punishment but celebration. Food became not comfort but fuel. Rest became not avoidance but a strategy.

Reflection and Action

Reflection: What is your body asking for right now—rest, nourishment, movement, or medical attention?

Action: Choose one act today that honors your body's request. Write down how it makes you feel afterward.

The Soul: Realigning My Compass

If the mind is the battlefield and the body is the vessel, then the soul is the compass. And mine had been spinning wildly, pointing everywhere but peace.

I had become so accustomed to doing that, I had forgotten how to be. My soul was crowded with noise: responsibilities, worries, and unspoken griefs. I didn't realize how disconnected I had become until silence forced me to listen.

My healing began with surrender—unpolished, unfiltered surrender. I stopped bargaining with God. I stopped presenting prayers as negotiations. I simply sat in His presence, messy and undone. And in that stillness, I began to hear His voice again.

Prayer became conversation, not obligation. Worship became a reset button, not just a Sunday ritual. Gratitude became a language, not just a list.

And slowly, my soul began to breathe again.

I started noticing beauty in the most minor things: the sunrise spilling through the blinds, the kindness of a stranger, and the way a song could soften even the heaviest day. My soul began to unclench. My compass slowly, tenderly, pointed back toward peace.

Hope, once fragile, began to take root.

Reflection and Action

Reflection: When was the last time your soul felt light, peaceful, or joyful? What were you doing?

Action: Schedule ten minutes today to reconnect with God—no agenda, no striving, just presence.

Unleash Her Voice: The Birth of a Mission

In restoring my mind, body, and soul, I stumbled upon something I didn't realize I had nearly lost: my voice.

For years, my words had been filtered through fear—fear of judgment, fear of not being enough, and fear of making others uncomfortable. I became skilled at speaking politely and apologetically, always checking the room before daring to share the truth.

But healing does something powerful: It peels away those filters. It demands authenticity.

My true voice emerged not all at once, but in fragile whispers that grew louder with practice. It was the voice rooted in conviction and compassion. The one willing to say, "This is my story," even if it trembled. The one that learned courage isn't the absence of fear but the decision to speak anyway.

That's why Unleash HER Voice was a calling, not as a catchy phrase or a motivational slogan, but as a mission. A mission to help women everywhere rediscover the power in their stories. Because when a woman speaks from a place of wholeness, she does not just talk for herself. She speaks for generations.

I remember one of the first times I dared to speak my truth in public. My knees were shaking, my palms sweating, but when I finished sharing my story, a woman in the audience grabbed my hand and whispered through tears, "That's my story too. I just didn't know how to tell it."

And that's when I realized my voice wasn't just mine. It was a bridge. A lifeline. A ripple of healing that could extend far beyond me.

Reflection and Action

Reflection: When was the last time you spoke your truth without watering it down?

Action: Write down one story from your life you've been afraid to share. It doesn't need to be public yet but acknowledging it is the first step toward freedom.

From 8 to 88: The Ongoing Process

Here's the truth: Whether you are eight years old or eighty-eight, you are still becoming.

There is no expiration date on transformation. No "too late" stamped on purpose.

I've seen children use their voices to challenge injustice and create change in their communities. I've seen women in their seventies and eighties publish their first books, start businesses, or mentor the next generation with wisdom only age can provide. And I've witnessed people rise from pain into purpose in ways they never believed possible.

Every season of life gives your voice new depth. Every challenge adds new meaning to your message.

So, if you're reading this thinking, "I've missed my moment," let me speak directly to your heart: No, you haven't. You're breathing. And as long as you're breathing, you're becoming.

Reflection and Action

Reflection: If you genuinely believed you were "still becoming," how would you live differently starting today?

Action: Write down one bold step you can take this week toward the life you want, then take it.

The Call to Action

Pause if you must, but do not stop.

You are not broken beyond repair. You are a masterpiece in progress.

The same God who whispered to me, "You are still My work in progress," whispers it to you now. Let those words breathe life into your weary places. Let them remind you that the story is not over. Your next chapter could be the one that changes everything, for you and for someone else.

In the pages ahead of your life, you will walk through silencing the lies, strengthening your truth, and unleashing a voice so clear and powerful that no one, not even you, will be able to deny it.

Because the world needs what only you can say, and it is time to say it.

Reflection and Action

Reflection: What is one thing your future self will thank you for starting today?
Action: Write it down. Say it out loud. Take one small step. Then take another.

Kimberly Tyler

https://www.linkedin.com/in/kimberly-tyler-a8849539/
https://www.facebook.com/profile.php?id=100094747320115
https://www.instagram.com/kimmijotyler/
http://www.brokenvesselholylight.com

Kimberly Tyler, M.Ed, is an international best-selling author with over 30 years in education and children's ministry leadership. A retired Education Director and dedicated teacher, she possesses a wealth of knowledge and experience in student success through positive learning environments and advocating for inclusive practices. Kimberly is an inspiring author with a profound gift for seeing others succeed despite any challenges that they may face. Residing in Northern California with her husband and extended family, she draws inspiration from the beautiful surroundings and close-knit community. Kimberly's writing reflects her genuine desire to uplift and empower readers as she shares stories that resonate with faith, hope, and resilience. Her unique blend of storytelling and encouragement has positively impacted the hearts of readers worldwide. An accomplished creative, her favorite mediums are fabric arts such as quilting and embroidery.

Confidence with a Purpose: The Proverbs 31 Woman as a God-Assured Businesswoman

By Kimberly Tyler

Have you ever looked at the Proverbs 31 woman and thought, *"I could never be like her"*? I know I have. She seems to do it all—manages her home, runs a thriving business, keeps her family happy, clothed, and fed, and still has time to speak wisdom and kindness to everyone around her. It's easy to read that passage and feel overwhelmed, maybe even a little discouraged. But here's what I've come to realize: She isn't a picture of perfection. We were never meant to read her that way. She's a picture of *"purposeful confidence."* And that confidence? It doesn't come from how capable she is—it comes from how connected she is to God.

The Proverbs 31 woman is a confident businesswoman, but her confidence isn't self-made. It's God-given. She's bold and strategic because she walks in step with the Lord. She makes wise decisions not because she knows everything but because she trusts the One who does. She shows us that real confidence—the kind that lasts—is born in faith, nurtured in trust, and lived out in love. And friend, that kind of confidence is available to you and me, too.

Rooted in God: The Source of Her Confidence

Let's begin at the foundation. Proverbs 31:30 says, *"Charm is deceitful, and beauty is passing, but a woman who fears the Lord, she shall be praised."* That verse is the heartbeat of the entire passage. Everything she does—every decision, every task, every act of kindness—flows from this reverent relationship with God.

When we think about confidence, the world tells us it comes from how we look, what we've accomplished, or how many followers we have. But this woman knows better. Her assurance isn't rooted in external things. She doesn't need validation from people to feel valuable. She has found her identity in the Lord—and that changes everything.

Her fear of the Lord isn't a fear that shrinks back; it's a deep respect, a surrendered awe that leads to wisdom, strength, and clarity. It's not a burden—it's a blessing. She doesn't waste energy trying to prove herself because she knows she's already approved by the One who matters most.

And that's the kind of confidence we're invited into. Not the kind that puffs us up or puts on a show, but the kind that whispers, *"Even when I don't have all the answers, I know the One who does."* It's steady. It's unshakable. And it's available every day we choose to walk closely with God.

When our confidence is rooted in Him, we no longer live to impress—we live to express His goodness through our lives. That's a firm foundation, one worth building every area of our life and business upon.

It's also worth noting that the Proverbs 31 woman didn't grow this confidence overnight. It was cultivated daily through prayer, obedience, and learning to listen for God's voice in every area of her life. Her relationship with God wasn't a side note. It was the anchor. And that's good news for us because it means we don't have to strive to be confident. We simply have to stay connected to the One who fills us with it.

She Plans, She Builds, She Trades: A Strategic Entrepreneur

If anyone tells you the Bible doesn't talk about women in business, just point them to Proverbs 31. This woman is not only spiritual and nurturing. She's also sharp, savvy, and strategic. Look at verses 16, 18, and 24:

"She considers a field and buys it; from her profits, she plants a vineyard... She perceives that her merchandise is good... She makes linen garments and sells them and supplies sashes for the merchants."

She's a planner. She studies the field before buying it. She reinvests her profits to create something even more fruitful. She recognizes the value of her work and doesn't hesitate to bring it to market. This is not passive faith—this is active, purposeful confidence lived out through smart decisions and God-led entrepreneurship.

It's encouraging to see that faith and business are not at odds in this passage. They're intertwined. Her relationship with God empowers her to make wise investments, build wealth, and provide for her family and others. That's the beauty of walking with the Lord. He doesn't just care about our hearts; He cares about our hands and what we do with them.

Whether you're selling handmade goods from your kitchen table, launching an online store, or leading a corporate team, your work matters. And when you surrender your plans to God, you can move forward boldly, knowing He is your guide and provider.

Strength and Dignity: Her Character Is Her Branding

Proverbs 31:25 says, *"Strength and honor are her clothing; she shall rejoice in time to come."* In today's terms, you could say her character is her brand. She wears strength and dignity like a well-tailored outfit. And just like clothing, it's something she puts on intentionally.

What stands out is that her strength isn't loud—it's steady. Her dignity doesn't scream for attention—it speaks through her actions. She doesn't rely on flashy marketing or performance. Her confidence comes from knowing she's doing what God called her to do and doing it with integrity.

We live in a world that often confuses confidence with arrogance. But the Proverbs 31 woman reminds us that true confidence doesn't push others down. It lifts them up. She doesn't need to compare or compete. She knows who she is and whose she is, and that alone gives her peace.

You and I can walk in that same peace. We don't have to be the loudest or the most polished. When we clothe ourselves in godly strength and dignity, it becomes our testimony. It shows up in how we speak, serve, and do business with grace and purpose.

She Leads with Wisdom and Kindness

One of my favorite verses in the whole chapter is Proverbs 31:26: *"She opens her mouth with wisdom, and on her tongue is the law of kindness."* Isn't that beautiful? This woman doesn't just lead with her hands. She leads with her words.

She's not harsh or domineering. She doesn't run her home or business with fear. Instead, she leads from a place of wisdom and kindness. That doesn't mean she's weak. On the contrary, it takes a strong woman to lead with grace. It takes true confidence to correct gently, to speak the truth in love, and to offer kindness when it's not required.

As women in business, we can sometimes feel pressure to be harsh or aggressive to earn respect. But the Proverbs 31 woman shows us a better way. She's respected not because she's hard, but because she's wise and kind.

Let's be those kinds of leaders. Let's run our businesses and lead our homes with the wisdom that comes from God and the kindness that reflects His heart.

Her Confidence Impacts Generations

Proverbs 31:27–28 says, *"She watches over the ways of her household, and does not eat the bread of idleness. Her children rise up and call her blessed; her husband also, and he praises her."*

This isn't just about productivity—it's about legacy. Her confidence, her business, and her leadership all have ripple effects. Her children are watching. Her community is impacted. Her husband sees the fruit of her labor and praises her.

And that's the bigger picture: Her work is not just about income. It's about influence. She's building something that lasts, blesses others, and points back to the God she serves.

That's the kind of confidence we're called to—one that goes beyond our own success and touches the lives of those around us. Whether you're raising babies or building brands, your faith-fueled confidence matters. And it doesn't just change your story—it changes generations.

Walking in God-Confidence

The Proverbs 31 woman isn't some superhero we have to strive to become. She's a woman who simply walks closely with God and that closeness becomes her confidence.

Her strength isn't in her schedule or her sales. Her confidence isn't rooted in her looks or her bank account. It's rooted in her relationship with the Lord.

And friend, you and I are invited into that same kind of confidence. A confidence that plans wisely, speaks kindly, leads with integrity, and impacts generations. All because we're leaning on God every step of the way.

So, let's let go of perfection and lean into purpose. Let's run our businesses, our homes, and our lives with the assurance that comes from knowing we are called, we are equipped, and we are never alone.

Here's the beautiful truth: Confidence doesn't begin with achievement. It begins with alignment. When our hearts are aligned with God's Word, when our plans are surrendered to His wisdom, and when His Spirit guides our efforts, we can step forward with bold, holy confidence. Not only will our lives be transformed, but so will the lives of those around us.

So start today. Start small if you must. But start knowing this: You are capable, you are called, and with God's strength, you are already equipped. Walk forward in faith. Your confidence is safe in His hands.

Tishana Meyers Eason

Brooklyn Beauty Bar
Self-love Coach

www.brooklynbeautybarga.com
www.brooklynbeautybar1.com

Tishana all so known as Brooklyn was born and raised in Brooklyn New York. At the age of 19 years old. She became part salon owner, where she began to counsel women behind the chair. She decided to get certified. Tishana is now a certified Self-love coach. August of 2017 Brooklyn Beauty Bar opened its doors for the very first time. The mission is to help others look and feel great about themselves In order to fulfill the mission. After her divorce Tishana turned her pain into purposes and became an author. The book is called "Living His Lie but Found the Truth." She had a passion for fashion so she ran after her childhood dream of becoming the couture fashion designer. Her fashion line is GioNyka Couture. Brooklyn is also known as the makeover queen for her amazing talents in the beauty industry.

Unleashing Her Greatness

By Tishana Meyers Eason

As she sat in her car, hands gripping the steering wheel, heart pounding louder than the traffic outside. Thinking about all the rooms filled with people who praised her silence but feared her truth and what lives inside of her. How she would shrink to make others shine. Feeling unworthy even to be in rooms of imperfect people who bleed the same way she does. The bondage of lack of self-love. Having invisible chains, controlled by low self-esteem as you master. But today was different. Today, she came to speak. It was just a matter of time that God would break those chains and that day is now.

Her name is Brooklyn. And like so many women, she spent years being everything for everyone: the good girl, the strong friend, the quiet wife, and the dependable stylist. She smiled when she wanted to cry. She stayed when she wanted to leave. She whispered when her soul was screaming for help. She is me and I am her. Just tolerating less than. She knew she had to unteach herself beliefs and habits that she learned throughout the years.

Brooklyn believed that being silent kept the peace, but all it did was break her piece by piece. Not having the ability to voice your opinion really takes away your peace. It took her falling into depression to understand what she was doing to herself.

The first time Brooklyn decided to speak up, her voice cracked. She was just nervous to hear her words out loud. It wasn't in front of a crowd. It wasn't polished or powerful. It was in front of her bathroom mirror, whispering the words, "I don't deserve this." That whisper became her anthem.

She started telling her truth—first to herself, then to her journal, and eventually to the people who had hurt her. Not to gain an apology, but to set herself free from the bondage she's been in.

Speaking up didn't change the past, but it unlocked her future. She found strength in her vulnerability and discovered that her voice had been waiting for her for a very long time. She was no longer a victim but a hero. Saving the lives of women like herself. Living a lie but found the truth. The truth was my marriage was falling apart, and she had low self-esteem because of the decision of ignoring the red flags and not sticking up for herself. Just people-pleasing. Dying on the inside.

When Brooklyn finally left the relationship that nearly broke her, she had nothing but her name, her beautiful children, and the desire for peace. But stepping up isn't about having it all figured out, because she didn't. She allowed God to order her next steps in life. Everything she knew was gone. It's about choosing yourself, even when it's terrifying or you don't know the future.

Brooklyn moved to Georgia and opened a salon with the little bit she had, which gave her purpose. She began with little changes in her life. The first thing was saying "no" without explanation. This was the hardest part for her. She wore bright colors again. She began to dance at church feeling free of what kept her down. She stopped apologizing for her dreams and being true to herself. That little girl on the inside needed to feel safe again. Brooklyn learned that this was a personal journey so there is no special date to heal. She allowed herself to feel her emotions instead of suppressing them. She would walk around with her journal so that she never had to keep it on the inside.

Every step forward was a rebellion against the lies she had been told: that she was too much, too emotional, too complicated, and not good enough. Truth was, she was powerful and

Brooklyn once hid from her story, ashamed of what people would think. Feeling like she was a failure.

But one day, she realized her survival wasn't a secret; it was a testimony.

She started sharing her story online and on podcast shows. Women like herself are starting to reach out stating, "You're telling my story."

That's when she knew—her pain had purpose.

Embracing her story didn't mean she had to relive it. It meant she had to own it. She was no longer just the woman who went through it. She was the woman who grew through it. I'm Brooklyn, the stylist, life coach, fashion designer, and author of *Living His Lie but Found the Truth*. Brooklyn turned her journals into a book that will help so many women like herself who are looking for change but are too scared to stand on faith.

Pay attention to red flags in friends or relationships. Here are a few:

- You find yourself walking on eggshells, afraid to speak up.
- Feeling drained or on edge more than you feel safe or supported.
- Someone not respecting you or your boundaries.
- Words not matching up with their actions.
- The conversation gets twisted so that you end up apologizing for something you didn't do.

If you see these red flags, learn to trust yourself. Unleash your greatness that lives inside of you. Let her blossom. Self-love is a MUST. Step into your power, worth, and voice so you no longer shrink for others or stay in spaces that harm you. Don't apologize for being true to yourself.

My story is not unique. It's for every woman who has ever felt invisible, silenced, or small, and chose to rise anyway. Sometimes it takes for you to find your voice to understand that your voice is important. Turn your pain into purpose. There is someone out there that needs your help.

Unleashing your greatness means giving yourself permission to be seen, heard, and be whole.

You don't have to wait until you have it all together. Don't wait for someone to choose you. You are chosen. Chosen to save lives and to bring out the greatness in others. You are the one others have been waiting for. Brooklyn no longer waits for anyone to give her the platform. She takes and owns it and you can, too.

Here are some daily affirmations to help bring out the greatness that lives inside of you.

1. I am powerful, purposeful and destined for greatness.
2. I release my fears and step into my boldness.
3. My voice, my story, and my truth are needed.
4. I am worthy of success, love, and abundance.
5. I rise above my doubt and claim my greatness.

Put this in your daily routine so that you can change your old beliefs on how you view yourself. Now it's time to Unleash Her for Greatness.

Poem

Looking into the mirror wondering who she is, well she is I, and that is me, a woman unleashing all this greatness into the world, a world that needs my pain to turn into purpose, purpose that will change lives forever. Platforms bigger than I can imagine. Imagine me holding on to my voice, with no one to rejoice and feel free, free from the very thing that is killing me, killing the most important thing in life, my legacy. Without my voice there's no empire I can build, so I'm honored and thrilled that I get to save a soul and not kill one.

Jennifer Ngulube MBE

African women Renaissance
Child protective specialist, charity founder African women Renaissance, life coach

https://www.facebook.com/share/172ZtNNxwA/
https://www.instagram.com/africanwomenrenaissance
https://www.africanwomenrenaissance.org

Jennifer Ngulube MBE honoured by the late Her Majesty The Queen for services to children in 2015. Jennifer is passionate about children in foster care and has fostered over 30 children in her home in the UK. Jennifer sits in several safe guarding children's panels which she is also passionate about. Jennifer is a founding member of the charity African Women Renaissance which supports vulnerable women and children in some African countries. Jennifer is a life coach, international motivational speaker and a best selling author of several books.

Unleashing the Voice Within

By Jennifer Ngulube MBE

People often say that we need to find our voices. I disagree with this idea, because our voices are not lost. We were born with them. What we often lose is the courage to use them. Each of us already carries a voice that is strong, worthy, and powerful. The real question is not whether we have a voice, but whether we choose to remain silent or to let it be heard.

One of my favorite sayings is, "If you want to empower a woman, give her a microphone." That simple image captures so much truth. Women do not lack ability, wisdom, or greatness—they often lack the opportunity, the space, or the confidence to speak and be heard. We are all capable of remarkable things, but life, circumstances, and society's judgments sometimes make us forget. That is why we must constantly remind ourselves of our worth, our resilience, and our potential.

Life can be hard. There are seasons when challenges weigh us down and self-doubt creeps in. The world has a cruel way of whispering lies that we are not enough, that we are failures, and that our dreams are too big or too unrealistic. When those voices grow louder, they can easily drown out our own. But it is precisely in those moments of discouragement that we must dig deep and remember who we are at the core.

When I think about voices, I often reflect on children—especially newborn babies. A baby enters the world with no fear of being too loud or too much. They scream with all their might to get the attention they need. No one tells them they should be quieter or that their needs are inconvenient. They cry out with confidence because they trust they deserve to be heard. That is a lesson for all of us. We were all once that fearless, unapologetic child. But as we grow, the world begins to shape us with its expectations and limitations. Slowly, society teaches us to minimize ourselves, to conform, and to hide our voices so that we fit into the molds created for us.

To unleash her voice, a woman must remember who she was before the world told her who to be. We must peel back the layers of doubt, fear, and imposed identity and return to the truth of our own authenticity.

I speak from personal experience. One of the most challenging chapters of my life was relocating from Africa to the United Kingdom. On paper, it was a fresh start and a new opportunity. In reality, it was a storm of stereotypes and silent battles. The community around me had already written my story before I could even introduce myself. To them, I was not an individual with dreams, intelligence, and ambition; I was simply an immigrant, an African woman to be boxed into their limited imagination of what that meant.

I remember neighbors suggesting jobs to me—not in fields where I could use my talents or my voice, but only as a cleaner, a shop assistant, or in other roles they assumed were my "place." It was painful to realize that in their eyes, I could not possibly belong anywhere else. They could not imagine me leading, creating, or speaking. They expected me to shrink myself into the shadows of their stereotype.

At first, I tried to brush it off. But as rejection letters from job applications began to pile up, a small voice inside me started echoing their doubts. Maybe they were right, I thought. Maybe I was not capable of more. Maybe I had reached too high. That is the dangerous power of repeated negative voices—they begin to sound like our own.

It took enormous courage to silence those lies. I had to keep reminding myself: I am enough. I am capable. I am here for a reason. Some days, it was harder than others. On the darkest days, the voice of defeat was deafening, almost convincing me to give up. But this is when unleashing our voice becomes not just an act of expression but an act of survival. To speak, to persist, to believe in ourselves even when the world refuses to, is the most radical form of resistance.

To every woman who feels beaten down by life's trials, let me say this: Do not give up. Lift your head high. Acknowledge the pain and the difficulty but never let them convince you that your story is over. Tough seasons are not permanent; they are passages, not prisons. You are not a victim, even if circumstances try to make you feel like one. You are a warrior navigating a temporary storm.

One trap we must avoid is adopting a victim identity. Life will present obstacles—sometimes unfair, sometimes heartbreaking—but we must not let those struggles define us. To unleash her voice, a woman must refuse to be reduced to her pain. She must rise and speak her worth even in the middle of hardship.

Healing and growth do not always happen in leaps. Sometimes, progress is slow and deliberate. I often remind myself that before we can run, we must walk, and before we walk, we must crawl. There is no shame in small steps. The world often pressures us to move faster, achieve more, and keep up appearances, but we must give ourselves the grace to move at our own pace. Each step forward—no matter how small—is still progress.

When we begin to embrace our journey, we discover something even more powerful: purpose. Each of us was created with a purpose, though the timing of its discovery is different for everyone. Some women find their purpose early in life; others search for it through years of trial and error. But the timing does not make one purpose greater or lesser than another. If you are still searching, your path is just as valuable as the one who seems to have everything figured out. What matters is not how fast you find it, but that you stay open to the process.

Unleashing her voice is not only about speaking. It is about living authentically, fully, and unapologetically. It is about refusing to let the world write our story for us. It is about stepping into rooms where we were told we do not belong and claiming our space. It is about raising our children, leading in our communities, building businesses, and telling our stories in our own words.

Every time a woman chooses to speak her truth, she unlocks the door for another woman to do the same. Our voices are contagious. When one rises, others see that it is possible, and they rise too. This is why silence is not an option. When we stay quiet, we not only rob ourselves of freedom, but we also rob the world of the gift of our perspective, our wisdom, and our strength.

I want every woman reading this to remember you already have your voice. It has been with you since the day you were born, loud and unafraid. The journey is not about finding it but about unleashing it. And when you do, you give permission for others to do the same.

So, stand tall. Speak boldly. Live unapologetically. The world is waiting for your voice, and it is more powerful than you know.

Ada Cook

Author & Artist

www.adacook.com

Ada Cook is a best-selling author, artist, and entrepreneur whose journey reflects resilience, creativity, and determination. An immigrant who built her life and career in the United States, Ada draws on her experiences of adapting, overcoming challenges, and carving her own path to inspire others through both words and art. Her work blends storytelling, self-reflection, and creativity, offering readers encouragement alongside space for personal expression. With an entrepreneurial spirit, her projects combine grace with purpose, empowering people to cultivate joy, confidence, and self-love. Ada's perspective is shaped by her multicultural background and her ability to see opportunity where others see obstacles. She is passionate about helping others discover their voice, embrace authenticity, and pursue meaningful success. Now living in New Braunfels, Texas, with her husband and two dogs, Ada continues to expand her writing and creative ventures, reaching audiences who seek both inspiration and transformation.

Roar, Don't Whisper

By Ada Cook

For as long as I can remember, women have been told to stay small. Be sweet, be polite, do not make a scene, do not be "too much." Smile pretty, even when you are breaking inside. Sit quietly, even when everything in you wants to shout. Somewhere along the line, we started believing that being silent is safer, that shrinking makes us lovable, and that keeping everyone else comfortable is more important than being true to ourselves.

Let me ask you something. When was the last time you swallowed your truth? When was the last time you wanted to say, "This is not okay," yet you forced a smile instead? Maybe it was last week. Maybe it was yesterday. Maybe you have been living like this for years.

Here is the part no one likes to say out loud. Silence does not protect us. Silence strangles us. Every time you bite your tongue, a little part of you disappears. Every time you say yes when everything in your soul is screaming "No," you sell pieces of yourself for approval. It is never a fair trade.

There were seasons of my life where I thought keeping the peace was the most important thing. I thought if I stayed quiet, if I kept my opinions to myself, if I tucked away my art and my ideas, maybe I would finally be enough. Maybe people would accept me. Maybe I would not have to deal with rejection.

This is what life taught me: Rejection is not the worst thing that can happen. Losing yourself is. Every time I silenced my voice, I felt smaller. My creativity dulled, my energy drained, and my joy slipped away. I was surviving, but not really living. I was that girl smiling on the outside while screaming on the inside.

Everything shifted when I started speaking, first in whispers, then louder. I started writing my story, creating art that told my truth, saying no to the things that drained me, and saying yes to the things that scared me but set me free. I realized my voice was not a random mistake. It was a gift. The moment I started honoring it, my life began to align. Your voice is not just words.

Your voice is your story, your art, your laugh that fills a room, your no that protects your peace, and your yes that changes your life. It is every piece of you that refuses to stay hidden. The world needs it. When a woman unleashes her voice, everything shifts. She speaks her story, and another woman feels less alone. She creates, and suddenly people see themselves reflected in her work. She sets a boundary, and suddenly other women feel braver to set theirs too. She dares to speak truth into a quiet room, and the atmosphere changes.

Your voice creates ripples. Ripples turn into waves. Waves turn into movement.

We all knew how powerful speaking up is, but why do we keep quiet? Fear. Fear of being called too much. Fear of rejection. Fear of judgment. Fear that people will misunderstand us. Fear can feel louder than faith. We convince ourselves it is easier to stay quiet, to let things slide, and to put our dreams on the shelf until later.

The problem is, later never comes.

Why are you staying quiet? Where are you hiding the words, the ideas, and the dreams that could change your life? Who gains from your silence, and who is losing out because of it? See, your silence does not serve anyone. The art you are scared to share, someone out there is waiting for it. The story you have buried deep inside, someone else needs to hear it. The boundary you are afraid to set—that no one could save your life.

Unleashing your voice does not mean you have to be the loudest in the room. It does not mean you need a stage or a microphone. It does not even mean people will always agree with you. It means you live in alignment. It means the world outside of you finally reflects the truth inside of you. It means you stop apologizing for being exactly who you are.

Start small. Say the truth to yourself first. Write it down. Whisper it in prayer. Look in the mirror and say it out loud. Sometimes unleashing your voice begins behind closed doors before the world ever hears it.

Practice boundaries. Stop apologizing for saying no. Stop overexplaining why you are choosing yourself. Give your yes to what is aligned and your no to what drains you. Every no you say without guilt is a yes to your peace. Every boundary you set is a line in the sand that teaches others how to treat you.

Tell your story, even if it is messy. Stop waiting until it is perfect. Connection comes from the raw, unpolished, real truth. Vulnerability is not weakness; it is magnetic. It draws the right people to you, opens doors you never expected, and ignites courage in everyone who witnesses it.

Create without apology. Whether it is art, music, business, or a dream you have been sitting on, stop waiting for someone to give you permission. Start trusting that the gifts inside you were put there for a reason. Your ideas, your energy, your talents, your vision—all of it is needed now, not later.

For me, unleashing my voice is tied to my faith. I believe God did not give me this voice for it to stay quiet. I was not made to shrink. My story matters. My truth matters. My voice matters.

Every woman has a voice. Not every woman uses it. That choice, to shrink or to rise, changes everything. Every time you speak, every time you create, every time you refuse to let fear dictate your actions, you are rewriting your story and inspiring others to do the same.

I may not know your exact story, yet I know this much. Somewhere deep inside you, there is a part of you that is ready to come out. Maybe it is a book you have been scared to write. Maybe it is a song you have been too shy to sing. Maybe it is a dream you have been hiding or a boundary you have been avoiding. Maybe it is a truth you have carried for years but never dared to speak.

Whatever it is, it is time.

It is time to stop shrinking.
It is time to stop apologizing.
It is time to stop performing for acceptance.
It is time to rise.

Your voice is not just for you. It is for every woman who needs to hear it so she can finally use her own. It is for every person who is watching how you live. It is for every friend who will find courage because you chose courage first. It is for a world that is desperate for the kind of truth only you can bring.

Fear will show up, I promise you that. Courage does not mean fear disappears. Courage means you speak anyway. Every time you choose to speak, to create, or to defend your peace, you remind yourself that you matter. You remind the world that you are here to shine, not hide. You remind the next woman, the next girl, the next person watching that it is okay to claim their voice too.

This is your moment. Your rallying cry.
Unleash her voice.
Unleash your voice.
The world is waiting.
Roar, Don't Whisper.

Kaila Nike

Author

https://www.tiktok.com/@kailanikeauthor
https://www.facebook.com/kaila.em.9
https://www.instagram.com/kailanike.author/
www.kailanike.com

Born and raised in British Columbia, Kaila Nike is a dedicated mother raising two wonderful sons. While she earned a diploma in social work, writing has always been her true passion. Finding solace and expression in her words, Kaila focuses on crafting engaging narratives through poetry and fantasy. Kaila is also on a life long journey of personal growth, and she enthusiastically shares everything she's learned over the years with others.

The Voice Within

By Kaila Nike

I used to believe that finding my voice meant speaking like an advocate at a protest rally or commanding a stage like a powerful woman. It felt like an external show of strength, much like the loud friend who steps in for others who are too shy. But I've come to realize that a true voice is not always spoken aloud. It is sometimes the quiet, internal power to advocate for yourself. The most profound voice I've ever found is the one that lives inside me, shaping my choices and holding me steady long after the noise of the world fades.

In the pages that follow, I'll share, with real-life examples, how I learned to listen to and unleash my inner voice, using it to build the life I have today. My hope is that by sharing my story, I can inspire you to pull up a chair for your own voice, giving it a seat at the table it deserves. This is a journey of becoming; a reminder that through truth, resilience, and courage, you can level up the version of yourself you wish to as well.

Growing up, there were many things that shaped me. Through those experiences, I learned to conform to the wants and needs of others, in turn shutting out my own voice. My voice felt unworthy. I eventually learned this through my relationships because I wasn't respecting myself. I wasn't listening to the voice within. It was mute. This led me into many harmful situations as I grew older. I hung out with people who were no good for me, I dated men who didn't respect me, and I put myself into situations that were dangerous, all because I was misguided and lost. Though I might have known right from wrong, my voice had no place at the table.

My story didn't begin in my early twenties, but that was where this chapter started. It was where the real turning points began to happen for me. Because of my past, I had little to no self-respect, and to be honest, I felt utterly worthless. This made me a perfect target for a toxic relationship that changed the trajectory of my life forever. What went on behind those closed doors is a story for another time, perhaps never to be told. But what I can say is that I lost everything: my friends, my confidence, and every last shred of worth and respect I had for myself. I was a high school dropout with no real direction in life, other than standing by a man who could never love me the way I loved him. I would have done anything for him. As naive as I was at the time, I wanted nothing more than to become a family with him and to carry his child. I partly got what I wanted; I became pregnant, but he didn't share the same enthusiasm. I hit rock bottom.

The relationship was a blessing in disguise. It had to happen that way, and I'm grateful I never stayed. At first, it wasn't my own self-worth that pulled me out of the situation. It was the fierce, protective love I felt for the life growing inside of me. I couldn't bring a child into the world I was living in, a world poisoned by fear and control. I faced what seemed like an impossible choice at the time: the man I wanted to build a future with, the trauma bond that held me, or the little bit of perfection that was growing inside of me. I couldn't pick both, for if I did, my child would never grow up in an environment he deserved.

I chose my child.

Choosing my child was probably the first time I consciously and actively listened to my inner voice. It was a single, silent declaration that said, *"This ends now."* From that moment on, I knew that if I was going to create a life full of love and security, I had to start caring for myself in a way I never had before. I had to learn to put myself first. *Was it hard?* The fight was brutal. Imagine taking a lifetime of subconscious programming and flipping it flat on its head. Of course, the healing didn't happen overnight, and my voice didn't simply return with a flourish. But it was the beginning of something powerful: the first stone laid on a new foundation for my life. This was the first time I truly listened to my inner voice. I not only chose my child, I chose myself.

After the split, it took a long time before I could even leave the house. I left at 8 months pregnant and stayed with my mom for a couple of months. Then, when my son was only a couple of months old, I rented a place with my brother. My family was there, and for that, I will be forever grateful. But I was so stuck in my own mind, I was alone. Of course, I left the house for the necessities, such as food, etc. But other than that, I just didn't have it in me to go out into the world. I was slowly beginning to build my friendships back up, but I was very much a homebody as I was on my own private healing journey. The world outside my door felt foreign and terrifying, a place full of judgment and unspoken expectations. The shame from the past weighed on me, keeping me confined. I still haven't shared with my family the reality of that relationship, and I don't plan to.

As time went on, my inner voice grew louder, and with it came a sense of purpose I'd never known. When my son was just a baby, I went back to school to earn my Grade 12 diploma before enrolling in college. As a single mother, I faced countless obstacles, but I was determined to do better, for myself, for my son, and for the community I wanted to contribute to. By the time my son was five, I had not only graduated from college but had also faced the dreaded court system and was granted sole custody. My transformation wasn't just internal. I started to get into the best physical shape of my life, exercising regularly and participating in races and obstacle courses. It wasn't always easy, but I was actively becoming the person I wanted my son to look up to and admire. I was becoming someone that I wanted to look up to and admire. It wasn't always easy, and even now, the journey is far from over. Know that I don't say any of this to gloat; I say this because if a high school dropout—a battered single mom can do it, so can you. Your voice is there, and it's worthy.

People often ask me, *"What was someone like you doing with someone like that?"* I always jokingly answer that *"He was just the wrong guy at the right time,"* but the truth is, I was broken. It took a lot of work and self-reflection to become the version of myself I am today. The most important thing I did for myself was listen to my inner voice. I allowed my voice the room it deserved, and in return, I was able to create a beautiful life for my son and me. Do I regret that relationship? Not entirely. The most amazing thing in my life came from one of the most terrible experiences. I wouldn't change that for the world.

Is healing linear? I learned with brutal honesty that it's not. My journey was never a straight line; it was a winding path with many two steps forward and one step back. I had countless ups and downs, and I continued to make mistakes. I still do. But the difference now is that I no longer silence my voice. I listen to that voice, that quiet compass inside me, and it guides me toward better decisions. That voice is the steady echo that reminds me of my worth, the vigilant whisper that keeps me safe, and the persistent hum that moves me forward in a positive direction.

If I hadn't listened to the voice within, I wouldn't be where I am today. It guided me to build a career as an author, a dream I had always held but lacked the courage to pursue. I've found that courage, and I am so grateful for the journey that I'm on. If you would like to check out some of my other work and connect with my story, please scan the QR code below, which will take you to my website (www.kailanike.com).

Be loud, be proud. You never know who or what you will inspire.

Sabrina Thomas

Sabrina Thomas LLC
Best Selling Author, Visionary, Advocate

www.linkedin.com/in/sabrinatspeaks
www.facebook.com/sabrinatspeaks
www.instagram.com/sabrinatspeaks
www.sabrinatspeaks.com

Sabrina Thomas is a Best-Selling Author, Speaker, Visionary, Advocate, and TV Producer with Zondra TV Network. She serves as a Know Your Lemons Global Breast Cancer Educator, Ambassador for the American Cancer Society's Voices of Black Women, and a devoted Caregiver. With over 20 years of advocacy experience, she is a powerful voice in the special needs community. Sabrina founded Girl Don't Count Yourself Out, an empowerment community focused on self-care, confidence, and self-worth. She also leads The Author Collective, a platform supporting authors and aspiring writers through training, brand elevation, and anthology projects. An 20x Amazon Best Seller and co-author of 21 books, Sabrina holds certifications in Advocacy, IEP Master Coaching, Speaker Training, and Life Coaching. Her work has earned numerous awards and magazine features. In 2021, she launched Color with Omar, a coloring book series created with her special needs son, celebrating creativity and their inspiring journey.

The Power of My Pen and My Voice: A Journey of Advocacy and Authorship

By Sabrina Thomas

I never expected that my voice would be the key to the confidence I now carry with me every day. Growing up, I was often quiet, reserved, and unsure of my place in the world. But over time, I came to realize something crucial: My voice, whether spoken or written, has the power to create change. It's the vehicle through which I advocate for the causes I believe in and share my story as an author. Through these roles, I discovered that confidence isn't something I was born with; it's something I had to work for, and it all began with choosing to use my voice.

The Early Years: A Voice in the Shadows

Growing up, I often stayed in the background, hesitant to speak up. Although I had ideas, the fear of judgment and rejection kept me quiet. I watched others speak confidently while I doubted my own voice. Academically, I thrived, but socially, I remained in the shadows, unsure of my place. I didn't realize then that my silence was a defense mechanism, protecting me from the vulnerability of being heard. But life, as it often does, forced me to confront that fear, and it was through my journey as an advocate that I finally began to find my voice.

The Awakening: Advocacy as a Call to Action

Advocacy entered my life in a way I hadn't anticipated. It wasn't something I initially sought out, but rather a path that opened up when I realized there were people, groups, and causes that needed a voice. I was compelled by the idea of fighting for justice, equality, and the rights of others. I was drawn to causes that ignited passion in me—causes that needed a loud, powerful voice to make change.

As an advocate, I quickly learned that silence wasn't an option. Every issue I encountered, whether it was about social justice, education, or personal empowerment, required bold action, and bold action required using my voice. In the beginning, this was incredibly intimidating. I remember standing at my first rally, a small, nervous part of me telling myself I wasn't ready to speak up. My heart raced, my palms sweated, but then I thought about the people who were counting on me to speak on their behalf.

That was the moment I realized that advocacy wasn't about me; it was about the cause. I wasn't just standing up for myself; I was standing up for others, for justice, for change. That shift in perspective helped me push past my fears. Advocacy isn't easy. It means speaking out against the status quo, confronting uncomfortable truths, and fighting for what's right, even when it feels like your voice is too small to make an impact.

But each time I spoke, whether it was in front of a crowd or in one-on-one conversations, I grew more confident. The more I spoke up, the more I realized that my voice could effect real change. I could rally people to take action, to get involved, and to stand up for what mattered. In those moments, I felt an overwhelming sense of purpose. My voice wasn't just something I used—it was a tool for transformation.

Writing as an Extension of My Voice: Becoming an Author

My advocacy work made me realize something profound: The power of my voice didn't end with spoken words. Writing became another powerful outlet for me to express my thoughts, experiences, and message to a wider audience. I decided to take the leap and write my first book.

Writing had always been a part of me, but it was only after I embraced my role as an advocate that I realized how deeply writing could amplify my voice. The process of writing became cathartic. It allowed me to distill my thoughts, frustrations, and hopes for change into something tangible. As an advocate, I had already seen the importance of using my voice to call attention to injustices and issues I cared about. As an author, writing allowed me to do that on a larger scale, to reach people beyond the spaces I occupied.

When I first started writing, I faced a lot of self-doubt. "*Who am I to write a book?*" I would ask. "*What if no one cares about what I have to say?*" But the more I wrote, the more I realized that my story—my voice—was unique. I was telling the story of my journey, the struggles I'd overcome, and the lessons I'd learned as an advocate. And I knew that if my words could help even one person feel seen, heard, or inspired, they were worth sharing.

The first time I held my published book, I felt an overwhelming sense of accomplishment. It was a culmination of years of building confidence, learning to speak up, and trusting that my voice had value. Writing gave me the opportunity to refine my message, articulate my experiences with clarity, and share the wisdom I had gained as an advocate.

The Intersection of Advocacy and Writing: Using My Voice for Impact

Both advocacy and authorship are driven by the same underlying principle: the belief that my voice can make a difference. In my advocacy work, I fight for change, raise awareness, and stand up for those who cannot speak for themselves. Through writing, I share the same message but in a way that allows it to resonate long after the conversation ends or the rally is over. The written word, like spoken advocacy, has the power to challenge the status quo, spark conversation, and inspire action.

One of the most rewarding experiences as both an advocate and an author has been the feedback I've received from others. When people tell me that my words have inspired them, empowered them, or made them feel less alone, it reinforces the idea that our voices—whether written or spoken—carry weight. They have the power to shift perspectives, change lives, and create communities. And it was through embracing my own voice that I found the confidence to take on both roles.

As an advocate, I often work to highlight the voices of marginalized or overlooked communities. But I also realized that my own voice matters because it's a part of the larger narrative. I am a living example of how finding and using your voice can lead to profound personal transformation. I have grown not only as an advocate but also as a person. Confidence, I've learned, isn't just about being heard; it's about believing in the worth of your words and the impact they can have.

The Courage to Keep Speaking: Confidence in Action

There are moments when the fear of judgment, failure, or rejection still lingers. Even now, when I stand in front of a room full of people or share a piece of writing with the world, there's a small voice inside me that asks, *"What if they don't care?"* But over time, I've learned to recognize that voice as a product of insecurity, not a reflection of my worth. The truth is, my voice will never please everyone, and it doesn't need to. What matters is that I'm speaking my truth, advocating for what I believe in, and using my platform to create the change I want to see in the world.

Confidence is not a destination; it's practice. And the more I speak, the more I write, the more I advocate, the more I realize how strong I've become. Every word, every sentence, every speech is an act of courage that strengthens my resolve and solidifies my belief in the power of my voice.

Looking Forward: A Lifelong Journey of Advocacy and Authorship

As I continue my journey as an advocate and an author, I know there is still much to learn, much to speak about, and much more to share. The world is full of voices that need to be heard, and I consider myself fortunate to be in a position where I can use my voice to contribute to those conversations. Through both advocacy and writing, I've discovered that confidence isn't about perfection or having all the answers. It's about showing up, using your voice with purpose, and trusting that what you have to say matters.

When I started this journey, I never could have imagined the depth of confidence and purpose I would gain from simply choosing to speak. But now, I can't imagine a life where I remain silent. My voice is my strength, my pen is my weapon, and together they give me the power to continue advocating for change, to share my story, and to inspire others to find their own voices along the way.

So, here I am, speaking up, writing down, and using my voice to make a difference—confidently, powerfully, and unapologetically. And I will continue to do so every step of the way.

Evelina Solís

CEO of Sol2Soul
Shine Your Light Christian Youth Camp and Programs, Co-Founder of Kingdom Youth Legacy, International Best-Selling Author, Inspirational Speaker, Certified Youth and Adult Transformational Empowerment Coach

https://www.linkedin.com/in/evelinasolis/
https://www.facebook.com/Sol2SoulwithEvelina
https://www.facebook.com/EvelinaSolis
www.Kingdomyouthlegacy.com
www.EvelinaSolis.com

Evelina Solis is an unstoppable powerhouse—a storyteller, inspirator, and joyful spirit with a heart as big as her love for tacos and Texas. As CEO of Sol2Soul Shine Your Light Christian Youth Camps and Programs, and Co-founder of Kingdom Youth Legacy, Evelina lights up every room with her infectious energy, empowering both youth and adults to embrace their God-given gifts. After triumphing over a battle with Lupus, Evelina became a champion for those facing Lupus, PTSD, and neurodivergent children. Her mission is to help others shine brightly and live a purposeful life with unshakable faith. When she's not speaking, coaching or leading dynamic youth programs, Evelina is cherishing memories with her daughter, Hope, traveling, enjoying the arts, playing sports or serving her church and community. She thrives on fiestas, food and laughter with her family and friends. Shine your light together by connecting with her at www.linktr.ee/EvelinaSolis.

From Deathbed to Destiny: My God-Given Voice, Miraculously Restored

By Evelina Solís

Flatline...

The piercing sound split the room, sharp, and unrelenting. Nurses rushed in, voices overlapping with urgency, machines blaring in protest as my body surrendered to silence. I was slipping, not once, twice, but three times, into the valley of the shadow of death. Seizures ransacked every part of me, and the doctors' verdict was grim: Lupus Cerebritis. My voice, once my greatest gift, was silenced. My future uncertain. My body fragile.

Even in that silence, prayer rose louder than any monitor. My words weren't audible, but God heard the cry of my spirit: "Lord, if You keep me here, You will have to perform a miracle. Raise me up as You raised Lazarus. Restore my body. Restore my voice. Use me as Your messenger. I will bring hope to the hopeless and be a voice for the voiceless."

I clung to Psalm 118:17 like a lifeline: "I will not die but live, and will proclaim what the Lord has done." It wasn't just a verse; it was a survival vow.

For 25 days, the hospital became my battlefield. Machines and medicine waged war for my body, but my faith anchored me to God's promise.

Recovery was not instant. It was long and grueling, one small victory at a time. Speech therapy became my battlefield of words. Words had always been my lifeblood. I had built a career as a TV and Radio Personality, CEO, Certified Transformational Empowerment Coach, Inspirational Speaker, Podcaster, Educator, and Mentor. I had spoken at colleges across the country, co-hosted shows, MC'd events, and shared stories meant to inspire. Then, I was silent, broken, wondering if I'd ever stand on a stage again.

Simple phrases like yes, no, thank you felt like climbing a mountain. I remember sitting in that chair, staring at the therapist's lips, my tongue heavy, my brain struggling to connect sound to meaning. Yet I refused to give up. When my first word finally broke free, it wasn't just a sound, it was resurrection. God was faithful. Each syllable I regained was a testimony. Each word I relearned was a weapon against the enemy's plan to silence me.

Physical therapy tested me just as deeply. Muscles that once carried me across stages, classrooms, running 5Ks, and bootcamp workouts now wavered like fragile branches. Every step felt impossible, but Isaiah 40:31 became my strength: "But those who hope in the Lord will renew their strength. They will soar on wings like eagles; they will run and not grow weary, they will walk and not be faint."

Occupational therapy pieced my daily life back together. I relearned to tie my shoes, write my name, comb my hair, and hold a spoon. Each movement was shaky, but each one a miracle. What many people overlook as ordinary became for me evidence of God's extraordinary grace.

The road back was slow, painful, humbling. Every whisper, every scribbled word, every trembling step was proof God was not finished. The first time I stood without support, I felt like a child learning to walk. The first time I heard my voice again, weak and unsteady, it felt like heaven broke into earth. That moment gave me hope and changed everything. God declaring: "Daughter, I'm not done with you yet. Your story is not over."

But I wondered: Why me? Why was my life spared? What lesson is God teaching me? How do I make a Kingdom impact with this second chance at life? How do I change the world and leave a legacy?

God had been preparing me long before that hospital room. My love affair with the microphone began under my kitchen table and in my grandparents' and parents' living rooms. As a little girl, I'd sneak away with my boom box, pretend I was hosting a TV show, interviewing imaginary guests, singing into a hairbrush, dancing for talent shows at family gatherings, and dreaming of stages where my words mattered.

That dream carried me into college, where I double majored in broadcast journalism and Spanish. My world opened in newsrooms, radio stations, newspapers, magazines, award shows, and red carpet events. I thrived in leadership roles and spoke at conferences, never imagining that the very voice God had blessed me with would one day vanish.

Luke 12:48 says, "To whom much is given, much will be required." Back then, I thought that meant working hard and climbing ladders, but after I lost my health, my marriage, my sense of self, I realized it meant something far deeper. God wasn't asking me to use my voice for success; He was asking me to use it for significance.

Even after physical healing, my voice went silent in other seasons. Not because of Lupus, but because of life. In an unhealthy marriage, I lost myself piece by piece. I was a wife, a bonus mom, a mother, a caretaker, but I was no longer Evelina. My dreams were muted. My gifts buried. I was alive, but not truly living. Surviving, not thriving.

I know what it feels like to go through the motions, to doubt your worth, to wonder if you'll ever get back to the person God created you to be. Maybe you know that feeling too. God is faithful. He didn't just restore me once in that hospital; He's been restoring me ever since.

One of the greatest ways He's done that is through my daughter, Hope. When I look at her, I see a younger version of myself: strong-willed, creative, determined, and full of potential. I also see her battles. She is being raised by a single mom, battling anxiety at times, and growing up as a teen under today's societal pressures. Some days she struggles to believe in herself and silence the lies of the enemy that tell her she's not enough. Does that sound familiar?

On those days, I remember the little girl under the kitchen table. I remember the woman given a second chance and the one who fought to speak again. I remember the silence I endured when I forgot who I was, and I refuse to let her or this generation grow up believing they must shrink back, play small, or silence themselves.

God used Hope to remind me of my calling. It's not just about me finding my voice. It's about creating spaces where she and others can find theirs. 1 Timothy 4:12 says: "Don't let anyone look down on you because you are young, but set an example in speech, conduct, love, faith, and purity."

That's why I created Shine Your Light Christian Youth Leadership Camp & Character Development Programs and co-founded Kingdom Youth Legacy. It's not just a program, it's a movement. We bring together community leaders, teachers, coaches, and creatives to equip youth with life skills, leadership training, and spiritual growth. We teach them to speak with confidence, lead with integrity, and shine using their God-given gifts unapologetically in a world that tries to dim them. Another way Hope and I decided to amplify youths' voices was to launch our first ever mother-daughter podcast called The Hope and Ev Show. The podcast bridges two generations over one conversation. It covers faith, family, life, and the next generation. It gives youth entrepreneurs, leaders, and creatives a platform to share what God is doing their live.

I tell students often: "You don't have to wait until you're older to make an impact. Your voice matters right now." I watch their eyes light up when they believe it for the first time.

Revelation 12:11 reminds us: "They overcame him by the blood of the Lamb and by the word of their testimony." Every young person who shares their story defeats the lies of the enemy and unleashes freedom, for themselves and everyone listening.

Here are 5 steps you can take to Unleash Your Voice Today:

1. **Pray Boldly** – Speak honestly to God about your fears, dreams, and the impossible. Ask Him to give you courage and boldness to act. (Esther 4:14)
2. **Write Your Story** – Journal your experiences, lessons, and breakthroughs. Your story doesn't need to be perfect; just document the truth of what God is doing in your life.
3. **Share with One Person** – Tell your story to a friend, family member, or supportive online or church community. Also, find yourself a coach and mentor who can help you develop it. Your words could be the survival guide someone else has been waiting for.
4. **Shine Your Light** – Use your gifts daily—speaking, teaching, writing, or creating to point others back to God. (Matthew 5:16)
5. **Lead, Bless, and Give Back** – Be an example of faith and courage. Encourage, educate, mentor, and guide others, especially the next generation, to find and use their voices. Invest into a cause or mission to give of your time, treasure, or talents. (Acts 20:35)

If you've ever felt muted by fear, trauma, or doubt, this is your wake-up call. Done is better than perfect. The perfect time is now. You don't need a microphone or a stage to begin. Start with your story. Share it with one person. Write it down. Speak it aloud.

Find groups online like LIGHTbeamers that are welcoming, loving, and supportive and will help you become a better storyteller. They helped me build up my confidence when I hit rock bottom.

In addition, say thank you to God for bringing you this far, and let gratitude grow your testimony.

You are not voiceless. You are not forgotten. You are not too broken, too late, or too small.

If God can bring me back after flatlining three times, give me my voice after silence, prepare me to grace many stages and media platforms, turn my mess into a message as an International Best-Selling Author in collaborative books with LIGHTbeamers and She Rises Studios, He can do the same for you!

This is your moment to rise, speak, and shine. Don't hide. Don't wait. Don't let fear win.

The world is waiting for your voice, and when you unleash it, you help someone else step into theirs. God turns your pain into purpose, and all things work together for good to those who love Him (Romans 8:28).

Let's shine brighter, rise higher, and make Jesus known! Follow my faith-filled journey at https://linktr.ee/EvelinaSolis.

WOMAN
SHE RISES STUDIOS
FENIX TV

Shelley Lynn Hines

Founder of She Rises in Wellness Women's Retreats
Master Evolutionary Astrologer

https://www.linkedin.com/in/shelleylynnhines
https://www.facebook.com/shelleylynn.hines/
https://www.instagram.com/shelleylynnhines/
www.shelleyhines.com

Shelley Hines is a Registered Nurse and Master Evolutionary Astrologer, whose calling is devoted to soul healing, empowering women through remembrance, and awakening the Divine Feminine. With over three decades of experience, she bridges science and mysticism to support U.S. and International clients in reclaiming their wellness and divine purpose. Her approach blends mindfulness, astrology, and creativity to illuminate the client's soul path and purpose. Her work involves the once-hidden sacred teachings of Mary Magdalene and cutting-edge information about the asteroid Magdalena. Bringing a revolutionary lens to modern astrology, she helps clients unlock the codes of inner sovereignty. During her signature She Rises in Wellness Women's Retreats(C) and personalized one-on-one sessions, Shelley creates sacred spaces for healing, awakening, and creative expression, where each woman is invited to rise into her sovereignty, wisdom, and truth. Her mission is clear: to help others remember who they truly are and rise in wellness.

Unleashing the Magdalene Story Within: When The Magdalene Rose, So Did I

By Shelley Lynn Hines

There is a voice within every woman; a voice that remembers who she is. Not the roles she plays. Not the rules or expectations placed upon her. But a deeper, ancient knowing that pulses in her heart and stirs in her bones. A voice that has been silenced, shamed, distorted, but never extinguished.

For too long, the story of Mary Magdalene has been misunderstood, relegated, misrepresented, or erased. But like a star that guides lost travelers home, her light has never truly disappeared. It merely awaited the moment when we, as women and society at large, were ready to remember.

In 2016, during a mystical experience, I was guided to help others (and myself) through the voice of the Feminine Divine. The voice of Mary Magdalene was never meant to be forgotten, and now is the time for her voice to be unleashed. Noting the surge in books, media, and spiritual communities, we see a need for spiritual books that influence the market, seeing a rise of over 12% in 2024 in these areas. We witness the 'unleashing' of Her voice, the voice of the Feminine Divine, and our voices as well!

In my book, *The Star of Mary Magdalene*, I explore Mary Magdalene as a historical figure and as astrological archetypes encoded in the sky through Asteroid 318-Magdalena. This celestial body has, unbeknownst to us, moved in quiet rhythm, holding keys to our personal liberation, particularly through our voices. It asks, "What and where is your message?"

Each of us carries *her essence* in our longings, our struggles, and our yearning to speak our truth without fear or apology. She is not separate from us. She is us. And when we dare to speak from our souls, without pretense or performative perfection, we activate something ancient and healing in our voice.

The power of voice on the Soul Path is essential to wellness for the individual and the collective. In my work as a Pastoral Evolutionary Astrologer, I've witnessed firsthand how a woman's chart is a sacred map, not only of her soul path but also of the wounds that have silenced her for lifetimes. Astrology, when practiced through a humanistic and compassionate evolutionary lens, reveals where the soul is longing to grow, what karmic patterns need healing, and how one's inner voice can be restored without shame, without dogma, and always through love.

This is not the voice of religion telling us what to believe or how to behave, or risk shame and damnation. This is the voice of Spirit, inviting us to become truly human. I walk with women of different faith backgrounds who are reclaiming their right to feel, to question, to create, to say no, and to say yes. To pray in their own way and, most importantly, to speak from the heart center of their beautiful beings!

My work is more than just astrology. It's about embodiment and permission. Permission to tell your story. Permission to name the pain, to trust your innate knowing, and voice it with confidence. When we do this sacred work together, whether through one-on-one mentoring, at She Rises in Wellness Women's Retreats ©, or in sacred circles, we are healing generations. We are rewiring our brains and reweaving what has been torn. We can stand in a truth that doesn't have to shout but can if needed. It also may come in whispers, songs, prose, and artwork.

Astrology's popularity is growing, and it is becoming a multi-billion-dollar market. According to the 2024 Harris Poll, 70% of Americans believe in astrology. My work bridges two worlds for the first time!

The spiritual voice of the Feminine Divine and Magdalene via Asteroid-318 Magdalena.

Another method I utilize to unlock your inner story is through Intentional Creativity®, where we allow the muse to meet the mystic. Many of us were taught that our inner critic was the voice of reason, but in truth, it's more often the voice of fear. Through this method, we can co-create from a place of sacred intention rather than self-judgment. We give form to our inner worlds, to what we sense, feel, and know before we have the "right words." Paintbrush or pen in hand, symbol by symbol, we begin to speak. Not always in sentences. But in shape, color, story, and sensations. It is where we allow the muse to meet the mystic and have a voice!

And the best part about this process is that it never requires talent, just a willingness and courage to step into you! It is in this dance between the canvas or paper and the universal cosmos that women rediscover themselves and The Magdalene within. She, who feels deeply, witnesses fully, and responds with grace. She, who has been cast aside, yet remains unwavering in her devotion to truth, healing, and love. The mystical message bearer. In these creative spaces, we don't just express ourselves. We remember and integrate. We reclaim our voices and step into our authentic stories.

For much of my life, I carried both a longing and a fear of using my voice. I often softened my words to avoid conflict or hid my truth behind the roles I played as nurse, midwife, mother, and teacher. Yet inside, I knew there was a deeper story waiting to be spoken. When I discovered asteroid 318-Magdalena in my birth chart, it was as if the cosmos itself confirmed what my soul already knew: My voice was sacred, and it mattered. Working with Magdalene as an archetype and guide helped me untangle lifetimes of silencing and shame. Through astrology, painting, and sacred circles, I began to speak again. Not just with words, but with color, story, and prayer. Each time I dared to express myself, whether in retreat circles or on the canvas, a part of me healed. The trembling in my throat became a song. What I once thought of as weakness revealed itself as a holy strength: the power of an authentic voice rising.

Allow Magdalene here to be an archetype, not an opponent. Some readers of this book hold deep Christian faith, and I honor you. Please know that my honoring of Mary Magdalene does not compete with Jesus. It complements the love, wisdom, and liberation he came to model.

The feminine was never meant to be silent in the gospel story. I do not believe the false narratives against her. History indicates Mary Magdalene was *the first witness*. Apostle to the Apostles, per Pope Francis in 2016. There are indications she was wealthy (supporting Jesus' mission) and a healer and a teacher. Her voice is no longer 'dangerous'; it is divine. In lifting her memory, I am not tearing down your belief. I am inviting you to see how broad and loving the table of Spirit truly is. My work is not to rewrite theology but to help women hear their own divine voice again.

This is a call to the woman who is ready. If you are reading this and something stirs in you, a flicker of remembrance, a whisper you can't quite place, then I invite you to follow it. Join me and other women on the journey to express our truth as we unlock our stories in the safety of circles.

Whether through a retreat, a private session, a painting, or simply sitting under the stars with your birth chart in hand, prayer in your heart, and knowing you have permission to seek and to question the old narratives. To awaken and to reclaim, but most importantly, to unleash your voice and to speak.

You are not "too much" or "too late." You are not broken, but you are on a healing journey of a lifetime. You are becoming your authentic story—unleash it! You were never meant to stay silent. You are a sacred voice, and the world is ready to listen to you.

This moment is more than a coincidence—*it is your invitation.*

She Rises in Wellness is more than a retreat—it is a remembrance of your wholeness.

The Star of Magdalene is more than a book—it is a map to your true north and a mirror to your soul's voice.

Aura Elena Martinez

Live to the Max™/Viva al máximo™
Self-Discovery & Empowerment Coach

https://www.linkedin.com/in/aura-elena-martinez/
https://www.facebook.com/AuraEMartinezCoach/
https://www.instagram.com/AuraElenaMartinez/
https://www.auraemartinez.com

Aura E. Martinez is a Self-Discovery and Empowerment Coach and creator of the Aura Blueprint™, and TEDx Speaker, helping women gain total clarity in their purpose so they can wake up to a life of daily fulfillment and certainty. She is also the founder of Live to the Max™/Viva al máximo™, and author of the book "Creating a Lifetime of Wellness: Start Having the Life You Deserve" and "Creating a Lifetime of Wellness Journal: Your Personal Coach to the Different Areas of Your Life." Her book has been seen on Spirituality and Health magazine, Psychology Today and Natural Awakening NYC edition magazine.

The Mirror, The Wound, and The Woman I Chose to See

By Aura Elena Martinez

I never thought it would be my hair.

It wasn't the years of feeling invisible. Not the relationships that drained me. Not the rooms I'd shrink myself in, pretending I didn't want to speak up. No, it all circled back to my hair, and I didn't even see it coming.

You'd think someone like me—ambitious, driven, constantly "working on herself"—would know what her wounds are. But pain hides in plain sight, and mine was coiled into curls I refused to touch.

My parents are from the Dominican Republic, and although I was born in the States, I grew up with many of my parents' customs and beliefs. In the Dominican culture, just like in most Latin American countries, curly hair like mine is considered "bad hair," so I didn't just absorb the idea that curly hair was undesirable; I felt and viewed my hair as something broken that needed to be fixed. Like it was a problem I was born with and now had to spend my life correcting.

The message came from all angles–family, friends, strangers, and perhaps the loudest messenger of all: the screen. I watched novelas religiously as a child, those glamorous Latin American soap operas where the heroines were always beautiful but never looked like me. Their hair was long and straight. Their skin was lighter. Their features are Eurocentric. They were the ones being fought over, rescued, and chosen. And even if no one said it out loud, the message was clear: *This is what beauty looks like. This is what success looks like.*

So, I learned early that if I wanted to be seen, I had to erase parts of myself. I had to earn beauty by conforming, and that meant straightening my hair, lightening my presence, and contorting myself into whatever the world said was worthy.

From a young age, I started straightening my hair, chemically and emotionally, trying to smooth down every piece of me that stood out, and hoping I could fit in and be accepted.

The truth? I never felt enough.

Not pretty enough to be chosen. Not polished enough to be respected. Not worthy enough to belong in the rooms I dreamed of. And definitely not successful-looking enough to believe I could lead, love, or be loved. I thought I didn't have "the look" of success, and a part of me thought I never would.

What we don't heal will shape our lives quietly. To the degree that we don't see ourselves fully, we will allow ourselves only a fraction of what we truly deserve. Our unworthiness will whisper in the choices we make, the love we accept, and the life we settle for. That was me, playing small while secretly dreaming big. Chasing validation in all the wrong places, including men.

The men I dated didn't really *see* me. And how could they? I didn't see myself. I ignored my intuition, second-guessed my gut, bent over backwards to be "chosen," and always came up short. Each relationship felt like a silent echo of the one before it: "*You're not enough.*"

The thing is, self-esteem doesn't travel alone. It always drags its cousins down with it: self-worth, self-trust, and self-confidence. When one is missing, the other ones will be missing as well. I didn't trust myself because I didn't believe in myself. I didn't believe in myself because I didn't *see* myself. I only saw what I wasn't because I had a layer that was covering my true essence.

And then came that event.

I went to my mentor's personal development/business event, not knowing exactly what to expect. At the time, for me, it was just another personal development event. But in one of the exercises my mentor had us do, we were asked to draw our inner child. No rules. Just whatever came to mind. And there I was, pen in hand, drawing a tiny version of me. She had big curly hair with glasses, and she was crying.

I stared at the paper, and suddenly, I wanted to cry as well.

We were teamed up with a partner for this exercise and as I was telling my partner what I had drawn, my voice cracked. I couldn't stop the tears. That little girl—me—was grieving. I didn't even know I was carrying that grief. But my hand knew. My heart knew. And that was the moment I could no longer avoid it. I had to face the wound I'd buried beneath years of straightening, pretending, and performing.

It wasn't just about hair. It never is. It was about identity. It was about rejection. It was about never feeling like I belonged—to others, or to myself. It was about breaking generational cycles. It was about reclaiming a voice I didn't even know I'd lost. It was about deciding that I no longer needed to fit someone else's mold of enoughness.

That moment cracked something open.

In my healing journey, I was paired with a coach who wasn't going to let me hide. One day, she had me stand in front of a mirror with my natural hair loose. Not brushed. Not styled. Just me. Raw and real.

I resisted. I didn't want to do it. I felt exposed, embarrassed, and even ashamed. But I did it anyway.

Standing in that mirror with my hair out was the first time I really *heard* that soundtrack. I heard every voice that had ever told me I wasn't enough. Every "tame that hair." Every "you'd be prettier if..." I realized how much of my life had been shaped by those voices and how many opportunities I didn't go for. How many conversations I stayed silent in and how many men I let into my life who were never meant to stay, all because I had never been taught how to stay with myself.

I realized how many times I had looked in a mirror and never really seen myself. I started to wonder how many times *we all* do that. We glance, adjust, apply, and critique, but we don't look. And if we don't look, we can't love. If we can't love, we can't lead. And if we can't lead ourselves, we hand over the pen and let the world write our story for us.

And that's the thing about cultural and societal conditioning. It becomes a soundtrack in your mind, playing in the background so long you don't even notice it. Until one day, you do.

After that mirror moment, the real work began. Undoing years of internalized rejection. Learning to speak to myself with compassion. Building rituals that honored, not masked, my identity. I started wearing my curls more often, even when it felt vulnerable. I began collecting images of women who looked like me, not just to see them, but to *normalize* them in my mind. I rewrote the beauty standard in my own head.

Healing wasn't linear. It was messy. Some days I felt like I was making progress. Other days I wanted to hide under a wig and forget I ever started. But something in me had awakened, and it refused to go back to sleep.

As I continued the work—inner work, mirror work, soul work—I noticed shifts. I spoke with more conviction. I stopped chasing people who couldn't love me properly. I said no without apology. I stopped outsourcing my confidence.

And one morning, I wore my hair out.

No straightener. No backup plan. Just curls.

I walked into a room, fully myself, and I didn't shrink. I didn't apologize. I didn't wonder if I was "too much."

That day, I wasn't "too much." I was just enough. I *was* the standard. Not someone else's version of it, but my own version.

The deeper truth I want you to get is this: Nothing outside of you can give you the worth you're withholding from yourself. Not a man. Not a title. Not a look. Not a number on a scale or a check in a bank account.

If you don't feel enough, look inward. That feeling didn't come from your true essence, which is your soul. It came from a moment, maybe many, when you started believing the lie that you weren't worthy. That moment needs your attention. That inner child needs your protection. That wound needs you to tend to it.

If you're reading this and feeling like something in you is still unseen, unclaimed, and unloved, start by looking within because we all carry messages we didn't ask for. Stories about who we are, what we're allowed to be, and what we must hide to be loved. But here's what I've learned: *Healing is remembering who you were before the world told you who to be.*

It's not just about loving your hair, your body, or your face; it's about loving the *you* underneath it all. The *you* that existed before shame entered the room, before comparison dimmed your shine, or before someone else's beauty became your burden.

This journey is not easy. You may cry. You may want to turn back. You may doubt if you're strong enough to confront the mirror. But I promise you, on the other side of that mirror is power. Not because someone gave it to you. But because it was yours all along.

You don't have to fix yourself. You must *face yourself*. And when you do, you'll remember what it feels like to come home to you. Because the woman you're looking for? She's been waiting; she's not broken. You just must choose her.

Lisa Jacovsky

Early Intervention
Professor of Psychology

www.linkedin.com/in/lisa-j-29351382
https://www.facebook.com/booksbylisajay
https://www.instagram.com/diverseinkbooks/
www.diverseinkbooks.my.canva.site/

Lisa Jacovsky is a Psychology professor at Union College of NJ and SNHU. Lisa began writing short stories when she was seven years old. Writing is a passion for her and one of the many things she enjoys. She is currently the author of the award-winning first four books in the Let's Talk! Series, Rascal Cat Brothers, Purrrfect as I Am, Spooky Ooky Dance Party, and others found at stores worldwide. Lisa lives in New Jersey, where she enjoys spending time with family and friends, traveling, and working on her next books. Keep up with her on social media to see what is coming next.

From Silence to Spotlight: Turning Passion Into a Positive Evolution

By Lisa Jacovsky

To be successful in my career, I have to speak in front of people. Many are surprised when I tell them I have social anxiety. It took years of personal growth, small acts of courage, and a deep connection to my purpose before I could confidently stand in front of others. My journey from silence to spotlight wasn't a dramatic leap but a steady, intentional evolution.

As a child, I was outgoing, confident, and unafraid to raise my hand first. I'd often finish tests early and would speak up without hesitation. I never thought twice about what others thought of me. I was simply myself, which was confident, expressive, and curious. That changed in middle school.

Middle school was the first time I was thrown into a world where I didn't know most of the people around me. My elementary school had merged with others, and suddenly I was surrounded by strangers. The comfort and familiarity of neighborhood friendships were gone. I didn't know how to act anymore. For the first time, I questioned how others saw me and whether or not I belonged.

That was when my social anxiety surfaced. Talking in front of the class became unbearable. I'd turn beet red, stare at the back wall, and hold my hands stiffly in front of me while giving presentations. I rarely raise my hand anymore. The vibrant, fearless girl I had been was slipping away.

High school and even undergraduate years followed a similar pattern. I made friends, mostly through work rather than school, but I stayed away from large groups. I felt safer on the sidelines. Whenever I was forced into the spotlight, I froze. I didn't know how to use my voice anymore. But life and purpose have a way of nudging us forward.

When I began my career in Applied Behavior Analysis (ABA), I was suddenly asked to lead training for newly hired staff. That meant standing at the front of a room filled with adults I had never met before. My anxiety told me to run, but my passion wouldn't let me. I had worked hard to get into this field, and I knew this was part of the job. So I forced myself to try. To my surprise, I found I was more comfortable speaking in front of strangers than I had ever been with peers. Each training got a little easier. Confidence began to take root again.

Later, when I transitioned to working with children with autism in home-based ABA, my anxiety flared up in new ways. I dreaded calling families to set up sessions. Email felt safe, and phone calls did not; however, it would take too long to get in touch through email. I had to switch phone calls to stay in compliance. Slowly, the dread eased, and I began to realize I was gaining confidence back.

This transformation came with a deeper realization that I no longer felt aligned with the ABA path. I loved the children, but something felt missing. Around the same time, I enrolled in a PhD program for ABA. It brought new opportunities and new challenges. Residencies were in person, and I often found myself paralyzed with anxiety until the moment I sat in the chair in the conference room. Live virtual classes were another hurdle. But each one was a brick in the foundation of my growth. I learned how to give presentations with confidence, speak in academic spaces, and navigate discomfort with a sense of purpose. I wasn't just finding my voice again; I was learning how to use it intentionally. I was becoming someone I hadn't seen in a long time: a leader.

It was during this program that I became a children's book author, and that's when the real evolution began.

Writing has been my dream since I was a little girl. Publishing my first book was exhilarating, but I quickly learned that writing was only the beginning. The real challenge was marketing. Publishing a book doesn't guarantee anyone will read it. Getting the story into people's hands requires visibility. And visibility means stepping into the spotlight.

Marketing pushed every button my social anxiety could find. It wasn't just about social media posts and catchy captions. It was podcast interviews, school visits, festivals, and book signings. It was calling schools out of the blue to offer readings. It was showing up in public and believing in my story enough to share it with strangers.

I'll never forget my first podcast interview. I was so nervous that I texted my best friend for hours beforehand. I changed my outfit multiple times, even though only my shirt would show. Just before going live, I had a full-blown panic attack. And yet, the moment the interview started, it all melted away. The conversation was so natural, so full of joy, that I forgot we were even recording.

When it was published, I started to feel some small panic all over again. I wasn't sure I could share it publicly. But I sent it to my family first, and their support gave me the courage to post it on social media. Since then, I've never looked back. I now host my podcast, interviewing inspiring individuals and organizations making a difference in the world.

I still can't watch or listen to my own interviews; I doubt I ever will. However, I've learned that doesn't diminish the value of my voice. My stories still matter.

Oddly, I wasn't nervous at all for my first school reading. Talking with the kids came easily and felt natural. What terrified me was my first book festival. I had no idea how to approach people, what to say, or how to bring them to my table. I panicked. But I did it. Now, I have a practiced intro and even enjoy the experience, though I still sometimes wonder whether to say "hi" first. It's the same with teaching. I still get nervous on the first day of every semester when I teach, but as soon as I start speaking, the nerves fade.

The first training I gave in person at a professional conference was a whole new ball game. You'd think that after podcast interviews, school readings, and countless staff trainings, it would have been a breeze. But I was so nervous I almost canceled. When I arrived and walked into the conference room, I immediately turned around and walked back out. I nearly left the entire event. Instead, I found a quiet moment in the bathroom to collect myself. Once I began speaking, that familiar confidence I feel when teaching returned. I ended up loving the experience. Since then, I've done a few more in-person presentations, and now, it's something I genuinely want to do more of.

I've come to understand that confidence doesn't mean the fear goes away. It means doing it anyway, over and over, until your voice feels like home again.

This journey of reclaiming my voice has taken years. It's been filled with discomfort, awkwardness, tears, and setbacks. But it's also been filled with joy, pride, connection, and the deep satisfaction of living my purpose. I've become an award-winning author, a college professor, and a podcast host. All things I never thought possible because of my anxiety. But passion, when pursued wholeheartedly, has a way of clearing the path.

The key to my growth wasn't perfection; it was persistence. It was showing up again and again, each time a little braver than the last. It was letting my passion be louder than my fear. And it was realizing that authenticity, not flawlessness, is what connects us.

I am still evolving. I still get nervous. But now, I also get excited. I have found my voice, and I continue to use it. Not just for myself, but for the children I write for, the students I teach, and the women who might be where I once was: silent, afraid, and unsure of their power.

To them, I say: Your story is worth sharing. Your voice matters. You don't have to be fearless; you just have to be brave enough to begin.

Amy Neumann

Founder of Purpose Queens Arise
Lead Visionary Consultant

www.linkedin.com/in/amy.d.neumann
https://facebook.com/amy.d.neumann/
https://instagram.com/purposequeensarise/
www.purposequeensarise.com

Amy is a wife, mom, and coach whose life transformed when God met her in the midst of overwhelming anxiety and self-doubt caused by perfectionism and striving to please everyone, teaching her to quiet the noise and hear His voice. Through that intimacy, she found healing in her identity, clarity in her Kingdom purpose, and confidence in her callings. Today, she empowers women to do the same: learning to hear and communicate with God, discovering their unique design, purpose, and assignments, and overcoming mindset blocks and management gaps that hold them back. Drawing on neuroscience-based and Kingdom truth-centered mindset practices, along with online business expertise, Amy helps women align with God's strategies for their business, find support in an iron-sharpening-iron, purpose-driven community of sisters, and steward their lives and callings with excellence.

My "Good Girl" Problem...

By Amy Neumann

Have you ever found yourself wearing a mask, unexpectedly catching yourself acting like someone else entirely?

I recall being at a social event one evening about a decade ago, mingling and chatting, when I suddenly had a moment of bizarre clarity, as if I were seeing myself from the outside. I had laughed in a way that truly startled me, which triggered this strange experience.

It wasn't MY laugh. It was my grandma's socialite laugh. In that moment, I realized I wasn't showing up as myself but as who *I thought I should be.*

My grandma loved social events. She was charming – full of smiles, good manners, and polite conversation. Although I don't remember any actual training in childhood on what it meant to be a Southern lady, and my mom did not really subscribe to the same traits as my grandma, I definitely absorbed years of subtle lessons about what "good girls" did and didn't do. Did you know that "good girls" do not have big emotions or talk about the internal ups and downs that come along when life feels overwhelming? Oh no! We must be pleasant, put together, competent, and helpful and always prioritize approval from and service to others.

Perhaps you also mastered these lessons and became an expert at reading the room and the people around you, putting on a mask and becoming the person you thought you should be?

After college, while searching for purpose, I joined a church that I would later realize was spiritually controlling. Messages from the pulpit, as well as those absorbed from the church's culture, reinforced my "good girl" childhood programming, as I learned that even God's approval and acceptance depended on performance. What I didn't see then was that I had no grid for grace, especially for myself. I had never truly experienced the personal, overwhelming, unconditional love of God and did not know what it felt like to have an intimate relationship with Him. I equated people-pleasing and boundaryless serving as righteousness. Since leaders often explained mindset or emotional struggles as a person lacking faith or needing to pray more or "nail their sinful nature to the cross," I continued hiding parts of myself that felt unlovely or imperfect.

I met my husband there, truly my perfect match (we're now going on twenty-five years!), and together we eventually followed God's prompting to leave that church. It was terrifying at the time, because we had been taught that leaving the church was like turning your back on God. We agonized a bit about whether we were being led astray by our "flesh/sinful natures," but after much prayer, we chose to trust that God's was the voice guiding us. His faithfulness proved bigger than bad theology, for it was at the very next church we belonged to that we learned that communication with God (rather than one-way talking to God and then hoping to find an applicable Scripture as an answer) was possible. The two-way journaling practices we learned there revolutionized our relationships with God and remain a significant part of our spiritual lives.

Still, even in that church and other grace-filled congregations we belonged to afterward, I carried the same "good girl" patterns of stuffing and hiding uncomfortable and difficult things and trying to earn love, approval, and belonging from others by presenting myself as I thought I should.

Years later, with four children and a hectic life as a homeschool mom, I realized I no longer knew who I truly was. I had poured myself so completely into being the "good wife," "dedicated mom," and "faithful volunteer" that I had forgotten who I was outside of those roles. I couldn't remember what I enjoyed or even list what I thought I was good at. I felt like a shell of the person I was meant to be.

At the time, I thought that the problem was that I didn't have a direction or focus outside of my roles as wife and mom, so in an effort to "find purpose" again while also helping my family, I started a business. For a while, it seemed to be working. I discovered gifts in writing, graphic art, website design, and leadership. I connected with visionary, growth-minded women and began to feel alive again. But eventually, the same old "good girl" patterns surfaced—the desire to earn approval, finding my identity and worth in pleasing others, and burying the uncomfortable parts of myself followed me into my business.

Online business coaching programs based on attraction marketing only served to reinforce those patterns. I overgave to my clients, spending hours creating beautiful resources that I often gave away for free, and I undercharged for all my offers. I learned that I should curate my message online and project authority, which, filtered through my "good girl" lens, meant that I diluted my authenticity, hid my struggles, and shaped myself into who I thought I should be for my audience. I took the attraction marketing tenet of serving my audience with value to heart, but with a lifetime of not knowing how to set boundaries or value myself, that pattern only led to burnout and exhaustion.

I had tried to heal my sense of being by *finding a new thing to do* when I started a business, but doing couldn't heal what true belonging was meant to. What I needed wasn't achievement. I needed restoration.

God met me in that quiet, depleted place—not with condemnation, but with compassion. He began peeling back the layers of disguise and performance I had worn for so long and gently uncovering and loving even the parts of me that I had deemed ugly and had hidden out of shame. I felt absolutely seen, unconditionally loved—and I finally discovered the beautiful and dynamic two-way relationship he wanted with me all along.

Life is messy and beautiful. Growth includes peaks *and* valleys. God is present in both chaos *and* calm and wants to journey with us through all of it. I'm learning that purpose is more about being authentically myself in EVERYTHING I do, rather than performance in any of my specific callings. I'm learning to live in the *and,* to embrace both progress and process, hard truth and tender grace, nurturing myself and serving others. I haven't "arrived." I'm walking this road alongside the women I serve, growing, healing, and realigning with God one day at a time.

Here are a few truths God continues to teach me along the way:

First, **restoration and transformation are meant to be ongoing.** They are part of a lifelong journey, not something to achieve or graduate from. It unfolds layer by layer as God lovingly removes the power of the lies and wounds that have led to misalignment and restores the parts of you that you once hid or disowned.

Second, **your worth isn't earned by doing.** It's revealed in simply being His. Before you ever accomplished a thing, God called you His masterpiece. He specifically created you to reflect his nature into the world in a unique way, and your highest lifetime work is uncovering and walking authentically in that design in everything you do.

Third, **true self-care is not selfish.** When you nurture your whole self—spirit, soul (mind, will, and emotions), and body—you can better steward the roles and relationships you have been entrusted with.

Fourth, **shame and fear are your enemy**. Being honest with yourself, with God, and with safe people who will hear you compassionately and yet also hold you accountable to God's highest and best for you is crucial for healing and transformation.

And finally, **you can live in the "and."** It's okay to be a work in progress and a vessel of impact at the same time. You can be growing while teaching and healing while leading.

These aren't lessons I've mastered; they are rhythms I'm still practicing. My certifications in neuroscience-based mindset coaching and Christian life coaching, as well as the two-year Kingdom-lens theological program I completed, were both part of my own healing and also intentional equipping so that I can help others in their journeys. And maybe that's the point: not to appear as someone who has arrived, but to be someone who is becoming alongside others who are also becoming.

If you are exhausted by years of wearing masks and trying to be everything you think people need you to be, you are not alone. You are not behind. You are becoming. God is inviting you, even now, to partner with him to find clarity, healing, and alignment and to impact the world through your unique design, purpose, and callings.

"Make a careful exploration of who you are and the work you have been given, and then sink yourself into that... Don't compare yourself with others. Each of you must take responsibility for doing the creative best you can with your own life." — *Galatians 6:4–5 (The Message)*

Ana Martinez

All Travel Worldwide LLC
Travel Advisor and Lifestyle Coach

https://www.linkedin.com/in/anamlv
https://facebook.com/groups/AllTravelWorldwide
https://www.instagram.com/MagicalMomentsNow
https://www.alltravelworldwide.com/
https://anatraviswygant.com/

Ana is a homeschooling mom of three daughters and owner of All Travel Worldwide LLC, a Cruise Planners franchise, who believes wellness begins with wonder. Her love for travel started early through family adventures. After years as a Registered Nurse and Certified Lactation Counselor in labor, delivery, postpartum, and hospice care, she learned firsthand that life is too short to keep waiting for "someday." Losing her mom, who was only 53, sealed that truth. Joy and memories can not be put on hold. Thus, travel became her way of living intentionally, making memories, and helping others do the same. She now specializes in travel solutions for families with kids under three from cruises and Disney vacations to tours and group trips. When she is not planning first-class adventures, Ana is dancing or traveling the world full-time with her family as modern nomads by RV or plane, always seeking new adventures.

What If You Are One Decision Away From The Life You Truly Want?

By Ana Martinez

Most people live life on autopilot. I know I did. I went with the flow, enduring hardships, and letting life happen to me instead of creating it. I also checked off all of the boxes that I thought I was "supposed" to, like high school AP classes, going straight to the university, graduating, getting married, having a baby, getting divorced, and grieving my mom's death... all by the time I was 26.

The truth is, the only intentional decision I made during that time was choosing how I birthed my baby (at home with a midwife). Everything else felt like it just happened *to me.*

I never gave myself time to pause, to breathe, or to grieve...not the loss of my old self, not the loss of my mom. Between changing jobs, co-parenting, and trying to chase joy, I spent years drowning in grief, postpartum depression, and anxiety, unable to let go.

Unfortunately, it took more than one traumatic experience to finally wake me up. I realized that no one was coming to save me from... me.

After the last traumatic experience, I knew I had to make a choice. I could keep surviving on autopilot or *finally* take ownership of my healing, my story, and my power.

As many couples do, Travis and I send each other videos we find interesting or that help each other. One day, he sent me a clip of Dr. Joe Dispenza. That single video, combined with the lessons of Alex and Leila Hormozi, became the spark that helped me. I began my journey into my inner world and started the process of ending my addiction to my old self.

The following lessons taught me to wake up, take ownership of my choices, and start creating my life instead of letting life just happen to me.

Lesson 1: Resilience & Recovery

Alex Hormozi once asked, *"How quickly do you recover from a bad moment?"*

Days, weeks, years? Many people never recover at all. That question struck me. Because if you do not build resilience, every setback feels like a nuclear bomb.

I realized resilience is not a talent. It is a skill you can build for your survival. In my experience, I have noticed that the more I work on myself and triggers, the easier it is for me to assess, process, and recover from a discussion with my husband or loved one. What I used to picture as an argument or accusation, I have had to slow down and ask myself why or tell him how I feel to stop assuming a wrong assumption. Otherwise, we could have an argument and I would keep score or hold a grudge for a very long time, which becomes resentment over time. Thus, resilience has been a tool to help communicate and recover from a bad moment.

Lesson 2: Why Wait to Change?

Dr. Joe Dispenza often says it takes a life-altering event for most people to change. However, he sends the message that you do not need to wait for a crisis to begin your journey.

The pursuit of change is only possible for those who seek it and take action. Waiting only prolongs your suffering. Thus, why wait for tragedy, loss, or trauma?

You can change today.

Lesson 3: Sadness vs. Anxiety

Alex Hormozi also explains the difference between sadness and anxiety in a way that clicked for me:

- **Sadness** is when you feel like you have *no options* → so you need to ***learn.***
- **Anxiety** is when you feel like you have *too many options* → so you need to ***decide.***

This reframe helped me see that no matter how I feel, there is always a path forward, either through learning or deciding. This distinction alone also changes how you approach your emotions and move forward.

Lesson 4: The Steps to Self-Development

Alex also shared 4 steps that made growth less overwhelming. The steps are:

Step 1. Self-awareness: Be brutally honest with yourself, or nothing will change.

Awareness is the first step.

Every day, you wake up carrying the signature of your old self. Your body remembers old wounds, old triggers, and old habits. It is addicted to repeating the same emotional patterns.

But here is the good news! **You are not your past.** Trauma and conditioning are programs, and programs can be rewritten.

So how do you disrupt old patterns and build new ones? By practicing new patterns! Not just imagining who you want to be, but *feeling* the emotions you want to embody.

For example, if you visualize making a free throw, you do not just picture it. You also feel the joy, pride, and gratitude of sinking the shot. This combination of imagery and emotion rewires the brain and body.

Step 2. Emotional intelligence: Learn to understand and regulate, not suppress, your feelings and emotions.

Create space between the trigger and response.

The next time you feel a negative emotion like anger, frustration, or sadness, do not fuel it. Just **notice** it.

The goal is not to control the outside world but to control your inner world.

Why? This is because emotions are not just psychological; they are also physiological. Your body gets addicted to the chemicals (hormones), like fight-or-flight. Every time you react in anger or frustration, you reinforce that particular pathway, like deepening grooves on a highway.

When a trigger hits (like your kid spilling milk), pause instead of reacting. This creates space between **trigger** and **response**. That space is where transformation begins.

When you pause, breathe, and observe why it is a trigger instead of reacting, you create space. That space is the beginning of transformation. It interrupts the old habit and opens the door to a new one.

By practicing new patterns, you build a new road.

Step 3. Understand your brain: Your brain is wired to keep you "safe," but fear is not the same as safety, which often means being stuck in survival mode.

Information is not transformation. Only repetition, presence, and practice will rewire your identity.

Pause, breathe, shift focus, observe, and choose new reactions without attaching a story. It will feel unnatural because the body is addicted and conditioned to feel the way it has for so long.

As mentioned before, if the typical reaction is frustration, it feels familiar even if it is destructive. Every emotion is a deeply ingrained pattern in the brain.

So what can you do? Practice, practice, practice to make a new reaction permanent. Practice being intentionally calm and *feeling* an elevated emotion like peace, gratitude, or love. **The brain does not know the difference between practicing and a real event.**

Step 4. No cookie-cutter formulas: Growth is not one-size-fits-all. What works for someone else may not work for you.

Practical steps to try, one at a time:

- **Start each day with gratitude.** Align with abundance now so life can match that energy.
- **Pause and breathe.** When triggered, question why it is triggering you before reacting.
- **Choose new emotions.** Practice feeling peace, love, and joy even when it feels uncomfortable.
- **Meditate daily.** Teach your body what your mind already knows. Close your eyes, focus on your breathing, and stop thinking. Only focus on feeling an elevated emotion.
- **Detach from old stories.** Detachment is power. Your energy is your responsibility.

These steps reminded me that transformation is not about a perfect formula. It is about experimenting, practicing, and adjusting what works for you.

At the end of the day, your energy is your responsibility. Even if you write and repeat affirmations, but you still feel like you are in survival mode, your energy does not lie, and in a state of desperation, it cannot create.

So when you wake up, wake up as your **future self** before your fears and triggers have a chance to hijack your identity.

Lesson 5: Self-Respect & Curiosity

Leila Hormozi teaches, *"You are a scientist, not a judge."*

Instead of criticizing yourself, study your behavior with curiosity. Ask:

- Why do I behave the way I do?
- What patterns am I repeating?
- What triggers me?
- Who would I become if I chose differently?

When I started approaching myself with curiosity instead of judgment, I began to rebuild my confidence and self-respect. Only then could I begin to change.

Leila Hormozi also teaches that true self-respect is not about demanding it from others. It is about living in alignment with yourself, which is not being selfish or arrogant. Below are six practices that changed my life.

#1 Keep your word to yourself. If you do not, why expect others to?

Every time you break a promise to yourself, you lower your own standard and teach others to do the same.

Instead of addressing misalignment early, we let resentment build. Eventually it comes out sideways. We then explode over something small and insignificant with our loved ones or closest people around us. That is due to unmanaged discomfort.

True alignment means telling yourself the truth and honoring it before it becomes resentment.

When disagreements come up, ask yourself before talking to that person:

- What outcome do I want from this conversation?
- What action do I want the other person to take when we're done talking?

This clarity keeps you from spiraling into "word vomit" and ensures your communication stays intentional.

#2 Leave environments out of alignment. Jobs, relationships, or places that suppress your true self are costing you peace.

I was good at doing this at work and had no problem switching jobs every one to two years when things no longer fit. Unfortunately, I was not good at it in my relationships. I stayed too long or prioritized how others would feel over how I was feeling.

At the end of the day, you are the one who lives with yourself. Why feel bad about where you are and who you are spending your time with? Life is too short to feel bad.

#3 Choose discomfort over self-abandonment. Growth requires facing the unknown instead of staying stuck.

I know from experience how uncomfortable it is to get divorced and co-parent. That pain was still better than staying in the wrong situation. In my second marriage, the discomfort came from staying and working on our marriage vs. getting divorced. When we bought a 21-foot travel trailer and lived in it full-time. It was the change we needed to start working on our marriage. We then moved to Florida and later Guatemala. It was another leap into the unknown that stretched me in ways I could have never predicted.

The truth is, growth always feels uncomfortable at first. If you avoid discomfort, you avoid growth and end up abandoning yourself in the process.

#4 Let consequences teach. Boundaries do not need to be announced. They need to be enforced.

A real boundary is set up internally and *beforehand*, so you already know how you will respond if the line is crossed. That way, you are not scrambling in the heat of the moment.

For example, if you decide you will not tolerate cheating, then when a partner cheats, you already know you will leave as a consequence. Do not beg them to change. This boundary is not about controlling the other person. It is about staying true to yourself.

#5 Master your emotions. Respond with calm action, not drama.

Mastery does not mean ignoring or burying your emotions. It means allowing yourself to feel your emotions without letting them take the wheel.

Show strength by distancing yourself and calmly exiting a situation. Drama demands energy, but calmness preserves it. Boundaries become far more powerful when enforced with silence and action rather than shouting and chaos.

#6 Stop arguing for respect. First ask, "What do you want me to do differently?" Then decide if it aligns with you. If not, walk away.

Choosing to step back is not giving up. It is growing up. Not every conversation needs to happen. If there is no change after the first time, it most likely will not happen after the fifth.

Walk away. Choose your self-respect over the situation.

Like fitness, self-respect requires consistent practice. You do not build it once but strengthen it daily.

Bringing It Back to You

These lessons were not just motivational; they were lifelines. They helped me rebuild after loss, depression, and years of running on autopilot.

Between Dr. Joe Dispenza, Alex Hormozi, and Leila Hormozi, one truth shines through:

You are one decision away from the life you truly want.

Here is the most important part: ***You do not need to wait for a crisis to begin your journey and wake you up***. You can start now. Build awareness, practice new patterns, and honor your self-respect.

When you align your energy, choices, and actions, you unlock your confidence, your power, and ultimately your true self.

- Start by noticing how long it takes you to recover from bad moments.
- Journal one behavior you want to study instead of judge.
- Choose one decision this week instead of spinning in anxiety.

Because sometimes, the smallest shift creates the biggest ripple.

What about you? When was the last time you chose to change before life forced you to?

Jacqueline Long

CEO of Elevate Your Biz Digital Consulting, LLC
Business Marketing Strategist & Expert

https://www.facebook.com/groups/elevatedfemaleentrepreneurs
https://www.instagram.com/elevatewithjacqueline
Amazon Author Page: https://shrtm.nu/JLongAuthorPage

Jacqueline is a Business Marketing Strategist, former Podcast Host, Master Certified Life, Transformation & Mindset Coach. She is also a Best-Selling Co-author of four Anthologies for professional women in business: Purpose Driven Paycheck, Becoming an Unstoppable Woman Entrepreneur II, The Force of Women CEO's and Women Decision Makers. Over the last several years, Jacqueline has helped women start coaching businesses, and master their digital sales and marketing strategies.

Jacqueline is the founder of Elevate Your Biz Consulting, LLC - her official brand dedicated to women achieving the next level of their dreams, by building profitable online businesses. Jacqueline holds three advanced degrees (Master of Science in Human Resources Management, Master of Public Administration & Master of Arts in Criminal Justice). Prior to starting her coaching business, she had a 20+ year career in non-profit senior management. She has formerly served as a Director of Case Management, Director of Social Services, Director of HIV Clinical Trials, and Vice President of Human Resources. Jacqueline is a native New Yorker who enjoys traveling, reading, listening to music, and spending time with her large family. She has two daughters, and she lives in the Atlanta Metro-Area.

Currently, Jacqueline is working her PhD in Education, specializing in online learning; she is ABD (All but Dissertation).

The First

By Jacqueline Long

"A woman with a voice is by definition, a strong woman." – Melinda Gates

We are all exceptional in our own individual ways and have an important story to tell, which can be helpful or inspirational to someone else. My story isn't one of trauma to triumph. But one of motivation, inspiration, and becoming the first...

Humble Beginnings

I'm the youngest child, "the baby," of 14 children. Yes, I said 14 children. This is something people often have a hard time believing. But people from the Caribbean islands, like my family, often have a lot of children, and they raise them with the support of family and the community. This was true of my family as well. However, my older siblings were all grown, with families and lives of their own, by the time my mom emigrated to the USA, and I was born in the early 70's. I was born in Queens, NY, but grew up mostly in East Flatbush, Brooklyn. My parents and family are from the twin Caribbean islands of Trinidad and Tobago. My mother was a short, pretty, mixed Afro-Caribbean, Spanish-Indian woman, and my biological father was Afro-Chinese Caribbean.

I didn't have a relationship with my biological father growing up. I was raised primarily by my mom and stepfather. I grew up in a tough neighborhood, where many in the community were statistics who had fallen to drugs, teenage pregnancy, prison, or worse. But my mother was strict and worked long hours to provide for me. I was a latchkey kid who went home from school, had a snack, and did my homework until my mother got home from work. My mother never allowed me to hang out in the neighborhood or socialize with the neighborhood kids. I often spent summers in New Jersey with family, Queens with my older sister, or Trinidad with other relatives. She always taught me that while we lived in "the hood," we were not "of the hood." She did her best to keep me out of trouble, well cared for, and focused on my schooling. So, I did just that. At an early age, I took a liking to school, got good grades, and followed the rules. I was a precocious child who was curious about the world and smart beyond my years. I loved to read, a skill and pastime that I still enjoy immensely to this day. However, I never knew at that time, as the youngest child in my family, my love for books and knowledge would grow into my becoming the first to do and achieve many things as a first-generation American in my family, even in the face of many challenges and adversities throughout my life and career.

Her

My family was working-class and even poor by economic means. But we didn't know it or feel it. I always had what I needed and a little more. We always had a house full of food, I wore good clothes, and my mother kept an impeccably clean and organized home. Most importantly, I was surrounded by family and family friends, who always believed in me and supported me. As a result, I learned that, although our family had little in money and success, as the youngest and first-generation American, I could have and do anything. My mother was my biggest cheerleader. She was the first to encourage and empower me to have a voice of my own. She saw and understood my passion for knowledge, and she pushed and encouraged me to do everything I wanted. She always said, "Whatever it is you want to do, do it." She would also tell me to think, "WHEN it happens, and never IF it happens."

My mother didn't have much and was of a very different generation of women. However, what she gave me was invaluable. She taught me to go after whatever I wanted and make sure I worked hard and asserted myself doing it. My mother was a strong woman who believed in gratitude, prayer, and speaking up for herself always. She was a woman with a "voice" who taught me that her generation of women didn't have the opportunities that I had and were often submissive and that I should never be subservient to anyone. My mother was feisty and outspoken. She didn't suffer fools gladly. She always spoke her mind and said what she meant and meant what she said. As a child, those were the qualities I observed in her, and I was often in awe of them. I admired her candor and ability to wear who she was on her sleeves and say whatever she was thinking. Those qualities helped me to become an assertive and confident teenager, and later woman, who was passionate about achieving my own goals. My mother was my biggest cheerleader. She doted over me as the "baby" of the family and assured me that I would be the first to do many things that would break many years of generational trauma and struggle in my family. She taught me that life was hard, unfair, and often scary, but to push forward anyway, be confident, and always assert myself. And when I was scared, she would tell me that just because no one I knew did it didn't mean I couldn't do it. She encouraged me to always "try, succeed, or learn something from failing." My mother was the first "voice" in my life who helped me to find my own.

It would take me years to realize that my drive, motivation, and fearlessness to try new things and accomplish my goals came from my mother. She gave me the most invaluable lessons that my formal education could never give me. She gave me the push and belief that I needed to be comfortable in being "the first" woman in a leadership position, managing the difficulties of a male-dominated field. Her encouragement led me to be the first to try new things, reach new career heights and be fearless doing it. From my mother, I learned that failing didn't mean I was a failure; it simply meant that I had more to learn. Her life lessons would play a profound role in the woman I would become, a woman with a voice of her own, who has never been afraid to be the first and lead the way in my life's journey. She taught me lessons that I would now pass on to my own daughters to help them find their own voices as young women.

My mother passed in January 2020. But her memories, words, and encouragement will continue to be a driving force in my life. My mother was a wise and intuitive woman. She prayed and was always grateful for the little we had. She always told me to think and believe in myself and my desires. She never demanded that I go to college. But her support and my love for knowledge helped me to find my own passion and pursue my own goals. I would go on to be the first in my family to graduate as valedictorian from high school and then the first to graduate from college. I would then exceed my own expectations and be the first to complete three master's degrees and finally pursue my doctoral studies in 2022 and achieve ABD (All but Dissertation) status this past summer, 2025.

For several years, I enjoyed a career with the HIV/AIDS population as a testing counselor and worked my way up to Director of Social Services and then Vice President of Human Resources. After 20+ years in a profession I enjoyed, I traveled the world, moved to Georgia, and decided to do something new. I left my profession and started my own business and podcast and became a multi-best-selling co-author. Today, I manage my own business, and I'm working on my PhD in Education. Along the way, I managed to raise two beautiful daughters, a 25-year-old now a doctoral student in business, and a 21-year-old graduate student in management.

Me

I'm now in my early fifties and experiencing a new chapter in my life as a doctoral student, business owner, and almost-empty nester. But I still have many dreams and desires to pursue, and I can hear my mom's voice saying, "Do it!" And when I look back at how far I've come and all that I've done and achieved, despite many life disappointments, losses, and setbacks along the way, I ask myself, "How in the world did I do it all?" Honestly, I'm not exceptionally talented or gifted, by any means. I'm simply a woman who was inspired by a strong mother to find my voice, make it heard, and pursue what I wanted in life. I worked hard, and I failed forward. I learned that being strong and fearless in pursuing my passion was my way of expressing myself, raising my voice, and sharing what I have to offer with the world as a woman, mother, business owner, professional, and leader. I thank my mother and pay homage to her for giving me the tools to be confident and empowering me to become a woman with a voice, passion, and purpose. Most importantly, I also thank her for teaching me that it's not so bad or hard to be "the first."

Alexis Long

Lex Vuitton Content
Doctoral Student, Social Media Manager

www.linkedin.com/in/alexis-long430
https://www.facebook.com/alexis.long.3367
www.instagram.com.lexvuitton_

Alexis is a passionate social media manager and content creator, dedicated to helping businesses grow through powerful and strategic digital storytelling. As the founder of Lex Vuitton Content, Alexis specializes in crafting engaging content and managing online presence for brands, helping them skyrocket their visibility and success. With a creative eye and a deep understanding of digital marketing trends, she empowers entrepreneurs and business owners to connect authentically with their audiences and achieve measurable results. Originally from New York, Alexis has called Georgia home for the past 12 years, bringing a unique blend of big-city drive and Southern charm to her work. In addition to running her business, Alexis is pursuing her Doctor of Business Administration (DBA) in Human Resources Management, further expanding her expertise in leadership and business strategy. Her mission is to inspire, create, and transform brands through innovative content solutions.

Finding My Voice Through Purpose

By Alexis Long

Losing Focus: Finding My Voice Through Purpose

There was a time when I didn't know who I was, where I was going, or what I was truly meant to do. Looking back, I realize I wasn't just searching for a degree or a career. I was searching for me. My journey to pursuing a doctorate in business administration wasn't a straight path but rather a winding road filled with detours, dead ends, and moments where I almost gave up completely.

I began my college journey back in 2018, eager and hopeful as I declared my major in business administration. At the time, it felt like the right choice, but deep down, I lacked clarity. I didn't have a clear vision of my future or my purpose. I was going through the motions, taking classes, checking boxes, and hoping that somewhere along the way, I would figure it out. But without a strong sense of "why," I quickly lost focus.

Searching for Direction

In my uncertainty, I made a bold move. I switched my major to criminal justice. Something about it at the time intrigued me, and I thought maybe it would give me the direction I was looking for. But soon, I discovered that it wasn't for me either. The excitement faded, leaving me feeling even more lost and frustrated.

After transferring to another school and still feeling unsettled, I made a decision that terrified me at the time: I walked away from school altogether. I told myself it would only be a break, but deep down, I questioned whether I would ever return. That season of my life was filled with doubt and shame. I saw friends and peers moving forward with their degrees, their careers, and their lives, while I felt stuck.

There were moments when I convinced myself that maybe school just wasn't for me. Maybe I was destined to simply work and survive, not thrive. My dreams felt too far out of reach, and I began to believe the lies my fear was telling me: that I wasn't smart enough, capable enough, or deserving enough to achieve greatness.

Choosing to Fight for My Dreams

But as much as I wanted to silence the dreamer inside of me, she wouldn't go away.

In 2022, something shifted. I can't pinpoint one specific moment, but it was as if a light turned on inside me. I realized that if I wanted more for my life, I had to fight for it. I decided to return to school, but this time, I chose with intention. I went back to my original major—Business Administration—because deep down, I knew that was where my passion lived. As I progressed through my coursework, something unexpected happened: I discovered a deep love for human resources management. For the first time, I wasn't just going to school to get a degree; I was building a career rooted in purpose.

Discovering My Purpose

Finding that passion gave me the clarity I had been searching for all along. Suddenly, school wasn't just about passing classes. It became about creating impact, about stepping into the woman I was always meant to be.

Fueled by this newfound purpose, I didn't stop at my bachelor's degree. I went on to earn my master's in human resources management and organizational development, a journey that stretched me in ways I didn't think were possible.

During that time, I worked two jobs to keep my dreams alive, often staying up late into the night to finish assignments after long days of work.

Life didn't pause for me while I pursued my education. I experienced profound loss during those years—family deaths and illnesses that left my heart heavy with grief. There were days when the weight of it all felt unbearable. I wanted to quit so many times. But every time I reached my breaking point, I reminded myself of why I started.

Perseverance Through the Pain

I wasn't just doing this for me. I was doing it for every person who believed in me, for every loved one who wasn't here to see me win, and for the version of myself who once thought she wasn't capable of greatness.

Despite the tears, exhaustion, and setbacks, I persevered. And with each challenge I overcame, I found my voice becoming stronger.

When I graduated with my master's degree, I didn't stop there. I boldly decided to pursue my Doctorate in Business Administration (DBA) with a focus on Human Resources Management. It was a decision that terrified and excited me at the same time. The little girl inside me, the one who once doubted herself, was now walking in rooms she never imagined she'd enter.

Walking Boldly in My Truth

Pursuing a doctorate has been one of the most challenging but rewarding experiences of my life. There are days when the workload feels overwhelming, and imposter syndrome whispers in my ear, telling me I don't belong here, but then I remember how far I've come.

I think about the girl who once walked away from school completely, unsure of who she was or what she wanted. I think about the woman I've become—resilient, determined, and passionate about her purpose.

This journey has taught me that purpose isn't something you stumble upon by accident. It's something you uncover through persistence, self-discovery, and the courage to keep going when everything inside you wants to quit.

Unleashing My Voice

My purpose is clear now: to advocate for others, to create spaces where people can thrive, and to use my voice to inspire change. Human Resources isn't just a career for me. It's a calling. It's how I serve others and leave a lasting impact on the world.

When I reflect on my journey, I see how every setback was preparing me for this moment. I remember sitting in my dorm room late at night, textbooks scattered across the bed, wondering if I had made the right choice in switching majors again. The hum of the desk lamp was the only sound as tears rolled down my face—not from defeat, but from the quiet realization that I wasn't giving up. I was simply rewriting my path. Taking breaks, mourning losses, and rebuilding myself each time weren't signs of failure—they were chapters in my story of resilience. Those challenges shaped me into a woman who refuses to settle, who dares to dream bigger, and who unapologetically uses her voice to uplift others.

Today, as a doctoral student, I stand proud of the woman I've become. My voice is no longer being silenced by fear or uncertainty. I know who I am, and I know why I'm here.

A Message to the Woman Who Feels Lost

To every woman reading this who feels lost or uncertain, I want you to know this: Your path doesn't have to be perfect to lead you to your purpose. There will be detours, obstacles, and moments when you want to give up, but those are the very moments that build your strength.

I almost didn't return to school. I almost believed the lie that my dreams were too big for someone like me. But by choosing to keep going, I discovered not only my purpose but also the power of my own voice.

This chapter of my life is proof that no matter where you start, you can create the future you deserve. You have the power to rewrite your story, to rise from the ashes of doubt and fear, and to unleash the voice that's been inside you all along.

Still Rising

My journey isn't over. I'm still climbing, still growing, still becoming. But today, I walk boldly in my truth, knowing that my voice matters. And if my story can inspire even one woman to keep going, then every struggle, every sleepless night, and every tear was worth it.

I found my purpose. I unleashed my voice. And now, I stand ready to help others do the same.

Mojca Klemen

https://www.linkedin.com/company/she-rises-studios/
https://www.facebook.com/sherisesstudios
https://www.instagram.com/sherisesstudios_llc/
www.SheRisesStudios.com

Mojca is a teacher, mindset coach, intuitive healer and author, devoted to guiding women through deep transformation. Her work blends spirituality, mindset mastery, archetypal wisdom, helping women rise from burnout to balance and embrace their authentic power - a journey she knows deeply, having walked through burnout herself twice and finding way back to wholeness. As a passionate student of archetypes, she explores an empowering path of self-discovery with her Andromeda Way. Her unique approach includes healing with horses and for horses, honouring the sacred bond with animals and nature. She writes fairytales carrying messages of Mother Nature's importance and our inner magic. With compassion and a fierce belief in women's potential, Mojca crates spaces where limitations are gone and confidence is born. As a co-author she shares her mission to help every woman unlock her story, reclaim her voice and shine unapologetically.

Healing My Inner Wounds: A Path to Self-Love and Empowerment

By Mojca Klemen

They are laughing at me and I have nowhere to hide. Why are they laughing at my tears?!

Those were the thoughts running through my 6-year-old mind. I had just finished my first year of elementary school and some adults, probably my parents' acquaintances, asked me about my school report. Let me tell you, I passed with flying colors. I should have felt proud, even excited, but instead a heavy shame would come over me as if my achievement was not OK. I didn't understand why I felt this way; I didn't even know why I was crying. And I believe now that they didn't know how I felt and I am sure they didn't want to make me feel humiliated by their laughter. Yet their response made me believe it is not good to do well or to be seen.

As a teenager, I was curious and fun but also reserved. Sometimes I would withdraw myself from the company of my friends. I didn't understand why. I mean, deep down, a part of me wanted to stay, but simultaneously, in my mind, there was this inner voice telling me to go and stay safe. Isn't it amazing what our mind can come up with based on something that happened many years ago or even based on how we interpret that event? So, that had to be the trace of that childhood scar still echoing in my soul, influencing how I interpret the world based on my own perception of that event. Even more, I thought something was wrong with me because I didn't want to hang out with my school friends after school. This pattern has stayed with me for years.

In my marriage, I loved my husband, and I didn't even realize that I had begun to adapt to his visions and expectations and slowly muting my voice. You know, I have always found, and still do, magic in everything around me. And one time when I was especially excited and opened my heart, the response I got was: "Behave according to your age." I guess he was just joking, but I felt as if that haunting memory started echoing even louder at that moment. And yes, I was still chasing approval, so I started changing my behavior and thus was slowly losing myself. When I became a mother, I was overwhelmed and really enjoyed this role, nurturing my children, playing with them, telling fairytales, ... I devoted most of my time and energy at home to them. I would put their needs first and forget about myself. Not really healthy, right?

At work, I poured my energy into countless projects. I took part in initiatives I loved and often even spent hours doing some extra tasks because I was passionate about my work. And from my own experience I can tell you that perfectionism isn't good. But I always loved the connections I made with people, the laughter I shared through the plays I wrote, the love I gave freely, and the healing I offered others. I enjoyed every moment of it, but somewhere along the way, I overlooked my health, my needs, and my boundaries. I believed that my worth was defined by how much I could give and how many lives I could touch. I motivated myself with the idea that 'this is what I'm meant to do' but was unaware that I was slowly burning out. The more I gave, the more I was losing my own light, risking my well-being just to keep others uplifted. I also realized that by working long hours and being in many different projects, I was actually running away from some issues that should have been looked into and dealt with. Maybe this sounds familiar to some of you.

Then, the exhaustion hit—it was as if my body and mind had reached their breaking point. I found myself functioning on autopilot, ignoring the whispers of my inner voice, which were becoming louder by day. I thought I was just busy and that this would stop just when I finished another project. Until one day, I collapsed, completely drained, both physically and emotionally. That was my first burnout. Sitting in that silence, I realized I had been running from myself all along and for far too long. I was doing everything 'right' on the outside but not on the inside.

The change didn't happen until my second burnout. I always say that the universe sent me the second message because I didn't answer the first one. This time, it was different. I couldn't even walk anymore. I was so exhausted, that my body simply refused to cooperate. Doctors told me that some of my organs were under severe stress, and it was a serious situation. I knew I had to make a choice. I had to shift my entire world—my priorities, my relationships, my perception of worth—if I wanted to stay in this world, alive. That moment was a wake-up call, an alarm that forced me to confront what really mattered: my health and my happiness.

A few months before my second burnout, I had signed up for a Tony Robbins online event. I could hardly wait to be a part of this transformational energy but due to burnout, I thought I wouldn't be able to attend. The day the event arrived, my family helped me set up a massage table in the living room so I could lie down comfortably and watch. My sister was there with me throughout the entire event. As I listened to Tony's words, something began to shift inside me. His energy, his passion, the tools and techniques he shared with us, and his message of owning your story started deleting those traces of doubt, shame, and self-judgment, cutting through all the BS stories I was carrying through the years, decades, maybe lifetimes. By the last day of the event, all the labels I'd worn and the opinions I'd held about myself—they started to fall away. In those moments, I realized I had a choice: I could continue dimming my light or I could finally step into my truth.

I started making small but consistent steps every day with breathwork, meditation, and taking time just for myself. Taking time for myself, putting me first—yes, believe me, it works. It is possible. Even though as women we are mostly programmed to put others first. But I persisted on my path to recovery. You see, I would sit in the sun, on my grass, grounding myself in nature. And I consciously chose to surround myself with kind, loving people who lifted me up. I chose activities that brought me peace or joy. Day by day, I was becoming more of myself—rediscovering the woman I was beneath all those layers.

My passion is to show women that true power, wisdom, and love are found in our strength, our pain, our dreams, and our light waiting to shine through the fears and labels that try to hold us back. Our worth is not measured by how much we give or what role we have in this world—it's rooted in who we truly are. When we embrace our authenticity, our inner wisdom, and our unique beauty, we ignite a power that cannot be dimmed. And what is even more important here is that we can then finally be the light for others and pass it on to them.

I am grateful for all those people in my life who mirrored back to me those parts that needed to be healed. Yes, it was painful, but once I became aware of that, I was ready to heal those shadows and bring them into the light and embrace myself with love and compassion.

I have 'Shine Your Light! Be You! tattooed on my arm as a daily reminder—a promise to stay true to myself. And also, the word 'Believe,' because I want to be reminded every day to never forget who I am, because I never again want to be who I am not.

When I finally stepped into my power with courage and love, I found my mission: to keep my light shining and, by doing so, to show others what has always been in them, see their potential, and give them the spark to shine their own light and fight for their dreams. I believe it was unconsciously in the beginning but soon I became aware of the effect my steps and my energy have on others (many people say that to me) and I realized that I started creating ripples of change—and I invite you to do it too, not just within yourself, but in the world around you.

Remember, the world needs your light, so find the compassion, grace and love in your heart and shine like the star that you are.

Shine Your Light. Be You!

Samia Pego Keating

Founder of Magical Magnetic Women
Coach

https://www.facebook.com/groups/boostconfidence
https://www.instagram.com/magicalmagneticwomen/
https://magicalmagneticwomen.com/

I help professional and entrepreneurial women rise in authentic confidence, unlock their magic, and step into feminine power with clarity and intention. My mission is to support women in embodying a higher expression of themselves — confident, authentic, magnetic. A woman who moves with alignment and is ready for more: more clarity, more presence, more expression, and a life that reflects who she truly is becoming.

Instead of pushing through life with pressure, perfection, or constant strength, I guide women to build confidence from the inside out. Through self-awareness, feminine energy principles, and soul-identity recognition — your particular magic — my work elevates how women show up, communicate, and make decisions.

This is where you shed outdated roles, step into your true identity, and move through life with a calm, steady magnetism. A woman who doesn't chase — she attracts. Effortlessly.

The Call Back To Your Authentic Confident Self

By Samia Pego Keating

Dear Woman,

There are moments in life when you won't understand why things are happening. You may feel you've lost your confidence, misplaced your magic, or silenced your own voice.

Life doesn't happen by accident; it happens to awaken us it's often a nudge, a quiet knock at the door of your soul, calling you back to your authentic, confident self.

Let me hold your hand, open your heart, and remind you that this journey can be magical if you permit it, if you allow it.

No one else needs to give you permission. Only you.

The permission to rise, to speak, to live fully. I know this because I had to give it to myself.

But there was a time it wasn't like that... a version of me from what now feels like a distant past...

Look at her face... if someone from the outside had seen me that day, they would have found me lying in bed — exhausted, drained of energy, silently asking where I could find the answers to improve my life.

I've never been the kind of person who only complains; quite the opposite, I've always tried to stay positive, to push forward, to make the best of what I have. But no matter how much I tried, the answers I was seeking never seemed to come.

And then, in the middle of all the confusion, something stirred inside me. I saw, with sudden clarity, that the environment I was in was slowly dimming my voice, eroding my values, and shadowing my light.

It was my ***aha*** moment. In that instant, something began to shift — a hunger for something different, a pull to return to myself. To uncover which parts of me had been shut down. To ask which parts I could finally allow to be expressed. To rediscover my life, my why.

It's a breakdown moment — when you finally see that the life you've been living is not what it seemed. And when it arrives, the emotions come in waves: anger, grief, confusion... and a constant, exhausting stress that no feminine body is meant to carry.

Yet somewhere beneath it all, there's a quiet whisper, calling you back to the woman you were always meant to be.

The Turning Point

It was the moment I decided — truly decided — that I would live a life true to myself, fight for what I believe, and go all in.

It felt like waking up from a dream state I didn't know I was in. For so long I was thinking that was all there is... until I opened my eyes and realized there was so much more waiting for me.

More possibilities. More joy. More magic. It wasn't the end of the story; it was just the beginning unfolding."

That's when the changes began.

At first, it felt like pushing mountains uphill.

When you want to change something in your life, it's like emptying out your entire closet — pulling everything into the open to see what serves you and what's out of alignment.

In the beginning, it's messy, uncomfortable, and confronting. But then... you start rediscovering every part of yourself.

You begin to understand that every obstacle you've faced was a blessing in disguise — shaping you, strengthening you, waking you up to your own power.

And with that awareness comes a vow to yourself: never again.

Never again will you allow yourself to be in a position where your voice isn't heard, your light dimmed, or your worth questioned.

Because here's the truth —sometimes people will try to take advantage, belittle you, or create false narratives about you.

It makes them feel better. And sadly, for many, diminishing someone else's confidence is like a sport they love to play.

But confidence — real, rooted confidence — it's like a **diamond in the mud** — no matter how dirty it gets, its brilliance and value are still there.

The perception might change, but the worth remains the same.

And along the way, you'll also meet people who will stand beside you, lift you higher, and help you cross the bridges you didn't think you could.

For those who played both roles — the ones who tried to diminish me and the ones who uplifted me — I only say thank you.

Because I know now that everyone will walk their own path, live their own lessons, and fulfill their own destinies.

And in the end, each one of them shaped the woman I chose to become.

Final Destiny: Your Authentic Confidence

There's so much more I could tell you, but in this fast-paced life, less is more. So here are the key truths I want to leave with you:

- Your past never equals your future.
- You can reinvent yourself as many times as you choose.
- Life becomes richer when you see it as an adventure waiting to be discovered.

✨ And your inner magic is far more powerful than you think.

If you're in a moment of confusion, unsure of your direction, or even believing it's impossible to rise from where you are...

I want you to know this — it all begins with one step. **One decision**. One spark.

That single step is the start of elevating your **authentic confidence** — the confidence that is true to you, aligned with your values, rooted in your soul.

The confidence that knows what you desire in life, business, love. The confidence that doesn't wait for permission but creates.

The confidence that unlocks the magic within you — a magic you may not even realize you carry.

I am share this with you because I know, deep in my bones, that change is possible.

My own life became proof of it.

I reconnected with my authentic confidence and everything began to shift.

I walked away from a relationship that no longer aligned with who I was becoming.

I found the courage to start over in a foreign country, without close family.

From the ground up, I built a coaching business that allowed me to speak with women from all around the world.

In the process, I didn't just rebuild my career — I recovered my energy, my joy, and my zest for life.

If I could rise from that place of uncertainty and create a life that feels true to me, then I know the same is possible for you. Imagine where your authentic confidence could take you.

Your journey doesn't end here — this is only the initiation of your beautiful path. Take this as your sign.

And never forget **Unlock your magic and keep sparkling.**

Connect with me on www.magicalmagneticwomen.com or Facebook

Tania Rizoski

Founder of Your Sanctuary Space
Burnout Prevention & Integrative Leadership Advisor

www.linkedin.com/in/taniarizoski
https://www.facebook.com/people/Your-Sanctuary-Space/100089766026184/
https://www.instagram.com/your_sanctuaryspace/
www.yoursanctuaryspace.com.au

Tania supports women who are overwhelmed, stuck, or on the verge of burnout to reconnect with their energy, values, and well-being so they can lead with integrity and ease. Blending coaching, Reiki, retreat facilitation, corporate leadership experience, and Human Design insights, Tania guides clients through small, sustainable shifts that create lasting change, without sacrificing themselves in the process. Her workshops, retreats, and 1:1 sessions focus on practical self-care, energy protection, mindset reframing, and restoring inner balance. Tania's approach helps women release pressure, let go of limiting beliefs, and align with their natural rhythm so they can thrive in life and leadership. Her message is clear: True leadership doesn't require burnout. It begins within and is rooted in self-worth, aligned action, and the courage to lead authentically.

The Voice I Didn't Know I Had

By Tania Rizoski

Success had never felt so empty.

I had just completed my MBA. I should have felt proud. I had climbed every rung of the corporate ladder, juggled my role as a general manager, a mother of two, and supportive wife, and somehow managed to complete a demanding degree. But instead of standing tall, I was lying flat, literally. I struggled to get out of bed. My body was completely drained. My mind was foggy. And my soul felt... hollow.

This wasn't just exhaustion. It was a full-body power failure. I was later diagnosed with adrenal fatigue, but long before the diagnosis, I knew something inside me had fractured. Or maybe something I had been suppressing for decades had finally erupted.

I remember lying there, tears streaming down my cheeks, not from sadness, but from a raw sense of grief. Grief for the version of me that had sacrificed so much to achieve so little of what actually mattered.

The truth was, I had spent my entire life succeeding by silencing myself. And now, I couldn't hear anything, not even my own heartbeat beneath the noise.

I was born in Macedonia and raised in a culturally traditional household in Australia, where men led and women supported. As a young girl, I watched my mother give so much of herself, quietly, endlessly. I internalized that silence as love, that sacrifice as strength.

My dream wasn't to be a CEO. It was to be a wife and a mother, to love and be loved. And by 27, I had achieved that dream. But what no one told me was that you can fulfill a dream and still feel like a stranger in your own skin.

When I moved to Sydney after I got married, a new world opened up. I climbed the corporate ladder with determination, rising from accounts assistant to executive assistant, and eventually into leadership. On paper, I was a success story.

But beneath the surface, I was still that girl who had learned to keep the peace, to smile when I wanted to scream, and to nod when I longed to speak.

The systems I had excelled in were built for performance, not presence. The cost? My health. My joy. My voice.

My body gave me no choice. It demanded surrender.

In the silence of burnout, I met myself. Not the polished version, not the achiever, but the tired, raw, questioning soul beneath the armor.

That's when the healing began.

For reasons I still can't explain, I booked a session with a psychic, something I had once dismissed out of fear or judgment. But in that space, I felt something I hadn't had in a long time: curiosity. Hope. A spark.

That session didn't give me answers. It gave me permission. Permission to explore my intuition, to soften, to feel, and to ask questions I had long buried. From there, I found Reiki, energy healing (including inner child healing), mindfulness, and a community of women who spoke a language I didn't even know I'd been craving. I wasn't just awakening; I was remembering.

I wept for the little girl who never felt safe enough to cry. I screamed into pillows for the woman who never felt safe enough to rage. I let go of generations of inherited beliefs that had taught me to be small, silent, and selfless to a fault.

Through that healing, I found not just rest but the voice beneath the roles I had learned to play. A voice that whispered, "There's more. You are more."

That voice kept growing louder. It didn't shout, but it sang. It hummed through my bones until I couldn't ignore it.

As I healed, I felt called to create something I'd never seen but had always needed, a sanctuary. A space for women to rest without guilt. To be seen without judgment. To breathe without apology.

I launched my business *Your Sanctuary Space* in secret and as a side gig, as I was still working full-time in my corporate role. I wasn't ready to explain myself to others. I was still becoming.

When I hosted my first retreat, I was terrified. I lit candles in the space with trembling hands, straightened the cushions at least five times, and whispered a silent prayer: Let this be enough. I wasn't sure what would unfold, or if the women arriving would even feel safe enough to open up.

But by the end of that weekend, something sacred had taken root. I watched one woman weep in the arms of another, neither of them speaking, just being with each other. I felt it in my bones: This was what I was meant to do.

It wasn't about teaching or fixing anyone. It was about creating space for softness, reflection, and connection. And in doing so, I was healing too. My voice wasn't in a speech or a business plan. It was in the quiet nods, the warm tea, and the deep exhale of a woman finally allowing herself to just be.

I knew this space had to exist. For every woman who had held it all together while quietly falling apart. For the women who needed permission to choose themselves.

From retreats came coaching. From coaching came certifications in Reiki, mindfulness, sound bowls, and human design. I was building not just a business, but a revolution of softness. A reclamation of worth.

Your Sanctuary Space is more than an offering. It is my voice, reborn, grounded, and finally free.

I spent years mastering masculine energy, doing, pushing, and controlling. It had built my career. It had earned me accolades.

But it had also burned me to the ground.

Learning to trust my feminine energy felt like walking barefoot after years in steel-capped boots. Unsteady. Vulnerable. But so incredibly real.

Resting. Receiving. Allowing. Feeling. These were not weaknesses; they were lifelines.

With every moment of stillness, I stitched pieces of myself back together. And in that wholeness, I found connection, not just to others, but to truth.

When a woman reclaims her voice, she doesn't need to raise it. Her presence alone shifts the room. I didn't need to be louder. I just needed to finally hear myself.

Today, my work is rooted in what I needed most: a blend of structure and soul. In my sessions and retreats, we explore the stories women tell themselves, the inherited beliefs, the burnout patterns, and the silence. Sometimes, we move through these with practical coaching tools. Other times, we sit in sacred stillness, letting the breath lead. I draw on Reiki, mindfulness, intuition, and lived experience to help women reconnect with the wisdom already inside them.

It's not about adding more. It's about removing the noise so they can hear their own voice again.

Today, I help women, especially those in leadership, redefine success as something sustainable, soulful, and aligned.

Leadership isn't about pushing harder. It's about leading from wholeness, creating spaces that prevent burnout before it begins, and integrating intuition with integrity.

Strangely and divinely, I've been called back into the corporate world. But this time, I'm not playing by their rules. I'm bringing *Your Sanctuary Space* into the boardroom. I'm helping women lead with their full selves, not just the polished parts.

My human design as a generator reminds me: I'm here to respond with passion, purpose, and aligned energy. This is my offering. This is my truth.

If your voice has been buried under titles, trauma, motherhood, marriage, or expectations, I want you to know:

You don't have to fall apart to begin again. But if you already have, know this: It might just be the beginning of your becoming.

You are allowed to pause.
You are allowed to rest.
You are allowed to be wildly, beautifully, imperfectly human.

You don't need to be fixed. You only need to feel.

Reclaiming your voice doesn't always start with a roar. Sometimes, it begins with a whisper, the kind that says:

"I am worthy. I am ready. I choose me."

If you're reading this and something in your chest aches, not in pain, but in recognition, I want you to know you're not alone.

I see you. The version of you holding it all together. The version that smiles while silently aching. The part of you that whispers late at night, "There has to be more than this."

There is.

You don't have to burn out to be worthy of rest. You don't have to break to be allowed to begin again. You just have to be willing to come home to yourself.

If I could go back to the woman I was, flat on the bed, exhausted and ashamed, I would whisper, *"This isn't the end. It's the beginning of your becoming."*

And if you see yourself in my story, I'd love to walk beside you. Your voice matters more than you know.

Gina Hornbogen

Founder of Illumine

https://www.facebook.com/gina.bernathornbogen/
https://www.instagram.com/gina.hornbogen/
https://illumine.world

Gina Hornbogen is passionate about helping people uncover their strengths, see new possibilities, and step into lives that feel more authentic and fulfilling. With nearly three decades in the corporate world of finance, she understands the demands of modern life and brings that practical grounding into her work. Alongside her career, Gina has followed a deep curiosity for personal growth and holistic wellness, blending both worlds to guide others toward lasting transformation. A lifelong learner, Gina earned a bachelor's degree in finance and has pursued numerous trainings and certifications to deepen her understanding of the human experience. She is certified in NLP, Art of Being, health coaching, Hermetic Alchymie, sound healing, and Reiki Master Teacher. Her diverse background allows her to meet people where they are and support transformation on multiple levels — mind, body, and spirit. Gina enjoys cooking, outdoors, time with her husband, three adult children, and animals.

Unapologetically Me

By Gina Hornbogen

Finding My Own Voice

I grew up in a house where silence felt like survival. On the outside, my family's life looked picture-perfect: a beautiful home, an in-ground pool, and fancy cars. People at school assumed I had it all—wealth, privilege, a life of ease. But behind closed doors, my reality was very different. I was the stepchild who didn't belong, not allowed on vacations, the live-in babysitter and maid, never really seen or heard. Emotional, physical, and psychological abuse left scars no one else could see. Most nights, I cried myself to sleep, never daring to show the pain outwardly.

And yet, even in that darkness, something inside me refused to be extinguished. People often asked, "Where did you come from?" They were puzzled by how I could handle situations with such calm and objectivity. Always curious, I asked questions, sought perspectives, and had a way of diffusing tensions.

I also learned something vital: Listening is as powerful as speaking. When we truly listen, we can take what resonates, leave the rest, and still create dialogue where everyone feels heard.

The Illusion of Safety

In my early twenties, still carrying the wounds of my childhood, I married a man much older than me. I thought stability lived in age and experience, but what I found was something else entirely. He was an alcoholic, and his jealousy, especially after the birth of our son, became unbearable.

The verbal abuse cut deep, but my son's presence gave me the courage I needed. I realized that staying would cost not just my happiness but my son's future. So I did the unthinkable: I left. Representing myself in the divorce, I gave up everything—the house, financial security, and savings—to give my son a better life. Some might have called that foolish. I called it choice.

Starting over was terrifying, yet it was one of the first real acts of claiming my own power.

The Pain of Rejection

Around the same time, I lost my biological father—not to death at first, but to silence. His decision to sever ties with my brother and me was devastating. I may never fully understand why, but I've come to see it was his choice, not mine.

As a little girl, I had been the apple of his eye, and I never stopped being his daughter in my heart. But suddenly, I wasn't his family anymore. Not long after, he died of cancer at a very young age. I never had the chance to mend what was broken, and I carried that grief for a long time.

Yet even in that loss, the inner voice I had always leaned on reminded me: His actions did not define my worth. That knowing allowed me to move forward with compassion instead of bitterness.

Finding My Way in a Man's World

Even as I carried the grief of losing my father, life demanded that I move forward and the workplace became the next arena where my voice was tested.

When I reentered the workforce, I landed in finance—at that time, a very male-dominated industry. From day one, the message was clear: "Keep your pretty little mouth shut." Many of my bosses took credit for my work, but I did not let that stop me.

I had already lived through silencing at home, and I knew what it cost. I wasn't willing to pay that price again. So this time, I spoke up.

I asked questions. I challenged assumptions. I sought out mentors who could see me for who I really was. Slowly, I carved a place for myself.

The secret wasn't playing by their rules. It was listening to my own inner compass—that quiet knowing I had relied on since I was a girl. Every time I chose truth over conformity, I grew stronger. Every time I trusted myself, I stepped further into my own power.

Learning to Trust Myself

For a long time, I was very alone, until I met my husband, Bill. Together we had twin daughters, and he became the most loving step-parent to my son. Through him and others who showed up at the right times, I learned that family isn't always blood. It's the people who choose to stand with you and who you choose to stand with.

I discovered the importance of community, no matter how small. Even one or two people who will listen, hold space, and encourage you to grow can make all the difference. Those relationships gave me the courage to keep listening to my voice.

My deepest strength, though, still came from within. That inner knowing reminded me I was enough, that I was capable, and that I could make decisions not based on others' beliefs but on what I knew to be true. The road was often scary, but it was worth it.

Reframing Life's Challenges

People sometimes ask how I endured so much—the abuse, the rejection, the isolation—and still sought more in life. My answer is simple: I don't see life in terms of lessons and punishments. I see life as a series of invitations.

Every experience is an invitation to grow, to expand, or to gather wisdom. Pain can be a gift, because it teaches us what we will no longer accept. Betrayal can be a gift, because it reveals the truth of who people are. Loneliness can be a gift, because it pushes us toward self-reliance and, eventually, toward the right connections. Sometimes the gifts are hidden, but if we stay open, every experience carries wisdom.

My experiences have shaped the lens through which I see the world. And through that lens, I see potential in everything—even the hard things, even the things that almost broke me.

The Power of Voice

Looking back, the common thread in every stage of my life has been voice. As a child, my voice was silenced. As a young woman, I gave it away to someone who couldn't value it. As a professional, I was told to suppress it in order to succeed.

Yet through it all, there was something more—a whisper deep inside, my inner compass, reminding me I was more than my circumstances.

At times, I believed my worth was tied to validation. I abandoned my own needs and molded myself into what others wanted. I thought I had kept the peace, but really, I had only silenced myself in another way.

I remember weighing the fear of leaving against the cost of staying in my first marriage. My mind wavered, but my inner voice grew louder, insisting I couldn't betray myself or my son by staying silent any longer. Eventually, that whisper became a roar I couldn't ignore. Choosing to leave was terrifying, but it was also a shift: Reclaiming my voice wasn't just about speaking, it was about choosing myself.

In my career, I faced another layer of silencing. I was told to blend in, to play the game, to not rock the boat. My ideas were dismissed, my opinions brushed aside, and my voice labeled "too much." But I had learned a pattern: Every time I dimmed my voice, I lost a piece of myself. And every time I honored it, I became more whole.

In the end, I discovered that my voice, especially the inner one, was my greatest gift. It was always there to guide me, steady and constant.

Today, I stand unapologetically in my truth. I know every person has a story worth sharing. Our world may try to teach us to silence or doubt our inner compass, but it is always within us—ready to protect, guide, and strengthen.

My deepest hope is that people everywhere learn to trust that voice, carve their own path, and shine light on the way ahead, even when it feels uncertain.

I would not change any part of my journey. Every tear, rejection, and triumph was an invitation to become the woman I am today.

And this truth is for anyone who has ever been silenced, overlooked, or made to believe they were less than: Your voice is waiting to be heard.

The most powerful gift we have is not just finding our voice but trusting it—unapologetically.

Angela Chademunhu

Pastor. Coach

www.linkedin.com/in/angela-chademunhu-114bb1332
https://www.facebook.com/angela.chademunhu
https://www.instagram.com/angelachademunhu

Angela Chademunhu is a Dynamic Pastor, speaker and Professional life coach, graduate in IT. Founder of "Hope of life church" and "Diamond In The Rough Foundation". She started her career 13 years ago, it is during her experiences in the struggles of emerging in her Pastoral calling as a young female Pastor in a looked down upon environment that writing books was inspired. With a dream of becoming an acclaimed author, She co-authored a book with HANNA OLIVAS and other authors in her debut first written published work in the USA BEST SELLER "PRAY DON'T PANIC" and her second book another USA BEST SELLER "WHOLE BODY BLESSINGS" with DR RENEE SUNDAY and other authors. I'm a philanthropist in my nation Zimbabwe Africa. As a certified coach, I help women who feel defeated and broken by life challenges experience a breakthrough, regain control and confidence so they can rise again and make a lasting impact on the world.

The Unleashed Woman

By Angela Chademunhu

The traditional roles of women have changed. No longer is the woman meant to bear children and clean the house and stay at home while her husband is busy scaling up the ladder in industry. Traditionally, our voices as women have been drowned out by what our grandparents, biological parents, foster parents, schoolteachers, authority figures, and society have taught us. We've been made to conform to ideals taught by male-dominated or masculinist culture systems that have left our voices in silence. The truth is, we are so desperate to be heard and express ourselves authentically as women.

Women still struggle for equality in many important spheres of influence, be it in politics, church ministry, industry, socially, economically, or physically. Women make less money. Society is also not doing enough to protect the women who have been victims for too long. It's up to us to figure out how to balance career and family. I'm so happy there is a newfound freedom for women in this world order. The new world order has birthed an unleashed, emancipated, evolved, strong, confident woman that cannot be suppressed: a woman that is financially empowered, a woman that inspires others, and a woman that is fearless, domineering, impactful, and growing and truly leading from the front. This new world order has brought about many opportunities and choices like never before for women, regardless of color, to be whoever they want to be. However, many of us women lack the right tools and stamina to navigate our way into becoming leading, unleashed women on the front line. In other words, many women are bound in chains like prisoners and that has kept them from being unleashed into their full potential.

What is the meaning of the word UNLEASHED? The dictionary meaning is " to free or let loose." Another interesting meaning is "to suddenly release a violent force that can't be controlled." All these meanings are a true description of many women's lives; they are tied up and it's time for them to be unleashed/let loose. I want to remind every woman, rich or poor, strong or weak, that it's your season to be unleashed. There are so many women out there looking down upon themselves, battling depression and trauma, and lacking confidence that it's time to snap out of this setback and be unleashed into power.

In my current position, I have been privileged to meet high-flying women in industry and politics, highly educated women, college graduates, college dropouts, and uneducated women. Despite their differences in society, all these women have one thing in common. They're longing for freedom. They want to be unleashed. Many have a vision of how their lives must be but don't know how to navigate to that final destination. Thus, exactly how I felt for a long time. I had always been that strong friend that everyone runs to when they need advice and a shoulder to cry on. I seemed to have all the answers to everyone's problem. I fixed everyone and everything, but along the way I became exhausted and worn out. I also needed love, support, and the same energy I gave others, yet I was constantly running at a support deficit. All this is good but you must first care about yourself before helping others. I longed to have a romantic relationship with someone that matches my vision and values so I embarked on a personal growth discovery journey and a strong, unleashed version of me attracted the right man to my life.

I know there are many women who do not enjoy financial freedom and this stands as a barrier for you to be unleashed. Can I tell you a secret? Your vision cannot be limited by the lack of funds. You have to shun negative voices that preach impossibilities and refrain from blame games and procrastination if you want to be unleashed. Many are victims of these obstacles that stand to block intelligent, conscious women from being unleashed into their greatness. I was once a victim of all these. In the midst of all this chaos, I learned that even if you cry, no one will save you. You have got to dust your feet and take the necessary steps towards where you want to go in destiny. Save yourself. You're your own superhero in this movie.

What are you called to amplify here on earth? I discovered that the greatest tragedy in life is to live a life without purpose. Nothing is worse than being alive and not knowing your purpose. Without purpose, life has no meaning. I am a woman of purpose/vision. I celebrate myself and I appreciate every step of progress in my journey. I might not have killed it but I got my foot on it. I wrote down my vision according to Habakkuk 2:3:

"For the vision is yet for an appointed time, but at the end it shall speak, and not lie: though it tarry, wait for it; because it will surely come, it will not tarry."

I plan to succeed. I do not plan to fail. My success is important to God. He is the creator of the brand and I am the product. My success is built into creation.

Deep inside me, I knew I was created for more. God created me here on earth to make a difference. I longed to create a career that honors my calling and gifting. Having discovered my calling, I realized it was not enough; I had to build on my success and achieve to impact others on a larger scale. I have been unleashed as a dynamic pastor, speaker, and professional life coach. I'm the founder of "Hope of Life Church" and "Diamond In The Rough Coaching Foundation." I started my career 13 years ago. It is during my experiences in the struggles of emerging in my pastoral calling as a young female pastor in a looked-down-upon environment that writing books was inspired. With a dream of becoming an acclaimed author, I co-authored a book with HANNA OLIVAS and other authors in my debut published work in the USA BEST SELLER "PRAY DON'T PANIC" and my second book, another USA BEST SELLER, "WHOLE BODY BLESSINGS," with DR. RENEE SUNDAY and other authors.

UNLEASH HER book is my 3rd anthology. I'm in the process of having my debut book published and it will be out before the end of the year. I'm a philanthropist doing philanthropy work in my nation, Zimbabwe, Africa. As a certified coach, I help women who feel defeated and broken by life challenges experience a breakthrough and regain control and confidence so they can rise again, create fulfilling, successful careers, have voices that can be heard and make a lasting impact on the world.

I am grateful to God for the privilege to be called to serve in ministry as a pastor but I learned the hard way and I thank God; I'm now unleashed. My advice to younger ministers of the gospel is to not go into ministry without financial backup. Ministry is hard work and more painful when you do not have money. It is high time pastors start projects that back them financially so that their children will not be at the mercy of the congregants, causing unnecessary embarrassment and ridicule, making them hate ministry yet it is noble and a privilege to be called by God.

Many women believe in luck. When they see a fellow woman doing well, they believe she is lucky, but believe me, there is nothing called luck. You have to adequately prepare yourself for opportunities. Orison Swett Marden once said, "Do not wait for extraordinary opportunities. Seize common occasions and make them great. Weak men wait for opportunities; strong men make them." What opportunities are before you? Grab them and make use of them. Every challenge or obstacle I have encountered on the way did not deter me from my pursuit. I know my vision. My mind agrees with my vision. I'm a woman that dreams with God and pursues my possibilities until they become a reality in destiny.

As a woman, what are you chasing? Go for it. We need women that pursue their visions and stand out to be counted. The UNLEASHED woman will pursue her vision like a trailer without brakes. A trailer that has lost its brakes will bulldoze anything or everything that stands in its way until it stops. It will take a new level of doing things to birth out a vision. It takes determination, focus, tenacity, and passion. For me, it took a different prayer life, a different hunger for the word of God and a lot of reading to birth out my vision. It was as if I was in an incubator being kept under the night temperature condition, waiting to break out. I felt it breaking. I was at the edge of my life; I broke out. I'm UNLEASHED. I'm a brand. I am unique. No matter how anyone tries to imitate me, they can never be. My brand is unique so I chose to keep developing my brand. In the Bible, I learned that Prophet Jeremiah and Prophet Isaiah prophesied in the same era (years) but with different assignments. This goes on to show that you can never be given the same specific assignment from God in this lifetime. I have been given a specific role to play by God, and if I do not play it before I die, I disappoint God and deprive my generation of that brand.

An UNLEASHED WOMAN is different. She knows what she stands for. She is financially independent and owns that company; she is a brand. Woman, wake up from that slumber and start that business, go in search of that job, go to school, pursue that degree, do that career course and learn a trade to earn a living. Wishful thinking without action will not bring you any results.

I'm AN UNLEASHED woman. AN UNLEASHED woman understands every generation is different. AN UNLEASHED woman knows the needs of her generation and serves it. I'm UNLEASHED with something different for my generation. I'm that UNLEASHED woman serving my generation with what they currently need at the time.

Angela Leapua

Lifestyles in Harmony
Holistic Health and Business Coach

https://www.linkedin.com/in/angelaleapua/
https://www.facebook.com/angelaleapua
https://instragram.com/angelaleapua
https://lifestylesinharmonycoaching.com/
http://beachybohoboutique.com/

Angela Leapua, M.B.A., M.Ed., NBHWC, MSCSIA, is a Wall Street Journal and Amazon bestselling author, freelance writer, college professor, speaker, transformational leader and holistic health coach. With over 20 years in higher education, several accredited certifications including a health coach certification from IIN, she specializes in Ayurveda, functional medicine, nutrition, mindset modalities and corporate business coaching. Her diverse background enables her to thrive in corporate, group, and personal coaching.

Angela's mission is to inspire positive transformational change. Her guidance helps individuals navigate life's transitions by promoting balance and harmony in the mind, body, and soul. She believes that everyone has the potential to raise their frequency by visualizing, manifesting, and actively working toward their goals.

Whether attending one of her lectures or courses, exploring her books, or visiting her health boutique, you'll discover that Angela embraces a natural, soul-centered, and stress-free lifestyle, inspiring others to live with purpose and harmony.

A Journey of Resilience

By Angela Leapua

Wow, congratulations! I am beyond excited for you because you are about to read the words that will guide you through the toughest moments and help you defy any obstacle in your life. So, take a moment, pause, breathe deeply, and say these words to yourself:

"I am everything. I am all that I need. I am strong. I am fearless. I am loved. I am capable. I am resourceful. *There is nothing I cannot do or achieve. Every challenge, every obstacle, every chaotic moment that life throws my way, I have everything within me to overcome it. All I need to do is dig deep, tap into my inner strength, and let it rise up to guide me. I have the power to shine through any storm, to protect myself from all that surrounds me. God is within me, walking with me every second, every minute, every moment. I am filled with power and courage because I am enough. I love myself. I love my life, and no matter what comes my way, I will power through, just me, myself, and I."*

I have spoken these words many times. They have gotten me through the worst of times. I have dug deep into the very core of my soul, with every ounce of strength I had, to get through the darkest moments of my own life. I faced sorrow, heartache, pain, and struggles that seemed impossible to bear. I walked through it all alone, but I made it. If I can do it, so can you.

We all have this inner strength. It's always been there, waiting for the right moment to rise up. It's in your deepest core, and you don't always realize it until life challenges you in ways you never expected. But trust me: It's there. Embrace it. Know it's within you and when the time comes, use it. You are stronger than you think.

My Life's Drama

As a woman who has endured life's most unimaginable challenges, I stand before you today as a testament to the resilience of the human spirit. My name is Angela Leapua, and my story is one of struggle, survival, and ultimately, triumph. This chapter is my story, but it's also the story of every woman who has been pushed down and told she couldn't rise. You *can* rise. I'm living proof.

Growing up in the heart of Indiana, I was the oldest of six children in a family close to poverty and hardship. We had no silver spoon, no inherited wealth, and no easy path to follow. My journey has not been defined by luxury but by sheer determination and the relentless desire to create a better life for myself and my family.

When I was a child, my parents were my role models. They were a young couple full of hope and love. Having their first child (me) right out of high school, they did the best they could with what they had. My father was awarded scholarships for college and had a promising future. We lived on a college campus, as both parents attended school and started to grow a family. Unfortunately, at the tender age of 15, my father passed away followed by my mother 10 years later. I felt like I was orphaned at an age when most are still sheltered by their parents' love and protection, I was forced to grow up quickly. Death to me seemed normal. During 6th through 10th grade, I lost my father, grandparents, younger brother, and a few friends. Attending funerals kept me numb to the pain of loss. I did not cry when death was near; I went into a state of survival and protection. Feeling sorrow but holding in the emotional pain.

After my mother passed away, I found myself feeling responsible for my younger siblings and endlessly fighting for freedom from my abusive stepfather. My stepfather was extremely abusive, and our mother somewhat protected us. With her passing, I took on the mother role. I thought we could start a new life without my stepfather, but that did not happen. I could not afford a lawyer, and the other family members did not want to help. Therefore, my stepfather took control of the property, my mother's family business and worst of all, custody of three younger children. I was forced to live on my own and became distant from my family. I was truly on my own. At age 25, I was dealing with my mother's death, grappling with the emotional and physical abuse, giving up control to my abuser and losing my home and family. I was at a crossroads. I was experiencing a life of turmoil, pain, and uncertainty.

Living without guidance or safety, I knew the harsh reality of fighting for survival. The weight of responsibility on my young shoulders was immense. As the oldest, I had to set an example, take charge, and bear the emotional burden of our circumstances. I had to grow up faster than I should have. But despite the overwhelming odds stacked against me, I refused to be a victim of my circumstances. There was no way I was going to fail! My stepfather degraded, belittled, and beat me black and blue. There was no way I was going to prove him right in thinking I was a waste of life and would fail. I pushed through the dark moments, determined that one day, I would rise above the limitations of my environment.

Throughout my teenage years, I sought solace in education, a lifeline that offered me hope for a future beyond the confines of my struggling home. With only a GED, little support and no financial resources, I always thought college was out of reach for someone like me. But deep down, I knew that education was my escape, my ticket to freedom. I was the life of the party and enjoyed the social scene. This was my escape from abuse at home. Hanging out with older friends, I would stay out all night and run off to college campuses every chance I got. Little did I know that the college lifestyle would lead me to becoming a college professor. The campus was a safe haven for me. I had many friends and a sense of family; therefore, I worked part-time jobs, took out loans or what ever it took to stay in school. Deep down I had an unwavering belief that I could defy the odds, I earned my college degree, a milestone that felt impossible when I first set foot on that journey.

But that victory was just the beginning. The struggles I faced didn't end with my education; they only morphed into new challenges. I found myself in more abusive relationships with men that had a heart but addictive behaviors. Physical abuse, I felt I could handle, but life with a drug addict was more challenging. I gave them excuses for their behavior and felt I could save them. After years of more abuse, I literally ran for my life. This time I ended up in a women's shelter not a college campus. From broken bones, bruises, homelessness, stealing, guns in my face, jail time, and losing it all, I had to rebuild my life and start over again. The scars from my past—the emotional wounds from the abuse, the weight of responsibility, and the isolation—were often hard to shake. Yet, through every setback, I learned to rise. Each failure was a lesson, each hardship a step forward. With every challenge, I found new strength.

Today, as a highly accomplished woman, I stand on the other side of adversity. Through self-belief, education, and perseverance, I've become strong, resilient, and unbreakable. This chapter reflects my journey, a story of empowerment that speaks to every woman who has ever faced the darkest of days and dared to rise from them. It is a reminder that, no matter where we come from or what we have endured, we have the power within us to shape our own destinies.

The Power of Resilience

Let's talk about resilience. It's a word we throw around a lot these days, but what does it really mean? Resilience is defined as the ability to bounce back from life's struggles and maintain psychological well-being in the face of challenges. For me, resilience was something I learned to embody simply by surviving. I didn't choose it. But as I look back, I see how I was shaped by it. When you're a child and you're dealing with abuse, neglect, and the loss of both parents, resilience isn't a choice—it's a necessity. I had no choice but to develop it. But I also didn't realize at the time just how much strength I was building, because all I could do was push through the pain and the fear.

Every single day felt like I was running on empty. Stress and pain were suppressed, and I had to grow up fast. I was doing the best I could, but I was carrying a heavy load. I learned to take on responsibility that should have been too much for me, and in many ways, I became hardened by it. But I also learned to be resourceful, to rely on my wits, and most importantly, to trust that I could figure things out. I had no fear. I did what I needed to survive and escape the heartache.

Resilience isn't about being invincible. It's about getting knocked down and choosing to get back up, even when you feel like you don't have the strength. I remember days when I had no idea how I would make it through, but somehow, I did. Somewhere deep down I always knew it would be ok. That positive attitude, or what some might say is "unrealistic thinking," kept me going.

When you're struggling to survive, you don't always have the luxury of thinking about long-term goals. But one thing I always had, even if it was buried deep beneath my fears, was hope. I believed that there was more for me out there. I believed that somehow, things could get better. The struggle taught me how to survive, but it also gave me the strength to start building a future that would be different.

Discovering Life Purpose: From Surviving to Thriving

As a child, my purpose was simple: Survive. But as I grew older, I realized that surviving wasn't enough. I didn't just want to get through life. I wanted to thrive. I wanted to find meaning beyond the pain, beyond the struggle. But how do you do that when you've never been taught what it means to have a purpose?

The search for purpose is a deeply personal one, and I didn't have a road map to follow. For me, it wasn't until I hit adulthood that I realized just how much I had been living in survival mode. I was always under stress, moving from place to place and most days seemed chaotic. Once I got through the basics—finding stable work, securing a roof over my head—the question became: *What's next?* The hunger for something greater began to grow, and that hunger led me to continue my education.

Finding my purpose became my pursuit. I had to explore various jobs, living situations, and experiences to find my pathway to purpose. It is not easy to feel content, happy, or full of life. For most people there is always a void and feeling of wanting more. Purpose in life comes from identifying what you really care about, what your talents and skills are, and how you can use them to make you feel connected, needed, and happy.

I didn't have a support system that could help me navigate my future, but what I did have was a fierce determination to create something different. Education became my lifeline. I went to college not just to get a degree but because I knew it was the key to unlocking my future. There was a fire inside me that told me, *You are worth more than your circumstances. You deserve more.*

I learned that the process of learning wasn't just about academics—it was about discovering who I was. I began to explore my passions and what truly motivated me. I started to realize that I wasn't bound by my past. I didn't have to be the victim of my circumstances forever. I could create something better.

The real turning point came when I realized that education wasn't just about building a career. It was about creating a meaningful life. That life was going to be based on something deeper than just surviving. It was going to be based on purpose. My purpose became clear—not just to get an education, but to make a difference. To prove to myself and others that no matter where you come from, you have the power to create the life you deserve.

Overcoming the Past and Achieving Happiness

I have realized that success doesn't automatically bring happiness. For years, I thought that if I could just get a good job, get out of poverty, and achieve some level of success, I would finally be happy. But I quickly learned that happiness isn't something you can chase by looking at external achievements. Happiness, I discovered, is an inside job.

I spent a lot of time thinking that happiness would just appear once I crossed certain milestones off my list—graduating from college, getting a "good" job, and finding financial stability. But once I ticked off all those boxes, I still felt a void. That's when I realized that the key to happiness wasn't tied to external markers of success—it was tied to the way I viewed myself, my past, and my potential.

I was still carrying the weight of my past. The emotional wounds from the abuse, lack of feeling loved, the pain of losing my parents, and the trauma of growing up without support—it was all still there. But something shifted in me. I realized that if I was ever going to truly be happy, I had to let go of the past. Not forget it but release it. I had to forgive—not others, but myself. Letting go of anger, regrets, shame, and guilt allowed me to free myself and find inner peace.

As I healed, I began to build a life that reflected who I truly was—not the broken girl from Indiana, but the strong, independent woman I had become. I found joy in simple things: exercise, spending time by the ocean, and taking care of my body. These activities became my tools for maintaining balance and peace in my life. The ocean became a sanctuary for me. Its vastness reminded me that life, like the sea, is full of ebbs and flows. The ups and downs are all part of the journey.

True happiness doesn't come from accumulating wealth or recognition. It comes from knowing that you are at peace with yourself. It comes from the freedom of letting go of the past and living fully in the present. It comes from understanding that you are enough, just as you are. And let me tell you, the more I embraced this mindset, the more happiness and fulfillment I found.

The Role of Self-Belief and Empowerment

One of the biggest lessons I've learned on my journey is the power of self-belief. For years, I allowed my past to convince me that I wasn't worthy of happiness or success. It was subconscious. I verbally told myself I was worthy, and I deserved it all. But deep down my soul was ill with lies. It was hurt and filled with sadness. I had to take a really good look at my mindset and true self-belief. I stopped looking to others for validation. I learned that true empowerment comes from within, not from external approval or validation.

Empowering yourself means saying "no" when necessary. It means setting boundaries with people who drain your energy and protecting your peace. It means taking care of your physical, mental, and emotional health. I've learned to prioritize my well-being—not out of selfishness, but because I understand that I cannot pour from an empty cup. I started putting myself first and not others. I realized that self-care isn't just about pampering yourself. It's about taking responsibility for your own happiness and well-being.

As I grew in confidence, I realized something important: Believing in yourself doesn't mean you won't face doubts or setbacks along the way. It means you'll keep going, even when those doubts arise. Perseverance is what makes self-belief so powerful. It doesn't require perfection; it just requires the decision to keep going.

Today, I used my experiences to empower others. Empowering others is one of the most fulfilling parts of my journey. When you help someone else rise, you rise too. The act of sharing your knowledge and supporting others creates a ripple effect that can reach far beyond what we can imagine. When women support each other, we create a community that thrives. By embracing our own power and helping others to do the same, we change the world.

Conclusion: The Triumph of Resilience, Purpose, and Happiness

Looking back on my journey, I realize just how far I've come. I went from a girl who had nothing but a broken home and shattered dreams to a woman who knows her worth and her purpose. I've learned that resilience, purpose, and happiness are not destinations—they are practices. They are ways of living that we choose every day.

If there's one thing I want you to take away from my story, it's this: You have the power to change your life. No matter what you've been through, no matter where you've come from, you can create the life you deserve. It starts with believing in yourself, finding your purpose, and embracing your own strength. You've got this. If I can do it, so can you.

Katina Rice-Davis

Best Selling Author, Journalist

https://www.facebook.com/share/16rKaT5FDW/

Katina Rice-Davis is a six-time Bestselling Author, Speaker, and Journalist with The Woodruff Times. A native of Cross Anchor, South Carolina, she studied at Winthrop University and USC Upstate. Her work has been featured in multiple magazines, and she has contributed as a writer and appeared on numerous podcasts. After the sudden loss of her husband, Eric M. Davis, in 2002, Katina turned to writing as a source of healing while raising their two young children, Mariah and Mon'eric. In 2023, she became a Bestselling Author through her first faith-based anthology project and has since earned the distinction of #1 International Bestselling Author. She is also a proud grandmother to Sa'Mauri. Katina is currently launching HALO (Healing After Loss Organization), a nonprofit supporting young widows raising children. Passionate about purpose and resilience, she seeks to inspire women to live boldly and unapologetically.

Rising From The Rubble—Finding My Voice After Loss

By Katina Rice-Davis

I never imagined I'd be a widow at 28 twenty-plus years ago. I never imagined I'd be standing over a casket trying to explain death to a four-year-old while bouncing a two-year-old toddler on my hip. I never imagined that my identity, once wrapped in love, partnership, and dreams built with another, would be reduced to rubble overnight. But life doesn't ask for our permission before it shifts. It simply moves. And sometimes, it breaks us wide open in the process.

Before that moment, I was a wife. A mother. A woman with a vision that included "we" in every plan. My husband and I were raising two beautiful children. He was on the road, providing for our family, and I was holding things down at home. Our love wasn't perfect, but it was ours. There was laughter. There was a struggle. There was hope.

Then one day, there was silence.

I received the news like a blow to the chest. My husband had been found unresponsive at a truck stop. Just like that, he was gone. No goodbye. No warning. Just an echo of the life we shared and the hollow space where his presence used to live.

Grief is not a straight line. It's a storm that comes in waves, sometimes steady, sometimes crashing. In the days that followed, I wore a mask of strength. People called me brave. But I was just surviving. Going through the motions. Feeding babies. Planning a funeral. Crying in the shower. Smiling at neighbors. Grief has a cruel way of making you invisible even when everyone is watching.

In the quiet hours after bedtime, I would sit with my pain like an old friend. I asked myself questions that had no answers: "Why him?"

"Why us?" "What now?" My identity—once so clear—now felt foreign. Who was I without him? How could I be enough for my children when I felt so shattered? How do I go on?

But pain, as devastating as it is, also has a way of peeling back the layers of who you thought you were. Beneath the sorrow and the shock, something else was beginning to stir: a whisper of resilience, a flicker of voice.

Redefining my identity didn't happen all at once. It started with small choices. Choosing to get out of bed when I wanted to disappear. Choosing to ask for help when pride told me not to. Choosing to tell my children the truth in ways their little hearts could hold. Choosing to honor my pain without letting it have the final say.

The old me would have stayed quiet. She would have smiled politely and swallowed the lump in her throat. But the woman rising from this loss, the woman who emerged from the ashes, knows the power of truth. She knows silence can be a cage. And she is choosing freedom.

There was a moment, a turning point, when I realized I wasn't just surviving anymore. I was evolving. I was parenting not just as a mother but as both protector and provider. I was learning how to fix things I once depended on him for. I was making decisions alone, and slowly, I began to trust my own judgment. Each time I did, my voice got stronger.

I started writing again. Not polished essays, but raw, messy thoughts. I wrote in journals, on sticky notes, and in the margins of my grief. I wrote to make sense of the chaos inside me. I wrote to remember him. I wrote to discover myself.

And something miraculous happened in the writing. I found clarity. I wasn't just mourning my husband. I was mourning the version of myself who only existed inside our relationship. The girl who deferred her dreams. The woman who didn't always speak up. The mother who questioned her worth. That version had died with him. But in her place, a new me was being born.

Healing was not only about letting go of the past but also about embracing a future I hadn't imagined. I realized that resilience doesn't mean pretending you're okay. It means choosing to keep moving even when you're not. It means allowing the tears to fall but still daring to dream again. It means finding moments of laughter, not as betrayal to your loss, but as testimony that joy still has a place in your life.

As the years passed, my perspective shifted. I began to see that grief was not my enemy. It was my teacher. It taught me patience when all I wanted was answers. It taught me compassion, not only for others but also for myself. It taught me to slow down and treasure the smallest details: the sound of my children's laughter, the warmth of the sun after a storm, and the sacredness of ordinary days.

I learned to lean into community, even when it felt easier to isolate. Friends, mentors, and even strangers spoke life into me during times when I doubted my ability to stand. They reminded me that I didn't have to be strong all the time. That it was okay to fall apart, so long as I kept finding my way back. And slowly, I did.

In time, I learned that grief and gratitude can walk side by side. I could miss him deeply and still give thanks for the years we shared. I could feel empty in one moment and full of purpose in the next. I discovered that grief was not just an ending but also an opening: a painful invitation to step into a version of myself I had never met before.

I am no longer just someone's widow. I am a mother. A nurturer. A truth-teller. A woman who carries both pain and power in her stride. My voice, once hidden behind circumstance, now leads the way. I became a best-selling author and a newspaper journalist where many can hear my voice.

One of the hardest parts of grief is loneliness. People check in less often. The world keeps turning. But I realized that while I had lost my husband, I hadn't lost myself. I was still here. And that counted for something.

Rediscovering my voice meant allowing myself to grieve in public. It meant saying "I'm not okay" without shame. It meant honoring my story, even the chapters I never wanted to write. That's what UnleashHER Voice is about. It's about stepping out from behind the curtain and standing in the spotlight of your truth.

In sharing my story, I hope another woman sitting in her own version of devastation feels less alone. I hope she sees that even in the darkest valley, there is still light to be found. Not because the pain disappears, but because you discover the strength that's been inside you all along.

Grief didn't just break me; it revealed me.

I began to parent with intention. I told my children stories about their father, not as a ghost, but as a part of our daily lives. Even though they are now young adults, we speak his name with joy, not fear. I show them what it looks like to keep going, to feel everything deeply and still stand tall. They saw me cry. They saw me laugh. They saw me rebuild.

And in those moments, I know they watched not just a mother, but a woman who refused to stay broken.

To every woman reading this, know this: Your voice matters. Whether whispered or shouted, it is worthy. You do not have to wait until you are healed to speak. Sometimes, healing begins when you finally do.

If I've learned anything through this journey, it's that grief and growth can coexist. That it's possible to miss what was while still embracing what is. That identity isn't a fixed thing. It's a living, breathing evolution.

I didn't choose this chapter of my life. But I am choosing to write it with honesty and heart. I chose to live out loud and raised my babies in truth and to never again silence the parts of me that ache to be heard.

This is my moment of redefining. This is the sound of a woman finding her voice in the ruins and deciding she is still worthy of rising. UnleashHER Voice is more than a title. It's a truth I had to embody. I have faced the darkest parts of life and dare to speak anyway. It honors those of us who've had to redefine ourselves when we feel the world stopped recognizing us. And in sharing this chapter of my life, I am choosing to unleash my own voice—not as the woman I was, but as the woman I became.

Closing Prayer:

Lord, thank You for turning pain into purpose and silence into strength. Remind every woman that her voice is worthy, whether whispered through tears or declared with courage. Help her see that healing and grief can walk hand in hand and that her truth carries power. May she rise from her rubble, speak boldly, and honor the woman she is becoming. Amen.

Srilasya Volam

CEO of Srilasya LLC

https://www.linkedin.com/company/srilasya/posts/?feedView=all
https://www.facebook.com/profile.php?id=61578165185348
https://www.instagram.com/srilasya_llc/
www.srilasya.com

I am the CEO of Srilasya LLC, a strategic consulting firm dedicated to helping entrepreneurs, small businesses, and nonprofits transform ideas into sustainable success. At Srilasya LLC, we specialize in strategic consulting, business development, and growth planning, offering hands-on support to both new ventures and established organizations looking to scale. Our approach blends creativity with critical analysis, ensuring every client receives tailored strategies that align with their unique goals and resources. Whether you are launching your first company, expanding operations, or strengthening a nonprofit, we provide the structure, guidance, and tools needed to thrive in a competitive environment. Beyond startup support, we emphasize systems building, efficiency, and long-term sustainability, helping leaders focus on growth rather than guesswork. We believe strong foundations and clear strategies transform ideas into impact. At Srilasya LLC, our motto says it best: "You Focus on the Vision. We'll Handle the Rest."

The Cost of Rest

By Srilasya Volam

The first time someone called me lazy, I had just pulled an all-nighter. I was getting ready for a biology exam after being awake for over twenty-six hours. I dropped my plate into the sink, fully intending to wash it later. My roommate, sitting nearby, looked over and said, "That's lazy—you could just rinse it."

She didn't mean it maliciously. English isn't her first language, and I knew she wasn't calling me lazy, just the action. But it hit me like she had. Because I've spent my entire life trying to be anything but lazy. That word has always felt like an accusation, like a stain I can't afford to have attached to me.

That moment didn't hurt because of the plate or because of her. It hurt because I had already pushed myself to the edge. I had denied myself sleep, food, and any kind of break. And still, somehow, it wasn't enough to avoid being seen as someone who doesn't do enough. It felt like everything I'd been holding together could fall apart with just one word.

Lazy.

That's my trigger word.

I haven't taken a week off in more than two and a half years. Not because I can't, but because I don't know what would happen if I did. When I stop, I fall apart. When I rest, I lose motivation. I lose structure. I spiral. It takes me forever to bounce back from stillness, so I don't allow myself to stop. I stay in motion. I fill every minute. I do and do and do until I crash for a few hours and get back up to do it again. On the outside, it probably looks like ambition. But for me, it's not about ambition—it's about control. And fear.

I didn't grow up with the kind of parenting people expect when you say "Asian household." My parents weren't overbearing or harsh. They didn't punish me for bringing home a B. My mom believed in independence, so both my brother and I were expected to learn how to cook, clean, and handle things on our own. And I really am grateful for that. But still, there were small things. Quiet differences. Expectations that weren't always spoken but still felt.

I always felt like I had to prove myself. My brother was naturally smarter. He got praised for picking things up fast. I got used to putting in the extra hours to catch up. No one ever said I wasn't good enough, but I just felt like I already wasn't. I started to associate being seen as capable with being seen at all. I knew what attention looked like when things went wrong, but success often went unnoticed. And so I worked harder. I worked for visibility. To be good enough.

There was another fear I carried—one that I didn't talk about, because it wasn't something my parents ever threatened me with. In many Asian cultures, the idea of arranged marriage exists, sometimes quietly, sometimes openly. My parents never talked to me about it. That conversation never happened. But I'd seen it happen around me, and that was enough to plant the fear. It didn't matter that they'd never said it. The possibility alone kept me alert. I've seen what people have gone through. I've watched the movies with the horror stories.

The only thing I knew for certain was that if anyone ever tried to force something on me, I wanted to be able to leave. And to leave, I needed to be financially independent. I needed to have an apartment of my own. A car. A job. A bank account. I needed the kind of security that let me say, "No," and back it up with a lease in my name.

So from a young age, I decided I wanted to be rich. Not for luxury. For leverage. For freedom.

Even now, I still want to be rich. I want to build things. I want to help people. I want to have the freedom to support my family and my community, not out of guilt, but because I want to. I want options. I want backup plans for my backup plans. I want a life where fear doesn't dictate my decisions. To me, wealth is not just about comfort. It's about having choices. It's about being safe.

That mindset has shaped my relationship with rest. Because when you grow up believing your freedom has to be earned and that your value comes from what you produce, rest doesn't feel like peace—it feels like failure.

And failure isn't just about not succeeding. Failure means losing control. It means needing someone else. And needing someone else means possibly depending on someone who could say no. That's what terrifies me.

This is where the gendered part comes in. And I want to be clear. I'm using "men" and "women" in a very general, socialized sense. But there is a pattern in how people are raised. In how boys are often taught to value their own time, and how girls are often taught to anticipate everyone else's.

Most boys are not explicitly told, "Don't clean, don't cook, don't notice." But they're not told to do those things either. Most girls are not told, "You have to take care of others before yourself." But they are shown—over and over again—that the ones who are praised are the ones who give, the ones who clean up, and the ones who remember what needs to be done.

And over time, those things stick. They become muscle memory.

I've been at dinners where the men keep eating while the women get up to clear the table. I've been in conversations where women know everyone's birthdays and keep the group chat alive, and no one notices. I've seen wedding toasts where the groom's friends say, "Say goodbye to your freedom," and everyone laughs. But when you think about it, the joke only works because many men are often raised to have freedom—freedom to focus on themselves, to put their needs first. For women, freedom isn't taken away at marriage—it was never freely given in the first place.

And the difference shows up everywhere. When men order takeout, it's "treating yourself." When women do, it's "bad with money." When men play video games, it's "unwinding." When women watch a show, it's "lazy." Men are expected to rest. Women are expected to earn it.

So when my roommate said, "That's lazy," she had no idea what kind of history that word held for me. She didn't mean anything by it, but to me, it was more than just a comment about a dish. It was a challenge to my identity. I have spent years building a version of myself that is self-sufficient, reliable, and constantly performing. I don't stop even when I'm sick. I don't ask for help unless it's an emergency. I don't rest, because I don't feel like I've earned it.

But I'm starting to learn that this isn't healthy. It's not noble. It's not sustainable. It's just what I was taught myself. And like anything that's been learned, it can be unlearned.

I'm trying to unlearn the guilt that comes with a quiet afternoon. I'm trying to unlearn the idea that rest has to be justified. I'm trying to believe that I can slow down and still be valuable. That I can do less and still be enough.

Some days, I still push myself past the point of exhaustion. But other days, I leave the dish in the sink. I try not to spiral when I do nothing. I try to remind myself that I don't have to collapse in order to deserve a break.

I may not always choose rest. But when I do, I choose it on purpose.

Not because I've earned it. Not because I'm breaking.

Because I want to.

Because I can.

Because this life belongs to me.

Now I ask you, the reader:

When was the last time you gave yourself permission to stop performing—and just be?

Nicole Toney

Founder and CEO of Healthcare Solutions Unlimited and Favored Not Forgotten

https://www.linkedin.com/in/nicole-toney-21a230353
https://www.facebook.com/nicole.toney.421106
https://healthcaresolutionsunlimited.com/
https://favorednotforgotten.org/

Dr. Nicole Toney is a multi-passionate entrepreneur, licensed mental health professional, 5-time Amazon best-selling author, and dedicated advocate for women's empowerment. With over 15 years of leadership and human services experience, she is the founder of Healthcare Solutions Unlimited and the nonprofit organization Favored Not Forgotten, which provides education, resources, and support to economically disadvantaged individuals and families. Dr. Toney holds a doctorate in Marriage and Family Counseling and is a certified educator, speaker, and mentor who equips women to overcome adversity, embrace purpose, and build faith-aligned, impactful lives. Her work spans from mentoring youth and consulting organizations to training caregivers and advocating for underserved communities. Dr. Toney is a dynamic force in entrepreneurship, mental health, and advocacy—passionately guiding others toward healing, abundance, and legacy.

The Silence That Shaped Me

By Nicole Toney

There was a time in my life when silence felt safer than truth. When being unseen was more comfortable than standing in the spotlight. When my story remained tucked away beneath layers of responsibility, shame, and fear—hidden even from myself.

Growing up, I was the "strong one," the dependable daughter, the strong sister, the one who kept it together no matter what chaos swirled around me. I wore that badge like armor, thinking that if I stayed composed, polite, and quiet, I'd stay safe. That strength became my survival. But survival is not the same as living, and silence, I learned, can become a cage.

I was seven when my mother married my stepfather. He came into our lives like a storm—loud, protective, and firm. But he also brought something I hadn't known before: stability and consistency. He raised me and my brother as his own, blending our family with his children. There was an adjustment period, of course, but overall family life was good. The outside world, however, was a different story. I learned that girls were expected to be seen and not heard, and I often felt it was safer to stay quiet than to voice my true opinions.

So, I learned to shrink.

I was the girl who sat in the back of the classroom, even when I knew the answer. The one who wrote poems in the margins of her notebook instead of reading them aloud. The one who smiled and nodded even when her heart was breaking. I mistook invisibility for peace. And I carried that with me well into adulthood.

But silence does not mean healing. And suppression does not equal strength.

It wasn't until years later—after becoming a wife, a mother, and a professional—that my body started to speak the things my mouth wouldn't. I was excelling on the outside: degrees, promotions, applause. But internally, I was unraveling. I couldn't sleep. My chest often felt like it was caving in. I started forgetting things, losing focus. No one could tell, of course. I had perfected the art of appearing okay.

Until one day I wasn't.

It was a Sunday night when everything came crashing down. I got up in the middle of the night to use the bathroom, but before I could make it, I passed out. When I woke up, I was lying in a puddle of blood, disoriented and afraid.

A syncope episode, they later said.

But in that moment, it felt like something deeper, a reckoning. A confrontation with the person I'd buried beneath years of composure. I realized I had spent so much of my life helping others find their voice while denying my own. Beneath it all, I was overwhelmed by the pressures of life and too afraid to speak up or take action about my own unhappiness.

That was the turning point.

I began a season of self-reflection and a journey of growth. During that time, I turned to writing, since I had always carried a love for reading and words. Writing became a safe place to process my thoughts and feelings, not for applause or performance, but for myself—for the little girl who had so much to say but lacked the skills to communicate effectively. And slowly, I began to unlearn the lie that silence was strength. I began to understand that vulnerability is not weakness—it is a doorway to freedom.

I remember the first time I stood on a stage and told my story—the real one. Not the polished version, not the résumé-ready highlights. The story of how I doubted my worth. The story of how I questioned God's plan for me. The story of how I lost myself in the roles I was expected to play. My voice shook. My palms sweated. But I did it. And when I looked out into the audience and saw women crying, nodding, and standing—I knew something sacred had happened.

They didn't need my perfection. They needed my truth.

So many of us walk through life hiding behind titles, degrees, filters, and curated versions of ourselves. We think if we reveal the messy parts—the brokenness, the confusion, the grief—we'll lose love. Or credibility. Or respect. But the opposite is true.

Authenticity creates connection. Honesty builds bridges. And when a woman tells the truth about her life, she frees others to do the same.

Since that day, I've made it my mission to speak up. Not just for myself, but for every woman who's ever felt silenced by shame, fear, trauma, or culture. I speak for the girl who was told to "stay in a child's place," even when the adults in her life were failing her. For the woman who looks strong but cries in the shower. For the professional who's scared to say she's struggling. For the mother who loves her children but is losing herself.

My voice is no longer a whisper—it's a weapon. A tool. A lifeline.

But finding it didn't come without cost. I had to confront the parts of me I'd tried to hide. I had to unlearn the beliefs that told me I had to earn love through performance. I had to risk rejection, knowing that not everyone would understand this version of me—this fuller, freer me.

And still, I chose to speak.

Because silence, while safe, never healed me.

Speaking up did.

It healed the part of me that believed I was too much and not enough all at once. It healed the shame I carried from things that weren't my fault. It healed the need to control everything just to feel okay. And it continues to heal me every time I tell the truth.

Truth-telling, I've learned, is not a one-time act—it's a lifestyle. It's choosing, again and again, to live with integrity. To say what you mean. To let people see the real you. It's not always comfortable, but it is always worth it.

Today, I mentor women who are learning to tell their stories for the first time. I walk with them as they face their fears, reclaim their identities, and stand in rooms they never thought they belonged in. And every time one of them speaks, I'm reminded of why I do this work.

Because every voice matters.

Every story has power.

And every woman deserves to be heard—not just the polished version of her, but the whole, beautiful, complicated truth of her.

So if you're reading this and you've ever felt like your voice doesn't matter, let me tell you: It does.

If you've ever been told to quiet down, to toughen up, to hide your feelings—hear me now: You are allowed to feel deeply. To speak boldly. To take up space.

Your voice is not too loud.

Your truth is not too much.

You are not too much.

In fact, you are the exact right amount of fierce, fragile, and powerful needed for this moment in history. And your story, with all its twists and turns, could be the key that unlocks someone else's prison.

Don't let fear keep you silent. Don't let shame keep you small.

Unleash your voice.

Tell your truth.

And watch what happens when you do.

Nikki Girard

Founder and CEO of Heart Energy X Me
5-time Award Winning Entrepreneur & Manifestation Expert

https://www.linkedin.com/in/nikki-girard-962601207
https://www.facebook.com/nikki.girard.311
https://www.instagram.com/nikki.girard.311
Website: https://highafadvantage.com/
High AF Advantage -Life & Biz Clubhouse Community:
https://www.clubhouse.com/house/high-af-advantage

Nikki Girard - 5-time Award-Winning Entrepreneur, Manifestation Expert & Strategic Business Advantage Architect. A 4-time #1 International Bestselling Author, Podcast Host & Creator of - the High AF Advantage, driving innovation. Force Magazine - Force Awards Awardee-Top 10 Entrepreneurs to Watch for in 2025. A Senior Level Executive Contributor, Expert Panelist & Awardee of the: CREA Global Awards- Brainz Magazine, & 2-time Brainz Magazine 500 Global List Awardee-alongside luminaries Les Brown, Jay Shetty, Marisa Peer, Oprah Winfrey, Rachel Pailing, Jim Kwik, Lewis Howes & more. Specializing in guiding individuals & businesses to develop custom-tailored strategies to create a life of abundance & financial freedom. Today, she empowers individuals & businesses worldwide to unleash their full potential through award-winning coaching, bestselling books & groundbreaking "High AF Advantage" methodologies.

Ultimate Manifestation: No-Excuses Solution to Success

By Nikki Girard

If you've come across this chapter, it's no accident. It means that you're searching for a solution...to finally breakthrough the success bubble...

Between endless strategies, programs, mentorship's, experts & other people telling you to ***"step out of your comfort zone"*** & ***"think outside the box..."***

Great , so now you feel flipping uncomfortable, confused, unbalanced & overwhelmed, looking over the edge of a slightly bigger box, congrats...

And...you paid how much for that ??...

Free yourself from outdated advice & tap into predictable success...

Your mind can become either your Personal Mental Prison or your Greatest Assets...

Escape the Matrix & Sea of Sameness

- Shatter the status quo with a fresh, holistic approach to manifestation.
- Rise above the noise and unlock the long held secrets of the 1% now....,*why wait?*
- Break free from limiting beliefs, self-sabotage & embrace continuous transformation
- Become a "manifestation master" boosting productivity up to 500%
- Effective, no-nonsense strategies, lasting change & expansion

Your time is Now...

Unlock your greatest potential with the innovative, "***High AF Advantage***": Your Quantum Core Blueprint to Success

Learn to:

- Smash limitations, unleash high achievers million dollar success mindset
- Unearth exclusive strategies of the thriving 1%
- Learn to "step into your comfort zone"
- "Think Outside the Box"...What Box?
- The Ping Pong Effect-the interplay between the conscious & subconscious mind
- The Maze metaphor & how to escape the matrix
- Effortlessly & easily integrate into daily life

For high achievers, Entrepreneurs, thought Leaders & Individuals who want to say goodbye to wild goose chases, shiny objects or imposter syndrome & more...

This program, is the antidote to what's been holding you back...

You'll Gain:

- Clarity, Focus, Purpose, Cutting-Edge Neurobiology, Cognitive Science, Positive, Behavioral & Social Psychology & more
- Achieve the freedom trifecta: Financial, time, personal fulfillment
- Match resonance frequency of manifestations, balance, inner peace & harmony
- Self Awareness, Mindfulness, Interconnectedness, expansion, holistic wellness & Life purpose
- And...there's no way to say everything...just need to read the book

Join the Coaching Revolution, experience the game-changing 'New Gold Standard' evolution...

Your Swiss Army knife, kick-ass holistic approach to Personal & Business development...*ninja style!*

This is not a so called - "quick fix"...

It's a permanent "fix"

And besides, I'm allergic to BS...

*"Connecting the Quantum Dots to create a Legacy of Success."—**Nikki Girard***

Starting or scaling your business?...

Want financial freedom & skyrocket your abundance?

The time freedom to do what you want to do, where & how you want to do it...setting your schedule...

Yet, most importantly, more time with those you love and care about & who light you up. *If that's you...*

It's Time to Take Inspired Action Now!

Embrace the ***High AF Advantage*** witness rapid returns, compounding progress & continuous transformation.

Why settle for mediocrity?

Join the ranks of high-achievers, invest in yourself, with expert guidance.

The Ping-Pong Effect

As we strive to achieve our goals, our consciously want success, yet our subconscious mind holds self-limiting beliefs & patterns that can hinder progress.

The Ping-Pong Effect is a psychological concept, the internal struggles between aspirations & self-doubt.

This mental tug-of-war manifesting as an oscillation between positive & negative thoughts, resulting in self-sabotage & indecision.

Remember...subconscious controls 95% of our thoughts & emotions...happening on autopilot.

This determines action or inaction in life as we are working towards our manifestations. To illustrate, consider an example of internal chatter:

1. ***Conscious Mind***: I deserve financial abundance and I'm capable of achieving it.
2. ***Subconscious Mind***: remember how you failed last time? You're not worthy of success.

The maze: metaphor

The maze, a powerful metaphor for the often disorienting success journey...

It's easy to become trapped with endless strategies, mentorships, programs, podcasts & information overload...

Each turn, a new approach or opportunity, possibly another "***failure***".

Bouncing between various paths, our internal ping-pong match intensifies.... Every dead-end, failed strategy...fuels self-doubt...

Invested time, energy & resources & find ourselves back at square one. Success is often filled with twists, turns & setbacks.

It can seem hopeless when you feel like all you got was a "***cheesy trophy***" for your efforts... *Like a mouse, in a maze, looking for cheese...always in search of another.*

Master Your Mind

Your mindset is the key that unlocks the door to your true potential, shift perspective & ultimately...your reality.

Limiting Beliefs

Limiting beliefs are self-imposed mental roadblocks that hold individuals back from reaching their full potential.

These beliefs often stem from past traumatic experiences, family and or religious dynamics, as well as cultural, societal pressures and other expectations.

For example, many people tell themselves,..*'I'm not smart enough,' 'I'm too old to start a new career,'* or *'I can't achieve success without sacrificing my personal life.'*

- ***Understanding***: *psychological underpinnings of limiting beliefs*, recognize & challenge them.
- ***Self-belief is a crucial element:*** a strong mindset allows individuals to have faith in their abilities, potential & worth.
- ***Positive Thinking***: is a game-changer, bolsters confidence, fuels determination & resilience.
- ***Emotional resilience***: crucial for navigating challenges, growth mindset & bouncing back from setbacks.

Transforming Self-Talk

- ***Identify disempowering thoughts or phrases***: Reframe to positive affirmations, boosting self-love & esteem.
- ***Monitor Inner Conversations:*** Notice negative thought patterns, consciously replace them
- ***Challenge Cognitive Distortions:*** Identify self-limiting beliefs, reframe with realistic, positive thoughts & beliefs.

Reframe thought example:

Disempowering Thought: *"I'm not as successful as my friends."*

***Inspiring Affirmation*:** *"I celebrate my unique accomplishments and working towards my future successes."*

This helps foster a nurturing inner dialogue.

Meet, Nikki Girard, 5-time Award-Winning visionary entrepreneur, exponential transformation & manifestation expert. 4-time #1 international bestselling Author, speaker, podcast host.

Founder & CEO of 'Heart Energy X Me,' combining over 38-plus years of experience with neuroscience, psychology, coaching, and quantum energy engineering & more.

Force Awards*: *Awardee: *Top 10 High-Impact Coach Award 2025 &* ***Awardee:*** *Top 10 Entrepreneurs to Watch in 2025-****Force Magazine***

A Senior Executive Contributor for ***Brainz Magazine***, Expert Panelist, **Awardee** of both prestigious: ***CREA* Global Awards** & 2-time ***Awardee: Brainz Magazine 500 Global List -***

So humbling, standing alongside luminaries such as: *Les Brown, Jay Shetty, Marisa Peer, Oprah Winfrey, Deepak Chopra, Rachel Pailing, Jim Kwik, Lewis Howes and more.*

"Think Outside The Box": What"Box"...?

Boxes...Great for Moving, Not for Manifesting...ha, ha, ha!

We love a good-solid box when time to pack up our belongings, store treasured keepsakes...oh yes, absolutely 100%.

Yet...in personal & business development...

Time, to ditch that "boxed" metaphor!

It was a fantastic concept when it was first introduced, encouraging us to push boundaries & explore new possibilities.

The catch...it only scratches the surface.

Think about it...

When you're thinking outside the box...

Where are you?...

You're still in a damn box, except now, just peeking over the edge! Whoo Hoo!

Yet, for high achievers striving to manifest their goals and dreams, it's crucial to recognize that there is "no box".

Realizing, there was never a box to begin with!...It's a powerful shift in perspective. Check out client results:

Meet Hysam—Entrepreneur/Attraction Marketing-Click to Clients

He experienced remarkable transformation, with Nikki's expertise resulting in a more balanced personal & business life,

He's consistently earning $100,000+ monthly income.

Clients saying:

- *"the things Nikki knows, blows my mind"*
- *"She's the walking encyclopedia"*
- *"Its an easy & seemless integration process"*
- *"The one stop shop for ultimate Transformation & Manifestation!"*

For more inspiring success stories-learn more: highafadvantage.com. Closing the gap *with a new effective - perspective...*

Discover what the movie ***'The Secret'*** didn't reveal... *oops!*

The hidden truths, which helps explain why manifestation has remained elusive for so many people.

Redefining the "Comfort Zone"

While traditional coaching stresses ***'stepping out of one's comfort zone'*** *to grow...* The ***'High AF Advantage'*** offers a refreshing alternative with its groundbreaking approach. Instead of pushing individuals beyond their limits...

Be equipped with the necessary tools and techniques, transforming the ***comfort zone*** *into a source of empowerment...*

A space of authentic alignment, inspiration & true personal power,...in alignment, *prioritizing self-love, mental resilience & coherence,* achieving manifestations faster, greater ease & clarity.

Place Your Cosmic Order

Imagine turning your wildest dreams into reality...

This is the world of cosmic orders, where intentions and alignment with universal forces... Understanding cosmic laws, such as:

- *Law of Resonance*
- *Law of Vibration*
- *Law of Attraction*
- *Law of Manifestation*

Just to name a few & tapping into limitless potential

To place your cosmic order:

- *Set clear & focused intentions.*
- *Visualize desired outcome as if you have already achieved it, in the present moment.*
- *Infusing positive energy, emotions, truly feeling into the gratitude*
- *Release resistance, take aligned action & trust the universe's support.*

Also the Founder & Mastermind Host : ***High AF Advantage: Life & Biz Hub***, *Elite Exclusive Clubhouse Community.*

It's a Free Membership - Experience a transformative journey, join deep discussions, ask questions...get answers...feel the High AF Vibes

Covering topics from the High AF Advantage & areas as it relates to personal & business development & success.

And grab your copy of the #1 Best Selling smash hit-book releases: ***High AF Advantage:****Your Quantum Core Blueprint to Success &* ***Mindset Mastery:*** *Unfunk Your Thinking, Rewire Your Brain, and Unlock Your Full Potential*

Or...to begin your journey...

Perhaps, even become the next million-dollar success story...connect with Nikki, apply today!

No excuses... just results!

The ultimate turnkey solution for manifesting your dream reality Now!

Rachel Tseng

Founder of RM Investment Group

https://www.linkedin.com/in/rachel-t-923655274/
https://www.instagram.com/notoxhealer
www.renouvelebody.com
https://thenotoxhealing.com

Rachel W Tseng is successful entrepreneur and a survivor of profound challenges, including narcissistic trauma, divorce, sexual assault, and financial ruin. Through these trials, she has emerged as a beacon of courage, resilience, and transformation. A devoted mother to two inspiring adult daughters and a young son, she instills in them the values of strength, compassion, and perseverance. With an entrepreneurial spirit, she has founded and worked in over 10 companies spanning nine industries, channeling her diverse experiences into meaningful ventures. Now in a new season of her life, she is passionately dedicated to helping others live happier, healthier, and more beautiful lives. Her story is a testament to the power of overcoming, rebuilding, and thriving, offering hope and inspiration to all who face life's adversities.

From Hustle to Wholeness

By Rachel Tseng

Owning the Room, Losing Myself, and Finding My Voice Again

I used to believe that confidence was something you either had or didn't. Like the lucky girls were born with it, long legs, bright eyes, and a kind of sparkle that drew everyone in. And then there was me, hustling so hard that I convinced myself the grind was confidence. If I worked more, earned more, launched more, I'd finally feel whole.

I was wrong.

My name is Rachel Tseng, and I'm a serial entrepreneur, a mother of three, and a woman who has started over more times than I can count. From real estate to testing laboratories, medspas to telemedicine, I have built and rebuilt businesses in industries most people would never imagine linking together. On paper, that sounds bold. In reality, it often came from survival.

I didn't always feel strong. In fact, for years I wrestled with deep self-doubt, crippling fear of failure, and the exhausting belief that I had to prove my worth by achieving something bigger, shinier, or faster than the last thing.

But this is not a story about hustling your way to success. This is about how I lost my voice, and how I learned, slowly, painfully, and beautifully, to unleash it again.

When the Hustle Becomes a Mask

I grew up with the idea that hard work was the ticket to safety. So when life knocked me down, I built businesses. When I felt unseen, I built brands. When I doubted myself, I reinvented.

There was a real estate brokerage that gave me credibility. A medspa that allowed me to blend beauty with healing. A coaching job that allowed me to help others find their own voices. A wellness platform that let me whisper to people everywhere, *you deserve to feel good in your own body.*

People looked at me and saw confidence. But what they didn't see was how much of it was a mask. Behind the polished branding, the logos, and the social media reels was a woman afraid that if she stopped moving, everything would fall apart.

The truth was, I didn't know how to sit still. Stillness made me feel my fear. And feeling my fear meant facing the uncomfortable truth: I didn't fully believe I was enough.

Breaking Points

Entrepreneurship is not for the faint of heart. For every highlight reel, there's a sleepless night. For every ribbon-cutting, there's a bank account stretched thin. I faced lawsuits, financial losses, betrayals, and the kind of exhaustion that no amount of green juice or affirmations could fix.

But my biggest breaking point wasn't financial,it was personal.

I looked in the mirror one day and didn't recognize the woman staring back. My skin was aging, my eyes looked tired, and my smile felt like it belonged to someone who had been pretending for too long. My life partner saw me more as a mother than a partner. My children saw me constantly working. And somewhere along the way, I had stopped seeing *me.*

I realized I had built businesses to help others heal, but I had abandoned my own healing.

The Rebirth of Confidence

Confidence doesn't come from the applause of others. It comes from daring to tell yourself the truth. My truth was that I was exhausted from chasing external validation. I wanted to feel radiant again, not just in my skin, but in my spirit.

So I began to rebuild. Not my businesses. Myself.

I said yes to therapy. Yes to writing. Yes to walks on the beach without my phone buzzing in my pocket. Yes to reconnecting with God.

Slowly, I began peeling away the layers of control I had wrapped around myself like armor. I gave myself permission to cry in front of my kids instead of being the strong one all the time. I started speaking in front of small groups, not just about peptides and anti-aging, but about resilience, intimacy, and the courage to keep going when life breaks you open.

The more I spoke, the lighter I felt. The lighter I felt, the stronger my voice became.

And that's when I realized something powerful:

Confidence is not built in the spotlight. It's built in the shadows, when you choose to face the parts of yourself you've ignored.

Redefining Beauty & Success

My businesses today and all the evolving brands in between, are no longer just about looking younger or slimmer. They are about aligning the inside with the outside. Because beauty without healing is just a mask. And healing without embracing your body often feels incomplete.

I tell my clients, "You don't need to become perfect. You just need to become honest."

I learned that lesson the hard way. For years, I thought my story was too messy, too scattered to be worth sharing. Who would care about a woman who pivoted a dozen times, who carried the scars of both business failures and personal heartbreak?

But here's the truth: every pivot, every scar, every failed attempt was my voice training itself to be heard.

And now, when I step into a room, I don't feel the need to "own it" like I used to. I simply arrive as Rachel; whole, messy, resilient, and real.

The Woman in the Room

My life partner once told me he fell in love with me because I owned the room. Back then, it was my energy, my confidence, my spark. Over the years, I lost that spark, buried under motherhood, responsibility, and fear.

But today, I own the room differently. Not with bravado. Not with hustle. But with authenticity.

When I walk into a room now, I bring my scars with me. I bring my laughter, my mistakes, my lessons. I speak about peptides and biohacking, yes, but I also speak about forgiveness, intimacy, and the audacity of women to rise again after life knocks them flat.

That is my voice. And it is finally unleashed.

Why This Story Matters

UnleashHER Voice is not just a book. It is a mirror. For every woman who has ever felt like her story was too small, too messy, or too complicated to matter. I am living proof that your story is exactly the thing that sets you free.

I am Rachel Tseng. I am not perfect. I am not fearless. But I am resilient. I am honest. And I am finally confident. Not because I built empires, but because I dared to tell the truth about the woman behind them.

And if my story can remind just one woman to stop hiding, to stop waiting until she feels “ready,” then I know I’ve fulfilled my purpose.

Because your voice, like mine, was never meant to stay silent.

Lucy Childers Burdett

Reserve Funding Corporation
(Retired) CEO

www.linkedin.com/in/lucy-childers-burdett-79bab449
https://www.facebook.com/lucy.childersburdett
https://www.instagram.com/childersburdett/

My life is enriched by four amazing children, nine grandchildren and two great grandchildren. Since retiring from my own business, I am now enjoying working part time with a nonprofit organization assisting fellow Georgians who need assistance with their gas bills. I cherish each moment spent with my husband. I love music of nearly all genres, reading and the work I do giving back to others in need.

Reflections and Future Goals I am grateful for the life experiences that have made me who I am. I took an unconventional path in life to make it as far as I did. Each, and sometimes harrowing episode, of my life along with innate skills did and still does prove blessings to me.

The next phase of my now, 76 years on this mundane sphere called earth, is to continue sharing my story as there are several chapters yet to be written.

The (Re) Birth Of Lucy

By Lucille Burdett

My story is not unique but it's mine to tell. I was married for 24 years to a man who reminded me almost daily how I was nothing, zero, less than zero, he would often repeat. "*No one wants you, you're too fat and have too many kids.*" It wasn't until I escaped, for lack of a better word, that I learned not only was he berating me with such words, but it turned out I was the exact opposite of what I had been fed a daily dosage of for all those years. I had always been able to secure good- paying jobs but was constantly reminded that I would never get any promotions because I didn't "know how to play the games," to which I replied, "I would not wish a promotion if I was unworthy except for playing games."

While raising four children, I encouraged and worked to support Bob as he earned a college degree. However, I began suffering what I later learned were severe anxiety attacks. I saw my doctor who took one look at me and exclaimed, "Your body is consuming itself as though a form of cannibalism!' He threatened to have me committed if I didn't get therapy immediately! I heeded his advice and started professional counseling.

One afternoon I decided to have lunch with a friend, a man I've known since I was 9 years old. I had just learned he lived in Atlanta also. I thought he would break my back; he hugged me so tightly. That lunch hour turned into a marathon. As he was my protector when we were kids, I felt I could tell him anything, and so I told him in detail what my life had been like all these years. He sat across from me with tears in his eyes and he said, "I'm getting you out of there!"

And so it was planned on the last day of school, he would bring a U-Haul truck, and when c "Bob" we'll call him, left for work, my friend and I loaded my furniture onto the truck, leaving not only half the furniture but also, I worked for a mortgage company, a Quit Claim Deed was drawn up and up, notarized and not only filed with the court but also a copy sent to the lender. He found it on the floor with a note to stick that house where the sun didn't shine! All was done in time to pick my son up from elementary school, which was over for the summer and move to the townhouse I had already rented. We moved everything in, left it in the middle of the floor and with that, I drove my car and parked it across town in my friend's garage, and rented a car. However, to buy time I had to first go to work and await my "check on me" call and once that came, I started my vacation, went to the bank to open a new account and warned the staff that he will come looking for information from them. I did the same with the utility companies, asking to flag my account so no information about my whereabouts would be released.

My 11-year-old son and I set out on Thursday to drive to upstate New York, where my eldest married daughter lives. My other two daughters were in college and had their own apartments. I never even gave them my new address so they would not have to lie when asked. Yet by that Friday, one of them called me and described where I had moved, saying her dad knew and described it to them. I was livid and knew it had to be either the bank or one of the utility companies. I soon learned it was the gas company when a representative sent me a letter stating she "accidentally" told the street I lived on but not the address. Of course, she gave the entire address since he went directly to mine when all the townhouses in the community were identical.

The reason, in case you're wondering why I took such precautionary measures, is because I tried to leave once before and Bob's position at a telephone company gave him access to be able to locate anyone in Georgia and it was how he found and harassed me until I was forced to return home. This time, I had the phone and even the townhouse in my friend's wife's name. So, one can imagine how upsetting it was to know all the precautionary measures taken proved futile.

Many called me a fool for leaving Bob the house, but I no longer wanted to live in the house where there were too many bad memories of how he mistreated me, both physically and emotionally. There was such negative air I could never even grow a plant. And besides, he was much more materialistic so I, foolishly as it turned out, thought he would be less likely to harass me if I did, including the Volvo financed in my name. It did not end quite so friendly. What helped was that he lost the house and was forced to remarry someone who had been eyeballing him for a while and she had a great career and could take care of him.

I decided to then throw all my time and energy into myself and work as an assistant for a mortgage loan officer so I could learn the business. One day, a customer told the president of the company that if I did not receive full commission for his loan, he would take his business elsewhere. He stated he never once met with the man I was the assistant to and that he only had worked with me and that I had done everything and it went so smoothly he just could not see anyone else pay for all the work I had done for him. I also had gone to other loan officers and asked for their files that had not been approved and they all said, “Sure, take them; they’re “dead!” Not only did I rework them until some or even half were approved but ALL of them were approved! And that was the day I put into motion opening my own company.

In less than a year, I became president and CEO of my own mortgage company and never once paid for advertising. My business was 100% by referral only. I had taken all the years of experience working for others and made it mine.

Drawing on my personal experiences, I provided guidance to underserved and vulnerable members of my community by visiting their churches and community centers. I encouraged them not to blame themselves for poor credit histories, recognizing that many, like me, grew up without parental guidance on financial matters due to their lack of knowledge and/or ability to have and use credit. When the housing and mortgage market collapsed in 2008 and many competitors closed, I stayed open and maintained normal operations. When I handled loans deemed high risk, I made sure to inform my clients about ways to repair their credit, helping them become eligible to refinance into a Conventional, FHA, or VA loan within six months to a year. But I also insisted that they do NOT sign a pre-payment agreement to get a lower rate. That is what was sold to the customers of my competition. Most of those loans used a Libor-based Adjustable-Rate Mortgage (ARM), making it unaffordable for borrowers once the interest rates changed. Because they signed the Prepayment Penalty Clause, refinancing would leave them without enough equity to cover the $10,000 or higher penalty.

That is only one example of how I took some of my life's trauma and turned into a positive to benefit others. Drawing from my experience with a harsh mother, I worked with abused children at a state-approved private school to help keep them with their parents. I also was a Group Home Mother for teenage girls. My commitment to supporting society's most vulnerable individuals developed into a purposeful drive to apply my writing skills effectively. When I was 27, I wrote a 33-page report that revealed the Executive Director of a nonprofit running four group homes had misappropriated funds. I was not only successful in removing him, I also solicited the aide of the Catholic Church to replace him.

This so-called "less than zero" woman wrote many such letters as described above to expose wrongdoing at other companies that resulted in positive outcomes. My lack of higher education may have stunted my growth to a degree, but never did it prevent me from moving forward. After 15 years of being a deliriously, happy divorcee, I remarried to someone I knew 40 years ago on 08-08-08 at 8:08 PM. My wedding theme was Chinese; I later learned that the 2008 Olympics in Beijing China started at the very same time!

Lovely LaGuerre

Founder and CEO of Pure Heavenly Hair and Beauty

https://www.linkedin.com/in/lovelylaguerre/
https://m.facebook.com/pureheavenlyhairboutique
https://www.instagram.com/pureheavenlyhair
https://www.lovelyinspireyou.com
http://www.pureheavenlyhair.com
https://lovelysellsvegas.com

Lovely LaGuerre is a powerhouse in the world of entrepreneurship an acclaimed Wealth Creator, Commercial and Luxury Real Estate, Amazon Best Time Seller, and International Bestselling Author. With a passion rooted in transformation and empowerment, she's become a beacon for women and leaders seeking to elevate their lives and businesses with authenticity, grace, and strategy. Lovely LaGuerre is a visionary real estate professional, committed to guiding people to financial freedom through real estate investing. Having a strong passion for real estate, she believes that "the best investment on Earth is Earth." Her areas of expertise include commercial and luxury real estate, wealth creation strategies, and market flexibility. She combines business sense with empowering others, which makes her an industry trailblazer. A transformational consultant and dynamic speaker, Lovely empowers individuals to unlock their fullest potential while thriving in both life and business. She combines deep industry expertise with heartfelt guidance, helping others lead boldly, create wealth intentionally, and make a lasting impact. As the visionary founder of Pure Heavenly Hair and Beauty Boutique, Lovely has redefined luxury in the beauty space. Her brand bridges the gap between opulence and accessibility, offering premium wigs and an exclusive cosmetic line tailored for modern professionals, go-getters, and beauty lovers alike. Her business isn't just about products it's a celebration of confidence, culture, and self-expression. "The path to success varies for each individual. However, becoming a true successful leader requires unwavering commitment, wholehearted dedication, and the ability to acknowledge and celebrate the success of others."

The Day I Chose My Voice Over My Fear: I Spoke, and Everything Changed

By Lovely LaGuerre

I still remember the day I almost gave up.

Not because I wasn't capable, but because I was tired, tired of second-guessing myself, tired of trying to be everything to everyone, and tired of hearing my own dreams whispered in the background while fear did all the talking.

There was a time I thought silence was strength. I thought staying quiet, doing the work behind the scenes, and not ruffling any feathers was the safest way to grow. I wanted success, but I wanted it to come without attention, without judgment, and without that feeling of being "too much."

However, as I would later learn, your voice isn't a burden; it's your birthright.

It started small, those moments of self-doubt that crept in between wins. You know, the "Who do you think you are?" moments that come when you dare to dream bigger than what's comfortable.

I had an idea, a vision really, to build something meaningful, a business that not only reflected who I was but also what I stood for. I wanted to create impact, not just income. Yet I kept shrinking when it was time to show up. I'd write the post but never hit publish. I'd rehearse what I wanted to say, but then I'd water it down because I didn't want to sound "too confident."

Fear had me editing my own brilliance.

Then one day, I realized that staying silent wasn't keeping me safe; it was keeping me small.

That was the day I chose differently.

It wasn't dramatic. No grand music played in the background. But inside, something shifted. I remember sitting at my desk, staring at my notes, and thinking, if I don't believe in my voice, how can I expect anyone else to?

That thought hit me hard and it was the beginning of everything changing.

I started speaking up in rooms where I used to blend in, in meetings where I used to nod quietly, and in conversations where I used to hold back. The more I spoke, the more I saw the truth: My voice wasn't just about me. It was about every woman who had been told to "tone it down," every dreamer who'd been told "not yet," and every leader who'd been told "you're too much."

Speaking my truth wasn't about being loud; it was about being real and authentically me.

Still, the journey wasn't perfect. Entrepreneurship has a way of testing your courage in the most unexpected ways. There were times I launched something and it flopped. At times I gave my all to projects that didn't move the way I hoped. There were long nights when I questioned whether I was really cut out for these moments when rejection stung more than I'd like to admit.

But looking back now, those weren't failures; they were lessons in disguise.

Each setback taught me something about trust. Trusting the process. Trusting the timing. Trusting myself.

I learned that trusting your instincts doesn't mean the path will always be clear; it just means you move forward anyway, even when the road is foggy. I realized that courage isn't the absence of fear; it's the decision to speak, act, and move despite it.

For one moment I stand out vividly. I was preparing for a business presentation, a big opportunity that could take my work to another level. I was terrified. My inner critic was louder than ever. But I remembered that promise I made to myself to choose my voice over my fear. So I walked into that room, heart pounding, and spoke with every ounce of truth I had.

I didn't aim to impress; I aimed to connect.

And for the first time, I felt the power of alignment, the power that comes when you're not trying to be perfect; you're just being you.

That presentation changed everything. It didn't just open doors. It reminded me that my voice had been the key all along.

After that day, I made it my mission to never dim that light again.

Business began to feel different. I approached challenges with calm confidence instead of panic. I stopped chasing validation and started creating with intention. I began building partnerships that felt aligned, not forced. And the more I trusted my instincts, the more things flowed, clients connected, ideas flourished, and my work began to reflect my values in ways that felt authentic and deeply fulfilling.

But here's the real beauty of it: Once I found my voice, I couldn't help but encourage others to find theirs.

I started mentoring women who reminded me of my younger self with big dreams but quiet voices. I saw their brilliance, their potential, and that same hesitation I once carried. I'd look them in the eye and say, "You already have what you need. You just have to believe and to know that your voice has power and your voice matters."

And every time I said those words, I was reminded of the day I finally believed them for myself.

The truth is, there's power in your story, even the parts that hurt, even the ones you'd rather forget. There's purpose in your pain and wisdom in your waiting. Every moment of doubt, every failed attempt, every tear shed behind closed doors is not a sign of weakness. They're the roots of your strength.

When I reflect on my journey now, I realize my voice wasn't just something I found; it was something I remembered. It was always there, waiting for me to stop whispering my dreams and start declaring them.

That's the message I want every woman to hear:

Your voice is the bridge between who you are and who you're becoming. It carries the story of your survival, your lessons, and your dreams. And when you use it, you give permission for someone else to rise too.

I've learned that leadership isn't about speaking the loudest; it's about speaking from the heart. It's about showing up authentically, even when your voice shakes. It's about being willing to go first to stand in your truth so others can see what's possible for them.

The day I chose my voice over my fear, I didn't just change my business; I changed my life.

And when I spoke, everything really did change.

Because I began to see that the real power wasn't in the success I built, but in the woman I became along the way.

A woman who no longer waits for validation.

A woman who no longer apologizes for her light.

A woman who knows her voice is both her weapon and her gift.

And that's what I want you to know too. Whether you're building a business, chasing a dream, or finding your footing again after a hard season, your voice is your power.

You don't need to wait for the perfect time or the perfect plan. You just need to take a deep breath, silence the fear, and speak.

Because the moment you do, the moment you choose your voice, you'll find that everything changes for you too.

Remember that **Your Voice is Your Superpower**!

Your voice carries the power to shift rooms, rewrite stories, and awaken hearts, starting with your own. Speak your truth, even when it trembles, because on the other side of fear lives freedom.

JOIN THE MOVEMENT!

#BAUW

Becoming An Unstoppable Woman

With She Rises Studios

She Rises Studios was founded by Hanna Olivas and Adriana Luna Carlos, the mother-daughter duo, in mid-2020 as they saw a need to help empower women worldwide. They are the podcast hosts of the *She Rises Studios Podcast* and Amazon best-selling authors and motivational speakers who travel the world. Hanna and Adriana are the movement creators of #BAUW - Becoming An Unstoppable Woman: The movement has been created to universally impact women of all ages, at whatever stage of life, to overcome insecurities, and adversities, and develop an unstoppable mindset. She Rises Studios educates, celebrates, and empowers women globally.

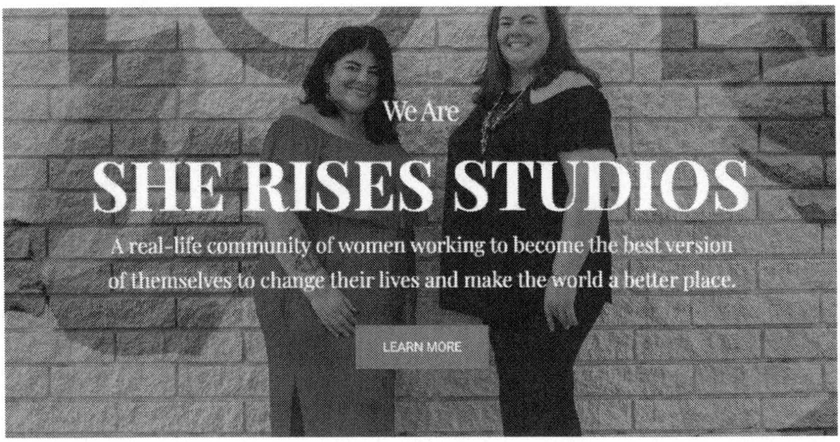

Looking to Join Us in our Next Anthology or Publish YOUR Own?

She Rises Studios Publishing offers full-service publishing, marketing, book tour, and campaign services. For more information, contact info@sherisesstudios.com

We are always looking for women who want to share their stories and expertise and feature their businesses on our podcasts, in our books, and in our magazines.

SEE WHAT WE DO

OUR PODCAST

OUR BOOKS

OUR SERVICES

Be featured in the Becoming An Unstoppable Woman magazine, published in 13 countries and sold in all major retailers. Get the visibility you need to LEVEL UP in your business!

Have your own TV show streamed across major platforms like Roku TV, Amazon Fire Stick, Apple TV and more!

Learn to leverage your expertise. Build your online presence and grow your audience with FENIX TV.
https://fenixtv.sherisesstudios.com/

Visit www.SheRisesStudios.com to see how YOU can join the #BAUW movement and help your community to achieve the UNSTOPPABLE mindset.

Have you checked out the ***She Rises Studios Podcast?***

Find us on all MAJOR platforms: Spotify, IHeartRadio, Apple Podcasts, Google Podcasts, etc.

Looking to become a sponsor or build a partnership?

Email us at info@sherisesstudios.com

SHE RISES
STUDIOS

Made in the USA
Las Vegas, NV
21 January 2026

39688851R00317